Bareboating

Lesley Newhart

Bareboating

□

Brian M. Fagan

International Marine Publishing Company

Camden, Maine

©1985 by International Marine Publishing Company

Typeset by The Key Word, Inc., Belchertown, Massachusetts
Printed and bound by Edwards Brothers, Inc., Ann Arbor, Michigan

Published by International Marine Publishing Company
21 Elm Street, Camden, Maine 04843
(207) 236-4342

Library of Congress Cataloging in Publication Data

Fagan, Brian M.
  Bareboating.

    Includes index.
    1. Boats and boating—Chartering. 2. Seamanship.
3. Yachts and yachting. I. Title.
GV775.F34 1985   387.5'1   84-47754
ISBN 0-87742-173-O

To

CAL CONRAD

Because of several memorable charters and because he became a
friend at a special time

Contents

About This Book

Bareboating is written from over 25 years of chartering experience in many parts of the world, a perspective that has left me with few illusions about the volatile world of yacht charters. The bareboat business is expanding rapidly, so you can charter almost anywhere these days. In part, the expansion is due to the growing number of people who want to spend their vacations on the water. It is also a reaction to the increasing cost of yacht ownership and, in the United States, a reflection of liberal tax laws surrounding the ownership of charter yachts.

For the beginner, the charter business is confusing, sometimes disastrous. If my experience is typical, a lot of people have problems with charter operations and charter boats. I have had companies go bankrupt a week before I was due to arrive, chartered yachts without engines, boats that literally came apart in our hands (one of the crew had to have stitches in his forehead when a mainsheet block came out of the deck), even a gorgeous 36-foot ocean racer.

Then there's the weather. My experiences on charter have included a cruise in an English snowstorm (we spent most of the time drinking hot whiskey toddies in pubs), a hurricane scare in the Caribbean, and being weatherbound for five days of a week's charter in the Channel Islands off France (surely the most frustrating cruise of all).

All this is before the joys and mishaps. I've enjoyed memorable beach bar evenings in the Virgins, run aground in Sweden, partied with flotilla charterers in the Greek islands, and eaten French food in a restaurant on Hydra in the Aegean accompanied by 24 fascinated cats. Yes, the world of bareboating can be traumatic and troublesome, but it can be hilarious fun as well. This book is an attempt to dispel some of the confusion and to distill some of my experiences for the benefit of others. Hopefully, having read this book, you will avoid some of the pitfalls that have caused me and others so many headaches.

Judging from the yachting magazines, bareboating is just a matter of fair winds, rum punches, and immaculate yachts. Of course, much of it is, but there's also a dark side that's ignored in the superficial articles published in the monthlies. Many of these are little more than marketing pieces—hardly surprising, since the magazines depend on advertising revenue for their livelihood. Most of the literature on bareboating consists of such articles. There is almost nothing for the beginner to turn to, other than the briefing materials put out by the charter companies. Some of these are excellent and very honest, but they are always at least in part self-serving.

This book is designed as an extended essay about chartering, about skills, preparations, and cruising grounds. I try to look at the world of bareboating as a whole, taking you on a tour, as it were, of many different areas of interest to both beginners and more advanced bareboaters. I try to describe things as they are. Far too many people have been burned by irresponsible charter companies for me to do otherwise.

Bareboating is divided into seven parts. I begin with the basic seamanship and navigational skills needed for a successful bareboat charter, because chartering is open to far more people than at first might appear. Many charter companies and some yacht brokerages have developed specialized training programs for beginners that can lead them to chartering on their own. Then I discuss such critical topics as anchoring and unexpected emergencies, sail handling, and reefing. I also tell you what to expect when you attend an instructional charter or a sailing school course.

Part II deals with the preliminaries for a charter, with the problems of selecting a charter company, a suitable yacht, travel arrangements, and the many advance preparations needed before you take off. What yachts are best for different charter areas? What equipment should they carry? How large a vessel should you charter the first time? For all the claims to the contrary, there are important preparations to be made once you have reserved your charter. What about travel plans? What should you take with you? And, above all, what about the make-up of your crew? All too many charter crews are formed in haste and regretted at leisure. My bias on this one is simple: personal chemistry is more important than a cheaper vacation or shared expenses.

Once on your charter, you are responsible for your yacht just as if you owned her. Part III covers these responsibilities and how they differ from those of an owner. What special navigational and seamanship problems are you likely to encounter? What about food, garbage, and snorkeling? How can you be the ideal charter client, the crew who are welcomed with a smile every time they return? Here again, my viewpoint is easily stated: every charterer should treat his vessel as if she were his own.

The remaining parts of *Bareboating* describe the major charter areas of the world. Once you have chartered a few times in familiar waters like the English Channel, the Chesapeake, or the Caribbean, you may want to venture farther afield. I take you on a brief tour of the major charter areas of Europe, the Pacific, North America, and the Caribbean. The objective is to give you the flavor of each area, outlining some of the peculiar charms and challenges of each region. I focus on special navigational or seamanship problems and describe the best anchorages and itineraries. For instance, English Channel charterers have to cope with unpredictable weather conditions, tidal harbors, and fast-moving streams. Charterers in Scandinavia navigate astonishingly narrow rocky channels, while Great Lakes bareboaters have to cope with bugs and sudden thunderstorms. What about customs in the Caribbean? What of the problems of chartering far from home in Tahiti, Tonga, Australia, or New Zealand? Should you combine chartering with land touring? These are a few of the problems we touch on.

Bareboating around the world presents unusual and fascinating challenges that will exercise the ingenuity of even the expert cruising sailor. Part VII describes some key resources for worldwide chartering.

As the costs of yacht ownership rise in years to come, we are likely to see a dramatic increase in charter opportunities, in chances to sail in parts of the world that were inaccessible to anyone except the most ardent full-time cruising people just a few years ago. With the wealth of bareboat fleets available even today, it makes sense for many of us to forget owning the large cruising yacht of our dreams. There comes a point when you think nothing of chartering a boat halfway around the world—to the envy of your boat-owning friends who have spent their all too brief cruising vacations in the familiar waters of home. There can be little doubt that, in a world of rising costs, bareboating is the wave of the cruising future, opening up even remote cruising grounds to people who have never sailed much farther than a few dozen miles from their home port, if at all.

In the past, there has been a tendency for serious cruising people to look down their noses at their neighbors in exotic anchorages who are mere charterers. All too often, bareboaters are thought of as a sort of second-class citizen. This sort of snobbish attitude is as dead as the poverbial dodo. It may just be that the crew of the 40-footer anchored a few feet away is an Admiral's Cup team taking a break from racing or, as once happened to me, a circumnavigator afloat again for the first time in three years. One of the joys of chartering is that it's a great social leveler, a wonderful way to meet people. So, next time you are anchored in the Bight in BVI or enjoying a cocktail at Catalina, row over and invite your neighbors aboard. There is no better way to meet people than chartering.

Acknowledgments

So many people have helped in the writing of this book that it is impossible to mention them all by name. I am very grateful to the many charter companies with whom I have done business over the years. Most of them have chartered me clean, well-found yachts, bless 'em! Some individuals deserve special thanks: Jack Culley of Sailboats Inc., Superior, Wisconsin, and Roger Miles of Rainbow Yacht Charters in the Bay of Islands, New Zealand, were especially cooperative in discussing the unique challenges of their business. The staff of Caribbean Sailing Yachts were also helpful on many occasions. Roger Taylor, Kathleen Brandes, Jon Eaton, and Phil Mason of International Marine criticized the manuscript at many stages. They made writing this book a comparative joy. Finally, my thanks to all those who have accompanied me on charters over the years. Sometimes we have suffered discomfort, but most of the time we have enjoyed every moment of it—and that's the purpose of the whole exercise!

Author's Note

Except in one or two specific and well-deserved instances, the mention of a company, service, or product in these pages in no way represents my endorsement of same. In the case of publications and sailing directions, I have given you my editorial assessment—for obvious reasons.

PART I: THE SKILLS

1 Bareboating

"There she is," said the charterer proudly. He pointed at a small orange-hulled yacht lying at the outer end of the dilapidated pier. Excitedly, we threaded our way through huddles of people loading their boats on a sunny English September morning. The tide would turn on the Blackwater River within two hours and everyone was anxious to be off. We looked down on our home for the next two weeks, a new 21-foot sloop fresh from the boatyard that lay only a few hundred yards downstream.

"She's only been out on one short charter and the people didn't go very far. She's as clean as a whistle and ready to go," said the charterer. He seemed impatient for us to be off. "Let me show you where everything is, so you can catch the top of the tide."

The provisions we had ordered lay on the starboard bunk in the cartons in which they had been delivered by the little store up the street. The charterer took us on a rapid-fire tour of the boat from stem to stern. He showed us where the propane shutoff valve was and how to operate the head and the battery-operated depth sounder, the only electronic device aboard. We looked around us feeling thoroughly confused.

"Any questions?" the charterer asked.

"Not offhand," my friend John assured him. Both of us felt a compelling urge to be on our way.

"Fine," smiled the charterer. "*Stella*'s little more than a dinghy. You should be thoroughly at home." Muttering a few remarks about laying out plenty of chain at night, he hurried away to sort out a huddle of families on a 30-footer just up the pier.

There was a long silence while we contemplated our new charge. This was the moment of truth. We had committed ourselves to two weeks in tidal waters in a small yacht without an engine, just a large sweep oar. Neither of us had ever skippered anything larger than a dinghy. We could hardly lay out a course and had never anchored a boat by ourselves before. Our total big-boat experience had been in large gaff-rigged yachts, converted oyster smacks owned by family friends. Yet the charterer seemed quite happy to let two inexperienced 21-year-olds sail off into the blue in a new, untried yacht. Finally I shook off my apprehension. "Let's get these provisions stowed and catch the tide," I said.

In the days that followed, we learned more about

sailing than we ever had before. *Stella* was ideal for two neophytes, a shallow-draft yacht designed for ditch crawling in the innumerable channels and muddy creeks of eastern England. She was forgiving of mistakes, of innumerable groundings, of inadequately laid anchors, and nights at 35 degrees on a sandbank offshore. Her hatches leaked copiously, the roller reefing jammed, and a new mainsheet block disintegrated in a 30-knot wind. But by the time we returned to base, we could turn her on a small coin and maneuver her into the tightest of berths with sail and oar. The bareboating bug had bitten us. Both John and I have chartered yachts all over the world ever since.

What is bareboating? You rent a fully equipped cruising yacht, a "bareboat," from a company or individual specializing in chartering and assume responsibility for sailing it yourself. The charter company takes care of all maintenance, insurance charges, unexpected yard bills, and permanent dockage of the yacht. All you do is pay your charter fees, sail your vessel with care and responsibility, and enjoy.

Although the charter business has been around a long time, it was rudimentary until very recently. *Stella* was an astoundingly primitive charter yacht by modern standards. That first charter of ours was over a quarter of a century ago, when charter companies were few and far between and most cruising sailors owned their own yachts or chartered larger vessels with a professional crew. Today, dozens of companies offer yachts for charter—some reputable, others real fly-by-night operations. In some areas like the Virgins, bareboat chartering is now a highly competitive industry, with dozens of companies vying for your business. But, while the competition for clients is sometimes ferocious, things have changed. No reputable bareboat organization would dream of sending two relatively inexperienced college students off on a boat like *Stella* without several hours of briefing and a firsthand check of their sailing credentials.

But the dream is still there, the dream of skippering a boat on a cruise you've planned yourself, usually a yacht that is far more elaborate and expensive than the modest vessel you own yourself, if you own a boat at all. The joy of bareboating is that it opens up the world of cruising not only to experienced sailors, but to small-boat owners who live thousands of miles from the ocean and hanker sometimes for blue skies and blue water.

Bareboating owes its current popularity to experienced sailors from the American Northeast and Midwest, Canada, and Northern Europe, who grew tired of long gloomy winters. They dreamed of flying south in midwinter for a week or two of sailing in tropical waters. Few people could afford to keep a yacht idle in the Caribbean for the sake of a few weeks' sailing each year, so a dentist named Jack Van Ost decided to do something about it. He founded a bareboat company, Caribbean Sailing Yachts, and put together a small fleet of charter yachts in the Virgin Islands. The idea caught on like wildfire, Van Ost's company prospered. Soon chartering turned into a profitable business and satisfied a lot of sailors' cravings, too. Now the Caribbean charter season has expanded beyond all expectations, to include not only the winter, but the spring and early summer months. Only in the hurricane season between July and late October can you expect to find the Virgins almost deserted.

Most people who think of bareboating automatically conjure up images of tropical beaches, palm trees, rum punches, and all the sybaritic glories of the Virgin Islands. True, the Caribbean is the mecca of bareboaters and the Virgins an ideal place to begin your chartering career. But today you can bareboat right around the world, flying direct from your home to cruising grounds thousands of miles away where a well-found vessel will be waiting for you. You can sail all year round as well, chartering in the Virgins, Grenadines, and Bay Islands during the cold European and North American months. Come summer, you can sail in the Mediterranean or cruise Maine, the Pacific Northwest, or the Chesapeake. Or you can fly far away to enjoy the tropical delights of Tahiti or Tonga, cruise the Bay of Islands in New Zealand, or savor the remote lagoons of the Great Barrier Reef in Australia. The more experienced charter skipper can explore the islands of Scandinavia or challenge the fast-running tides of the English Channel. Ireland's west coast and western Scotland are ideal charter areas for hardy crews, while Brittany, Corsica, Sardinia, and Greece are irresistible. Bareboat fleets are located in most of the world's premier cruising grounds.

Thousands of sailors, experienced and inexperienced, charter every year—to escape the winter, to take their cherished vacation far from home, or simply for a change of pace and sailing scenery. Avid racers leave the racecourse and their sleek IOR racers for a week's lazing in the Virgins. A group of Ohio teachers, who are dinghy sailors, charters a 39-footer in the Aegean Islands. Some people charter to try out a yacht of a type they are thinking of purchasing. A few ambitious sailors (and not necessarily people living inland either) spend their spare time bareboating and prefer not to own a yacht at all. For them, the reward of bareboating is the experience of skippering a different kind of vessel in exotic waters each year, often a yacht they could never afford themselves. They arrive to find the vessel of their choice fully provisioned and ready to go. Within a couple of hours they are on their way. No worries about blocked injectors, peeling brightwork, or fraying jibsheets. After a relaxed cruise in a new area, they return the yacht to base and fly away, to charter somewhere else next year. Their responsibilities to the yacht cease when they sign off at the end of the charter. Bareboating as a cruising lifestyle makes eminently good sense to many people in our busy and complex world.

I remember meeting two middle-aged Swedes, a man and his wife, on a 33-footer in Mykonos Harbor in the Aegean. They berthed alongside our 41-footer, coming stern-to the quay with a quiet display of competent seamanship that was a joy to watch. I complimented them on their boathandling and we visited over the inevitable glass of wine.

Inga, the wife, smiled. "Ah," she said, "this is easy after Brittany with its terrible tides."

We fell into a long discussion of ports and anchorages, tiresome officials, and places to visit. It transpired that they were on a bareboat charter from Athens and had done the same thing all over Europe and in the Caribbean. They spent up to two months afloat each year, changing areas each season. We had even chartered from the same English companies.

"Why do you do it this way?" I asked.

"Less trouble," said Svein laconically, looking over our cutter's brightwork (we had been varnishing all day). "We have a little Folkboat at home, but charter every year as well. How else could we afford to sail all over the world so cheaply? Besides, we can spend the winters at home near our grandchildren and have the families out on our charters sometimes."

I could sympathize with his viewpoint. Bareboating solves three problems: how to avoid the high costs of ownership, how to make optimum use of valuable vacation time, and how to move your yacht from one cruising area to another hundreds, even thousands, of miles away. Above all, bareboating is ideal for those who want to try out the cruising life without committing themselves too deeply at first, and for those serious cruising people who have only limited vacation time.

Owning or chartering?

Owning a yacht is said to be one of the greatest emotional experiences a sailor can have. But it is not for everyone. Some people must own their own yachts, those deeply committed to long-distance cruising, who want to take off on the high seas for months, years, even a lifetime. Some are sailors of independent means or retirees. Others have elected to live from hand to mouth, from freelance writing, yacht maintenance, and other irregular sources of income. Obviously, anyone living aboard permanently will own his own vessel, for his yacht is his home, office, and most prized possession.

Then there are many families who take off on a long cruise for a few years, selling everything and sailing over the horizon. Here again, yacht ownership makes sense, certainly for the duration of the cruise. A friend of mine took off on a two-year cruise from Southern California up the U.S. East Coast and through the Caribbean. He bought a fine 35-footer for $55,000, maintained it carefully, and recouped his temporary investment at the end of the cruise. He fulfilled a lifelong dream and now is happily back at work in a stimulating job. He now charters several times every year for a fraction of the cost of owning a yacht of equivalent size.

I once met a busy and sweating gentleman on a superb 44-foot ketch in Marina del Rey, California. Most of his diesel engine lay on sheets of newspaper in the cockpit.

"When are you taking off?" I asked, for his boat was festooned with every conceivable piece of oceangoing equipment.

"I don't know," he replied, as he reassembled the water pump. "It's difficult for me to leave my business for more than a few days. When we do take a summer vacation, there's always so much to do around the house and Catalina is so crowded. Besides, just keeping up with the boat takes so much time."

I quietly agreed, but privately wondered how long a successful and financially sophisticated man could keep such a valuable long-distance cruiser lying idle. If ever there was a skipper who should have been chartering, it was this one.

In the final analysis, the economics of yacht ownership come down to some simple questions that you should confront early on:

• Do you get such deep emotional satisfaction from owning a yacht that your life is empty without one?
• Can you afford the cost of buying and maintaining a yacht of the size you want? Are your hard-earned dollars, which would lie dormant in the equity in your boat, better invested where they would yield a profit?
• How much do you plan to use the vessel? For 3 to 12 weekends and a single 2-week cruise a year? For purely local sailing or for extended passagemaking?
• Where do you want to sail? In home waters and a radius of, say, 100 miles? In the Caribbean, Europe, or the South Pacific?

Owning a large yacht makes no sense unless you plan to sail at least two months a year. You can round the Fastnet Rock off southern Ireland in a bareboat, too. (Courtesy Irish Tourist Board)

● How much do you like routine maintenance and the hassles of interior and bottom cleaning? Are you prepared to commit several weeks a year to brightwork, engine oil, and interior and bottom cleaning?

If you have reservations about your answers to any of these basic questions, then you should seriously consider the bareboat option.

It is very difficult to generalize about the cost of yacht ownership, since so much depends on how many months a year you use your vessel, on the local climate, and on such variables as age and construction of the yacht, slip fees, insurance rates, property taxes, financing, and so on. Those who hire a yard to carry out all routine maintenance can expect to pay far more than those who do all the work themselves. So will those who keep their boats in fashionable harbors or marinas rather than on remote moorings. *Practical Sailor*, a U.S.-based newsletter for boat owners, recently sent questionnaires to its readers and reported that most of the respondents spent about 5.5 percent of the value of their yacht on annual running costs. The editors were surprised the figure was so low, because their own figures, on a 34- and 47-footer, came to between 8 and 12 percent of value, this without allowing for upgrading of equipment. They concluded that a figure from 6 percent to as much as 10 percent or more was realistic.

The respondents to the *Practical Sailor* questionnaire said they used their boats for an average of 62 days a year, a figure the editors thought was skewed by responses from sailors in warmer climate zones. They pointed out that three of their editors had a *combined* use on their three boats of much less than 60 days a year.

Taking these figures and a 35-footer that cost $70,000 new, a conservative sum these days, your 62 days of sailing are going to come out as an expensive proposition:

Annual maintenance at 8 percent of $70,000: $5,600
$$\$5,600 \div 62 \text{ days of use} = \$90/\text{day}$$
(The 8 percent figure includes very modest financing, not the sort of double-digit rates commonplace today.)

It is safe to say that relatively few owners will use their boats so much, even in warmer climate areas, so your daily cost is likely to be higher. Furthermore, you have at least 25 percent of the purchase price of the yacht tied up in a depreciating asset, when it could be earning double-digit interest somewhere.

In contrast, the skipper who charters has only two costs, the charter fee and travel expenses to reach the yacht (assuming that both owner and charterer have equivalent food expenses). For example, the price of a two-week Virgin Islands charter in the winter months of 1983 (high season) for a 39-footer for a couple living in California (a long distance away) was as follows:

Charter cost for two weeks at $2,100/week:	$4,200*
Return airfares from West Coast to BVI:	1,400
Hotel and other minor expenses:	250
Total:	$5,850

$$\$5,850 \div 14 \text{ days} = \$418/\text{day}$$

*This does not include provisioning, a common expense for both owners and charterers.

The equivalent ownership rate comes out to $400 per day, without any traveling expenses. The daily figure for chartering can be reduced dramatically if more than two people share expenses. Assuming our California couple wanted to spend 62 days chartering in one

stretch in high season, their cost would be $110 per day, before long-term charter discounts of 10 to 20 percent are taken into account.

If our hypothetical couple were to charter for five weeks in high season in the Caribbean, their costs would work out to:

---

5 weeks of a 39-footer at $2,100/week:	$10,500
Return airfares at $700/head:	1,400
Miscellaneous costs:	250
Total:	$12,150

$$\$12,150 \div 35 \text{ days} = \$347/\text{day}$$

And their $17,500 equity would be working away—indeed, the interest could pay as much as 25 percent of their annual charter expense. Taking just the basic figures, and making no allowance for long-term charter discounts, depreciation, tied-up equity, taxes on interest, and time spent on maintenance, it appears that chartering is cheaper than owning for Americans at somewhere around 60 days' use a year. Undoubtedly, the figure is much lower—and for many people the drastically reduced hassle makes chartering a sensible option.

The costs for a British sailor chartering in the English Channel would come out roughly as follows:

---

5 weeks of a 35-footer at 1,500/week:	$7,500
Rail or road travel to charter base for two:	250
Miscellaneous expenses:	150
Total:	$7,900

$$\$7,900 \div 35 \text{ days} = \$226/\text{day}$$

Another recent option is timesharing, a scheme whereby you have unrestricted use of a yacht for a specified period a year. The timesharing concept comes to cruising from the real estate industry, where it is a well-established way of offering low-cost vacations in resort areas. You buy a share of the vessel or a "right to use" her, together with all the other users. The cost for a share of a 40-foot yacht, where you own part of the vessel, can run about $300 per day, or $350 for "right to use," assuming the company can keep the boat running for as many as 42 weeks a year. This is far more than any charter company aims for. Their outside limit is about 30 weeks a year, and that's pushing it. Some companies aim for between 15 and 20 weeks, a more realistic figure. The maintenance needs and costs are simply too high to make chartering any more economic.

Jervis Inlet, British Columbia. (Bill Berssen, Pacific Boating Almanac)

As any yacht owner can tell you, boat timesharing companies are dealing with many unknowns as far as maintenance and use time are concerned, unknowns that no real estate company has to deal with. Best steer clear of timesharing until the facts and figures are better established.

The world of bareboating

The objective of bareboat chartering is to have a good time. This may seem a ridiculous truism, but it is amazing how many charterers you meet who are having a terrible time. There are those who are seduced by the blue skies and smooth oceans of the advertising agencies. They buy a charter on impulse and are bitterly disillusioned. We once met two couples and a skipper on a Morgan 43 in the Virgins. They had spent vast sums on gourmet food and had encountered high seas and torrential rain. The tensions aboard could be cut with a knife. Everyone was out of his element, no one was enjoying himself, and you knew none of them would ever charter again. Five Norwegian doctors in the Bight at Norman Island were a dramatic contrast. Expert sailors they, escaping from the Nordic winter, their trip planned carefully in advance. While the rum flowed, they extolled the joys of Caribbean sailing and urged us to visit them in Oslo. One day, perhaps, we'll charter in Denmark and sail north to their home port.

Your enjoyment of bareboating will depend to a great extent on several critical variables:

● Adequate experience to handle a bareboat charter.
● Careful selection of a charter company and yacht.
● Matching the charter area to your interests and plans.
● Thoughtful advance planning.
● Extremely careful selection of your crew: never take potluck with the people you charter with!

This book is designed to make the balancing of these variables easier and to introduce you to the many bareboating options that await even the neophyte cruising sailor. Lack of experience should not deter you from bareboating, as you will see in the next chapter.

2 Acquiring the Skills

Thousands of people dream of cruising under sail, even if they have never set foot in a sailing vessel in their lives. They buy books about sailing, subscribe to the magazines, and dream. Many of them live hundreds of miles from the ocean and have never had the chance to sail anything larger than a dinghy on a lake or river. A charter vacation offers a unique way to live out the dream. Many people realize this but end up frustrated when they discover that bareboating is not a beginner's sport. Not only do you have to know how to sail, but you have to be able to navigate, anchor, and berth your boat as well, skills that seem arcane to many eager beginners. You can hardly blame charter companies for asking questions about your sailing skills. After all, you are in charge of an expensive yacht, and it is only reasonable for the owners to be satisfied that you have the skills to operate her safely and responsibly. A basic knowledge of sailing and some cruising experience are needed before you can charter on your own. But how can you acquire such experience? What skills are needed before you can skipper a charter yacht on your own? This chapter covers some of the ways in which you can acquire the skills to skipper on your own.

The basic skills

The basic skills for becoming a bareboat skipper depend, to some degree, on the area where you intend to charter. There is a world of difference between a cruise in the relatively sheltered waters of the Apostle Islands on Lake Superior or the Virgin Islands and a two-week charter in the English Channel. The latter, with its strong tides and unpredictable winds, requires navigational competence and seamanship of a much higher order than those needed for an area where fogs are unknown and tidal streams minimal. The beginning skipper should plan to gain experience in a relatively undemanding area before taking on more dangerous waters.

Reputable charter companies define the levels of experience they require with considerable precision. Their brochures often lay out the qualifications needed to skipper various sizes of yacht. Some organizations, such as Caribbean Sailing Yachts, insist on different levels of experience for the Virgin Islands and their operations in Saint Vincent and the Bay Islands of Honduras. Every company requires you to fill out a

questionnaire that lists your experience; some may ask for verification and references. And every charterer is carefully scrutinized as he or she prepares to take off. The companies are concerned about two things: the level of sailing skills you possess and their adequacy for the size of vessel you are chartering. Clearly, a tiny trailer yacht requires less skill than a heavy-displacement 44-footer. So the company watches closely as you prepare to depart. Some demand comprehensive trials (one California company even insists on a full-length two-to-three-hour sea trial, for which they charge you $50). However stringent the examination may be, the primary concern is your safety. If there is any doubt about your competence, the company will insist that you take along a local skipper for a few days—at your expense (normally between $50 and $75 per day). This is as much to safeguard yourself as the yacht. After all, the company wants you to have a pleasant vacation so that you will return as a repeat client. If you make inquiries, you will find that most reputable companies have a substantial repeat business, sometimes as high as 70 percent of their clientele—so it makes good sense for them to develop a long-term relationship with you.

A typical questionnaire will ask such questions as these:

● Have you chartered before as a skipper? If so, give specific details.

● Do you own a boat? What type and size, and how much do you use her? Where do you sail her?

• What navigational experience do you have?

You will also be asked to list your cruising and sailing experience.

Although the level of sailing experience will differ from area to area, here are some basic guidelines for the aspiring skipper. To charter a smaller yacht in the Great Lakes or the Virgin Islands, you should have the following experience:

• Be able to sail! This may seem self-evident, but it is amazing how many people try to go bareboating with little more than a book knowledge of sailing. The marina staff are experts at sniffing out book learners from practical sailors. Don't try to fool them—the stakes are too high. But the good news is that anyone who has learned to handle a small dinghy or trailer yacht on a river or lake will have acquired the instinctive behavior with mainsheets, jibsheets, and halyards that is essential in larger, heavier-displacement yachts. So your apparent lack of big-boat experience may not limit you as much as you had imagined.

• Have some experience of sailing under varied conditions in a heavier-displacement boat of a size comparable to that of the boat you plan to charter. To skipper a bareboat, it is not just enough to have been along for the ride on many different boats. You need actual experience not only of helming and actively crewing, but also of making the sorts of decisions that every skipper routinely encounters, decisions that can range from elementary navigational calculations to the tactics of reefing and handling in winds of 25 to 30 knots.

• Know how to read a compass, lay off a course, take bearings, and use a chart. Areas like the Virgin Islands or the Great Lakes do not require vast navigational expertise, but there will be occasions when you will need to take bearings to establish your position in a squall, to line up your course into an anchorage, or to decipher soundings on a chart. Some exposure to eyeball navigation in tropical waters is invaluable, indeed essential, and can only be acquired by sailing over sandbanks and reefs.

• Above all, have practical experience of anchoring in bays and small coves in a vessel of comparable size, especially under congested conditions. Every skipper should be able to lay an anchor properly, know the principles of adequate scope and swinging room, and be experienced in using "Bahamian" moors and second anchors.

• Have some experience of handling yachts over 25 feet under power. You should know how to maneuver in close quarters, how to use wheel and throttle correctly to turn and reverse your yacht. A knowledge of engine maintenance, while helpful, is not essential

in most charter areas: the company will come out and take care of you.

Anyone with these basic skills should be able to charter in the Virgin Islands, the Bahamas, New Zealand's Bay of Islands, and other relatively undemanding areas safely and enjoyably. The great advantage of most charter yachts is that they are rigged for simple handling. They have roller-furling jibs and simple reefing gear, as well as strong anchor and sheet winches. With such simple, robust gear, you will find that your sailing skills will mature rapidly once you are out on your own.

There is one golden rule for the beginning charterer: *Be honest about your sailing experience both with yourself and the charter company*. It is only fair for both of you. Self-deception is bound to catch up with you.

I remember talking to one Danish charter operator, who had just refused to let two German families take out a 27-footer on a week's charter. He had returned their money after angry complaints and recriminations.

"How often does that happen?" I asked.

"Not very often, thank goodness," was the reply. "These people lied about their experience. They didn't even know the difference between a halyard and a sheet. Why didn't they realize that we could spot their inexperience at once? It would have saved so much unpleasantness." As a result of the stupidity of these clients, the charterer lost precious business at the height of the short summer season.

Part of the fault was the company's. They had been pretty casual about their questionnaire check. Even today, this often happens. One small English company asked me to fill in a short form that asked for my name, address, and the yacht clubs I belonged to. There was one other question: "Is there anything unusual about your sailing background?" One wonders what they meant by "unusual." Oddly enough, the 32-footer we ended up chartering from this somewhat idiosyncratic company was one of the nicest charter yachts I have ever cruised. The Caribbean companies are much more careful. Anchorages are congested, many more people are chartering, and insurance companies are becoming increasingly demanding about client qualifications.

Acquiring bareboating experience

The hardest part is taking the first step, acquiring practical rather than book knowledge. There are a number of ways to do this:

• Sailing with knowledgeable friends.

● Attending a sailing school or signing up with a yacht brokerage that offers sailing instruction and bareboating as well as sales.
● Going on an instructional cruise-charter run by a charter company.
● Taking a flotilla cruise.

Until very recently, most cruising sailors learned the hard way, by sailing with friends and gaining practical experience. This is a wonderful way to learn, *if* you have sympathetic friends, live near the ocean or a large lake, and have a skipper who is prepared to take the time to teach you the basics. I learned my cruising from a retired naval commander who owned a 17-ton converted oyster smack without an engine, and I learned fast. He had a tongue like a whip and believed in hard work. His harsh lessons in seamanship are with me to this day.

It is easy enough to acquire the basic sailing skills by crewing and helming on a well-handled yacht. My teacher was an expert at anchors, mooring lines, and tackles. He had to be. His yacht had no winches and we towed or warped her everywhere. The skipper had learnt his sailing on a naval sailing brig and taught as he had learned—from example. In some ways it was probably easier to learn from him than it is from a husband, wife, parent, or friend, who finds it difficult to switch into the role of teacher. If you are learning from friends, you are best advised to take some navigational courses at the same time. U.S. Coast Guard Power Squadron courses are taught all over the country and are excellent value. The RYA and Polytechnic courses taught in Britain are extremely good, too. Charter companies respect them as part of your qualifications. A number of commercial outfits offer correspondence courses in pilotage and coastal navigation that are of high quality—but firsthand experience is also essential.

I would strongly advise anyone planning to skipper his own bareboat to go on a charter with someone else first, if possible in the area where you plan to cruise by yourself one day. You can then learn about the boats at first hand, see how the company checks out the skipper, and visit the most attractive anchorages without the responsibility of being in charge. Insist, however, that you are not just going along for the ride and that you have the opportunity to skipper the boat into congested anchorages and to supervise the actual anchoring operation. This is the sort of hands-on experience that makes all the difference between enjoying your first skippering experience and hating every moment of it. I have one friend who wanted to step out on his own after crewing with several experienced sailors. So he chartered a 30-footer in the Virgins, enjoyed himself, but decided he needed more

experience before skippering a larger yacht. Now there's a wise and honest man, who has appraised his abilities and tailored his chartering accordingly.

More and more people are learning how to sail and charter not from friends, but from formal courses of instruction. There are literally hundreds of such courses to choose from all over Europe and the Americas, but I would recommend if possible that you combine the course with some firsthand experience with friends. A good school has well-trained instructors and a curriculum that is designed to give you a week or more of balanced, hard-nosed instruction and get you out on the water and into real-life situations from the start. As one well-known sailing instructor remarked to me: "It all boils down to ship handling, and that's where we spend the time."

Once you have taken a beginning course, it may pay you to follow through the whole spectrum of the school's offerings, right up to courses on electronic navigation and deep-water passagemaking. By the time you graduate, you will have all the formal instruction you need to charter almost anywhere.

Sailing schools

Sailing schools have proliferated in recent years, catering to an apparently insatiable demand for basic instruction in cruising and racing. You should choose your sailing school with care. Look carefully at the location and size of the school. Does it have a successful track record? Ask for the names and addresses of previous clients in your area to whom you can write or talk. Do the courses cover exactly what you are looking for? Do they serve as adequate preparation for a bareboat charter? Are the instructors properly trained and qualified? You will learn much more from experienced and thoroughly prepared teachers than you will from any number of the sun-tanned deck apes who sometimes masquerade as sailing instructors in between ocean races. Your best bet is to go to one of the large, well-established companies like Annapolis Sailing School or Steve Colgate's Offshore Sailing School. Another option: Sailboats Inc.'s large charter operation in the Midwest, which caters specifically to beginners. Some brokerage companies are going into chartering, arguing that a streamlined instructional charter-ownership program is a good way to foster continued yacht sales. There are, of course, many respectable smaller operations, but it is sometimes difficult for the beginner to choose a suitable one. Best play it safe first time. All sailing schools offer week-long or part-time beginners' courses, where you combine sailing sessions with lectures. After the basics, most schools divide you into racers and cruisers. The prospective charterer is more likely to be interested in basic and advanced cruising courses. These break down into a number of categories:

• *Basic cruising courses*, where you daysail in smaller yachts (about 25 to 30 feet) and learn basic pilotage, anchoring, and boathandling. The week includes a short cruise and some lecture sessions. This type of course covers getting underway, basic sail trim and handling under power, passagemaking, reefing, anchoring and safety, as well as elementary pilotage. Take a course like this first. You will enjoy the more advanced and intensive courses far more as a result. Sailboats' courses on the Great Lakes are excellent examples of this approach.

• *Live-aboard courses* last a long weekend or five days and consist of a cruise in company with an instructor. The larger yachts ship an instructor along with the students, perhaps your entire family. This way you have supervision all the time. Another option is a cruise in company, where the instructors supervise several smaller yachts that sail together. I would recommend the former because you are there to learn and you can have the instructor looking over your shoulder all the time. Insist, however, that you do the work, not the instructor. These courses are designed to give you practical experience of the basics you have already learned. Some companies offer you the chance to spend a week on board what is really a charter yacht in the Caribbean with an instructor aboard. Personally, I would settle for a week's intensive instruction nearer home—you would probably learn more and spend less time as a passenger.

• A few companies offer more ambitious *cruising-learning experiences* that combine passagemaking with everything from engine maintenance to electronic navigation. One company offers a "Learn-to-Cruise" course that includes two 140-mile nonstop passages off western Florida. You can sometimes pick up longer instructional passages as well, delivery trips taking charter boats down to the Caribbean or up north for the summer months. Be careful, however, before you select one of these alternatives. On many, the instruction is minimal, the mileage tough, often a long beat to windward. You are little more than a pair of convenient hands.

Armed with certificates from two or three intensive cruising courses, you should be qualified to bareboat in a relatively straightforward area like the Virgins. But I would still advise going on a basic bareboating course taught by one of the charter companies, for these are taught by people who spend their working lives dealing with the very problems that you will encounter in charge of your own yacht.

Sailboats Inc. of Superior, Wisconsin, is a sail brokerage company that offers sailing instruction and bareboating as part of its total service to cruising sailors. They specialize in introducing complete beginners to bareboating, and sometimes to yacht ownership, through intensive three-day courses that include eight hours of classroom instruction and two days' actual sailing. The classroom portion can even be taken as a short correspondence course. A successful graduate of the course is given "Bareboat Charter Certification," which allows him to charter one of the company's yachts. This highly structured, intensive course is taught by rigorously trained instructors and emphasizes boathandling and safety. The company claims that it teaches you to sail in three days. They have certainly introduced thousands of beginners to bareboating, and the Apostle Islands near the company's home base are an ideal training ground for beginners.

Sailboats Inc. also offers a four-day advanced course on a 38-footer that takes you across Lake Superior to Isle Royale National Park. The curriculum includes Loran and night sailing. This is an excellent introduction to open-water sailing. There are advantages all around in the Sailboats Inc. system. The beginner can take a basic course, be chartering within a few weeks, then graduate to large boats and more advanced courses in a few seasons. In due time, he may elect to buy a yacht, then put it in charter with the company. The company benefits in increased sales and in building up a regular clientele of repeat customers.

Sailing and learning in a bareboat

Discerning skippers charter the Caribbean in the late spring or early summer when the rates are much lower. Bareboating in these areas is a seasonal business, determined by the vagaries of the winter climate up north and by the hurricane season, which lasts from mid-July to October. Some of the best sailing in the Caribbean is to be found in the summer months, however, when the trades blow weaker and sailing conditions are often perfect, much less boisterous than in midwinter. The charter companies offer all sorts of incentives for you to bareboat in these months, some even promoting a two-week charter for the cost of one week's rental. Another way they attract clients, and enhance their business at the same time, is to organize week-long courses for prospective charter skippers.

Perhaps it is a misnomer to call such experiences courses—they are more like cruising under supervision. The company sends along a member of its staff on a lead boat to keep an eagle eye on a small group of yachts that sail in company to different anchorages each night. Some instruction is given in basic navigational skills, boathandling, and anchoring. The instructor in charge of the course moves from boat to boat, each couple in turn taking charge as skipper for a while. By the time you finish the week, you should be certified to go off on your own—if you have taken trouble to work hard on improving your skills. Instructional cruises like this are fine if you have some basic sailing experience, but are not for complete beginners. The great thing is that you can make fairly drastic mistakes under supervision—and learn how to get out of them.

Most charter companies stress anchoring and boathandling skills in their courses. Every company I have spoken to finds that its charterers tend to have problems in three basic areas:

● Anchoring: Many charterers do not understand the niceties of laying out an anchor so that it will not drag, do not know how to select the right place to anchor, and fail to pay out enough scope. The problem is compounded by chronic congestion in many locations and by unpredictable weather conditions or surge. So the charter companies place great stress on anchoring expertise.

● Use of sails and engine: Many charterers fail to realize that a sailboat is not a motor cruiser. Few have auxiliaries powerful enough to drive them against the wind into a 30-knot blow to arrive home on time. All too often, sails are flogged to death when motoring to windward or torn when reefs are tucked in badly. Too many charterers run their engines at maximum revolutions, waste fuel, or fail to check water and oil levels. Often, you pay for the damage.

● Use of the yacht's mechanical and electrical system: Improper use of these systems sometimes results in severe damage. Alternators are burnt out by running the engine with the ignition switch off, outboards are run aground at full speed, anchor rodes are wrapped around propellers by careless maneuvering.

Charter companies' courses are well worth taking for another reason, too. You'll learn how to cook on board and become familiar with the provisioning package offered by the charterer. Such knowledge can add immeasurably to the enjoyment of future charters. Have you ever craved French mustard in the Bahamas or your favorite brand of coffee when on vacation? This is a good way to find out what you should bring for the galley.

Flotilla charters

Flotillas are cruises in company, where a group of small yachts sail from port to port on a more or less fixed itinerary. Flotilla cruises are especially popular in the Mediterranean—the south of France, Greece, and Turkey—but they are catching on in Florida and the Caribbean as well. You can even flotilla cruise as far afield as New Zealand. The first flotilla programs were developed by nonprofit organizations like the Yacht Cruising Association in England, which maintained a small fleet of 25-footers in Greece under the supervision of a group of expert young sailors. The organization members then cruised regularly in company, but with enough flexibility that they could go off on their own for part of the cruise. In recent years, commercial companies have developed the original concept still further, and new fleets appear in the most unexpected places each season.

We once harbor hopped with a flotilla cruise, from Epidavros to Poros, Hydra, and Navplion in Greece. We first met the flotilla of 12 red-sailed boats in Epidavros, where they berthed near us in the tiny port. Each was manned by a family or a crew who were complete strangers when the cruise began. The fleet was supervised by a skipper, an engineer, and a hostess in a lead boat. They would enter harbor ahead of the other yachts and be on hand to take lines, offer advice, or even take charge if things got out of hand. As the fleet went from port to port, the lead boat would enforce a strict convoy, indicate a suitable course to sail, or leave everyone alone. But she was always on hand to deal with mechanical problems or to assist in an emergency. When we met some of the crews in local tavernas, they spoke enthusiastically of the chance to cruise in company, their anxieties minimized because expert advice was at hand. Six days of the two-week holiday were given over to independent cruising. You could visit new ports, sail to your heart's content, or simply lie on the beach. In practice, most flotilla leaders will let you go off on your own most of the time if they are satisfied that you know what you are doing. A flotilla cruise is not an instructional course, although you can learn a great deal by staying close to the leaders. People of every sailing background, from beginners to expert sailors, go flotilla cruising. This is a good way to get practical experience once you have learned the basics, and it also makes some tricky or relatively remote cruising areas, like Turkey and the Ionian, accessible for short vacations.

At present, the flotilla cruise business is dominated by European clients, flown in as groups from major northern airports. The cost of a flotilla cruise is

Flotilla sailing in Greece offers a safe and easy way to learn bareboating in congenial company. (Courtesy Yacht Cruising Association)

normally packaged to include airfares and is highly competitive with land-based package vacations. (In 1983, an Ionian two-week cruise from England for a family of four cost about $2,600, including airfare.) It has to be, because the operators cater to a broader clientele. Many of the people attracted to such holidays are complete strangers to sailing looking for a different vacation experience.

My advice for the more expert bareboater would be to avoid flotilla cruises, unless you want to familiarize yourself with a new charter area. And those interested in more systematic instruction are best advised to go with a sailing school or a charter company cruise.

Qualifications for more advanced bareboating areas

To acquire the necessary experience to skipper a bareboat in the Virgins, Southern California, and other relatively undemanding areas is straightforward enough—in this day and age not even a matter of knowing people who sail. You can take a series of courses, graduate from each, acquire a modicum of practical experience through chartering with others and flotilla cruises, and then go out on your own, just as a neophyte owner does. But there comes a time when even the most unambitious bareboater feels restless and looks farther afield.

Most return clients to the Caribbean simply graduate to another area—to the Grenadines, the Bay Islands, or perhaps to the Bahamas. But with charter companies operating as far afield as Europe, New Zealand, and Australia, there are abundant opportunities to bareboat in very demanding waters. Your worries about your ability to charter on your first trip are magnified tenfold at the prospect of the tide-ridden English Channel or the windswept Aegean islands. Many of these fears can evaporate in the face of common sense and good seamanship, for the same rules of sound cruising practice that apply in the Caribbean work just as well in the most demanding of charter areas. Two or three charters in the Virgins and farther afield in the Caribbean should give you a sound basis for bareboating more or less anywhere, *provided you do your homework ahead of time.*

One of the cardinal rules of seamanship is to be prepared. The rule applies with double force in cruising areas far from home. It is not enough just to choose a yacht and arrive ready to cast off on your charter. You should acquire charts and cruising guides well ahead of time and study them carefully. The introductory chapters of cruising guides like Donald Street's admirable Caribbean volumes are a mine of information on tides, weather conditions, and other hazards. They will enable you to assess your skills against the potential challenges. If possible, check some cruising books out of your local public library and read how other sailors have fared where you are going. Many cruising people seem to have a compulsive urge to write about their experiences. If Lin and Larry Pardey or the Hiscocks have not been there, someone else will. These sources will give you an idea of the best seasons for cruising, what types of yachts to expect, and some data about tides, currents, and harbors (European cruising guides tend to be much more comprehensive than those commonly found in North America). Another useful source, if you can find them, are the annual volumes entitled *Roving Commissions*. These are cruising yarns written by members of the Royal Cruising Club in England that cover just about every area of the world from Singapore to Finland (R.C.C. Press, 4 Coval Lane, London, SW14, England). Another useful source is the Cruising Information Center, Peabody Museum, Salem, MA 01970, which specializes in cruise planning and can advise you about more or less any charter area in the world. A modest fee is charged for their services.

Preparing for a charter in a totally unfamiliar area is somewhat different from entering a new cruising ground as part of a longer cruise. Someone cruising to an area receives a gradual initiation as he approaches the new landfall or skirts the coasts that lead to it. The short-term charterer does not have this luxury. An average charter lasts only one or two weeks. Your first encounter with the new area comes as you cast off from the dock in a totally unfamiliar yacht, perhaps with unusual gear. Within a few minutes you may be facing a complex tidal problem or some intricate navigational challenge that long-distance cruisers can postpone or even avoid, because they have more time. There is only one solution to what one can call the "cold turkey" problem: *very careful advance preparation*. This preparation will give you time to practice any new skills you may need.

Judging whether you have the experience to charter in a totally strange area is a subjective business, for you must be self-critical in ways that a charter company will never be. European companies, for example, are about as careful as Caribbean charterers about the qualifications of their clients. But, since they operate in tidal waters, they tend to assume that every sailor with experience has sailed in strong tidal waters or that he has moored a yacht stern-to a quay, when this is common local practice. If you feel up to the challenge and the company passes you as fit, take the time to read up on tidal navigation and, if possible, practice any unusual skills beforehand. You should have no trouble if you plan carefully, begin with undemanding passages, and brief yourself on local conditions as thoroughly as possible. Not that this will eradicate all your worries, but you can reduce them.

A classic example where advance preparation is essential is when crossing from the English Solent to the Channel Islands off the Normandy coast of France. The critical element is the passage of the Alderney Race, a maelstrom of current and tide that flows between the island of Alderney and the French coast a little over 7 miles away. The tides can reach 9 knots over the ground in this notorious place. You must catch a favorable tide to pass through, which means that you must time your arrival off the race with some precision. The first time I made the passage in a 32-foot chartered sloop, I worried for days. We left the Solent in the evening with a 15-knot breeze and smooth seas, our hearts in our mouths, 10 hours in hand, and a favorable window of 3 or 4 hours in the morning for the passage of the race. We arrived 2 hours early. So we hove-to for breakfast. When the tide turned, we let draw and sailed swiftly and comfortably before a fine easterly into Saint Peter Port, Guernsey. What a load off my mind! Undoubtedly, careful preparation made all the difference. We had calculated when to be where and had allowed enough time for the passage across the Channel to Alderney.

A bareboat skipper with broad charter experience in Caribbean waters need have no fear of even the most demanding charter areas, provided he does his homework beforehand. The greatest fear is that of the unknown, one that attacks even the most experienced cruising people before they set sail. I once asked a venerable member of the Royal Cruising Club whether he ever felt afraid at sea. He fixed me with a pitying gaze. "My boy, I am often afraid. Anyone who says he is not is a damned liar," he remarked flatly and changed the subject. It was obvious to him that I had asked a stupid question. The bareboater is no different in this regard.

3   Bareboat Seamanship

Writing books about basic sailing skills has become such an industry that it may seem superfluous to add to the literature. I am unrepentant, however, for many newcomers to bareboating are rightly bemused by the seamanship apparently required of them. This chapter plots a course through the basics and stresses the fundamentals that any fledgling bareboat skipper should be familiar with.

Even many expert sailors find the transition from a small dinghy or trailer yacht to a 40-footer hard to make the first time around. The dinghy spins on her own length and is easily rowed, controlled under outboard, or brought to the dock. But a bareboat yacht weighs many thousands of pounds more, moves slowly, even ponderously on her way, and can carry awesome weight downwind into a slip, taking everything with her. Small wonder many first-time charterers are daunted by the prospect of sailing on their own. Fortunately, most charter companies have chosen easily handled, relatively predictable yachts for their fleets. With a little forethought and some practice, you can sail them easily and with confidence, knowing they will take you

through any weather in reasonable comfort. This chapter describes some of the basic maneuvers you should practice on the first days of your charter. Eliminate the surprises of unpredictable boathandling, and you should feel much more confident on your own.

Preparing to leave

You have boarded your yacht, stowed your gear, checked the provisioning, and a member of the company staff has given you a quick run-through above and below decks. Your crew is milling around, the sun is shining, a perfect sailing breeze is blowing, and you are eager to be off. But confusion reigns. The instructions given by the briefing staff spin in your head. You are on your own. This is the point at which you should sit down, have a leisurely soda, and look over the rig and sails, the engine controls, and safety gear. Good bareboat seamanship starts at the company dock. Take a few minutes to identify every halyard, its winch, the sheet leads, the reefing gear, and the anchor windlass controls. Make sure, too, that every member of the crew does the same, so that you begin to move about the boat instinctively from the very beginning.

Every time you leave a marina or anchorage, run through a short checklist. Here is a typical example:

- *Battery switch ON.* If there are two battery banks, the indicator should point to BOTH. When not using the engine, keep the switch at "1" or "2," alternating the position each day so that you discharge batteries evenly. Always run the engine with the switch at BOTH, so that all banks are charged.
- *Secure all loose gear,* bring fenders aboard, haul the swimming ladder up, and check for trailing sheets or other ropes. Close all hatches and ports and tighten them down securely.
- *Pump bilges dry.* This should be daily routine anyhow.
- *Tie dinghy astern,* with two lines. Remove outboard and secure on stern bracket.
- *Start engine,* checking that the ignition switch is on, batteries are charging, and oil pressure is reading normally. Check that controls are functioning as they should be.
- *Secure the anchor* in its chocks forward once it is aboard. Make sure all the line is down in the chain locker.

This checklist is almost fail-safe and can save even the advanced sailor problems underway. It is amazing how lines dangle overboard and fenders or oars are forgotten when there are six people aboard a 40-footer.

Once away from the marina and in open water, you can turn your attention to making sail.

Rigs and rigging

Most charter yachts are either sloop- or cutter-rigged, since bareboat companies try to keep everything as simple and robust as they can. Maintenance on a second mast merely adds to their yard bills.

After a small dinghy or trailer boat, the forest of lines confronting you may seem a little daunting. But take heart. The charterer has rigged the yacht as simply as possible, both for ease of maintenance and for easy handling and safety in rough weather. Unlike privately owned yachts, most charter vessels are sent out with working sails and only a relatively small jib. While you may have to reef your mainsail, you will not, under normal circumstances, have to change headsails on a bumpy foredeck. Almost all charter boats are supplied with roller-furling gear—some of them allow you to reef the jib by partial rolling. Be sure to check this out with the charterer, however.

It is, of course, very difficult to generalize about charter-boat rigs, because there are many variations on the simple theme. The company will show you the setup, but you will find common features.

Mainsails are normally of moderate size, easily handled by one person in even heavy winds. The CSY-44 cutter, for example, has a total sail area of only 905 square feet, sufficient to sail comfortably under most conditions, but not a rig that will overburden an inexperienced crew.

Most mainsails are conventionally rigged, with a halyard and a single, deep "jiffy reef" with reef points. Dacron sails tend to deteriorate in the sun's ultraviolet rays, so many companies supply mainsails with protective cloth that serves as a sailcover as you stow the sail on the boom. A length of shock cord along the boom is pulled over the sail onto hooks on the other side, securing the sail tightly to the spar. Before you leave the dock for the first time, loosen the sail and check whether there are battens in the leech. Most charter companies have eliminated them or sewn them in place. If there are battens, make sure they are all in their pockets and that none are broken. It is a good idea to ask for a few spares to carry aboard during your charter. Also check the inboard ends of the batten pockets for wear. The company will have set the tension of the outhaul on the boom. Do not alter this.

Another golden rule: Check to see that the bitter end of the main halyard and sheet are secured. Nothing spoils a charter more than losing a halyard aloft.

Some larger yachts have roller-furling mainsails. The more expensive ones vanish into the mast, while others are on rollers just aft of the spar. These loose-footed sails are less efficient than conventional mains, and I have had bad luck with them. The procedure for setting and furling is basically the same. It is important to turn head-to-wind and to maintain tension on the outhaul as you furl the sail.

Most charter yachts have heavy mainsails, often made of 9-ounce Dacron. This makes them somewhat harder to handle on the boom than conventional mainsails, but you soon get used to it.

Jibs on bareboats are usually roller-furling, relatively small working sails that give you little driving power in light air and do best in winds between 12 and 20 knots. While I have chartered yachts where genoas, storm sails, and even a spinnaker are provided, this is unusual. The charterers rig their boats for moderate weather and assume that most sane bareboaters will stay in port if it is blowing hard. At the same time, they have to allow for

Roller furling gear is standard equipment on many bareboats, especially in the Caribbean. (Brian M. Fagan)

their yachts' being caught out in a blow. So a moderate jib area is the sensible rule.

I hate roller-furling gears and they hate me. Just the sight of me aboard is license for them to jam in a 25-knot wind, to tear the jib, or to end up with snarled furling lines. But to give the charter companies their due, most of these problems are my fault, for there is an art to handling roller-furlers.

Most yachts are equipped with well-known roller makes like Hood, Hyde Streamstay, or a Stearns rig. The furling line is normally led down the starboard side of the yacht, with a cleat close to, or on, the cockpit coaming. Always make sure the line is under tension and bent around the cleat, so you can find it quickly in an emergency. All roller-furlers are rugged, troublefree pieces of equipment, provided you obey the rules for handling them:

• Unfurl the jib carefully, maintaining light tension on the furling line so that it winds properly around the drum at the bow.

• *Never* use brute force or a winch to unwind or furl the jib.

• When furling the jib in anything but light to very moderate air, turn the boat downwind so that you relieve the tension on the sail. You can furl the blanketed sail with ease even in the heaviest weather. Maintain some tension on the sheet as you haul in, so that even coils form round the forestay. Do not let the sail flog uncontrollably, especially downwind. You will find that the sail and sheets wrap around the forestay. The penalty is a horrendous muddle that can only be cleared by some precarious foredeck work. The last

time this happened to me was on a rainy night in the middle of the Gulf Stream off the Florida coast. We had to bring the jibsheets forward and wind their coils around the stay about a dozen times before we could free the sail and stow it properly.

Most roller-furling gear allows you to sail with a reefed jib, that is to say, with the sail partially unrolled. Check this with the company before you leave. Again, if you want to reef, run the boat downwind so that you can furl canvas with the sail blanketed behind the mainsail.

Most people enjoy the advantages of roller-furling gear and seem to have little trouble with it. Do not interfere with the jib halyard, which maintains a proper tension on the forestay roller. The company sets this up and most prefer that you not touch them, except in grave emergency.

Staysails are found on CSY yachts and some other charter boats and provide a convenient way of breaking down the sail area up forward. Personally, I like staysails. They are easily set and are a marvelous accelerator on the kind of beam reach you can enjoy in Caribbean waters. The rig is simplicity itself—a halyard, a single sheet and track, and a short boom where the sail is stowed out of the way with the same sort of shock-cord arrangement as the main. A staysail is, of course, a much smaller sail than the roller-furling jib. It adds driving power on a reach, can be used upwind, and is a useful inboard sail up forward when it is too rough to fly the jib. Many first-time charterers have never met a staysail before and are reluctant to use it. Properly set and trimmed, it can add a knot or more to your boat speed. The best way to learn the staysail's effectiveness is to try to set it while watching the knotmeter. If the sail adds to your speed or steadies the boat, use it.

Spinnakers and drifters are rarely found on Caribbean charter boats and on only a few bareboat yachts offered in Europe or on the Great Lakes. Most companies find the wear and tear on them too expensive to justify the cost—nor are they happy about unleashing inexperienced sailors with such a powerful sail as the spinnaker. For all intents and purposes, the average bareboater can safely ignore such exotica.

Some European yachts are supplied with storm jibs, since the odds of being caught out in a blow are somewhat higher in northern waters. They are normally set on the forestay or on the staysail stay if a roller-furler is carried. If you do charter a boat with a storm jib aboard, check how the sail is set before you need it in earnest. In particular, be sure that the correct wire spans and snap shackles are in place on the jib, so that you do not have to find them in 45 knots of wind.

Once you have mastered the details of the rig, it is time to take off and to see how your boat handles.

Handling under power

The charter company will have shown you the engine controls and emphasized the importance of never running the diesel without the ignition switch on. Clearing the marina will be straightforward enough. Many companies insist that their staff take you out into open water before leaving you alone. Once you have plenty of sea room, spend a few minutes discovering how your yacht maneuvers under power.

First let her come to a complete standstill. Then try going astern. Remember that the effect of a clockwise-turning propeller is to kick the stern to starboard, so that the bow goes to port. This effect is, of course, reversed when going astern. You should turn the rudder in the opposite way to counteract the starboard sheer of the bow. A heavy-displacement, full-keel boat is often tricky to maneuver astern. You may find that a considerable distance and quite a lot of throttle are needed before she obeys the helm. With practice and bursts of stern power, you should be able to place the stern of your boat just about where you want it. Better to practice in open water with no danger of hitting anyone else.

Put the engine out of gear and let the boat lose steerageway. She will turn stern to wind. It follows that it is easy to turn a power-driven yacht away from the wind, but much harder to turn into it under engine alone. The windage and propeller effect can combine to make this almost impossible in strong winds, even using near-full power. Try turning into the wind in the moderate conditions of your first day and know what your boat can and cannot do ahead of time.

Now try hard-over turns ahead to port and starboard. Owing to propeller effect, you will find that your yacht will have a tighter circle to port or starboard, depending on the direction the propeller turns. It is important to know which is tighter, for there are bound to be times when you will need to turn away from, or into, the wind in crowded anchorages. Most charter boats will turn in about one and a half times their length and are practically impossible to turn very tightly by going forward and astern and using the rudder. The best way is to use short bursts of power ahead and astern, using the natural turning movements of the vessel to turn her round. Again, practice this in open water before you need to do it in a hurry in close quarters. The success of the maneuver depends on many variables such as current, the wind direction, and the individual performance of your boat.

Coming alongside or bringing up to anchor requires an ability to place your boat exactly where it needs to go. With a little practice, you should be able to power your boat upwind at very slow speed. You can juggle the throttle while watching a mark on shore. Cut back the power or increase it very slightly until the landmark is absolutely stationary abeam. Having mastered this, return downwind and try reaching the same spot, gradually cutting your speed, then using the engine controls to remain stationary. Once you are proficient at this, you should have no trouble approaching an anchorage.

How often have you envied a professional fisherman or expert powerboat skipper his uncanny ability to berth alongside with the minimum fuss? In fact, the skills are easily learned, provided you understand propeller effect and how your boat handles under power. In currentless waters, you can use the propeller effect to bring yourself alongside piers or, when coming in on the "disadvantaged" side, to slow down gradually as you approach, so the stern does not kick out. The problem of berthing is compounded by the windage of a sailing vessel, especially when stern or cross winds are blowing or, even worse, currents are acting against the wind. Marina berthing can be very tricky indeed in strong crosswinds (see figure below). Best to play it safe if you are in a heavy yacht. If there is room to do so, berth across the end of one of the fingers temporarily, get lines ashore, then warp the yacht into her berth. Lighter-displacement vessels, but probably few charter boats, may be able to steer into the berth and secure quickly before the wind catches them, but your crew must be alert and ready to jump ashore to take turns around cleats. If you have any doubts about your abilities under power, lie off, send two crewmembers ashore with long lines, and use the lines, winches, and engine to berth safely. Needless to say, keep the lines clear of your propeller.

Some common marina and harbor situations are described in the accompanying figure.

When maneuvering under power, make sure you know the limitations of your astern power, and *always* be prepared for unexpected engine failure. When entering or leaving a harbor or marina, have bow and stern lines ready and the anchor available to let go if need be. If anchoring, have the gear broken out well ahead of time and sails ready to cast off so you can sail downwind out of trouble if need be.

By now you will be tired of engine work, and a fine sailing breeze may be beckoning. So hoist the canvas and find out how she handles under sail alone.

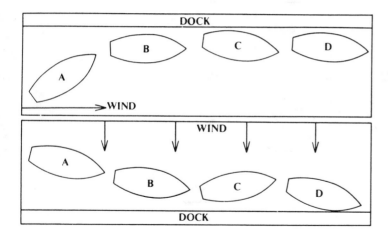

Left: Coming alongside a wall. Upper diagram: *Wind is astern, no current or adverse current. Yacht comes in at an angle, turns parallel to the wall and goes astern. This should move the stern in. Crew members have to do quick work with lines ashore to stop her.* **Lower diagram:** *Wind abeam. Almost certainly the bow will turn to leeward as you slow down, so to compensate you sheer away from the way.*

Below: Two ways of turning your charter yacht in a confined space. *Yacht 1 runs parallel to the starboard quay, then runs astern across the channel before returning the way she came. Yacht A steers across the channel, reverses to port, then proceeds. Needless to say, you need the channel to yourself for this maneuver!*

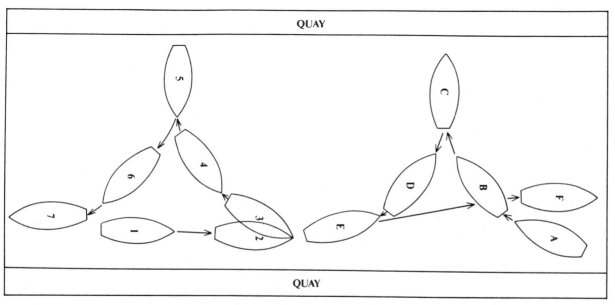

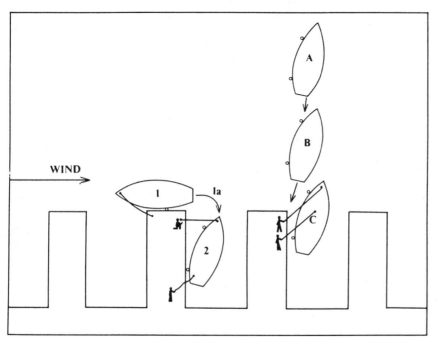

Docking in a marina under power with a cross wind. *Of course, you can come straight in and rely on your engine to stop you. But this can be risky.* **Two alternatives:** *Left-hand vessel has played it safe, secured alongside an end tie. She then warps into the dock with two crew members ashore handling the lines. Right-hand vessel is highly maneuverable, especially astern. She approaches in reverse, her stern sheering across the wind, fenders in place. A crew member jumps from the stern with a line, then another jumps from the bow. The boat is eased into her berth.*

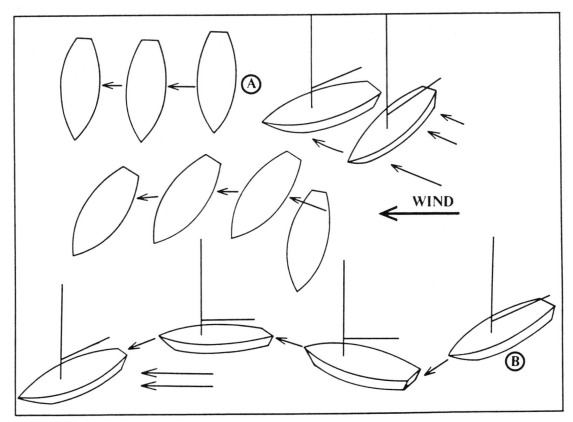

Drifting and balance

The drifting charter yacht. A. *A modern yacht when drifting with rudder free tends to seek the wind with her stern. She lies almost abeam, or with stern to the wind. Try this with your yacht and determine her tendency as early in the charter as possible.* **B.** *Steering downwind under bare poles in any strength of wind can sometimes get you out of a nasty spot when your engine fails. Know your boat's behavior. Some have excellent control downwind; others drift out of control. Here's a typical behavior pattern.*

There is a world of difference between a small trailer yacht or a centerboard dinghy and even a 30-foot charter boat. Smaller vessels respond almost instantly to changes of course and sail trim, to lowering the centerboard or turning downwind. Everything on a larger yacht is more deliberate; you have a little more time to think. Theoretically, this makes everything less complicated, but in fact, new factors like windage and the pushing-pulling effects of tide and current can enter into your maneuvering.

One of the best ways to learn how your charter yacht behaves is to find some sheltered, tideless, open water where you can find out her drifting and handling characteristics. If weather conditions are benign, turn off the engine and let the boat drift. In all probability her stern will turn toward the wind, but the angle to it may vary from beam-on to stern-to wind. Some designs make a little headway, others progress slowly downwind.

Let the rudder swing free. Your vessel will probably drift to leeward, yawing slightly. The amount of leeward drift depends on the hull shape, displacement, and windage aloft. Heavy, full-length keel yachts will tend to drift more predictably than fin-keeled boats. Let her drift for a while and find out how she lies. Then lash the wheel or tiller amidships and again see what happens. This information is of vital importance in rougher weather and when you have to heave-to for some purpose like bailing out the dinghy.

Next, try steering the boat downwind and see how much control you have. In moderate air, you may be able to steer her quite precisely. This is an invaluable quality in some tricky situations—for instance, when your engine fails and you have to drift clear of other boats in a crowded anchorage, in water too deep to anchor.

All this may seem a bizarre way to begin a charter, but a few minutes observing the behavior of your boat under bare poles and then under sail will relieve many of your anxieties later on. For example, you may have to sail into an anchorage or wait offshore while you fix a minor problem with your engine. I once saw this happen in the Bahamas. The skipper hove-to off the anchorage entrance while he and his crew lowered the main, prepared the anchor, and examined the bay for a suitable berth. Then he let the jib draw and sailed slowly toward his chosen spot, well clear of other yachts, where he anchored safely. This particular crew had a good idea how their boat handled with reduced rig and no sails at all.

Next, set the mainsail and jib. Immediately, the behavior of the yacht changes, for she is subject to the forces of the wind. Put her on a close-hauled course, balance the sail trim, and let go of the wheel. Some yachts will continue to sail themselves to windward, luffing occasionally in the puffs. Others will head into the wind, cast off on the other tack, and lie hove-to with the jib aback. A few vessels may even bear away to leeward and jibe downwind. Most heavier charter yachts behave well, if ponderously, hard on the wind. You are likely to be able to lash the helm for a few minutes, while the boat self-steers. Whatever the behavior of the yacht, you will at least understand it from the beginning. The attitude of the yacht when close-hauled is a useful piece of knowledge when your engine fails and you have to beat out of an anchorage, or when you want to heave-to for lunch or a swim.

Now turn the yacht on a beam reach and again let go the helm. Most charter boats will tend to head into the wind and stop with their sails flapping, even tack and heave-to. Once again, the average yacht is predictable in its behavior, once you have taken the trouble to identify it. Take the helm again and turn downwind with the main and jib goose-winged. Again let go. Most yachts will veer to one side and either jibe or throw the jib aback. There is no need to jibe all standing, just allow her to go through the initial turn before taking control again.

How will your yacht handle under main alone or with only the jib? Take a few minutes to experiment. These maneuvers will give your crew invaluable experience of halyards and sheets that will stand them in good stead later on. Try going to windward under both sails alone, measuring the amount of leeway and the progress you make to weather. Then try running and reaching, to gauge how much control and steerageway you have under various combinations of reduced rig. Should your main tear or your roller-furling jib jam, you will then have much greater confidence in your ability to work the yacht under reduced canvas.

Finally, set both sails again and heave-to. Then practice reefing the mainsail several times, so that your crew is letter perfect should the wind come up suddenly later in the cruise.

Every yacht varies in its behavior with weather conditions and according to her hull design, displacement, and windage. Your best insurance of confident boathandling on a charter is to run your boat through these simple maneuvers right at the beginning.

Getting the feel

By now you should have some sense of how your bareboat maneuvers under sail. This should give you an idea of her predictable behavior in open water and under different combinations of sail area. Now sail her for a while, on passage to your first anchorage. Let everyone steer, trim the sails, try different points of sail. The more predictable her handling to you, the more enjoyable and safe your vacation will be.

Pretty soon you are going to be sailing in more confined quarters. A wise charterer will practice a number of critical maneuvers before entering congested waters. Among other things, you should be able to predict how your yacht will carry way, to control your speed under sail, and above all to pick up an object that falls overboard.

Carrying way

A dinghy or small trailer yacht that is luffed head-to-wind will carry her way for a very short distance before falling off. A heavier-displacement charter boat will keep going for a considerable distance, perhaps as much as several lengths in light air, much less in a strong wind. Knowing how your boat carries way is vital when anchoring under sail or power, picking up mooring buoys, and recovering objects from the ocean.

The first passage of the charter is the best time to learn your boat and also a good moment to train your crew for emergencies. If the weather conditions are suitable, tie a weight of some sort (perhaps a stone from ashore) to a fender and throw it overboard. The submerged weight will minimize drift in current-free waters and you can practice recovering the fender at your leisure.

First, imagine that the fender is a mooring buoy you have to recover with a boathook. Approach it from downwind, luff head-to-wind, and try to stop the bow right over the buoy so that you can hook it aboard. In a light breeze, you will have to allow several boat lengths for the yacht to stop dead, while in strong winds you must luff almost at the fender, for the yacht will soon pay off out of control at mercy of wind and waves. You will probably misjudge when to luff the first two or three times. Station a member of the crew on the bow to indicate where the buoy is underfoot. Make sure that at least one other crewmember practices this, in case you are ill or incapacitated.

Now try a variation on the same maneuver. Approach the fender downwind. Once just past it, luff sharply into the wind and head for the float. You will find that the abrupt action of the rudder stops the boat almost immediately. Again, practice this until you feel your judgment is finely tuned.

Using the fender as a marker, try approaching it on a reach, slowing down to as close to a dead stop as you can. Let out the main and jib as far as they go. The boat will slow, but the process of slowing will bring the apparent wind aft and she will tend to pay off. As the bow moves away from the wind, the sails will fill unless they are let right out. Even then, stopping dead in the water is a virtual impossibility. Nevertheless, try the maneuver, so that you know how your boat behaves in an emergency.

Even nicer judgment is needed to pick up the buoy downwind, something that can only be done with a current or tidal stream against the wind. Here you use your sail area to control your movement against the current. Sail well upwind of the fender, drop your jib, and then the main. Station a crewmember at the main halyard, telling him to be ready to hoist or lower the peak. Now judge the speed of your boat against the current under bare poles. Add sail, if necessary, to bring you right up to the fender. This maneuver takes the nicest of sailing judgment and considerable experience. It is tricky even under power.

Finally, take the weight off the fender and practice picking up the float as it drifts. Make certain that at least two other members of the crew try this. You might be the person who falls overboard.

Stopping the boat under sail

Every bareboater needs to stop while under sail, perhaps to have a leisurely lunch underway on a longer passage, to reef, read a chart, or to bail the dinghy in rough weather. It will pay you to practice stopping very early on in your charter.

One simple way to stop is to let out the jib and main as far as they will go, then head slightly into the wind, and lash the wheel or tiller to leeward. The yacht will then lie beam-to the wind. As she loses way, the apparent wind will move farther aft and the main, which can only be let out to the shrouds, will fill again. So the vessel will back and fill while drifting slowly forward. This temporary way of stopping is best in light or very moderate airs, when the sails will not flog to ribbons.

Heaving-to is the best way of stopping in both moderate and rough weather. Full-length keeled vessels heave-to well with the mainsail sheeted in and the jib hauled aback. You lash the rudder to leeward and the boat should lie comfortably with the wind forward of the beam. Fin-keeled charter yachts may yaw around much more, in which case try lowering the mainsail or slacking it somewhat. Experiment with your main until you find the ideal settings. Few, if any, bareboaters will ever have to heave-to in gale conditions. Under these circumstances, you would rely on jib or main alone. It is surprising how many even quite expert seamen have never learned to heave-to, for to do so is simplicity itself. The best way is to tack the boat without letting go the jibsheet. Bring her about and lash the helm to leeward. The effect is dramatic. The boat stops fighting the waves and lies comfortably at a slight angle of heel. You can eat, reef, navigate, or whatever, in comfort. When you are ready to move on, simply unlash the helm, let the jib round on the other side, and away you go.

Motorsailing

Bareboat charterers tend to use their engines or to motorsail more frequently than people who own their own boats. This is partly because of tighter schedules and partly because no one wants to ruin a short vacation by bashing to windward. All too often, charterers place undue strain on themselves and their boats by trying to motor directly into the teeth of boisterous tradewinds or steep seas. Better to take a little longer, using the sails and engine to make your

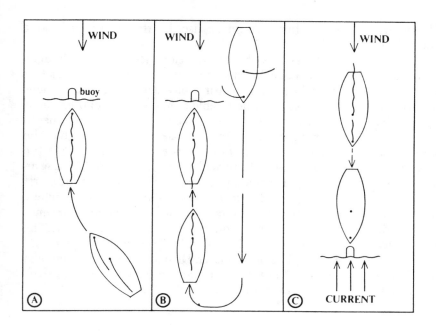

Picking up a mooring under sail. A.
*No current. You approach the buoy
close-hauled, then go head to wind and
lose final way at the moment you pick
up the ring.* **B.** *Approaching the buoy
downwind with no current. Pass the
mooring, turn head to wind, and carry
your way up to the buoy.* **C.** *Wind
behind you, current against it. This is
tricky. If the current is strong, approach
the mooring downwind against the
current; lower sails to reduce speed.
The adverse current will help you stop
at the buoy.*

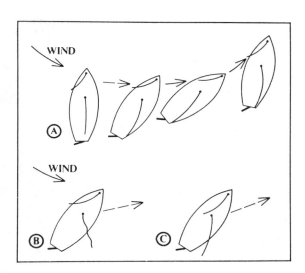

Heaving-to. *Vessel A is hove-to with the jib aback and the
helm down. Some designs will vacillate in this mode. Vessel
B is lying with main flapping and stays quiet. Vessel C is
also lying quietly because both jib and main are sheeted less
hard, the jib only just amidships.*

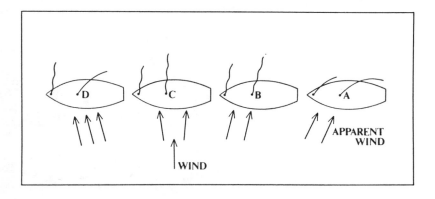

Stopping. *The wind is abeam. You let
go the sheets; the apparent wind moves
aft gradually until the mainsail begins
to fill again (diagram, left). At this point
you will drift slowly ahead, luffing and
laying off in turn.*

way to windward. If there is any wind at all, you are foolish to motorsail. You will get there just as fast, if not faster, by sailing.

The secret of effective motorsailing is to use the correct balance of sail and power. When working to windward, you are best advised to set the mainsail or, in stronger winds, the reefed main. This will steady the boat, give you some additional drive, and at the same time keep the yacht upright enough for the propeller to get a good grip of the water. Very often, setting the jib will heel the boat too much for the engine to be fully effective.

The engine is often used on heavier charter yachts to give the boat more speed against a lumpy sea. Again, do all you can, if necessary by reefing, to reduce heeling.

Never motorsail into a congested anchorage. Lower sails first and enter under power, keeping the sails ready for emergency use in the event of engine failure.

The secrets of bareboat seamanship are forethought and practice. With some careful preparation and a few short hours on the first day devoted to experimentation, you should be able to handle your chosen yacht with ease. Twenty-five percent of bareboat seamanship is preparation, common sense, and forethought. The rest you can gain only from experience. Naive is the sailor who thinks he will never get into trouble, drag an anchor, or scrape someone else's boat. One of the worst anchor drills I ever saw was in Bimini, Bahamas, where a seaman of vast experience had to re-anchor four times before his yacht would stay put in the current. "The worst foul-up in 25,000 miles," he called it over a well-earned glass of rum later. He had simply miscalculated again and again. It can happen to the best of us—the sooner you start learning, the better!

4 Anchoring

You have enjoyed three hours of idyllic sailing, away from the rush of airlines, baggage inspections, and company check-outs. The wind is dropping gradually and your thoughts turn idly toward your anchorage for the night. Then, suddenly, the truth hits home. You are about to anchor an unfamiliar yacht in a strange anchorage. Several other boats are obviously converging on the same spot. As the cove comes into sight, you see a few vessels already comfortably anchored in the shelter, their crews idly watching your approach. Mentally, you run over the steps you will need to take. The sails have to be furled, the engine started, the anchor gear prepared. Will there be enough swinging room? How much scope will you need? The prospect of anchoring becomes suddenly menacing and slightly frightening, especially in front of an audience.

Take heart! You are not alone. Nothing worries most crusing skippers, even experienced ones, more than the mechanics of anchoring safely and staying in the same place when they have done so. Most charter company and sailing school courses concentrate heavily on anchoring. They regard it as the most difficult skill for a

novice charterer to master, for there are many variables to consider as you approach an unfamiliar anchorage to spend the night. When I told one charter company manager that I was writing a book on bareboating, he was pleased. "Please emphasize anchoring," he begged. "We have more problems with charterers who anchor badly and damage their boats than with anything else." The manager is right. You should pay careful attention to learning about anchoring—some people would say almost to the exclusion of anything else—long before you embark on your first charter.

You are almost certain to have some anchoring problems when you first begin, especially if the wind pipes up and anchorages are crowded. Again, take heart! Even the most experienced skipper sometimes gets into trouble and makes silly mistakes. Congested anchorages have been the scene of some of my greatest cruising triumphs and worst traumas. Perhaps the worst was when I had to anchor in a 45-knot gale at Vivero in northwest Spain. We anchored twice in the windswept anchorage and dragged 30 fathoms of chain each time. Then we laid out two anchors in a fortunate lull and stayed where we were. Two hours later, an English yacht anchored right on top of us and dragged ever closer. It took half an hour to persuade her to re-anchor, but by the time she did we were fending her off from our rigging. It was not until 0200 that everyone was settled down for the night. Moments like this tempt one to give up sailing forever. But the occasional moments of triumph make everything worthwhile, like the time when the clutch on our chartered 34-footer failed and we had to anchor under sail in the congested waters of the Bight in the British Virgins.

The Bight was crowded with large bareboats. Everyone was lying head-to a 20-knot breeze blowing down the middle of the anchorage. It was cocktail time. It seemed as if everyone was watching. We beat up to the yachts, heeling sharply to the gusts. Anxiously, I surveyed the anchored yachts, while briefing the crew on the sequence of orders to follow.

"There's a gap," cried one of the crew, pointing to a space among a group of 40-footers. There was just enough water for us to swing if we laid the anchor in the right spot—but no margin for error.

"No engine, no second chances," I murmured. "Let's go."

There was silence as we beat through the anchored boats and lowered the genoa well ahead of time.

"What about your engine?" yelled one skipper.

"The clutch is shot," I yelled. He shrugged his shoulders and sat back to watch, obviously ready to fend off if we ran into trouble.

"Now." The crew dropped the main in a few seconds. We turned in to the wind, lost speed, let go the anchor in just the right place. The wind carried us back to a firm snub. We lay in just the right place.

I breathed a sigh of relief. Then I heard the applause from the neighboring boats. So I stood up, raised my sun hat, and bowed. What else could one do? It was a *very* special moment!

The secrets of successful anchoring

Yes, we executed a perfect maneuver, and I did have a relatively experienced crew. But things would have gone much less smoothly if we had not taken care to prepare for all sorts of eventualities ahead of time. Every member of the crew knew exactly what to do. The dinghy was brought close astern, so that it would not swing into other boats. We had cleared away not only the main anchor, but had the second anchor and line on deck ready to let go if the first one dragged or we were set down on our neighbors. Insofar as it was

possible, we had thought out every eventuality ahead of time.

The first secret of anchoring is careful and methodical preparation *before* you enter the anchorage and are close to other yachts. Everyone has seen them, the hasty skippers who charge into a crowded anchorage at full speed, dump the anchor and a pile of chain overboard, and then go below without a second glance at their neighbors. These are the yachts that drag when the wind gets up, the boats that every experienced charterer dreads, the people who enjoy no peace of mind from one day to the next. If such skippers spent a little more time on careful preparation, they and their neighbors would sleep so much better. So, make ready ahead of time.

In moderate weather, you can make many of the necessary preparations while still on passage. Heavier conditions may require that you reach shelter before furling sails and breaking out an anchor. But the same rule applies. Lower sail and get ready to let go anchor well clear of other boats. Frantic, last-minute gropes for the anchor will lead to inevitable trouble.

The second secret is to use your engine in congested anchorages. Purists may protest, but they are being unrealistic. Your primary responsibility is for the safety of your crew and for the expensive yacht you are skippering for a few short weeks. Even if you are experienced yourself, you may be maneuvering in the vicinity of much less expert crews, who may not know what to do in an emergency. So use your engine, if only out of consideration for others. You must, of course, be prepared to sail up to anchor if your engine fails, but practice this in open water long before you need to and, if possible, anchor clear of others or in an uncongested anchorage.

The third rule is to be fanatically careful of how and where you drop anchor and lay out the line. Good holding ground, adequate scope, and a hard snub are primary secrets of good anchoring. It is remarkable how few skippers pay careful attention to snubbing their anchors. Then they wonder why they drag when the wind pipes up.

Lastly, be prepared for trouble. Brief your crew ahead of time as to what to do if you drag or someone comes down on you in the middle of the night.

If you obey these rules, think of others, and avoid overcongested anchorages, you should minimize the traumas of anchoring.

Ground tackle

Most charter yachts are equipped with two anchors,

Plow anchor is the most common design used by charter companies. (Brian M. Fagan)

more than adequate ground tackle for the local cruising you are likely to be doing.

Debates about the best type of anchor to use on different holding grounds rage wherever bar admirals assemble and in the pages of the yachting literature. Fortunately, the charter companies have done the thinking for you. Most use either CQR (plow) or Danforth-type anchors. The former are the best all-round anchors except on rocky bottoms, while Danforths are especially good in hard mud, but tend to skip over coral, grass, and gravel. I have had nothing but good experiences with both. You will be quite safe with whatever ground tackle the company supplies. They know local conditions and equip their yachts accordingly.

Most larger yachts have a CQR bower or main anchor of appropriate size (normally around 35 pounds for a 40-footer), a 30-to-50-foot length of chain, and up to 250 feet of nylon anchor line. The plow is stowed on a bow roller and lashed in place, while the chain and line are kept below in a special chain locker forward. Many companies mark their anchor lines with lengths of small stuff or labels every 50 feet. Be sure to ask them about this at check-out time. The bitter end of the anchor line is normally secured to the yacht inside the chain locker. Quietly check this before you leave base. I once saw a beautiful charter yacht anchor off Mustique

in the Grenadines. The CQR snubbed beautifully. The boat coursed astern as the anchor dug in. They laid out more and more scope, until the bitter end flew out of the chain locker and went overboard—much to the entertainment of the other boats in the anchorage! Fortunately, the crew were able to anchor with the kedge and recover the line by diving into 25 feet of water.

Most charter companies have given careful thought to anchor leads, bow cleats, and anchor windlasses. The cleats should be placed where you can take a rapid turn round them to check a running anchor line or a warp under strain. Larger yachts are equipped with simple electrical windlasses with foot or hand controls. Be careful to use these only when the engine is running; many companies wire the switches so that the windlass will operate only under power. The electric motors drain batteries at record speed. But always use the engine to bring the yacht up to the anchor. The windlass is designed to help break the anchor out of the ground and should be used primarily for this purpose.

The first time you use the main anchor, carefully inspect the warp as it goes over the bow. Many bareboat anchors get hard daily use. Their lines sometimes become chafed and previous charterers either do not realize it or do not bother to report the damage.

Windlass and fairlead arrangement aboard a CSY-44. This layout works well in the Caribbean. (Brian M. Fagan)

The second, or kedge, anchor is normally a Danforth type, considerably smaller than the CQR at the bow. The kedge normally resides in a cockpit locker or a lazarette, together with a 30-foot length of chain and some 150 feet of line. You may go through an entire charter without ever using your kedge, but all too often you will need it to lay a stern anchor, to lie-to a Bahamian moor, or to haul yourself off the sand.

If the anchor is stowed in a cockpit locker, I would recommend bringing it out on deck, coiling the warp down and stopping it with fine thread, tying down the end to a cleat, and then securing the anchor to the stern

pulpit. You can then get at it in short order when you need to. Lazarette stowage is ideal if the yacht is large enough, because you can leave everything out of the way, the anchor lying on top of the chain, and the warp ready to run out in a hurry. Again, make sure you secure the bitter end ahead of time.

The kedge line is usually somewhat smaller than the main anchor line. You can control it from the cockpit with one of the genoa winches, but be sure the line leads clear of the pulpit or stanchions.

Most Caribbean charter yachts carry a small Danforth dinghy anchor, which is invaluable when you are snorkeling or diving. You can also use it to anchor your dinghy clear of beach breakers or over the stern to keep her from fouling a dock.

European charter boats have somewhat more variable anchor gear. Many English yachts carry 20 to 30 fathoms of chain on their main anchor, leaving nylon for the kedge. Chain gives you a great deal more weight on the bottom in strongly running tidal waters, but is much heavier to hoist and lower, less flexible, and can "growl" on the bottom at night. A windlass is almost essential for anchor chains on yachts over 35 feet.

The anchor gear on most charter yachts is robust and simple. It will hold your vessel in almost any weather. The variable is the way in which you, the charterer, use it.

Preparing to anchor

With a little luck, your first passage will be in moderate weather, so that you can practice your anchor drill at leisure. Start the engine and lower sails well ahead of time. This is the moment when you should clear the cockpit of surplus towels, beer cans, and other impedimenta that could be trampled underfoot. Then station the crew at their regular places for entering harbor.

If you have a large crew aboard, one person should stand at the stern, ready to bring the dinghy close under the stern, so that there is no chance that the painter winds around the propeller. Someone else should be stationed amidships, ready to transmit orders from the cockpit or information from forward. It is amazing how often communication breaks down between bow and cockpit.

This is the moment when you station the most experienced crewmember forward, with instructions to clear away the anchor. The anchor should be unlashed from the bow roller, the chain ranged on deck, leaving only rode in the locker. Above all, the foredeck crew should make sure that everything is ready to run free,

Anchor compartment with windlass on a Nicholson 32, an English design. Many European charter yachts come with chain rather than rope. (Brian M. Fagan)

often impossible for the anchor crew to hear orders from the cockpit and for the helm to understand what is going on at the bow. Your best bet is to communicate with hand signals, like those given in the figure below. I have found these to be highly effective even in emergencies, and especially when steering the yacht up to a mooring buoy or when lifting anchor under power. It is worth training everyone in these signals. Some skippers even go so far as to use a whistle as a signal to drop anchor. This is very effective and for some reason creates a profound stir among one's neighbors! Above all, insist that only one person (the skipper) give orders, and impress on your crew the importance of obeying instructions at once and of making sure that the cockpit knows exactly what is happening with the anchor once it is in the water. One skipper of my acquaintance insists that his crew repeat all orders upon receipt. This old navy custom works very well, even if it seems a little arbitrary. "I like it," one of his crew told me after a hectic anchoring session. "The skipper knows that we understand what he said—and blasts us to hell if we make a mistake!"

Once everything is in place, sails furled, and the anchor cleared away, make your approach to the anchorage. Motor slowly into the cove and make a slow traverse through the anchored boats. Make no attempt to anchor, simply feel out the situation. Where is the most sheltered water? Is there space to swing clear in the best spot? What about depth? Can you anchor inshore of other boats, leaving room to swing if the wind or tide changes? Where do you land a dinghy? What is the holding ground? Give yourself adequate time to juggle the many variables in your mind. Lie clear while you decide where to anchor, then share your plans with the crew, rehearsing rapidly the sequence of orders you will be using.

Clear orders and signals are vital. Here is a sequence of commonly used instructions:

"Starting final approach." This is the moment when you have entered the anchorage and are taking up your final course for the spot where you will drop the anchor.

"Engine's in neutral." Signals to the foredeck that you are losing way.

"Stand by." The anchor crew should now slide the anchor off the roller ready to let go, keeping chain in hand. The yacht will be close to the anchor spot, almost stopped, the engine now engaged astern.

"Drop." As the boat gathers way astern, the crew drops anchor and pays out the line.

"Snub." The order to take a turn of the rode around the bow cleat to snub the anchor. Once the snub is made, you pay out ample scope at your leisure.

that the bow cleat is clear, ready to take the rode when you snub the anchor. A large crew should have two people up forward, one to let go the anchor, the other to give signals to the cockpit. Ideally, the same crew should raise and lower the anchor several times, so that you have a regular team to use in rough conditions, when coordination and familiarity with the gear are important.

Communication between bow and stern is not nearly as straightforward as it appears. What with the noise of the engine, casual conversation, and the wind, it is

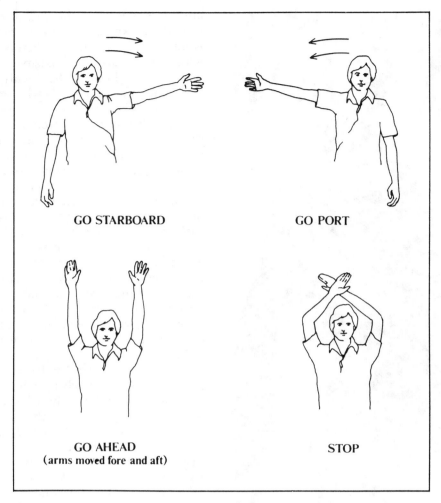

GO STARBOARD

GO PORT

GO AHEAD
(arms moved fore and aft)

STOP

Hand signals for coming up to anchor or maneuvering in confined spaces (looking from ahead).

Choosing the right spot is largely a matter of experience. In an empty anchorage, your primary criterion should be the most sheltered location, with sufficient room to swing to wind, current, or tide, whichever way they turn. You should have good holding ground, adequate protection from wind and surge, and easy access to shore. Congested anchorages, commonplace in many charter areas, present many more problems. The most sheltered places have usually been taken hours before you arrive, although there is always an off chance that someone will have just left. Look for a place where you will have room to swing freely. This may mean anchoring outside the other boats. Check, however, whether there is space close inshore, in deep water where other yachts are afraid to tread. There are, for example, a few anchorages in the Virgin Islands where you can lay out a stern anchor and lie just off the beach with your bow secured to a convenient palm tree. If conditions are quiet, this may solve the congestion problem beautifully for you—but such opportunities are few and far between.

Once everything is ready, set the yacht on a straight approach course to the spot where the anchor will be dropped. *Always* approach from downwind (or down-current if this is stronger), if there is space to do so. You must stop the vessel dead at the exact place where the anchor will lie below water, *not* at the spot where the yacht will finally end up. Control your speed very carefully, creeping forward dead slow. This gives you time to keep an eye on other boats and to react if the engine fails or some sudden emergency occurs. Mentally rehearse what you would do if the engine failed or

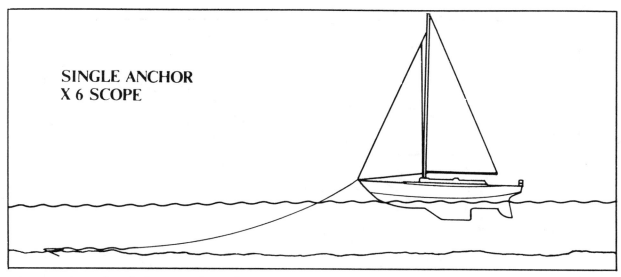

SINGLE ANCHOR
X 6 SCOPE

The properly anchored charter yacht, with six times scope, and short length of chain weighing anchor on the bottom.

someone fell overboard, so that you are prepared for all contingencies. If you are not satisfied with your first approach, go around again—the extra effort is well worth it. As you approach, check the fathometer carefully until you reach your chosen depth.

Once the yacht is positioned exactly where you want the anchor to be dropped, put the engine astern at slow speed. As the boat gathers way astern, and not before, drop the anchor and let the chain and rode run free, accelerating astern until you have good way on the vessel. Once a considerable amount of line is overside, some 75 feet or so, yell "Snub." The anchor crew should be paying out the line around a bow cleat. They now take the strain, watching the rode until the line becomes bar taut and the anchor hooks deeply into the bottom. If there is enough space to leave the helm unattended, the skipper should go forward and watch the snubbing line. He can then rest assured that the anchor is well laid.

Make careful preparations, study the anchorage closely, use an easily understood sequence of orders, and you should find anchoring much easier.

Dropping anchor

There is only one way to become expert at anchoring, and that is to go out and do it —again, and again, and again. But each time obey the fundamental rules of safe anchoring:

● *Adequate ground tackle.* You can assume that your charter yacht has the right gear for the job.
● *Proper holding.* Your anchor should take a deep bite in the ground and be snubbed into place.
● *Sufficient scope.* No anchor will hold without sufficient scope of chain and rode to absorb the snubbing weight of the yacht.

As far as is possible, you should standardize your anchor drill, so that the same sequence of maneuvers and instructions is used, even in the most congested or tiny anchorages. The drill then holds no surprises for either skipper or crew, and you can concentrate on putting the yacht in the right place and on laying the anchor properly.

A good snub ensures that your anchor is hard in the ground, for a well-designed plow anchor properly buried will hold up to 30 times its weight with ease. Adequate scope will make sure you stay there. Once the snub is made, pay out more line until adequate scope is over the bow. There are many formulas for adequate scope. No two sailors agree on any one of them, except for the principle that you cannot have too much line overside. A common formula calls for five times depth at low water for chain and rode, and three times depth for chain alone, but these figures apply to moderate conditions only. You are well advised to lay out much more, so that the rode lies close to the bottom (see figure above). The more scope you lay, the less likely the yacht is to snub at its cable when a gust comes. You will also reduce your sheer while at anchor. The first time you

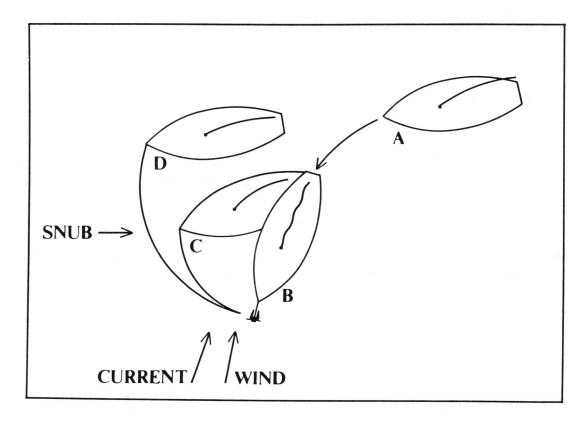

Dropping anchor under sail, wind, and current in same direction. The yacht comes head to wind under main alone (A, B), drops anchor when vessel is stationary. Boat drifts off to starboard and main fills as anchor line is paid out (C), the warp being snubbed when sufficient scope is over the bow (D). Sail is then lowered.

anchor, check in the chain locker how much line is left below, then adjust your scope accordingly. You can then mark the rode with thread to indicate adequate scope for that depth of water in the future.

Dropping anchor is more complicated under sail or when there are currents to contend with. Under sail, you should try to approach from downwind, luffing to bring the bows to a stop at the spot where you are to drop the anchor. If you are obliged to come to anchor on a reach or run, reduce sail so that you have complete control of boat speed. Downwind, you can creep ahead, dropping the anchor underfoot, snubbing it, and laying out the scope as you sail gently ahead. Once approaching the desired position, you lower sail and the yacht turns head-to-wind on her anchor. The anchor crew should be warned to drop the anchor at once when the boat is under sail, for the bows will pay off rapidly at the mercy of the wind. You must sheer the boat away from its anchor to avoid fouling the flukes with chain.

The charter companies have astounding tales to tell of anchoring glitches by inexperienced (and sometimes experienced) bareboaters. They tell of crews who dump chain and line overboard in a heap and are then surprised when their boat drifts towards the beach as they are drinking ashore. Then there are the charterers who motor into an anchorage, drop anchor and line as they are moving ahead fast, snub the cable, and stop engines. The wind blowing down the anchorage carries them astern, flips the anchor through 180 degrees, and they drag. One Florida charter manager complained about scope. Only the week before, he had had a yacht anchor in a sheltered spot in the Keys in 25 feet of water. The crew laid out about 40 feet of line and went to sleep. They woke to find themselves drifting on the open sea. Fortunately, they had drifted clear of the coral reefs astern. "Surely it's simple common sense," he complained. "The more line you lay out, the safer you are..." So lay out plenty of scope, you'll sleep better.

Staying anchored

Once safely anchored in tropical waters, go for a swim with a mask and snorkel and check your anchor. Is it buried in the bottom? If not, run your engine astern and achieve a proper snub. (In more temperate climates, row out in your dinghy and peer over the side with a mask.) Then check again and take some anchor bearings, throwing your bearing compass onto one or two easily identifiable landmarks ashore, preferably ones you can see at night. Make a note of the bearings and check them occasionally. Such a precaution is wise in high winds, where the bearings may give you vital early warning of a silent drag.

In light or moderate weather, your only concerns will probably be your neighbors or new yachts coming into the anchorage. If someone tries to anchor close to you, show him where yours lies, and tell him whether you are lying to two anchors. (A polite skipper will ask anyhow, but it is better to make sure.) If someone does anchor right on top of you, insist politely and firmly that he move to a safer berth. The unspoken law of congestion is that the first comer has priority. If the newcomers won't shift, don't get into a shouting match. Pointedly shift your berth—not that your exercise in tact will have much effect, but at least you will have peace of mind.

If the wind pipes up, check your anchor bearings and let out more scope, if necessary bending the kedge line or some other warp to the bitter end of your rode. The best way to do this is with two bowline knots. Place cloth, a length of hose, or some other chafing gear around the anchor line at the roller. If conditions become extreme enough to merit it, set an anchor watch (two hours each is enough), the crewmember on watch checking anchor bearings every few minutes. The watchkeeper should also keep an eye on your neighbors. Keep fenders handy for use against unwelcome guests who drag down on you in the depths of night.

With adequate scope and a properly set anchor, you will probably stay where you are, but your neighbors may not. Your first warning of a dragging visitor may be frantic hails or a loud bump. Awaken the crew at once, place one person at the helm ready to start the engine, and concentrate on keeping the dragging vessel from fouling your rigging or anchor line. Allow her to lie alongside with fenders for sufficient time to recover her anchor, *no longer*. Your primary concern must be your own yacht and crew. Someone should check constantly for lines over the side that could foul either boat's propeller. You should also make a careful note of the incident, the circumstances and time of the collision, and of any damage to your boat in case your charter company wants to file a claim against the owner. Above all, keep calm and do all you can to assist the other boat. The skipper is probably scared, upset, and anxious for any help available. After all, it could be you in the same predicament.

Raising anchor

Raising anchor is straightforward enough in moderate conditions. Use the engine to ease the boat up to the anchor, with one of the anchor crew giving hand signals to indicate where the line lies. Use the electric windlass only to break the anchor out of the ground. Again, station crewmembers to watch the dinghy painter as you motor away from your berth, and look out for the wind swinging the bow before you get way on.

Breaking out the anchor under sail is much trickier, especially when there is a current against the wind. When there is no current to contend with, hoist the mainsail and have the jib ready to unroll at short notice. Then hove in the rode until it is almost clear of the ground and right up and down. Then unroll the jib and back it so that the bow pays off on port or starboard tack, depending on the space available.

It is very difficult to get underway under sail in a congested anchorage. One possible strategy: hove the anchor short, then turn the boat bow for stern, unrolling the jib as you break the anchor out of the ground. You can then sail away downwind. If there is a current against the wind, you should break out the anchor, then sail clear under jib alone until you have room to round up into the wind and hoist the main.

The great secret of raising anchor is to let the boat do the work. Use the engine and the natural sheering of the boat on the rode to bring in the slack. Under normal circumstances, the windlass should give you sufficient power to break out the anchor. If it does not, check to see if the anchor is fouled on a mooring line or someone else's anchor. The latter is quite common in congested anchorages. To clear it, you are probably best advised to lie to the kedge while you pass the line around the other yacht's rode from the dinghy. If the water is shallow enough, you may be able to snorkel or dive to clear your anchor from an underwater obstruction. You can sometimes clear a fouled anchor by passing the bight of another line down the rode, but this requires patience.

Fortunately, it is rare that you cannot recover a fouled anchor. In waters where there is obvious danger of fouling, you can buoy it by tying a fender to a light

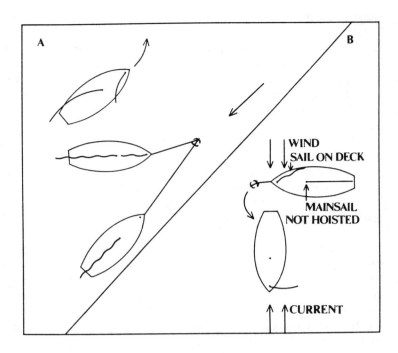

Breaking out the anchor under sail. A.
Mainsail is hoisted, then jib raised when cable is vertical and anchor almost off the bottom. The jib is then backed so that the anchor is broken out of the ground and yacht sheers off to port clear of dangers. **B.** *Wind against current. Lift anchor, then sail out of danger under jib alone.*

Hand signals for raising anchor (looking from ahead).

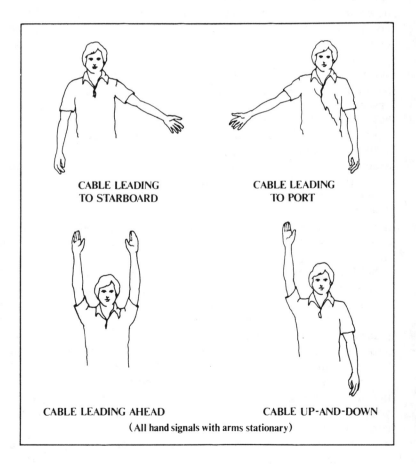

CABLE LEADING TO STARBOARD

CABLE LEADING TO PORT

CABLE LEADING AHEAD

CABLE UP-AND-DOWN

(All hand signals with arms stationary)

line attached to the eye on the anchor. Hopefully, you will be able to cockbill the fouled anchor and lift it vertically from the underwater obstruction. Sometimes the rode is fouled around coral heads in clear water. You can often unscramble the coils from the dinghy with the aid of a mask and snorkel. With a little ingenuity, a fouled anchor should not delay you long.

Laying two anchors

Lying to two anchors can give you welcome peace of mind in very strong winds and in situations where there is limited swinging room or a strong tide that flows in two directions up and down a channel. Charterers in southern California use bow and stern anchors in offshore island anchorages to minimize surge from Pacific swells, while the so-called Bahamian moor is popular in the Caribbean.

Laying a second anchor is an inconvenience, something that you should do only when strictly necessary. Many people lie to both kedge and main anchor even when they are by themselves in a well-sheltered anchorage, on the grounds that it will give them more security. This seems like overkill, except under very severe conditions. In congested coves, you will have to lay a second anchor if even one other yacht is doing so, otherwise your wider swinging circle will lead to inevitable collisions and angry words.

A common way to lay out a second anchor is to do so with your dinghy. You anchor in your desired berth, then lower the kedge and chain into the dinghy, rowing or motoring out as the crew pays out the warp from the deck. The skipper watches as you lay out the rode, giving hand signals to steer you to the right place. The anchor and chain are cast overboard, the line tightened until the yacht is securely moored fore and aft or from the bow.

You can, of course, lay out two bow anchors from the boat by dropping the bower, then motoring to the site for the kedge, paying out the main rode until you can drop the second anchor. Then you pay out the one and haul in on the other until you are in the right spot. Beginners are probably better off laying the second anchor from the dinghy until they can find an uncongested anchorage to practice in.

The Bahamian moor has been popularized by Caribbean sailor Donald Street and others as an ideal way of swinging on a single spot. You lay one anchor from the bow, the kedge 180 degrees in the opposite direction, bringing the line to the bow fairlead. The yacht will then swing in its own length. The Bahamian moor is especially useful in congested bays and in

places like Bimini, where the tide runs fast through the main channel. It is vital, however, that both anchors are well dug in and that ample scope is laid both bow and stern. All too often, people lay the second anchor with inadequate scope. The effect of the Bahamian moor is lost as the second anchor drags.

When entering an unfamiliar anchorage, check whether the other yachts are lying to two anchors. If in doubt, inquire of a neighboring boat and follow her lead. Nothing is more irritating than a single antisocial vessel lying to two (unnecessary) anchors when everyone is lying to one.

Anchoring and mooring

There are occasions, especially in the Mediterranean, where you will have to lie bow- or stern-to a quay, or even, as in Scandinavia, to a convenient rock or tree.

Many Mediterranean harbors require that you berth stern first. This is a somewhat trickier maneuver, one that requires nice judgment, especially in a strong wind. The trick is to lay your bow anchor well offshore, snub it in hard, then go astern until you can get a line ashore or to any neighboring yachts. Few heavy-displacement charter yachts handle precisely under power when going astern, so practice stern boards in open water before you approach the shore.

Personally, I prefer to lie bow-to, so that you have some privacy. Casual quay walkers seem to get a tremendous kick out of watching one eat dinner. On more than one occasion in Greece and Spain, I have been tempted to hang up a noticeboard with the menu printed out for all to see!

Lying bow-to and stern-to makes me somewhat nervous, largely because of the potential for damage to rudder or bow in shallow water or against a sea wall. And on more than one occasion, I have had to leave harbor in a hurry when a strong wind has threatened to blow us into a quay. Mykonos Harbor in the Aegean is an attractive place in calm weather, but murderous when offshore winds blow. Within a few minutes, steep, vertical-sided seas push into the harbor, bouncing around even the largest yachts berthed at the sea wall. I once had to leave at a moment's notice at dusk when an unexpected wind blew up. Fortunately, there are plenty of sheltered anchorages within a few miles and we were able to weather the gale at anchor in comfort.

A tremendous mystique surrounds anchoring, one that seems to fascinate even the most experienced cruising people. But there is nothing mysterious about

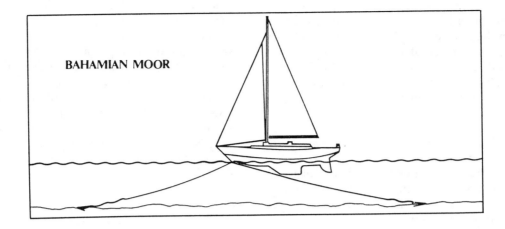

Allows the yacht to swing in its own length. Especially useful in tidal channels and restricted waters.

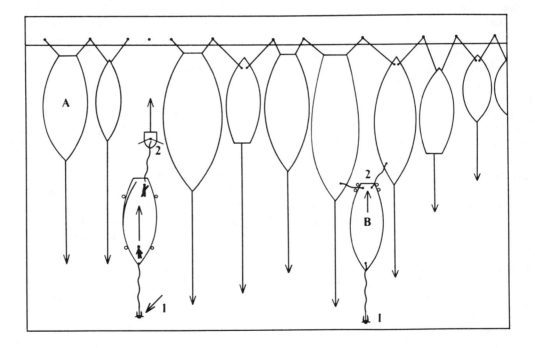

Securing stern-to a quay, Mediterranean style. Vessel at left has dropped anchor opposite a gap at (1), then gone astern under power. As she approaches other yachts, she launches a crew member with a stern line in a dinghy; crew member secures the rope to the quay, so that berthing can proceed (2). Yacht at right is securing at a congested quay. She lowers anchor at (1), then drops astern until lines can be thrown to bows of larger neighboring vessels. Stern is well padded with fenders (2).

successful anchoring. Time and time again, people drag anchor or have problems in congested berths because they fail to prepare beforehand, neglect to snub the anchor with a sharp stern board with the engine, or lay out insufficient scope. Invariably, the moment you are careless or casual with anchoring, it will catch up with you. We once anchored in the tiny harbor of Gavrion in the Aegean, a sheltered bay with limited swinging room only, what with ferries and fishing boats. It was a lovely evening, so we laid out 10 fathoms of chain in 25 feet, without checking whether the anchor was well dug in, close to a shallow sandbank. In the small hours of the morning a terrific thunderstorm blew up, with gusts over 50 knots. It took two hours of back-breaking work and constant relaying of anchors to haul us off the sand. The crew has not forgiven me to this day. Never again will I be casual about snubbing an anchor and giving myself adequate swinging room.

There is only one way to learn about anchoring—go out and do it for yourself. This is one area of chartering where experience counts. Fortunately, you can gain this experience in areas like the Great Lakes, the Virgins, or the Bahamas where the winds are benign and there is plenty of room to make mistakes.

5 Hazards and Mishaps

We were sailing from Bequia to Union Bay in the Grenadines on a perfect fall day. The wind was blowing at 15 knots on our port quarter, *Maria* was surging along at 6 knots plus. John was at the helm. Everyone else was reading, drinking rum, or just dozing in the sun. It was an idyllic, dreamy afternoon.

"What's going on up ahead?" John suddenly cried.

I opened a sleepy eye from my comfortable berth on the starboard cockpit seat. "Porpoises?" I asked.

"Looks like someone's in trouble," he said, peering across the leeward bow.

I sat up and looked under the staysail. A yacht was motoring in circles, its main flapping. The crew were gathered in the stern gesticulating at something in the water.

"Let's bear away and look." I eased the main and jib, while the rest of the crew bestirred itself.

We were soon within hailing range and could see the reason for the circling. A man was splashing frantically in the water, the crew of the yacht were shouting at him, lowering the main, and trying to motor up to him. No one seemed to be in charge.

"Do you have a dinghy?" I yelled.

"No, just an inflatable," they called back. "Can you pick him up with yours?"

We rolled up the jib, hove-to under staystail and main. John and another crewmember motored over to the man overboard, who was floating tiredly in the calm water between the two yachts. He grabbed onto the transom, and they rowed him over so the crew could help him up the swimming ladder. It turned out he was the skipper—and the only person on board who knew how to sail.

"They were lucky," remarked John as we unrolled the jib and sailed on. "That guy was really exhausted and they were all a little drunk. They hadn't a clue what to do, didn't even have the sense to stop the boat and let the skipper swim to a life jacket or something. The water was dead calm."

For the rest of that charter we trod more carefully than usual, for the experience had reminded us that the sea is a harsh mistress. Even when you sail in the most benign of waters, accidents can happen without warning. Sound seamanship requires being prepared

A well-equipped charter yacht, with two horseshoe lifebuoys, stowage for emergency lights. Man-overboard pole is stowed in transom at bottom right of picture. Life raft is kept under helm seat. This vessel is used for English Channel charters and is somewhat more comprehensively equipped than many Caribbean yachts. (Brian M. Fagan)

for the occasional emergency. Your peace of mind and the safety of all aboard will benefit. This chapter covers some of the common hazards of bareboating that can confront even the most experienced of charterers.

Safety gear

Every charter company equips its yachts with safety gear appropriate to the waters in which they operate. Caribbean yachts carry relatively little gear, equipment suitable for daylight sailing and for cruising within easy reach of base. European yachts tend to carry more comprehensive safety inventories, for night sailing is essential if you are to cross the English Channel or the North Sea. As the charter company checks you out, locate all safety gear on the boat *and make sure that every crewmember, however inexperienced, knows where key items are kept and how to use them.*

Life jackets will be provided for every crewmember. Make sure that everyone knows how to put them on. Insist that nonswimmers wear them when out of the cockpit or in the dinghy. Ideally, they should be stowed within easy reach of the helm.

Life cushions are normally to be found in the cockpit lockers. These make nice informal cushions for sunbathing, but always remember that their fundamental purpose is for flotation. On passage, it is wise to keep one on deck attached to a light line, so that you can throw it overboard at short notice. (They also make nice floating tables for soap or drinks, if you are swimming.)

The *lifering* is normally on a bracket on the stern pulpit. Check this carefully and make sure that the attachments for the grablines have not rotted in the sun. I once had them pull out, fortunately during an exercise. I like to keep the lifering attached to a rope coiled ready for immediate use, attached to the pulpit.

A length of Velcro is ideal for keeping it in place.

Fire extinguishers are essential on any yacht. Most charter companies provide at least two, one in a cockpit locker, the others mounted in the main saloon and perhaps in the aft cabin. Again, make sure everyone knows where they are located and how they operate.

Bilge pumps are as important as extinguishers. Most charter yachts have an electric pump in the main bilge, which you should run every day. Then there is a manual backup, normally located in the cockpit. Make sure everyone knows where the handle is stowed.

Flares are provided on every yacht and should be located in a locker close to the cockpit or chart table. Do not wait until an emergency to read the instructions.

A bell is required aboard all U.S. vessels, but you will probably use it only at anchor in a fog.

Foghorn. Either a freon horn or a manual design will be provided. Foghorns are useful for bridge signals in places like Florida, but are unlikely to have much use in the Caribbean, where fog is almost unknown. It is wise, however, to set up a signaling system for your crew, to be used if you want people to return aboard as soon as possible in an emergency or when there is a tide to catch.

Flashlights will be provided by the charter company, but you should check at once to see that they work. Ask for spare batteries and bulbs. It is also a good thing to bring a trusted reliable of your own. The skipper should keep one close to his bunk, while the other is kept on, say, the chart table, where it can be found at once in an emergency.

First-aid kit. The company will provide a small automobile kit sufficient for minor cuts and bruises. Their (very reasonable) assumption is that you will be relatively close to base throughout your charter and that a real emergency can be handled with their chase boat or in a nearby port. Be sure to bring with you whatever personal prescription drugs and medications you need.

VHF. A VHF radio is found on virtually every charter yacht. Check that every member of the crew knows how to operate it and call for assistance on Channel 16, the international distress frequency. The charter company will give you specific instructions on how to use the radio to speak to their base in the event of mechanical failures and other problems. They will also be able to tell you what channel to use if you want to talk to yachts cruising with you. Chatting with a buddy boat can be great fun and the repartee highly entertaining, provided you restrict it to the proper channels and do not clutter Channel 16 with unnecessary talk. The proper procedure when calling another yacht or shore station is to call on Channel 16, asking them to

suggest another channel, such as 6, 12, 68, or 71. Remember, however, that not all bareboat radios have the same channels, so if you are cruising in company, verify ahead of time what channels your buddies have and, if possible, arrange to monitor that particular one rather than 16.

European yachts normally will be equipped with man-overboard lights, safety harnesses, and radar reflectors, all of which are essential for night sailing in congested waters. VHF radios are not as common in Europe as they are in the New World, but are being seen more often.

Personal emergency gear is something you should bring along for yourself. *A sharp knife and shackle opener* are essential for the serious sailor. I have sailed thousands of miles with a stainless steel knife, pliers, and spike-shackle holder in a leather holster slung around my waist. You can buy them in the U.S. for about $30. *A safety harness* is essential on any trip. Many's the time we have crossed the Sir Francis Drake Channel in the British Virgins in a tumbling 30-knotter, when a safety harness increased our comfort and security on a heaving deck. The Lirakis (about $60) is an admirable design, but there are many others. At least two harnesses for a crew of six is advisable, preferably more. *Flotation jackets* are commonplace these days and are well worth their steep price tag if you are serious about chartering. Many of them now come with a harness built in (about $350).

An adequate inventory of safety gear will help you a great deal in predicting and coping with unexpected problems.

Preventive safety

The key to safe bareboating and enjoyable vacations is to be prepared for mishaps and to practice what we may call preventive safety at all times.

Most preventive safety is common sense, following a few elementary rules from the beginning of the charter. At the beginning of every vacation I get the crew together for a drink and discuss safety and the few elementary and inviolable rules aboard. Here are my preventive safety rules, for what they are worth. All skippers have their own.

● The skipper is in charge, and his or her orders are to be obeyed in an emergency. This may seem elementary, but it is worth repeating. You may wish to rotate skippers every day, but the rule should not change.

● Everyone is to learn where the liferings, fire extinguishers, and life jackets are. They are not to be moved from their permanent positions without the skipper's permission.

- When moving around the deck while underway, hold on at all times. The old adage, "one hand for yourself and one for the boat," still holds true.
- Nonswimmers are to wear life jackets on passage at all times and in the dinghy. Everyone is to wear them, or flotation jackets, in rough weather or when the skipper orders it (normally when going forward in rough water).
- No one is to dangle his legs over the side at any time (this may seem unduly strict, but the habit is lethal in port). Also, no one is to fend off other boats with his feet. I once saw a crewmember's foot crushed between a yacht and a fishing boat, and I've never forgotten it.
- All ropes are to be coiled after use, and mooring lines are to be stowed in lockers while underway to avoid having trailing lines foul the propeller.
- All those using the dinghy or going ashore must carry oars in case the engine breaks down. They must tell someone where they are going. This may seem stupid, but large crews have been known to leave people behind.

Then follow some housekeeping rules—about dumping garbage, using the head, cleaning toilets, and washing up (we rotate these duties religiously). I end by informing people that we will be practicing reefing and man-overboard drill on the first passage—whether they like it or not. Then everyone has at least some idea of what to do in an emergency. I remember talking to a family on a 37-footer in Cane Garden Bay on the first day of a Virgins charter. We had left the marina together. They had sailed on, while we practiced and maneuvered all over the place on the way.

"What the hell were you doing?" asked the skipper.

"Practicing man-overboard drill," replied one of our teenage crew. "It was fun! I had a wonderful swim off the boat and they hauled me out with a rope!"

The skipper raised his eyebrows and changed the subject. Nothing more was said, but I noticed them doing the same thing next day.

Man overboard

No emergency strikes more dread into a seaman than the cry "Man overboard!" This is the eventuality you should guard against at all times, even in the most sheltered of charter areas.

Recovering a crewmember who falls overboard in light or moderate weather is straightforward enough. You simply send someone out in the dinghy to collect him or bring the yacht close so that he can swim up to the boarding ladder or a rope bight. But what if the victim is injured or you are in rough weather? This is where practice and forethought come in.

If someone falls overboard, the person who sees the mishap should shout "Man overboard!" at the top of his lungs *and keep the victim in sight at all costs.* The skipper should immediately instruct someone to watch the person in the water all the time, so that there is no danger of losing him in the tumble of the waves.

If possible, the lifering should be thrown as close to the victim as possible, so that he has something to swim to. If the swimmer is too far away, keep the ring on board because you may need it later.

The skipper should roll up the jib immediately and start the engine. Keep the mainsail up for the moment and steer, jibing if necessary, to a position that enables you to approach the victim *from downwind.* At no time lose sight of the swimmer.

In approaching, your aim should be to arrive right alongside the person in the water. Come alongside very slowly. As soon as you have secured the victim, *stop the engine.* It is not enough just to place it in neutral.

At your first approach, come close enough to pass the lifering to the swimmer, so that there is something to support him in the water.

Most charter yachts have strong boarding ladders. These are safe to use in calm weather, but suicidal in bumpy conditions. Approach the victim a second time, aiming to stop the boat so he can climb aboard up the ladder. This is the best recovery method if the victim has not been in the water long. Keep the yacht to windward of the person in the water, so as to form something of a sheltered lee.

If you are towing a dinghy, you can pull an exhausted swimmer into the dink, if necessary by turning the victim outboard and hauling him aboard, lifting him by the armpits.

If all other methods fail, you can try to lift a weakened swimmer into the cockpit with a bowline loop under the armpits. You may have to use the jib halyard for this, but you will need to knot an extra length of rope onto the tail end to reach the swimmer. Another method that is especially effective with heavy, exhausted victims is to lower the main, drop the boom right into the cockpit, and lash it down tight. Then release the main slides from the mast track, bundle the sail overboard, drag the swimmer into the mass of Dacron, and haul the body up to deck level. I have never tried this myself, but it is said to be effective.

You may never have to resort to these drastic methods, but it is essential to practice the recovery of a floating object in the early part of your charter. Give

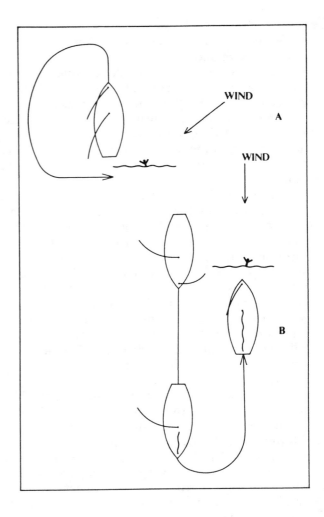

Man overboard drill. A. *On a reach, gybe round and approach the crew member head to wind.* **B.** *Downwind, run beyond the victim, keeping him close in right, then sail upwind to recover swimmer, approaching from downwind. The yacht must be stopped dead at pick up point.*

each member of the crew a specific task, and throw the lifering or some other item overboard without warning. You will be amazed how rapidly everyone knows what to do instinctively.

The one thing every charter crew, however experienced, should practice on the first day is man-overboard drill.

Heavy weather

You are most unlikely to encounter any really severe weather on a well-planned bareboat charter. Even if you sail in the Caribbean during hurricane season (mid-July to late October), you will normally have days of warning to get into shelter, and in any case the charter company will give you specific instructions on what to do. You are almost certain to encounter strong winds of up to 30 knots in many areas. The winter trades blow hard in the Virgins, northers can be gear-busters in the Bahamas, and an unexpected English Channel low can catch you in the middle of congested shipping lanes. So

it is good to be prepared for strong winds and rough seas.

All charter boats are equipped and designed to withstand far stronger weather than you will ever encounter. The weakness is more in their crews, especially since many charter crews tend to be inexperienced. The first rule of heavy-weather sailing on charter is to monitor the weather forecasts. If you do not hear them, ask other yachts. The second rule for comfortable sailing is to stay in port if the wind is forecast to blow more than 25 knots. This may seem a cowardly rule to the more adventurous among us, but the objective of bareboating is to enjoy oneself. Only a foolish sailor sets off in the teeth of a gale warning or strong winds unless it is absolutely necessary. The only time during a charter when you may have to defy the elements is when you have to return a boat at the end of a vacation. The golden rule for arriving back at base on time is to spend your last night in an anchorage close to home. You can then enjoy a leisurely breakfast and short sail back to the marina. So your rough-water

Rough weather. The first rule of heavy weather sailing on charter is to monitor the weather forecasts. Marianette II *on the Solent. (Beken of Cowes)*

passage, if it has to be made, is of the shortest possible duration.

If you must sail in heavy air or are caught out, you should have two primary concerns—the safety and comfort of your crew and boat.

As with all bareboating, the first rule is to be prepared. If you see gathering clouds and clear signs of a squall or bad weather, see if you can find a convenient and sheltered anchorage nearby. If no such berth is available, *shorten sail ahead of time.* Roll up some of the jib and reef the main while you are still in sheltered water or before the bad weather reaches you. Many charter skippers hang on to a full main and jib for far too long. Better to be under-canvased temporarily. You will be laughing while the yachts that overtook you are wrestling with sail changes. A few hundred revs on the engine will maintain your speed until the wind strengthens.

Insist that all crewmembers don foul-weather gear as spray first comes aboard and that they keep warm. A tired, wet crew does not function at its full potential.

Check that there are no trailing lines, that all loose gear is securely tied down, and that halyards and sheets can be reached easily.

If on passage, check your position and check the sailing directions for your anchorage that night. Is the approach easy? Is it sheltered from the direction where the strong wind is to come and from anticipated wind shifts? Decide whether you should divert to another port, and have some alternatives up your sleeve in the event that your first choice turns out to be too crowded or offers inadequate shelter. I once had to anchor in three different bays in the Virgins during a series of 40-knot squalls. Only the third offered uncongested shelter from the gusts.

Reefing is so easy on most charter yachts that you can complete the whole process in a few minutes. Do not try to reef while beating to windward or when sailing at full speed. Heave-to and put your reefs in at your leisure.

Most charter yachts are equipped with modern jiffy reefing that is extremely easy to use. Here's an easy-to-follow procedure that works like a charm:
- Heave the yacht to, if possible on a tack that leaves the jiffy-reef controls on the windward side, where they are easy to reach.
- Slacken off the mainsheet, if necessary hauling in on the topping lift to clear it from the boom gallows.
- Now loosen the jack line that holds the lowermost mainsail slides to the sail. (Many yachts do not have the lower slides fed into the track.) This enables you to
- Slacken off on the main halyard until the cringle

eye on the luff can be hooked into the hook at the boom gooseneck.
- Haul in on the reefing line that runs along the boom and through another cringle eye on the leech of the sail. Bowse this down tight, using the winch provided on the boom, until the eye is right at the boom.
- Tie the reef points that extend along the sail around the bag of sail at the foot, using reef knots.
- Finally, tighten the halyard until the sail is taut, retrim, and let draw.

The best way to reef the roller-furling jib is to run off downwind, blanketing it with the reefed main. You can then roll in as much as you wish, taking care not to wrap the sail around the forestay.

Shaking out the reef in the main is, of course, the reverse of the same process. Be careful, however, to untie the reef points. Failure to do so is an invitation to a torn sail and a loss of both sailing time and part of your deposit.

When should you reef? Most charter yachts will take quite a weight of wind before becoming overpowered. Your best guide is the steering. Is the yacht laboring and coming up to the wind in the puffs? Is there very strong weather helm? Do you have to work hard to keep the boat on course off the wind? Is she heeling excessively, with water lapping along the lee decks? A reef will have dramatic effects. You will feel in control again, the wheel will be easy to handle. Your primary criteria for reefing should be ease of handling and the comfort of your crew. These criteria should make you reef earlier rather than later.

Strategies of heavy-air sailing

Most bareboats are based in areas where sheltered anchorages are relatively close together. So you should not have to dally too long in exposed water if the weather pipes up. When setting out on a heavy-air passage, have several alternate anchorages in mind, so that you can change plans at short notice. Avoid long beats to windward; you can always visit those anchorages another day or on a future vacation. Another sound strategy is to do your windward work in the early days of your vacation, so that you are upwind of the charter base. Thus, you can ride in front of rough winds on your return journey—assuming, of course, that the heavy air comes in from the prevailing wind direction. For example, charterers in the Virgins are well advised to sail out to Tortola and Virgin Gorda from Saint Thomas in the first part of a week's charter. They can then return in leisurely hops without worrying about strong northeasterlies.

Your primary concerns at sea will be squalls, navigational hazards, and your dinghy. Squalls are a fact of life if you sail in the tropics. Keep a constant watch to windward for grey clouds cascading rain. The clouds will gather and lower, then move toward you. Almost certainly, line squalls and temporary strong winds will precede the rain. If a squall is bearing down on you, make the effort to roll up the jib or reef the mainsail before the wind strikes. Tropical squalls can cause the winds to rise from a mere 15 knots to 45 in few minutes. You can be out of control and close to a threatening shoreline in a few terrifying minutes. Well reefed down in advance, you should be able to weather even extreme squalls. Above all, if you are flying a spinnaker, lower it well ahead of time. I once had a 1.5-ounce spinnaker blown out in a 45-knot squall in mid-Atlantic. It took a long time to clear up the mess. You should keep a constant lookout for squalls even on fine days. Beware also of strong blasts blowing down passes between mountains to the leeward of some Caribbean islands. The judicious skipper sails in such waters with a constant eye to windward.

Navigation in heavy weather is uncomfortable at best, but even more hazardous in restricted waters. Your heavy-air passage may take you through narrow channels or intricate reefs. Avoid making such passages if strong winds are blowing or you are relying on eyeball navigation. The water colors will be confused by the wind and waves and the margin for error is small indeed, even for the expert skipper. If you are caught out in hazardous waters, you are probably better off anchoring in as sheltered water as you can find rather than entering a difficult anchorage. It may be uncomfortable in your temporary berth, but at least you avoid the danger of running aground and possibly wrecking the vessel.

Almost certainly you will be towing a dinghy when you encounter rough weather. Most bareboat tenders are too heavy to bring on deck, but a lighter dinghy can be hoisted aboard with the main halyard and lashed securely on the side or foredeck, wherever there is room. But in most cases, you will be towing it. If setting out on a rough passage, take the outboard on deck, or, if this is impossible, put an extra safety line onto the motor. Reeve two painters and remove the oars and all loose gear. Most heavier dinghies will look after themselves fairly well, even in very heavy following seas. Give them enough painter so they can make their own way. If the dinghy is swamped, heave-to and bring it along side to leeward. A life-jacketed crewmember equipped with a safety harness *should* be able to bail it out, provided you secure the dink alongside against some fenders and the motion is not too violent. This is

at best a difficult operation. Try to avoid swamping by reducing speed. If the dinghy is completely full and the weather too rough to bail it out, you will probably be unable to tow it. Your only recourse is to cut it loose, and that will cost you your security deposit.

Heavy weather is nothing to be afraid of if you charter a well-found yacht. Reef early, make sure the crew stays in the cockpit, and stay in port if you possibly can. Even the most enjoyable heavy-weather passage can be uncomfortable. Far better to snuggle down in port and wait for another day.

Running aground and stranding

Sailors who tell you they have never run aground are liars or have never sailed in shallow water at all. Sooner or later you are going to run your bareboat aground. You may make a simple navigational error, the engine may fail in a narrow channel, or you may encounter an uncharted shallow. Ten to one, you will make a silly mistake and the boat will come to a (we hope gradual) shuddering stop.

First, a word of encouragement. Ninety-nine times out of a hundred, you will be able to extricate yourself without external assistance. It is rare indeed that a stranding is so drastic as to result in official rescue or total loss.

Should you ground, the first rule is not to panic. If you ran onto the reef downwind, lower sails at once to prevent yourself running even harder aground. Turn off the engine, to avoid sucking sand into the cooling system. Then examine the situation and identify where the deeper water lies. You may be grounded on an isolated coral patch or sandbank surrounded by deeper water. More commonly, the greatest depth lies astern or on one side of the boat. Above all, don't despair, there are many ways of getting off.

If you ran onto the ground under sail and there is deep water all around you, try heeling the boat under full sail, using both the canvas and the weight of the crew to reduce your draft. With a little luck you will come off quickly. If success eludes you, start the engine and try powering off. Do not run the motor for long, you may suck sand into the cooling system.

Still stuck? It is time to try kedging yourself off. Using your dinghy, run your second anchor and line out for about 80 percent of its length into deep water, at an angle where you can winch the boat off in the shortest distance. Bring the line through a fairlead or chock to the most powerful sheet winch on board, then crank the vessel clear, using the engine to help when you feel her moving. It may take several anchor lays to turn and move the boat, even with the use of both kedge and bower anchors. Experts say that the Danforth anchor is much more effective in sand, digging deeper for much greater leverage. The best anchor of all is a tree or some other stout post ashore. Do not make the mistake a friend of mine made in the Bahamas. He pulled out the base of a lamp standard on a quay—and that cost him money! Make sure, too, that the anchor lines run clear inboard, for they can bend expensive stanchions in a few seconds.

Objects ashore can also be used to careen the yacht, reducing her draft until she slides off into deeper water. We once went aground at the entrance to Cat Cay in the Bahamas, deviating to starboard just off the marina entrance and running hard aground just off the deeper cut. With a help of a knowledgeable skipper from Texas, we ran the main halyard ashore from the masthead and cranked the boat down to an angle of about 40 degrees before she came off the sandbank. This is a pretty drastic method and should only be used *in extremis.*

Accepting a tow off the mud can be a tricky business, for the laws of salvage can apply in many situations. If a friendly yacht offers to help tow you off, that is one thing, but be especially careful with fishermen and other commercial vessels. Agree on a price beforehand and use your own gear, allowing none of the other boat's people aboard. Salvage claims result when the towboat's owner argues that he saved your boat from destruction and the crew from peril. This can mean expensive, lengthy claims and certainly the loss of your deposit. Many yachts will, of course, give you a tow in an emergency without a thought of salvage. Judge the situation carefully and behave accordingly. Your charter company will have specific instructions about what to do if you ground. Make sure you follow them. Tell them if you have hit the bottom at the end of your charter. This enables them to inspect the bottom for damage.

Stranding in rough water or in the open sea is a much more serious matter. The yacht will pound and shiver as the keel hits the bottom. If possible, lay out an anchor in deep water and keep tension on it. As the boat rises on a wave, haul in the slack on the line with the anchor winch. If the anchor is well dug in, you should be able to winch her off. It will be uncomfortable, but the technique works. If conditions are too rough for launching a dinghy, lay an anchor underfoot, in an attempt to prevent her driving farther on the reef. If you are on a lee shore, your only hope is to be towed off. The boat that tries to do so will have to lie off in deeper water and float a warp down to you with a life cushion or a fender on the end. Secure this around your mast, but have a knife handy in case you have to cut it in a hurry. If the situation is desperate, radio for assistance and *stay with the yacht.* Abandon ship only if the boat is breaking up. If you ground in rough conditions, you should contact the charter company by radio at once. They may send out a chase boat to stand by and summon a salvage company to your aid—but you pay.

Few charterers wreck their yachts. Those who do almost invariably venture into areas that are specifically off limits to bareboaters. Some time ago, a relatively inexperienced crew left on an almost new 50-footer from Tortola, BVI. The company gave them a chart that showed in red the areas that were off limits. One such area was the narrow channel between Mosquito Island and Virgin Gorda that leads to the Bitter End and its famous restaurant. The crew were hungry one evening. They took a short cut through the channel, ignoring the red on the chart, and ran hard aground. The yacht was a total loss. There was no insurance coverage, because they were off limits. They had to pay for the boat.

Lines around the propeller

Again, this happens to the best of us. You can pick up a trailing sheet, an anchor line, or a lobsterpot wire. Often your first warning is when the engine stalls as you put it into gear, so it is wise to check that everything works before entering an anchorage or marina.

Your best protection against fouling lines is preventive safety. Check frequently for trailing sheets, mooring lines left on deck that have washed overboard, or ropes trailed overboard for swimmers to hang on to. The dinghy painter is a frequent villain. When maneuvering in harbor, tie the dink in close to the stern, so that no loops come near the screw. Keep a sharp lookout for fish pots. Unfortunately, the markers are small and often weedy—bleach bottles or tiny cork floats. Unfortunately, too, they sometimes have wire mooring lines, which are the very devil to free.

If you foul your propeller in calm water, inspect it with the aid of a mask and snorkel first. If the wraps result from a trailing line entwining a freewheeling prop, you can sometimes clear them by putting the engine in reverse and literally unwinding the coils. All too often, the only solution is to send someone down to untangle the line from the shaft. This is best done with a dinghy alongside, with a safety line attached to the snorkeler, so you can pull the swimmer up when need be. It will take several dives to free the line. We once had to clear a fouled anchor line in the main channel at Bimini in a current of 3 knots. The snorkelers were attached with a safety line around their waists that was kept taut all the time—not an experience one wishes to repeat.

The final resort is to cut the line free. A serrated knife with teeth about 4.2 serrations to the inch is said to be best. Some charterers carry one in their baggage, partly to cut free anchor lines, but also because they find the kitchen knives aboard too blunt.

Fire

Fires aboard are rare. They are the most terrifying of all disasters. Careless smoking is one cause, cooking flare-ups are another. Anyone who smokes in a bunk is crazy, but it happens. Best outlaw this practice aboard.

Most company fire extinguishers are designed to handle all types of blazes except alcohol conflagrations, which are doused with water. Two ½-pound extinguishers are the norm, a size sufficient to cope with smaller fires. However, they will soon be exhausted if you are tackling a large galley flare-up. Then you are in real trouble.

Your best protection against fire is advance preparation. Make sure everyone aboard knows where the extinguishers are and how to use them

If fire breaks out:

● Shout "Fire!" at the top of your voice.
● Grab the fire extinguishers and aim them at the *base* of the flames.
● Make sure everyone not fighting the fire goes topside as soon as possible.
● If the fire is not coming under control, get the dinghy alongside. Send a crewmember to neighboring yachts to obtain more extinguishers. I once saw a major fire on a 39-footer that was doused only with the aid of 20 fire extinguishers from other yachts in a congested anchorage.
● If there is the slightest danger of a propane explosion, order everyone except the firefighters to abandon ship, if necessary by jumping into the water. And the firefighters should join them if the fire goes near the propane bottles or lines.

Fires at sea are the worst fear of the cruising seaman. Evacuate as many crewmembers as possible from the fire to the unaffected parts of the deck. If the fire is going to gut the vessel, attempt to get out a distress call on the radio and to gather up essential survival gear in the dinghy. If you are near shallow water, ground the yacht in the hope she will not become a total loss.

Flooding

Your first indication that something is wrong may be water lapping over the cabin sole. Your immediate concern should be to keep water away from the engine and batteries. Turn on the electrical bilge pump or man the hand pump at once, and investigate the cause of the leak.

The first thing to check is the automatic bilge pump itself, if one is fitted. Sometimes the non-return-valve flap jams open when you stop the pump, so water flows into the boat. Start the pump and run it until it sucks dry and leave it to run for about 15 seconds more. This should clear the problem. If it does not, repeat the process several times until the valve frees.

If the bilge pump is working right, check through the boat systematically, starting with the engine compartment:

● Has an intake hose on the cooling system broken?
● Is there a catastrophic leak around the stern tube?
● Is any through-hull fitting broken and leaking uncontrollably?
● Is water siphoning through the head or galley seacocks?
● Is a bilge pump hose disconnected, causing water to pour in when the yacht heels?

Once the problem is located, take immediate steps to block the flow of water. Hose leaks can be stopped by closing the seacock outboard of the damaged pipe. Radio the charter company for a new one once you reach port. Damaged seacocks are harder to block. Try stuffing a rag into the orifice, lashing it into place with tape, line, and a tough plastic garbage bag. Even better, find a chunk of wood and hammer it into the inlet. A piece of broom handle is sometimes effective for this.

If none of these fixes work and you are unable to stem the flow of water, or if you have a hole in the hull caused by collision or hitting a rock, sail into shallow water and try to ground the yacht in a place where she can be repaired temporarily and easily refloated. Stay with the boat, unless she actually sinks. Even then, stay nearby in your dinghy until help arrives. Contact the charter company at once by radio if the problem is of serious proportions.

It is rare indeed that a charter boat sinks. Most

operate in relatively constricted waters where you can run for shallow water or anchor within reach of assistance before the problem becomes critical.

Collisions

The most commonplace of all charter accidents, collisions occur nearly every day. Most are but casual bumps or grazings, with no damage, except to one's pride, involved. Check the boat for damage, apologize if it is your fault, and learn from the experience. It is best to make a note of the incident in your log, if you keep one, just in case questions arise later. More serious collisions generally occur in port. A yacht may drag her anchor in the middle of the night and run down on another vessel, breaking a shroud or snapping a lifeline. An inexperienced charterer may motor into the neighbors with a fouled propeller and bend a couple of stanchions. In these cases, your first responsibility is to render assistance to the other yacht if she needs it. Then inspect the damage and discuss it with the other party. Make a careful note of the circumstances of the accident, inventory the damage, and take down the number, name, yacht type, and name and address of the owner of the other vessel. Each charter area varies in its requirements for reporting accidents. Radio the charter company and report the accident at once. They will initiate the necessary reporting procedures and insurance claims, contacting other charter companies involved if necessary. It is particularly important to do this in cases of injuries. As soon as possible after the incident, write out a detailed report of the accident for the charter company's insurers.

Torn sails

Charter yachts' sails are subjected to more wear in one season than many privately owned vessels' sails undergo in five. Thus, they are more likely to give way during a squall. Worn stitching parts, seams unravel, sometimes roller-jib covers come away from the parent sail. Such mishaps are not your fault; they come under the category of fair wear and tear. Lower the sail at once, sail or motor to a convenient anchorage, and radio the charter company. They will bring out a replacement or repair the sail on the spot. If you are chartering far from base, find a sailmaker to make repairs. Above all, do not keep the damaged sail hoisted. Small tears can be patched temporarily with rip-stop tape or duct tape, so I recommend that you carry some of this with you.

Sometimes, sheer carelessness rips a sail—catching a staysail on an untaped cotter pin, or some other minor mishap. Inspect the tear carefully. Normally, you can repair this yourself with some thread or tape, and report it at the end of the charter.

Roller-furling jibs should be handled with care, for a partially rolled up or wrapped sail can sometimes flog itself to ribbons around the forestay in high winds. If such an accident occurs, try to unwrap the snarl, unroll the sail quickly, and lower it on deck before the damage gets worse. Do not leave it flapping aloft. The repairs will only become more expensive, you could damage the rig, and the entire sail may have to be replaced—to the detriment of your security deposit.

If your mainsail has battens, check the pockets daily. They have a tendency to chafe at the inboard ends.

Mechanical failures

Bareboaters seem to suffer from more mechanical breakdowns than other cruising people. Nothing can be more infuriating than an engine failure in the middle of your vacation, especially when you are about to enter a congested anchorage or spend an idyllic day off a deserted beach. You cannot blame the charter companies, most of whom are careful to keep engines on a regular maintenance schedule. It is just that the diesels are used (and misused) week in and week out, so that wear and tear is inevitable. But take heart, the problem is often a trivial one, something that you can fix yourself with some elementary detective work.

If you experience mechanical failure, your first priority is the safety of the ship. If you are approaching an anchorage, work the yacht into an outside berth under sail or try towing her in with your dinghy (Chapter 7). The latter may be difficult in windy conditions. Your best bet is to anchor in as sheltered position as you can, then to radio base.

The company will start by asking you the nature of the problem. I once had problems starting, so we got on the radio. The mechanic fired a series of questions at us:

- Was the ignition switch on?
- Was the engine turning over? (It was not.)
- Were the batteries topped with water and the terminals uncorroded? (We checked and cleaned them. They were fine.)
- Had we checked the tension of the alternator belt? (When we did so, it was too slack. The mechanic told us how to tighten it, we jump-started from a nearby yacht, and we were on our way.)

In this case, the company's logical questions saved them a trip and us a day's sailing. But in many instances, with starter failure, water in the cylinders, and so on, they will come out and take care of your problem.

When the company checks you out at the marina, they will go through the engine controls and the routine checks that they expect you to make daily: freshwater level, alternator belt, oil level, and possibly the weed trap on the saltwater intake. They will also urge you to keep a close eye on the control panel dials, especially the electric charge and the water temperature. Should either of these deviate from the norm, check the engine immediately.

The common mechanical problems seem to be the following:

• Engine failing to turn over or charge because of low battery capacity, a poor connection, or a loose alternator belt. Sometimes the alternator will fail completely.

• Overheating, caused by a blocked saltwater intake, insufficient water in the heat exchanger, a split engine hose, or most commonly a failed water-pump impeller. Many companies supply spare impellers.

• Engine failing to turn over although the electrical system is working properly. Almost certainly a defective starter or starter solenoid. You will have to call in the company on this one.

• Water in the engine, identified by foamy substance in the crankcase and failure to start. Call the company at once. They will clean the antisiphon valve and lift the injectors.

• Failing to start because of fuel starvation. Check that you have fuel in the tank or that you have switched from one tank to the other. If you have run out of fuel,

you will have to bleed the fuel supply. Call the company, they will probably be able to tell you how to do it over the radio. If the engine is a diesel, and you have not run out of fuel, chances are you have fuel pump problems or dirty fuel filters. Once again, call the company.

Above all, do not be afraid to call in. Far better to use the radio than to run into real trouble. But make sure you have checked the obvious first. We were on the first day of a charter in a 27-footer from Copenhagen, excited about getting away early on Sunday morning. But try as we might, we could not start the engine. Eventually we dug the owner out of bed. He drove 20 miles, poked around for three minutes, and turned on the fuel. Admittedly the cock was in a relatively inaccessible place, but there was no excuse. The owner was very nice about it, but were our faces red! So before radioing in, check the obvious things. Nothing is more embarrassing than having a mechanic travel miles to clean a battery terminal. Fortunately, charter companies have a vast experience of their engines. Their questioning will eliminate many of the most obvious problems. Do not attempt major repairs yourself, even if you are an expert with your own tools on board. That is the company's job and they have the spares in inventory. And if you have to wait a little while for them to get to you, be patient. They may be fixing someone else's engine. Remember, they are as anxious as you are to get you on your way.

In some ways, this chapter reads like a chronicle of problems, disasters, and menacing hazards. Do not be deterred. By applying some elementary rules of preventive safety and thinking ahead, you can avoid many of the minor hazards of a charter and cope efficiently with the major ones.

6   Bareboat Pilotage

Whether you fly in from Europe, the U.S., or Canada, starting a Caribbean charter is always a strange experience, for the contrasts are striking. Coming from California to the Virgins, we normally fly overnight, arriving in the islands the night before the charter begins. Then, bleary from lack of sleep and jet lag, we stay in a hotel before picking up our yacht the next morning. Groggy from a short night, perhaps from rum punch as well, we cast off from the marina and head into unfamiliar waters without further ado. Navigationally speaking, you jump right in at the deep end.

Like everything else about cruising, navigation has been surrounded with a mystique that few experts, or navigation schools for that matter, make any effort to dispel. This may be either because they want to make money from teaching you the arcane arts of pilotage, or because many deep-sea navigators cherish the aura that surrounds their uncanny passagemaking. Do not be deterred! Navigation, like "local knowledge," is largely a matter of common sense, and the skills required in most "beginner" charter areas are elementary at best. I once heard a neophyte charterer talking to his more experienced neighbor at the dock in Tortola, BVI.

"What course should I lay off for the Bight [on Norman Island]?" he asked nervously.

His neighbor, a stout, weatherbeaten Midwesterner, got up and stretched. He took the neophyte's arm.

"See Pelican Island?" He pointed to the conspicuous islet off the western end of Norman.

"Sure," said the neophyte.

"Head to pass midway between Pelican and Norman, stay on course until the Bight opens up to port and the coral reef off the west end on the chart is astern, then turn into the anchorage," he said. "You don't need a course: the landmarks are obvious from the chart."

The neophyte agreed dubiously and the expert went on his way. A few minutes later, I saw the newcomer quietly laying off a course on his chart. A sensible precaution, perhaps, but hardly necessary when the landmarks were plain to see and easy to identify on the chart. A few days later, we came across the neophyte in Stanley's Bar.

"Still laying off courses?" I asked.

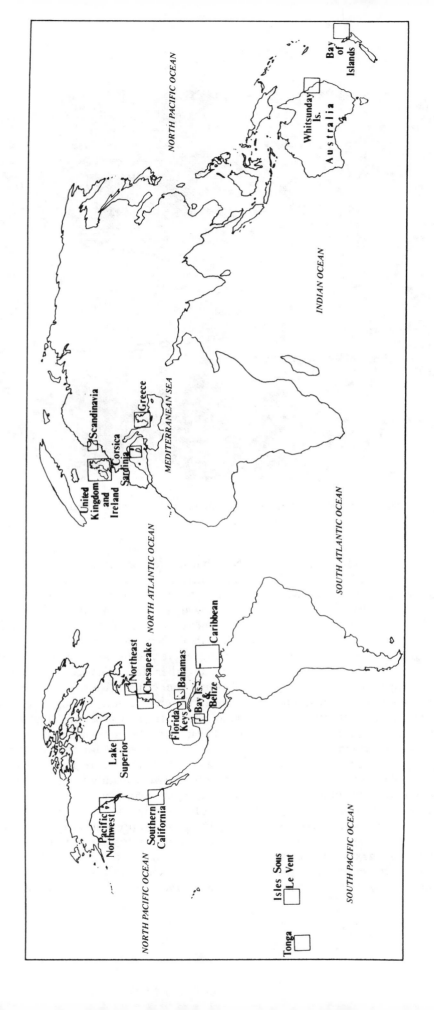

Major charter areas of the world described in this book.

NORTH PACIFIC OCEAN

Bay of Islands

Whitsunday Is.

Australia

INDIAN OCEAN

Scandinavia

Greece

United Kingdom and Ireland

Corsica Sardinia

MEDITERRANEAN SEA

SOUTH ATLANTIC OCEAN

Northeast

Chesapeake

NORTH ATLANTIC OCEAN

Bahamas

Caribbean

Florida Keys

Bay Is. & Belize

Lake Superior

Pacific Northwest

Southern California

NORTH PACIFIC OCEAN

Isles Sous Le Vent

Tonga

SOUTH PACIFIC OCEAN

The essence of successful chartering is to enjoy yourself. (Brian M. Fagan)

"Hell, no!" he replied. "I'm just following my nose and the chart."

Ninety percent of all charter navigation is eyeball, common-sense pilotage in good visibility.

Pacing, preparation, and pilotage

The essence of successful chartering is to enjoy yourself, to balance the distance covered with sailing time, shore excursions, and all the other activities that make up an enjoyable cruise. Every crew, every charter, has its own pace and formula for enjoyment. The best charter I ever took was in the English Channel many years ago, when we covered a total of 300 miles in the Channel Islands in two weeks. The 60-mile cross-Channel passages were the only long trips in the entire vacation. The weather was perfect, we swam, walked miles on Jersey, Guernsey, and Sark, and puttered from one rock-bound anchorage to the next. The worst charter was a mere week, spent traveling from the Florida Keys to Bimini and back in appalling weather.

Not that my fellow charterers were unpleasant; quite the contrary, they were delightful. The organizers of the charter tried to go too far in too short a time, making no allowance for weather or mechanical breakdowns. We spent all our time motoring to keep up our schedule. So pace yourselves.

Long before you fly out for your charter, gather your crew together for a congenial evening and start planning your cruise. (Alternately, if your crew is flying in from different places, arrange a formal meeting as soon after arrival as possible.) If you are going on a Caribbean trip, the company will probably have sent you the cruising guide for the charter area, together with a sketch chart of the region. If they do not, you can acquire them very readily from a marine bookstore or by ordering by mail from such outlets as the Dolphin Book Club, Camp Hill, PA 17012, which stocks most cruising guides. European cruising guides and charts can be obtained from a London source: J.D. Potter Ltd., 145 The Minories, London, EC3 1NH.

Spread the charts and sailing directions out on a table and let everyone take a look at the area. Then fill in the details like weather patterns, tides, currents, and unusual navigational features. Next, go through the major ports and anchorages, briefing everyone on what can be expected there and what activities are available ashore. Then turn to the boat, describe the accommodation plan, and talk about the provisioning package, if one is available. When everyone is fully briefed, pour another glass of wine and open the meeting to discussion. Begin by raising the basic questions:

• How strenuous a cruise do you want? Do you want a lot of sailing or sybaritic puttering? If long passages are needed, do you want them spaced out through the cruise or all in one lump of time? The answers to these questions will enable you to set a pace for the charter.

• What onshore activities appeal to everyone? Do people want to visit picturesque villages or spend all their time diving? What about snorkeling, diving, or windsurfing? Or do they want a combination of all of these?

• Are there any places that crewmembers particularly want to visit, places that might require special effort or an extra-long passage? If so, are they prepared to sacrifice other anchorages to get there? The answers to these questions will help you plan the outline of the cruise, to organize time for as many different activities as possible.

• Do different members of the crew want to do different things? Can the diving enthusiasts, for instance, be sent off in the dinghy, while the yacht moves a few miles away to visit an ancient temple? Everyone will have varying priorities, and you should try to accommodate as many of these as possible. Nothing is more soul-destroying than crewmembers who are frustrated because they cannot do what they want.

Once you have developed some idea of people's priorities, come up with some alternate flexible cruise plans that accommodate as many of these preferences as possible. Discuss alternatives with the crew, but leave room for the vagaries of weather, unexpected deviations, and so on. When you have reached general agreement on a possible cruise plan, put away your notes and leave the detailed planning until you are alone. In most cases, your companions are quite content to leave the details to you. "I like to be left alone to do the detailed planning," one experienced, but slightly egoistic skipper told me in the Bay Islands. "Then I can surprise people with unexpected anchorages and impress them with my navigational virtuosity!"

This is also a good moment to discuss domestic matters with the crew. Who will sleep in the aft cabin?

(A wise skipper claims this as captain's prerogative!) Does anyone have dietary problems that have to be considered in ordering the provisioning package? Are there any foods that should be brought along to complement the stores aboard? For example, many charters to the Virgins take supplies of French mustard and spices with them, to liven up the rather bland menus of many provisioning packages.

European charter companies generally expect you to do the provisioning yourself, although they will sometimes arrange for your order to be delivered to the yacht. If you are going on such a charter, use the pre-cruise meeting to sketch out some menus and to make up shopping lists. Then they are done well ahead of time, so that you waste no time with frantic list-making in the aisles of an unfamiliar supermarket.

Above all, don't delay your planning until you are airborne. You will be far too excited and there will be no space to spread out your charts.

Your congenial evening or first meeting at base may well be the most important element in your charter, for it will enable you to mate crew and itinerary with everyone's interests in mind. The information gathered in your living room will make your planning much easier.

Your next step should be a quiet evening of solitary cruise planning with the charts, some dividers, a pencil and notebook, and the sailing directions. Aim to emerge from the session with an overall plan for your trip that takes into account not only your crew's preferences, but prevailing weather patterns, tides and currents, the distances between anchorages, and the length of your trip. Your real concern should not be to develop a highly detailed cruise plan, but rather an overall strategy that provides you with the most sailing enjoyment. It is amazing how many experienced charterers you meet who have not bothered to figure out the easiest way to cruise from one end of a charter area to another when one way is against the wind!

Here are some of the variables:

• *Prevailing winds* are obviously a major factor. In charter areas like the Virgins or the Bay Islands, the winds blow mainly from the northeast, so you will find yourself battling headwinds in one direction as you sail the length of the islands. How do you make the most of it? The best strategy is to work hard the first couple of days, beating all the way, say, from Saint Thomas to Virgin Gorda. You complete all your windward work at the beginning and can then putter downwind all the way home. (If your luck is anything like mine, the wind will change onto the nose as soon as you start back!)

In many tropical areas and in Southern California, the nights and early mornings are often calm, while a fine wind rises during the middle of the day. You can make your windward distance either by motoring in the calm hours or by falling into a comfortable routine of afternoon sailing. Dawdle at anchor until the afternoon breeze fills in. Then enjoy a few hours of exhilarating sailing, before anchoring early in the evening as the wind drops. This strategy works well in areas where anchorages are close to one another, but not in places where harbors and coves are farther apart. Charterers in Southern California bound from Los Angeles to Catalina Island, or from the south to the Santa Barbara offshore islands, are certain to have some hours of motoring before them if they are to reach their destination before dark.

• *Bad weather* is always an uncontrollable variable. The only way you can reduce the risk of being weatherbound is to charter during months when unsettled conditions are least likely. For example, you can be fairly sure that you will have good weather in the Bay Islands of Honduras between June and September, while the Virgins have a risk of hurricanes during the late summer and early fall.

If you charter in the winter months in either the Grenadines or Virgins, you are almost certain to encounter some strong winds. Your advance planning should allow some flexibility for days spent at anchor weatherbound. And if the weather is really unsettled, figure on staying close to base, working your way up to windward on the calmer days. Thus, you will be able to return downwind at the end of the charter if the weather is poor, rather than having to flog your way home. Above all, do not rely on your engine to get you home in rough weather. You may not have the horsepower to make headway against 35-knot head-winds.

• *Tides and currents.* These are not significant in the Caribbean, but figure large in European cruises. The only way to cruise the Channel Islands or the Brittany coast is to play the tides. You head west when the tide is ebbing, east when it floods. If this means leaving at 0400, then you leave at that ungodly hour. Check the distances between ports, tidal streams, and tide tables to figure out a cruise plan that accommodates the tides.

If making a longer passage, say, west from the Solent to the English West Country or to the Channel Islands, you must figure out the correct times to use the Portland Bill inshore passage or to traverse the Race of Alderney. You should do this in advance, so that you can plan your cruise around the timing of these points.

• *Mechanical problems.* Few charter yachts offer 100 percent mechanical reliability. Given the heavy use they receive, you can hardly expect it. It is best to allow for a half-day or more spent at anchor awaiting assistance from the service boat. Only one of my eight Caribbean charters has been troublefree, and that was in a brand-new boat.

• *Your crew.* This is the most important variable of all, and the one on which you should spend the most time. It is here that you plug in the results of your congenial evening, blocking out a cruise plan that coincides with the interests of your companions. A group of serious sailors might choose to cruise the more remote anchorages of the Virgins, including an open-water passage to Saint Croix. In that case, you prepare a cruise plan that includes several long passages that satisfy everyone's desire for hard sailing. Another group might prefer to putter within 20 miles of Saint Thomas or Tortola. Again, you plan accordingly. When putting together such a cruise plan, select a part of the charter area where the anchorages are close together, so that you never have to sail far. Where are the best snorkeling reefs? Can divers enjoy themselves, too? Where are the best sunbathing beaches? Checking out these little variables can make all the difference between a superb vacation and a cruise that does not quite seem to come together. "Everyone had a good time, but if only we had...," is often heard. At best, everyone resolves to return to do all those things later; at worst, the crew end up hating one another.

By the time you pack for the charter, you should have a rough cruise plan in mind. Work out the overall pattern of the cruise. Where will you spend the first and last nights? What are the safe refuge ports in a blow? When will you make the longer passages? Where will you dawdle to snorkel, dive, or just laze in the sun? Make your cruise plan no more complicated than this, and fill in the details day by day as the charter progresses. Such an approach should guarantee that you will not be caught unaware by an unfamiliar area. And your crew will be impressed by your virtuoso performance as a navigator.

Navigation equipment

"Fog is unknown." "Pilotage is absolutely straight-forward, for the water is as clear as glass." "Even the beginning navigator will have no worries." These are quotes from charter company literature. In a sense they are right, for the navigational skills needed to charter in the Virgins, Grenadines, or Scandinavia are relatively minimal. The straightforward pilotage in these areas is reflected in the navigational equipment aboard charter yachts. Few companies provide more than a depth meter, a pencil, eraser, parallel rulers or protractor, a pair of dividers, and a simple bearing compass, together with a cruising guide and a sketch chart, often a reproduction of official publications. The exceptions are European companies that operate in northern waters. They supply a much more comprehensive inventory that includes radio direction finder, a much more expensive hand-bearing compass, a complete folio of charts for the charter area, and normally a far more detailed cruising guide, as well as Reeds Nautical Almanac or its equivalent and a tidal atlas. You can wager on using all of this equipment during a normal charter in these waters; the companies are not over-reacting.

Despite reassurances to the contrary, I have used every item of navigational equipment aboard my Caribbean charter yachts. I have laid out courses for the 35-mile passage from Norman Island to Saint Croix with the dividers and parallel rulers, and used the bearing compass to check anchors during a blow and to establish my position off Virgin Gorda in a rain squall when the visibility shut down to a quarter-mile. Most of the time you will be happy without parallel rulers, but when you need them, you will need them badly.

I am one of those strange people who like to carry their own navigational equipment with them, so I normally take along my favorite parallel rulers, dividers, and a notebook, pencil, and eraser with me. My faithful hand-bearing compass has sailed thousands of miles on my own boats and would be very offended if I did not take it along. In any case, it is normally in much better condition than the heavily used compass aboard.

Most charter companies supply binoculars, but you are much better off taking your own along. Almost invariably, previous charterers have scratched the lenses of those aboard, or the adjustment mechanism is corroded to an obstinate stiffness. A good pair of binoculars is probably one of the best investments a serious charterer can make. Why not give yourself a present of a pair? Although they cost more than $300, the Fujinon 7x50 Meibo marine binoculars are absolutely superb.

By all means, take along your own charts if you wish. The Chart-Kits published by the Better Boating Association, PO Box 407, Needham, MA 02192, cover such areas as the Bahamas, Virgins, Pacific Northwest, and Southern California. The yachtsmens' charts published by Imray, Laurie, Norie & Wilson Ltd. for some European waters are an excellent Old World and Caribbean equivalent. They are an easy, compact way of ensuring adequate coverage.

The charter briefing

However thorough your preparation, you are bound to feel some misgivings about a new and unfamiliar cruising ground. Many of these fears should be alleviated by the advance briefing given by the charter company on the first day. The company staff will go over the major features of the area with you. They will describe the major anchorages, discuss possible hazards such as unsettled weather conditions, and tell you which areas are off limits—normally places where the underwater obstacles or fast-running currents are too hazardous. Much of this information will be familiar to you, but you should pay careful attention all the same, even if you have been to the area before. What the charter staff offers is not only prohibitions and instructions, but a vast store of local knowledge that the company has built up over years of chartering in the area. This type of knowledge is worth every moment spent sitting through familiar briefings. Ask questions, more questions, and still more questions. Bring up points that may have worried you while planning at home. Ask about good snorkeling spots and check on the local restaurants. They come into fashion and change chefs with mind-boggling frequency. By the same token, when you return, make a point of telling the staff what your experience was. They, and later charterers, will be grateful.

When attending a briefing, I always take my charts along and mark them with all kinds of information—on rocks, restaurants, and holding ground. On one occasion, I was able to slip into a quiet, empty anchorage on the south side of Saint John on a rough day in the Virgins, simply because of a scribbled note, "Good anchorage here in a norther," on my chart. My crew thought it was magic.

Above all, mark your chart in bright colors to delineate the off-limits areas. Be aware that in many cases your insurance will not cover you if you stray into these places. Nice clear shading on your chart will keep you out of trouble.

The royal and ancient art of eyeballing

It is true that the pilotage skills needed to bareboat in such straightforward areas as the Virgins or Grenadines are relatively few. How to lay off a course, to take bearings, and to use a depth sounder intelligently are the basics taught in most elementary cruising classes. It is easy enough to navigate in a comfortable classroom, where everything stays still. The fun starts when you begin to apply these skills on a yacht that is heeling and pitching on the open sea. But even more important than your ability to lay off courses and to apply the fundamentals of pilotage is some knowledge of eyeball navigation.

Eyeball navigation is one of the great pilotage skills, with many unsung and expert practitioners. At its most refined, eyeballing is the craft of gunkholing and shallow-water navigation raised to a fine art. I have seen two skippers of 27-footers vie with one another over a week's charter to see who could find the most sheltered shallow berth to lie in in the Abacos. The winner collected her bottle of champagne by leading us up a tiny, barely discernible swatchway off Great Abaco Island. It was a pleasure to see her standing at the bow of the boat, indicating minute changes of course with a hand gesture, occasionally stopping to examine the channel, then moving cautiously ahead in a new direction. We ended up anchoring in a sheltered pool with barely 6 inches of water under our keel at low tide.

Be warned—this type of navigation can become an obsession. But few navigators go to the extreme that an elderly friend of mine goes to. He has chartered among the mudflats of eastern England for as long as I can remember. He arrives for each charter carrying a 12-foot red and white pole marked at every foot. This is his "gunkholing stick." He feels naked afloat without it.

There is only one way to learn eyeball navigation—go out and do it. No one can teach you a skill in the classroom that can only be acquired at the bows of a boat. The best way to learn is to ship aboard a yacht skippered by a maestro gunkholer and to apprentice yourself under him. I was lucky enough to learn the basics from two experts: one, my English friend with the gunkholing pole; the other, a Florida sailor who sailed regularly in the Bahamas. By standing at the bows with them and asking questions, I learned some of the subtleties of water color and bottom texture, the arts of controlling boat speed and of conning the vessel from the bow. If you are unable to ship aboard an expert's boat, do not despair. Eyeball navigation is largely a matter of experience.

The translucent waters of the Caribbean and the Bahamas are ideal for learning the basics, for the sunlit water colors are a magnificent indicator down as far as 50 feet or more. But successful eyeballing begins with overcoming the fear of shallow water. Most inexperienced charterers stick sedulously to deeper water and anchor well offshore, often in more exposed water. They suffer, as do many experienced sailors, from a fear of taking their boats into water much shallower than about 15 feet. I will never forget giving a lecture to a California yacht club about cruising in the Bahamas.

When I said that we had sailed in water shallower than 15 feet for more than two months, there were gasps of disbelief from the audience. They were used to deep-water harbors and anchoring at the offshore islands in more than 25 feet. The only way to overcome your (quite reasonable) fear of shallow water is to take your boat in sunny weather into a safe shoal area where you can go aground and get off easily. Then you can take a careful look around you and get used to the idea of less than 6 feet of water under your keel. An experienced eyeball navigator can call out the depths as accurately as the best of electronic depth sounders.

Shallow-water pilotage in the tropics depends on the water color. The basic principle is simplicity itself. Over a constantly shallowing bottom, the color gets paler as the depth diminishes. The clear waters of the Bahamas or the Caribbean are like a pale-blue filter. So the darker the color, the deeper the water. It does not matter whether the bottom is sandy or rocky, patchy coral heads or grass. The black-brown and yellow of the coral surrounded by white sand will become blue-black surrounded by lighter blue when the water is deeper.

Bright, sunny days, with the sun high and behind you, are the best conditions for eyeball pilotage, when underwater hazards show up clearly at a considerable distance. Beware of overcast weather or of the hours when the sun is low and straight in your eyes—the bottom will be obscured. Never tackle a tricky channel under such conditions. Watch out for deceptive signs, too. Small clouds passing across the face of the sun can often cast shadows on the bottom that look just like rocky patches. Avoid such patches unless you are absolutely sure they are clouds. Another danger signal: coral heads on a grassy bottom. Fortunately, they are often surrounded by a circle of white sand. Avoid such circles if you can. Never try eyeballing at night.

The best places for eyeball navigation are the bow, the roof of a deckhouse, or the spreaders, if you can reach them. You will be able to look down *into* the water rather than gazing ahead at a shallow angle. Try wearing Polaroid glasses. They do much to eliminate the surface glare. Make sure, too, that there is easy communication between the navigator and the helm, for you may have to signal course changes at very short notice. A whistle code (one blast, turn to starboard; two, to port; three, stop) is sometimes used, or you can employ the same hand signs you use when anchoring.

When first trying eyeball pilotage, station one of the crew by the depth meter and get him to call out the depth every 15 seconds or so. After a while you will be able to match the water color with the depth and distinguish even subtle gradations in the bottom. Once your fear of shallow water is overcome, you will be able to explore apparently inaccessible anchorages and channels in complete safety, provided you have a shallow enough draft.

Your practiced eye will pay off when anchoring, too. Many Caribbean bays have grassy bottoms with occasional patches of sand and coral. Use your eyeballing skills to lay your anchor in the middle of sandy zones so that you grab the bottom right the first time, then check your holding with a mask and snorkel.

Eyeball navigation is much harder in more temperate areas, where the water is not so clear or tides are constantly churning up the bottom. Under these circumstances, you must rely more heavily on your depth meter or use a measuring pole to feel out the shallows. The difference between 20 and 12 feet in many California anchorages, for example, is a matter of a subtle lightening in the water color from dark to lighter blue, and then only when the bottom is sandy. With practice you can identify some of the telltale signs, but it is far harder than in tropical waters.

Conventional pilotage

Eyeballing navigation becomes second nature in the Caribbean, but even there you will have to call on the conventional techniques of coastal pilotage, especially when bound down-island or from, say, Saint Croix to Saint Thomas. Any basic book on coastal navigation will tell you how to lay out a course, to take bearings, and to allow for currents and tidal streams. The tideless waters of the Caribbean are the ideal place to try out your book learning, especially if you combine these rudimentary methods with eyeball techniques. There are, however, many small wrinkles that you will learn from hard experience, and it is worth mentioning some of them here.

Many beginning charter crews know well enough what a plotted course means, but they have difficulty steering an accurate compass course. They become mesmerized by the compass, forget to keep an accurate lookout, and often end up steering less accurately than a more casual helmsperson. This can be hazardous in well-traveled waters. I once came on watch in the middle of the North Sea after an afternoon nap. Two large freighters were overtaking us on either side and were little more than a half-mile away, coming upon us rapidly. Meanwhile, our watchkeeper was peering at the compass conscientiously.

"What about the ships?" I asked gently.

"Huh, where?" he asked bemusedly.

He glanced astern and almost jumped out of the cockpit.

"My God, how long have they been there?" he asked.

Not much was said, but I noticed that he never hogged the compass again. Just as well, for it proceeded to blow very hard for the next four days and a close lookout was vital.

When in sight of land, encourage your watchkeepers to choose a landmark to steer on, one that coincides with the course you have set. This can be a building, a headland, even a tree or colored patch of cliff. Out of sight of land, train your crew to feel the wind on their cheeks or in their hair. At night, use stars to steer by, as sailors have for centuries, glancing at the compass every couple of minutes or so. The horizon gives you a perspective on your course, so that the helmsperson subconsciously corrects the course according to the motion of the yacht. Remember—you may lay a course of 180 degrees magnetic, but no helmsperson alive will be able to steer this with greater accuracy than 5 degrees in any sea. However, small steering errors will average out over a tideless, open-water passage. You should arrive right where you planned, unless someone is making a consistent error to windward or leeward.

A common problem with inexperienced crews is subconscious error caused by a fear of jibing down-wind, for example, or of undue heeling when squalls pipe up to windward. If sailing downwind, even in sheltered water, you can help an inexperienced crew-member by rigging a rope guy from the end of the boom through the bow fairlead to an anchor cleat, to prevent the spar's flying over unexpectedly. Excessive weather helm on a reach or beat in strong winds will produce a consistent error. Reduce this as much as possible by reefing the mainsail, by careful sail trim, or by playing with the mainsheet traveler. A good rule with inexperienced helmspeople is to reef earlier than necessary. The anxiety level aboard will drop sharply.

Your depth meter is one of the most useful aids to navigation on your bareboat, especially in hazy weather. Your charts will give you not only shallow-water depths, but the 5- and 10-fathom lines or more. (A fathom is six feet.) You can sometimes use these to approach land in thick weather, provided there are no outlying dangers. Maintain your course at reduced speed, watching your depth meter. When the gauge shows 10 fathoms, you will have at least a general idea of where you are. Then you can either lay off until the weather clears or feel your way closer to the land. (It is worth noting, incidentally, that European charts and

Shipping is a constant hazard in congested waters like the English Channel, and especially in fog. (Lesley Newhart)

some French Pacific surveys give depths in meters rather than in feet or fathoms.)

Fog is an unknown hazard in the Caribbean, but it is pervasive in many charter areas like Maine, Southern California, and the English Channel. However, even tropical waters can be hazy, making landfalls and close-in pilotage much harder than usual. Fog can be dense or patchy, giving you visibility of a quarter-mile or even a few feet. Southern California summer charterers will spend much of their time navigating in marginally foggy conditions, when the visibility is between a quarter- and a half-mile. It is only occasionally that California fogs are really dense, in which case stay in port or do all you can to keep out of shipping lanes. Many summer fogs are caused by the differing temperatures between the warm land and the cool ocean. They will burn off during the day, filling in again at night.

If you get caught out in a thick fog, keep clear of major shipping lanes. If it is safe to do so, move into shallow water where the big ships cannot navigate. Sound the prescribed signals for navigating in fog and listen for ships' sirens. Remember that fog tends to distort sound. Your first warning of a ship may be the thump of her propeller or even her bow wave, in which case you can do almost nothing to get out of the way. It is no joke to hear a siren in one direction, then to see a slightly thicker fog in another and the dark wall of a ship's side as it slides by a few yards away. Big ships

navigating in major traffic zones are so busy looking out for each other that they may not even see the minnow of a yacht on their bow. Fortunately, most fogs occur in calm weather, but the rare ones that form in the warm air streams in advance of low-pressure systems are extremely dangerous, for winds are strong and the yacht's radar signal may be lost in the wave clutter that appears on big-ship screens.

Maine charterers live with fog as a fact of life and soon learn to navigate from buoy to buoy, or from island to island, in comparative safety, timing their passages for the clearest part of the day, normally the afternoons. Fogs are far more hazardous in places like the English Channel, where the big-ship traffic has to be seen to be believed. If you are unlucky enough to be scheduled for a cross-Channel charter during pro-longed anticyclone conditions, when a high settles over northern Europe, you may as well forget a Channel crossing. The visibility will probably be less than half a mile in the great separation zones that slash through the Channel. Only an idiot would take a small yacht across to France under such conditions. Plan a coastal cruise to the English West Country instead and try for a cross-Channel excursion some other time.

Fog and haze can make landfalls very much harder than they would be in clear weather. Sometimes mountains and hilltops, even TV masts, can be helpful. Their peaks can appear over a bank of surface haze or fog and provide a lead into the land, *provided* you know which peak to steer for. Beware of approaching steep-to land masses in thick weather. You can literally be within touching range before seeing the land. Sometimes a telltale line of white breakers or even the sound of a swell breaking on the rocks will be your only sign that land is close. Under these circumstances, use your depth meter to find a suitable fathom line and wait for conditions to clear. Watch for sudden fog swirls that may billow away and reveal the land for a few fleeting seconds. Many's the time when such a sudden clearing has shown me exactly where I am and the correct course for port. A few quick bearings before the fog descends again, and you are on your way. You are asking for trouble if you approach a shoal-protected coast in foggy conditions, unless you have superior local knowledge.

Even experienced charterers can become confused when first conning their yacht in a completely unfamiliar area. Coming directly from the airport and suffering from jet lag, the disoriented skipper is capable of identifying headlands incorrectly or of taking a false turning in a narrow channel and going aground. It is especially easy to become disoriented in areas like Maine or the Swedish archipelagoes, where there are hundreds of islands that look alike. You have to develop a strong sense of horizontal direction, keeping the islands in sight in their correct relationship to one another, relative to your course. The best way to do this is to take bearings, identify key landmarks on them, and then orient these constantly as you sail along your course or a twisting channel. This is particularly difficult when the wind is strong and you are sailing fast. Under these circumstances, reduce sail and take your time with the navigation, making sure you identify every landmark in good time.

Few charter yachts ever make long passages, but a cross-Channel dash or an offshore sail from Saint Thomas to Saint Croix raises the spectre of making a landfall. A wonderful sense of anticipation will come over you as you approach the unfamiliar coast of your destination. But beware! A tired crew can often make silly mistakes, especially at night. The distance from the horizon on the average charter yacht is about 3.5 miles, so objects beyond this distance will be hidden from view. A distant coast may appear as an imperceptible line on the horizon. The high ground of Saint Croix, for example, will be in view long before the low-lying coast or individual buildings come into view. Resist the temptation to steer for the peak. Maintain your course until coastal landmarks are clearly in sight and identified. You will probably end up sailing a much shorter distance in the end.

Darkness compounds the problems of making a landfall. Your first view of the land will probably be a flashing lighthouse, or several of them. At first the lights will seem intermittent, for they may be low on the horizon and hidden by larger waves. Be patient and wait until you close with the land a little more. Then time their flashes with your watch until you are *absolutely* sure you have identified them correctly. Check your identification against the chart at once and do not alter course unless you are sure you are in the right place. It is all too easy to make mistakes. Crossing from Bimini in the Bahamas to Key Biscayne some years ago, I was delayed on passage and knew I had been set north by the Gulf Stream. Unfortunately, the portion of coast we were approaching was little illuminated by long-distance lights, except for the Port Everglades entrance beacon, which was obscured by squall clouds. Rather than close with an unidentified coast in the dark, I decided to heave-to offshore until we could see where we were. At dawn, Miami Beach was straight ahead, so we hardened sails on course to Biscayne Bay. On this occasion, biding our time paid off handsomely.

When navigating purely visually, it pays to study the charts very carefully beforehand. A distant headland may appear to be your destination, when in fact the actual point is hidden behind a fold of land that lies ahead. You can guard against this common error by keeping a mental picture of the coastal topography ahead. A great deal depends on the angle at which you approach the unfamiliar land. It is far better to err on the side of caution, especially when using local navigational marks and buoys. Make sure that you identify each one and that you keep carefully to the middle of narrow channels. This minimizes your chances of going aground. You may have to find shelter from an unexpected squall. Check from chart and sailing directions whether your ultimate destination is adequately sheltered from the blow. If you have the slightest doubt about this, divert to a more sheltered berth even if you have to travel farther to reach it. The extra hours spent at sea will all seem worthwhile when you are snug in a quiet cove with the wind howling topside all night.

Bareboat pilotage is a matter of common sense and careful use of eyeballing techniques in shallow water. It is only when you charter farther afield, in northern Europe or Greece, that you will need more advanced skills in order to deal with tidal streams and sudden weather changes. And even these skills are well within the capability of the average charterer.

7 Dinghy Work

Some of my finest moments on charter have been spent in the dinghy, snorkeling, rowing quietly up a narrow swatchway, or exploring the backwaters of a European fishing village. You are bound to spend hours in your tender. Your children will probably live in her from morning until night. You go shopping in your dinghy, visit neighbors, row away to be by yourself. Any well-prepared charterer gives careful thought to the dinghy at check-out time.

I never used to worry about the dinghy very much until some years ago in the Virgins. We were in a hurry to get off from Tortola, the check-out was complete, and the wind was blowing from the northeast. "Let's go," I cried.

The staffer who had checked us out nodded enthusiastically. "There's a lovely breeze," he said, clipping his ballpoint pen to his workpad. "Let me see about your dinghy. She's up at the bow."

I had clean forgotten about the tender and outboard, but climbed down into the battered dinghy under the bows. The charter manager leaned over the rail. "The engine's nice and new," he said. "It starts just fine. Just make sure you pump the gas line. No need to check it over, is there?"

I looked over the engine and located the oars and oarlocks. We passed them up on deck. "Wait a minute," I said. "Look at this delamination by the port buoyancy tank. The stern's separating from the hull."

The manager joined me, while the crew waited impatiently on deck. "That won't give you problems," he said reassuringly. "Quite a few of our boats have had this happen, it's just cosmetic."

It took me five minutes of strenuous argument to persuade him to give me another dinghy. It was just as well. Three days later we met another boat from the same company. A few hours before, they had had a hair-raising experience. Halfway between the yacht and the shore, the stern of their dinghy had separated from the hull at full speed, because an identical delamination had given way. Fortunately, the skipper had managed to grab the engine, while another crewmember rowed frantically for the beach. Everyone else had jumped overboard to lighten the boat and they beached in time. They had to wait for two hours before they could hitch a ride back to the yacht and rescue the remains of their dinghy. The company had ferried a new dinghy out to them, but I would like to have seen the manager's face when he saw the consequences of the "cosmetic" delamination. I would imagine it was a while before he was so casual about a dinghy again. Interestingly enough, they were quietly fixing a series of delaminated sterns when we returned to base.

The moral of this story is to check your dinghy as carefully as the boat itself.

The charter dinghy

I have strong views on charter dinghies, for I have suffered all manner of them, from wonderfully stable to highly unsafe. Perhaps the most memorable was a beautiful English mahogany pram, 9 feet of superbly crafted clinker planking that handled like a dream under oars. Her only vices were a tendency to bump the stern at night and her crazy antics under tow in a following sea. I rowed her over 20 years ago, long before inflatables and fiberglass dinghies had come into fashion. The worst tender I ever lived with was a flat-bottomed, outboard-powered monstrosity that tried to bury itself in every wave, even at half throttle. You could barely row her, even in calm water. It was a pleasure to walk away from this toy dink at the end of the charter.

You may sail away with an inflatable dinghy on a European charter, but most American and tropical charter companies supply you with a fiberglass tender, normally about 9 to 10 feet long. Most come with a 4-to-6-horsepower engine and will carry three to four people comfortably. Most show signs of a strenuous life, for bareboaters tend to treat their dinghies and outboards mercilessly. They drive them at full speed, batter them against docks and run them onto gravel beaches at high speed, grind them on sharp coral, and let them fill up with water when towed on rough days. They dunk the engines, let the fuel tanks stand in bilge water, bend the oarlocks, and fray the towing lines. Small wonder the average charter dinghy is a battered workhorse. Most companies buy the most robust dinghies possible and figure on replacing them regularly. A few even build their own to exceptionally tough specifications.

Most charter dinghies are designed with outboards in mind. They have easily driven hulls that will move along at about 4 or 5 knots with a 4-to-6-horsepower engine. They have ample built-in flotation and buoyancy tanks that keep them afloat even when swamped.

Unfortunately, very few of the more frequently used designs can be rowed at all comfortably, especially against a stiff wind or current. This definitely makes me nervous when crossing a large anchorage at night, for I like the safety of a good pair of oars. Besides, oars make laying out anchors and lines from the tender so much easier. If you have a choice of dinghies, go for one with strong oarlocks and solid oars.

Maybe I am old-fashioned, but I vastly prefer to row myself around or, better still, to sail between yacht and shore. Only one charter company, Rainbow Yachts in New Zealand's Bay of Islands, has ever provided me with a sailing dinghy. They never supply outboards, arguing—rightly in my judgment—that they are very expensive to maintain. We had great fun sailing in the anchorages. Underway, the sail and spars stowed nicely on deck. Most of their charterers loved these dinghies, but of course the distances traversed by tender in this cruising ground are short and an outboard is ideal for lengthy snorkeling expeditions.

When you take over your dinghy, the following gear should be provided:
- Outboard engine, fuel tank, safety line, and spare shear pin. Evinrudes and Johnsons are the most common power units in the Caribbean and elsewhere, but you will sometimes be supplied with a Japanese engine or even with an antique British Seagull. Make sure that you know the starting procedure and ask about any idiosyncrasies as well; some outboards have curious habits when they are cold. Check that you are supplied with a spare shear pin. Many companies tape it to the tiller. The damaged pin is easily replaced with a pair of pliers when you lose one after a collision with coral or sand.
- A pair of oars and oarlocks. Check that the oars fit the oarlocks and that the latter swivel the way they are supposed to. Do not get caught as I did once at Bimini in the Bahamas with a defunct engine, a fast-running tide, and a jammed oarlock that I had never checked. Eventually we paddled our way to a sandbank and managed to restart the engine, but there were some anxious moments.
- A bailer, attached to the dinghy with a lanyard.
- A light dinghy anchor and at least 30 feet of line.
- Two painters, one for everyday use, the second to serve as a double towline when on passage.

All of these items should be aboard whenever you use the dinghy, but loose gear must, of course, be taken out of the tender when on passage. Most charter yachts have an outboard bracket on the stern pulpit for carrying the engine while underway. Make sure that you use it, for dinghies have been known to flip over on rough days, and it's your deposit that's at stake.

Typical Caribbean charter dinghy with basic equipment and outboard engine. Like all such tenders, it shows signs of hard wear. However, this particular one was completely trouble free. (Lesley Newhart)

Dinghy handling

You see some incredible dinghy maneuvers in crowded Caribbean anchorages. There are the macho types, who believe in motoring through the anchored yachts at full speed, even when there are swimmers in the water. These are the people who pass under your bow, shouting drunkenly at all and sundry, as you are coming to anchor. Fortunately, such idiots are a rare breed. Then there are the partygoers, who persist in ferrying their crews in grossly overloaded boats at full speed. They often end up swimming and diving for their engines next morning. Beware of inveterate snorkelers. Sometimes they anchor their dinghies in deep water and swim off to nearby reefs. Look out for children motoring around in convoys. A few times, I have even seen dinghies drifting while their helpless owners swim after them from the beach. They failed to pull the tender high enough in the surf. In short, dinghy handling can be hazardous to your health, so exercise caution at all times.

More bareboat accidents occur in dinghies than on yachts themselves. This is because many charterers are inexperienced in the ways of light craft. People step on the gunwale instead of in the middle of the boat, overload their dinghies, get lines caught in the outboard prop, or run the tender hard onto coral heads. Incredible as it may seem, there are even charterers who find themselves stranded with a defective engine and have no idea how to row! Many mishaps can be avoided if some elementary rules are followed.

Never overload your dinghy. This is a matter of judgment. The numbers you can carry depend on the designed loading capacity of the tender and on weather conditions. You can transport six people from yacht to yacht on a calm evening, but only three in the same boat if it is blowing 20 knots or the tide is running strongly. The ideal for most charter dinghies is two to three people, placed forward, aft, and amidships, so that the boat rides evenly.

If the weather is the slightest bit chancy or you are traveling in open water, carry life vests for every member of the crew. *Children should wear them at all times.*

When loading the dinghy alongside, have one crewmember holding the painter aboard. The helmsman gets in first and sits in the stern. He then lowers the outboard into the water, primes the fuel system, checks that it is in neutral, and prepares for starting. First load the bow, then amidships, everyone being careful to step into the middle of the boat. This enables you to load the boat evenly. If you are carrying baggage, you should pack this as soon as two people are in the boat. You can then adjust the trim accordingly. The last person into the boat lets go the painter, while the others hold on. Only when everyone is loaded do you start the engine. The helmsman is responsible for adjusting the trim, and everyone should sit where he is told to.

Never, never operate a dinghy if you've had too much to drink. It is so easy to capsize a dinghy while boarding or to dunk yourselves in the breakers so that the tender turns over on top of you. This once happened to me in the Bay of Islands after a hospitable evening with some sportfishermen. The blind panic that hit me as I surfaced under the upturned boat convinced me never to fool around with alcohol and dinghies again.

While underway, keep a constant lookout, especially in congested anchorages. Beware of boats coming in to anchor, tenders appearing at full speed around the bows of anchored vessels. Keep a sharp eye out for lobsterpots, anchor lines, and coral heads. In shallow water, it pays to have the crewmember in the bow eyeballing for underwater obstructions. Never let anyone stand up in the boat while underway. I once saw a standing man lose his balance and fall overboard from a dinghy going at full speed. Fortunately, the helmsman had the presence of mind to cut the engine, so the propeller missed him—just. You sometimes see people standing in the bows of a dinghy going at full speed, holding the painter as the wind streams through their hair. This may look impressive, but is downright dangerous if something unexpected happens. For the same reason, never allow people to dangle their legs over the side of a speeding tender.

It pays not to accelerate or decelerate fast. In extreme cases, the stern wave can flood into the dinghy as you slow down, and the sudden speed changes are uncomfortable for your crew. By the same token, it's unwise to turn sharply except in dire emergency. You may take in water over the heeling gunwale if the dinghy is heavily laden. Adjust your speed according to conditions, keeping your crew's comfort and safety in mind at all times. This is especially important when you are breasting a head sea or running before small waves, when downwind control or dryness are paramount considerations.

Sometimes even the most reliable engines give trouble or stop without warning. Obviously, never cast off until the engine is running smoothly in neutral. Give it a minute or so to warm up before putting it into gear. Whenever you are underway, make sure that someone is strategically placed to grab the oars and row if necessary. The oarsman can keep the boat head-to-wind or prevent its drifting too far while you try to restart the engine. In tidal waters, do all you can to reach shallow water, a dock, or a yacht where you can lie safely while the trouble is fixed. Your dinghy anchor may save the day in these situations, so never leave the yacht without it.

Coming alongside a dock or a yacht, or landing on a beach under power, is largely a matter of practice. I always try to take the dinghy for a run the first night out and spend a few minutes learning her quirks. It's fun to try coming alongside the boarding ladder a few

times. In still water, it is a matter of learning the deceleration characteristics of the engine and tender. Try to arrive at the ladder with no way on the boat, without going astern. The secret is to come in at the correct angle and to allow too little, rather than too much, way. It is far easier to accelerate than to slow down, so take it easy. Your passengers won't have to grab the swimming ladder and nearly tear off their arms in the process. When landing at a dock in a strong wind, in tidal waters or a current, always approach against the stream or wind.

Beaching can be a very tricky maneuver indeed, especially if the breakers are up. Most Caribbean beaches are relatively easy to approach, for they shelve gradually, and you can land crew knee-deep in the water, sometimes even outside the breakers, without having anyone get cold. Just make sure that those who jump over the side take the painter with them and hold the boat stern-to the waves while everyone else disembarks. In calm water, the most important thing is to cut off the engine and lift it clear of the water, while another crewmember uses the oars, if necessary, to take you inshore.

Landing in rougher water requires more skill and good timing. If you can, time your landing for a calm period between sets of higher waves. These do occur at regular intervals, and it is worth standing off the breakers and watching the sets for a while before landing. Choose a smoothly shelving part of the beach with no hidden rocks, and ride a calmer set into the beach. The crew should be ready to jump out as soon as the helmsman gives the order, with everyone else following suit as the first people out pull the dinghy as far ashore as possible. A motorized landing requires precise timing, because you have to cut off the motor and raise it while still maintaining enough ground speed to ride the surf. Keep the stern to the waves at all costs, so that you expose the minimum surface area to the breakers. If you are swamped, the waterproof engine cover should keep the motor dry through a transitory dunking. But check the exposed parts and plugs, and turn it over as soon as you are on dry land. Some people prefer to land stern first, but this is a mistake; the engine can dig into the sand and cause you to spin around in the breakers. Plan on getting wet when landing in surf. I normally carry cameras, shore clothing, and documents or money ashore in plastic bags.

If you do capsize or are swamped by wash in open water, or some freak accident occurs, first make sure that everyone is accounted for and that no crewmember is stuck underneath the overturned dinghy. *Then insist that everyone stay with the boat.* Do not attempt to swim for help or to shore unless you are really close in. In most places, your combined shouts will bring help far more quickly than a heroic swim. Relatively few bareboating dinghy mishaps occur in remote waters. If you do run into trouble far from other people, again stay with the boat—having made sure that someone on board the yacht knew beforehand where you were going.

Towing and securing

Most charter dinghies are too heavy to hoist aboard on longer passages, so you are hampered with a tow, even on rougher days. This is not a serious problem, for most charter areas are in relatively sheltered waters. You are rarely in heavy seas for long, and yacht tenders are normally very buoyant and docile at the end of a towing line.

The first and most obvious precaution is to tie the towlines as securely as possible. Dinghies and outboards are very expensive items of equipment to lose, so insist that your crew all secure the tender in the same way, at the full length of the line. Take the spliced loop at the end of the towline and pass it through the opening at the base of the cleat. Then bring it back over the arms of the cleat and pull the line tight. Most companies are tired of losing dinghies, so they provide a second towline as a matter of course. Tie this in the same way as the first and your dinghy won't go anywhere. Even a nonsailor can master this technique. In the event the cleats have no opening, secure the line in the normal zigzag manner and put a half hitch on top. I am so paranoid about losing a dinghy that I tend to check the line every time someone returns from a trip ashore. It's a good idea for the skipper to do this. You will sleep better at night. Whether at anchor or towing, secure the tender at the full length of the two lines, running them to cleats on either quarter.

Many dinghy lines are made of polypropylene, which floats. Even so, you must be very careful to see that they do not become fouled in the yacht's propeller. If you can spare a crewmember, station him at the stern when you are anchoring or reversing. By gathering in the slack of the towlines, you can minimize the risk of a propeller wrap. Or hove the lines in short so that the dinghy is right under the stern while you maneuver. And when running the outboard, check that the dinghy painter is safely inboard.

Unless passagemaking for a short distance in gentle breezes and calm water, take everything out of the dinghy and stow it safely on board. The engine should be brought up to the stern pulpit bracket and secured inboard. If you do tow it, tilt the outboard up on its stand, so that the dragging propeller does not loosen the clamps. Even in the smoothest water, have one crewmember in the dinghy to lift and another at the pulpit to hoist. Even a 4-horsepower engine is quite a deadweight to bring aboard. Ever since I had to go diving for a beautiful new Evinrude in 15 feet of water, I've secured a safety line to the engine when lifting it from the dinghy—just in case. And it's come in handy, too. Once, a crewmember's oily hands slipped on the engine casing and the outboard tumbled over the gunwale, only to be brought up short by the safety line. Once again, better safe than sorry. The fuel tank is normally lashed with rope or shock cord to the pulpit as well. Wherever you stow it, check the filler cap to make sure it is tightly closed.

The dinghy will normally look after herself, although she may fill in rough seas. Towing a swamped dinghy is not only a heavy drag, but also dangerous, because you run the risk of fouling your propeller or losing her altogether. Should your dinghy become swamped, hove-to at once and bring her alongside on the sheltered leeward side. Except under extreme conditions, you should be able to secure her against a couple of fenders. If the boat is heeling, you may be able to bale her out with buckets. But more likely, you will have to send a life-jacketed crewmember into the dinghy to empty her. Put a safety line around his waist and secure it aboard before he climbs down.

Should your dinghy be light enough, you can lift her aboard and stow her on deck, over the cabinhouse or on the foredeck. The main halyard and a simple sling made by securing the painter to the thwarts or painter rings will make the task easy. Be sure to empty the boat of loose gear and bilge water first, so that nothing falls into the water.

Dinghies are docile at anchor, but may be less well behaved at night, when current, tide, or wind can cause them to bump against the stern. The old-fashioned remedy was to lash a galvanized bucket over the tender's stern, but in these days of lighter dinghies and plastic buckets, you are better off bringing the tender alongside and securing her with a fender and two lines amidships.

Securing a dinghy ashore is just as important as tying her up properly afloat. I am amazed at how often a beached dinghy drifts away in the breakers simply because her owners have neglected to pull her up high enough on a rising tide. The day is hot, the beach inviting, so the crew beaches the bow and leaves the painter unsecured. Presto, a rising tide or the wind and waves carry her off, leaving them stranded. Better to take a few moments to bring her up high and dry where even the largest waves cannot move her. And, by the

Typical modern fiberglass tender with built-in buoyancy tanks, towing eye forward, and provision for both outboard and rowlocks. Note the canvas fender around the gunwale, essential for charter operation. (Brian M. Fagan)

same token, take the anchor ashore and dig it well in, or tie the painter to a tree. Most places, you can still leave your dinghy and engine unattended. But at some ports like Bequia in the Grenadines, little boys will demand money to "watch" your boat. This is little more than thinly disguised blackmail. If you don't pay them, they will cast off the boat as soon as you are out of sight. Best fork out and enjoy yourselves with an easy mind. The fee may not prevent the boys from playing in your dinghy, but at least it should be there when you return.

Most times, you will have no trouble finding a safe spot to leave your dinghy, out of the way of other traffic. Tying up is easy enough at a floating marina, but much trickier in tidal harbors. In places like the Channel Islands or Britanny, you need a long painter, so you can allow enough scope for a tidal range in excess of 20 feet. All too often, you tie the line to a ring that is submerged at high tide, so you have to wade for the knot. Wherever you tie up, it's good manners to leave space for later comers and to tie your knots in such a way that those who got there before you can move their dinghies without disturbing your boat. I always try to leave the boat on a long line, so that it floats clear of the others. Tie your oars down, and maybe take the oarlocks with you, if they are removable. I have lost something like a dozen oarlocks in 20 years of chartering, most of them (I suspect) to other charterers.

The outboard

Let me admit to a bias: I dislike outboards. The finest

dinghy excursions I have ever made have been under oar or sail. Sailing up the Kerikeri Inlet in New Zealand's Bay of Islands takes you through a narrow, buoyed channel to the basin below the old mission station. A fortified Maori village broods over the channel above your head. Freed of the worry of navigating a deep-draft yacht on the rising tide, you have time to savor the green farmland and mudflats on either shore. This was an idyllic excursion under sail and oar, but there are times when an outboard is useful.

I will never forget exploring the canals that connect the small settlements on the north shore of Roatan in the Bay Islands, Honduras. The narrow waterways that connect the villages tunnel through mangrove swamps. The tradewind carried us downwind through the canals, with an occasional touch of the oars to keep us on course or to take us close to the stilt houses that line the canals. We felt much closer to the landscape with the engine silent on the stern. But it was nice to have the engine to bring us back 3 miles against the wind!

My morning and evening rows are among the favorite moments of my charters, but there have been times when I have been glad for an outboard. One blesses a reliable engine on rough days when one has to ferry several boatloads of crew to and from a yacht with the wind gusting hard across open water and the boat pitching to her anchor line. So it pays to treat your workhorse kindly. Here are some pointers:

● Always use the correct grade of gasoline, normally 85 octane regular, and the correct ratio of outboard motor oil, usually $1/16$ pint per gallon (U.S.), 50:1 gas-to-oil ratio. The charter company will normally send you off with a full tank. Always give this a shake before starting, and never fill it with more than 3 gallons or so, allowing room for the gasoline to expand in hot sun.

● Always check the clamps on the transom before starting, and make sure the safety line is attached to the engine and boat. This may seem elementary, but you will be surprised at how often the clamps work loose, even under normal use.

● Check that there is enough fuel for your journey. Have you ever run out of gas 200 yards from shore, with no oars aboard? I have.

● Most charter engines are fitted with recoil starters. Treat them with care, for the recoil springs may break if you pull them out all the way to the stop too frequently. If that happens, remove the engine cover and use a piece of knotted cord to start up.

● Outboards are obstinate beasts and are especially susceptible to gasoline flooding. If the engine fails to start after half a dozen pulls, sniff around for gas odor, a sure sign you have flooded the cylinders and crankcase. Open the throttle wide and pull the starting cord *slowly* a couple of dozen times. Then close the throttle and try a proper start. If that doesn't work, remove the spark plugs and dry them.

Most modern outboards are very reliable, provided they are fed the right mixture and are serviced regularly. They also thrive on hard work. As one charterer once said to me: "Work the beast as hard as you can, it loves it." He was right; outboards run most reliably when used for long runs and when warm. Look out for lots of short trips, with too much stopping and starting. Moisture can build up inside the engine under such conditions, making starting harder. Try rowing instead. Maybe this is why I have had better luck with engines in the Bahamas and Bay Islands than I have had in the Virgins, where motoring distances are shorter.

Sooner or later, every outboard owner or bareboater dunks an engine, sometimes by complete accident, more often through carelessness. This can cost you plenty, but you may be lucky if you take the drowned engine ashore or on board immediately and remove the plugs. Pour fresh water over the entire motor and into the cylinder head. Then pull the starting cord to flush the seawater out of the cylinders. Repeat the process two or three times, but with fresh gasoline. Then try starting the outboard in the usual manner. With luck, it will start. Immediately take it on a workout of at least 30 minutes' duration to dry it out. Be sure to tell the company that the engine has been drowned. They will want to overhaul it completely before sending it out again.

Should your outboard fail to start and flooding is not the cause, check that the fuel line is properly attached and that you have not run out of gas or tampered with the fuel mixture. You should keep an eye on the cooling system, because a defective water pump will surely cause overheating. Whatever the problem, you will almost certainly not have the spares on board, so you will have to call for assistance from home base.

The dinghy as workhorse

Your dinghy is an astonishingly versatile vessel: a tender, diving platform, lounging place, even a plaything for kids. You can even carry your garbage in her, stacking the plastic bags on the bottom boards until you find a trash container. But the tender is far more than a convenience. She can play a vital role in your yacht handling as well.

An outboard dinghy can be used as an auxiliary engine. Imagine that your engine has failed and that you have to enter a congested anchorage to wait for assistance. The entrance is too narrow for you to sail in. This is where your dinghy comes in handy. Bring the tender alongside and secure the painter around the shrouds and cleat it securely. Then place a couple of large fenders between the yacht and the dinghy, and lash the stern securely so that the outboard can operate freely. One or two breast lines from tender to yacht will keep her close alongside. Station one crewmember at the helm of the yacht, two others in the dinghy, so that she is level in the water. Start the outboard and accelerate slowly, checking the strain on the lines. You can then rig springlines if they are necessary. As the yacht gains steerageway, the helmsman can control the tow from the wheel. Eventually, you should be able to reach a speed of about 2 knots with a heavy 40-footer, even more with a smaller yacht, but realize that you have no braking power and that the boat will carry her way for a considerable distance. Changing direction requires extreme care, so take it easy!

There may be times you will have to use your dinghy for anchor work. This is when your fiberglass tender comes into her own. She will carry a heavy weight of anchor, chain, and rode. Even a 9-foot boat will provide a comparatively stable platform for lifting ground tackle off the bottom. A dinghy is essential when rowing out lines or anchors when you go aground. You will soon master the best ways of moving around with anchors and lines. I never use an engine to run out anchors and lines, for it means one more set of controls to operate while I am worrying about signals from the yacht. Use your oars and take your time. Apart from anything else, you can hear shouted instructions better.

Inflatable: "I vastly prefer the British-built Avon as a yacht tender, simply because its row-locks are properly designed for real rowing (the author)."
(Lesley Newhart)

When laying out an anchor, back the dinghy up under the stern of the yacht, and lower the anchor, chain, and a small length of rode onto the bottom boards of the tender. Rely on the crew to pay out the line from the stable platform above you. Then row out along the chosen line, watching for direction signals. Once the line is passed out, throw the anchor and chain overboard, making sure that the flukes are not fouled and that everything runs clear. You can then lie off in comfort while the crew digs in the line. Some purists lash the anchor itself in the water over the stern of the dinghy and then cut it loose, but this seems unnecessary with modern plow designs. Just make sure everything is stowed so that it can run free in an emergency.

I prefer to lay out anchors alone, but I always take another crewmember with me when lifting them. While one person keeps the dinghy steady with the oars, the other hauls in the rode, then gives a strong vertical pull to free the anchor from the bottom. Never try lifting an anchor from the side of the dinghy. You may well capsize if it comes home suddenly. Once the anchor's in the dinghy, relax. If your crew are the kind souls they should be, they'll pull you back home as they coil the line.

Inflatables

Very few Caribbean bareboats come with inflatables, but they are common in North American and European waters. They have the advantage of being readily stowed on deck, where they can double as makeshift liferafts. I normally semi-deflate mine, so that it's ready in an emergency. The modern inflatable is a tough creature, capable of taking a great deal of punishment. You can carry three people comfortably in a 9-footer even in quite rough water and beach it in steep breakers without getting too wet. The greatest problem with inflatables is their light weight. They are difficult to row against strong winds and far from ideal for laying out anchors and other hard dinghy work. They can be a liability when towed and can even fly aboard in a strong tail wind—a somewhat alarming phenomenon! Count on bringing them aboard whenever you are on passage.

But inflatables have important advantages as well. They are soft-sided and will not grind your topsides, and they are tolerant of rocks, gravel, and sharp dock walls. If you are unlucky enough to puncture an inflatable, you can patch and repair it in a few short minutes with the first-aid kit supplied with the dinghy. Check, however, that the synthetic adhesive provided is still fresh before you leave. It does not last forever, and many people never check it before they need it.

Most charter inflatables are about 9 feet long. Anything smaller is useless in all but the calmest water and with the tiniest crew. I vastly prefer the British-built Avon as a yacht tender, simply because its oarlocks are properly designed for real rowing. Those on the French-built Zodiac and other models are often weak, stainless steel swivels that inhibit a solid stroke in the water, which is critical if any wind is blowing. Plan on inflating the main tanks hard and the seat slightly softer for rowing. You will then have less of a floating sensation as you row and better control. The secret of inflatable rowing is the moderate, well-dug-in stroke, which uses the blades to achieve a smooth sweeping motion through the water. This gives you momentum between strokes and a better, more relaxed stride that is much less tiring on long trips. The most successful inflatable rowers are the relaxed plodders, the people who have learned that an economic, smooth style is better than the short, sharp paddling espoused by so many oarsmen.

Personally, I prefer to row inflatables. Indeed, most companies who use them with their fleets supply them without outboards. You can normally pay extra for an engine, in which case the company will supply the rigid floorboards and mounting bracket. Unless you rent a sport boat, the power unit will be a small one like a British Seagull. You can probably row almost as fast.

There is nothing quite like rowing an inflatable through a quiet anchorage on a calm, moonlit night. The black water shimmers in the moonlight, you can hear the drips from the oars as you paddle between the yachts and out toward the open sea. Your companion places a hand in the water and the gurgle seems obtrusive in the stillness. You sit and drift, talking of nothing in particular, almost part of the water, like a raft in the middle of nowhere. Moments like these make a charter truly memorable. A dinghy adds so much to the enjoyment of your adventure that it is well worth taking time to explore her potential to the full.

PART II: PREPARATIONS

8 Charter Areas and Companies

Perhaps the trickiest part of bareboating is choosing the company and the charter area with which to begin. Here you are very much on your own, although there is no lack of information to signpost the way. Some years ago, I was commissioned by a sailing magazine to write a piece on bareboating in Europe. As part of the research, I wrote away for brochures from various companies large and small, mainly in England. Within a few weeks, I was sitting on a pile of color leaflets over 4 inches thick. Some of the companies are still sending me literature to this day. The pages of the yachting magazines drip with tantalizing advertisements touting the virtues of different charter areas and bareboating companies, from the Virgins to Martinique, Tahiti to the Greek islands. Each of them claims to have that special something, that special luxury yacht, the ultimate in gourmet provisioning, and service beyond your wildest dreams. Beckoning views of tropical beaches, tradewind sailing, even of charter brokers themselves, gaze out at you in serried rows. All this is a carefully contrived fantasy land of perfect weather and idyllic cruises. Reality is, of course, something else. The weather may be lousy, the boat an ill-maintained dog, the provision package inadequate. Navigating these tortuous waters is as tricky as sailing the narrowest channel in the Abacos. What should you look for in making your final choice?

Choosing a charter area

Your best source of information on the major charter areas is a subscription to a national sailing periodical. In the United States, *Cruising World*, *Sail*, and *Yachting* (in Europe, *Yachting Monthly* and *Yachting World*) carry regular articles on charter cruises in every part of the world. American journals run special charter supplements each year, normally extra sections with a few feature articles on carefully selected areas, accompanied by an inventory of bareboating companies, mainly in the Caribbean and North America. *Sail* tends to be more ambitious in its coverage, running features on bareboating as far afield as Australia and Scandinavia. Unfortunately, however, the need for advertising

Lesley Newhart

revenue forces magazine editors to be somewhat circumspect in stating their opinions of different areas and companies, many of their pieces being written as a result of a promotion trip organized by a charter company. It's only fair to say that most writers make this clear in their articles, but *caveat emptor*.

You can use the magazines and their advertisements as a guide to what's available. They are an admirable basis for your preliminary research. A well-written charter piece will give you a good general idea of what a cruising area is like. Such articles are normally written from personal experience, so they give you valuable impressions of places and local conditions. Skim through the articles on different areas, borrow back issues from a sailing friend if necessary, and set the articles up against the questions you should pose right from the beginning.

- Which general area do I want to charter in? Tropical or temperate? Ocean or fresh water? Close to home or far from base?
- What time of year can I get away? During winter, high summer, or spring? For how long? Two weeks, three weeks, two months?
- How experienced are we? Have we sailed a large yacht by ourselves before?
- How large is the vacation budget? Are there creative ways of reducing the cost?
- What sorts of things do we want to do besides sail? Diving, snorkeling, bar hopping, or lying in the sun? Do we prefer gourmet restaurants or visiting Scottish fishing villages? Is the charter part of a longer vacation on land?

The first thing to do is to match your experience against the available charter areas. If you are a beginner, I most strongly recommend a charter in the Great Lakes or the Virgins. The bareboat courses and sheltered cruising grounds offered by Sailboats Inc. on Lake Superior are an ideal way to charter for the first time. The weather is mostly predictable, the summer season warm, and the Apostle Islands especially attractive. Another option is a charter in western Florida, either with Sailboats Inc. or one of the other instructional charter outfits that are springing up in this area.

The granddaddy of all beginning charter grounds is, of course, the Virgin Islands. The waters are warm, the navigation forgiving, and the winds normally predictable. The cost of reaching Saint Thomas or Tortola is not excessive by modern airline standards, and large fleets of bareboats are available. You can sign up for an instructional charter in these waters and choose from every sort of shoreside or waterborne activity, from windsurfing to gourmet dining. This is a good place to learn bareboat chartering at first hand, to make mistakes, and to benefit from them. Not only that, you are surrounded by people who are doing the same thing. The Virgins are set up for chartering, both ashore and afloat. Indeed, bareboating is the major industry in the British Virgins. Many people begin on the Great Lakes or in Florida and graduate here next.

If you are more experienced, I would recommend chartering somewhere different, *if your experience matches the challenges of the area*. You must be absolutely honest with yourself about this. The beginners' areas like the Virgins can suffer from chronic congestion. You can find 50 or more charter boats anchored off the Baths or sheltered off the Bitter End. Better to charter in some less popular locale like Southern California or the Pacific Northwest. The Grenadines are a popular choice for more experienced sailors, as are the Bahamas, where the navigation can be challenging and eyeball skills are needed. I would not recommend that American beginners charter in Europe, the South Pacific, Belize, or the Bay Islands until they have bareboated several times. You need a considerable degree of navigational expertise to handle European waters safely, and both the South Pacific and Bay Islands areas are relatively remote. Help is not as easy to come by in these places if you have problems. However, European beginners should not be deterred, as the necessary pilotage and anchoring skills are taught in all introductory cruising courses in northern Europe—they have to be.

Perhaps the most important decision after the charter area is the season in which to take your cruise. Plan carefully at this point—you can spend your whole charter vacation holed up by rain and strong winds. You must balance a number of variables: the season of finest weather, the time available for vacation, and the advisability of avoiding the peak season when anchorages are most crowded, boats in strongest demand, and rates at their highest. Consult charter company literature, borrow cruising guides, or examine government sailing directions to find out what the annual weather patterns are. Then choose the best time for your charter. You should do this research before you book your trip. It is sometimes almost impossible to move the dates because of congested booking schedules.

The Virgin Islands are a good example. Caribbean weather is very predictable, except for hurricanes and occasional strong northers, the tail ends of weather systems far to the north that sweep across more temperate latitudes. Hurricane season is from mid-July through October. Most charter companies virtually shut down during these months, although you may be able to take advantage of very low rates then. The late summer and fall are always slow, so some companies even offer two weeks for the price of one just to keep their boats busy. Others shut down completely and give their staffs vacation, as well as carrying out annual maintenance. Lower rates can mean potentially hazardous weather.

I have chartered only once during the hurricane season, in the Grenadines. The first few days were hot but delightful. Then the hurricane warnings began, far off in the Atlantic. The tension rose as Hurricane David swept toward Barbados. We listened in horrified fascination as the island shut down, storekeepers battened their windows, and gas supplies were shut off. By this time we had contacted the charter company by radio. They sent us to a hurricane hole among the mangrove swamps of Carriacou. There we found six more boats from the same company as well as 60 other yachts, many of them privately owned. Under the supervision of company staff, we laid out anchors bow and stern, tied ourselves into the swamps, and unrigged the sails, putting everything loose below. Some French owners simply anchored their yachts and went ashore, leaving no one aboard. The air was hot, buggy, and still, the sky grey with menacing clouds. We ate a silent dinner, then battened ourselves below as Barbados Radio charted the inexorable course of David ever closer. The hurricane was due to hit at 0300. You could feel everyone waiting, and waiting, and waiting. But the silence lasted all night. Then, at dawn, the shout came: "David's moved north!" You could feel the tension dissolve and laughter renew as everyone ate breakfast in the clear, fresh sunshine. We were soon on our way, chastened but safe. The weather was calm except for a huge hurricane-spawned swell. The only legacy of this experience was an attack of dengue fever from a swamp mosquito that laid me flat for five days with a temperature of over 103 degrees. I will never charter in the hurricane season again.

The winter months in the Virgins can be a gamble. The winds often blow strongly, and the weather can be unsettled for days on end as the rain falls and grey clouds scud across the sky. Many Americans and Canadians take the gamble and make a beeline for the islands between Christmas and March. So most charter fleets are very busy during this high season, despite the strong winds and chance of rain. The logical choice of months for a Virgin Islands charter is between late April and early July, when the weather has normally settled down. The trades are steady but weaker than they are in the winter, and the sun shines with predictable regularity. Caribbean veterans, like Donald

Street of *Iolaire* fame, recommend these months above all others—and I would agree with them. There are fewer people about, the magic is still there, rates are slightly lower, and you do not have to worry about hurricanes.

Each charter area has its own seasonal quirks and best months. For example, you can charter in Southern California any month of the year. But you are taking more of a gamble in the winter, when southeasters and strong post-frontal westerlies can kick up coastal waters to dangerous heights. Spring can be windy, but the summer months are predictable, though often foggy and hazy. I would recommend a charter in late spring or late summer, because the foggiest months are late May and June. Unfortunately, Catalina is very congested during these months. Avoid October through December; these months often bring strong and dangerous downslope winds known as Santa Anas. These mast-bending winds turn most of Catalina's anchorages into wave-tossed lee shores. It is no coincidence that the local Indians brought their canoes ashore in October.

It is worth taking the trouble to research your cruising area beforehand, so that you take as few chances with the weather as possible. You should be able to find a few uncongested, fair-weather weeks almost anywhere. In Scotland, for example, some of the finest weather can occur in June or early September, both relatively quiet charter months. If you are prepared to take a gamble, you can sometimes enjoy spectacular weather off season. My finest charter ever was years ago during an English Channel October. We had two weeks of blue skies, summerlike temperatures, moderate winds, and the Channel Islands virtually to ourselves. That time, we took on fate and won. A day after we landed, it blew Force 8 from the southwest.

Choosing a charter company

The charter company you choose can make or break your vacation. On the whole, I have been exceptionally lucky over the years. Only once have I dealt with a bad firm, a small outfit with only six yachts. The trouble was that they skimped on their scheduled maintenance. The diesel overheated—the company had forgotten to check the freshwater level and we blithely assumed they had. Then the engine would not turn over one morning—they had omitted to check the distilled water in the batteries. Two hanks tore out of the genoa because the Dacron was tired. A jibsheet parted in a 20-knot breeze, nearly decapitating a crewmember who was sunbathing. Altogether a most

Leaflets, leaflets, leaflets . . . (Brian M. Fagan)

unsatisfactory experience, but what was sobering was that we saw the charterer send the boat out the same day we brought it back, with plenty of urgent work to be done. It was partly our fault we had trouble; we should have insisted on checking things for ourselves before we left at the beginning of the cruise.

Your best protection against making the wrong decision is knowledge—knowledge gained through careful research, questioning of others, and then, as you charter, from quiet observation. First, scan the advertisements in one or more major sailing magazines and send away for brochures. (Or call the toll-free number that many companies maintain in the United States and ask for literature.) You will soon be flooded with brightly colored leaflets that try to lure you away to paradise with pictures of yachts sailing in perfect weather against a background of swaying palms. Read through the blurb once, then turn to the specifications of the company's yachts. If they do not include such details in their literature, throw the pamphlet in the trash and look elsewhere. The yacht specifications

from the different companies will be one of the key elements in your list of potential opportunities.

While waiting for your leaflets, locate some back issues of your chosen magazines from a year or two earlier. Check whether the companies you contacted were in business then. Chartering is a very volatile business. Many companies failed during the difficult years of the early 1980s, stranding dozens of charterers who had paid their deposits in good faith. These failures were healthy, in that several fly-by-night and undercapitalized operators were put out of business early on. Even now, you should be careful. The recession is still claiming victims, and one hears constant rumors of even major companies running into trouble. Be especially cautious in booking a charter with a new company, unless it is obviously backed by ample resources.

Once the flood of pamphlets dies down, lay them all out side by side on a table and compare the various companies. Ask a number of tough questions:

• How long has the company been in business? Is it listed with Dun and Bradstreet? Does it offer bankers' references or financial statements to demonstrate fiscal health?
• How many yachts are there in the company's fleet? On a first-time charter, eliminate all companies that have less than six yachts unless you know the owners and their boats well. They are unlikely to have the necessary spares or back-up boats to replace yours should serious mechanical problems develop.
• How old are the vessels in the fleet?
• Have any of your sailing friends chartered from any of the companies you are considering? What was their experience?
• Does the company own its own facilities? Is chartering a full-time activity or merely a sideline for a brokerage business? Are you being sold a charter or a boat? Go for full-time charter companies. They are in the business of providing service, not selling yachts.
• What types of yacht does the company charter? Do they satisfy your particular requirements as far as size and accommodations are concerned? Do they operate standardized fleets or many different designs? Your best bet is probably a company that maintains many yachts of the same type. Standardized fleets mean better service, simplified maintenance procedures, and more easily obtained spare parts. In all probability, a company operating many different designs simply maintains these yachts in charter for individual owners. Almost certainly, their spares inventory is much smaller. You could lose valuable days while the company locates, say, a starter.

● Does the company carry out its own maintenance, or is this contracted to a nearby boatyard? Do they have sufficient back-up yachts and service boats to deal with breakdowns—seven days a week? Can they let you have another yacht if yours develops really serious problems? Avoid companies who subcontract their maintenance work at all costs. They may not be able to deliver when you really need it.

● What is the turnaround time from one charter to the next? Anything less than 24 hours is going to be chancy.

● Are their prices competitive? If there ever was a business where you get what you pay for, this is it. Ten to one, a company that shaves its prices way below the competition is skimping on something—normally maintenance. Another variable is the newness of the charterers' yachts. Charter fleets that are leased back from owners at high interest rates or managed yachts financed with high monthly payments are going to cost you more. Make service and the type and age of the yacht the primary criteria. If you want a cut-price vacation, either prorate the cost between six or eight people or charter off season. Far better to pay a little more for reliable service and back-up. It will pay off when you least expect it.

The charter business is so volatile that it is sometimes hard to build a lasting relationship with a single company. Fortunately, some of the larger organizations that have been around awhile are realizing this. As competition intensifies in the Caribbean, some of them are looking for new ways to keep their boats working, especially in off-season months. For instance, one company offers a club membership requiring an initiation fee in the form of a lump-sum payment in the first year (normally between $1,500 and $2,000) and monthly payments (normally below $75 per month) for the duration of the membership. Such a membership entitles you to one or two weeks' free charter in mid- or off-season months and to a substantial discount in the busy time of the year. Such an arrangement appeals to regular Caribbean charterers, especially if they go in large parties. The company usually offers you other inducements, such as travel discounts and reductions on additional days. The system makes sense for both sides: the company keeps its boats in operation, repeat customers get a better deal. Be sure, however, that you want to make Caribbean chartering a regular part of your precious vacation time for five years before signing up in a club scheme! You could end up seriously out of pocket.

Once you have made a short list of companies, write or call them to ask them any questions that are not answered by their literature. Confirm the rates for the period you want to charter, find out if the yacht of your choice is available for that time, and ask for the names and phone numbers of at least three previous clients who have chartered from the company at different times whom you can contact. Any reputable company will be glad to provide such names, for it is proud of its repeat business. Compare the answers from each company, then make a firm booking. (This process is especially easy in the United States, where most larger companies maintain toll-free numbers.) The charter company will now send you a letter confirming what dates and yacht they are holding for you, together with sailing experience questionnaires for the skipper and crew, and an invoice for the deposit required, normally 50 percent of the charter fee. A verbal reservation will hold the booking for about 10 days only. The company will make final confirmation of your reservation when they receive your deposit and evaluate your sailing experience as acceptable. You will then be asked to sign the charter contract. Most companies ask you to pay your security deposit (normally $500 to $750), the balance of your charter fee, and any provisioning costs 30 days before your charter begins.

What happens if the charter company goes bankrupt or reneges on the deal? Unfortunately, it is often the charterer who suffers. Many bareboating companies have failed in recent years, some of them stranding dozens of clients, whose vacations were ruined and deposits were forfeited. Your only protection is to choose a reputable company and to check its references very thoroughly. The bareboat business is almost totally unregulated, so theoretically you are taking a risk when you enter into a contract ahead of time. If the company you are dealing with fails, you will probably have to start again with another company and suffer the loss of your deposit from the first company.

Another irritating, and regrettably persistent, problem occurs when a charter company tells you at the last minute that the yacht you chose is no longer available. This situation normally arises with managed fleets, when the boat is damaged or, more commonly, the owner decides to pull the yacht out of management at short notice. In this case, the charter agreement should bind the company to finding a comparable substitute, returning your deposit, or making reasonable arrangements on your behalf. Most management agreements allow far too much flexibility to the owner, with the result the company can lose the use of a boat within days. Your only defense is to check into your charter agreement very thoroughly before you sign and to confirm in writing with the company precisely what contingency plans are put into effect if the yacht of your choice is not available.

In most areas, you should have no trouble finding a reputable company. Your assessment should rely heavily on referrals from earlier clients and on the length of time the company has been in business. In the Caribbean and the South Pacific, go for the larger companies with standardized fleets. European charter companies tend to be much smaller, with a greater emphasis on personal service by the owners. Here you will have to rely on mail contact, but you can still get bank references and the names of previous clients who could tell you what the companies are like.

Wherever you charter, make your reservations as early as possible. Peak months are usually fully booked a long way ahead. You may have to make your reservations a year in advance to spend Christmas in the Virgins. Many European companies are fully booked for June through August by the New Year. (The same holds true for airline reservations, especially to small Caribbean islands.)

Some more experienced bareboaters charter regularly from private owners, some of them over periods of

Does the company operate standardized fleets? The Pearson 303 is a widely used charter design, especially on the American East Coast. With its 4-foot, 4-inch draft, the 303 is especially suitable for shallower waters. Her 25-foot, 4½-inch water-line makes her easily driven in stronger winds. This is an ideal charter boat for inexperienced crews, with a deep cockpit and very easily handled rig. Her interior sleeps four in comfort for a charter of a week or more. A Yanmar diesel provides ample power. I especially liked the anchor well up forward, which makes for a clean foredeck and easy anchoring. (Courtesy Pearson Yachts) years. This is fine, provided you are satisfied that the owner is properly insured and you can inspect the yacht beforehand. Insist on examining the insurance policy and see that it is endorsed for bareboat chartering. When you inspect the vessel, make a list of problems to be fixed in advance and insist on an agreement *in writing* that the charter is void unless the vessel is in full working order. Finally, *never* sign a charter agreement that does not spell out who is responsible for routine and nonroutine maintenance. Far too many privately owned yachts in bareboat charter are inadequately insured and poorly maintained. Some are downright dangerous. Unless you can develop a close working relationship with the owner, forget it, especially if you are a beginner. A large charter company is far better. They know their business and are set up to cater to all your needs. Yachts chartered from them cost very little more, and above all, you know what you are getting into. Not that all private charter arrangements are unsatisfactory. I have one experienced sailing friend who has chartered the same 36-footer in Saint Thomas for more than 15 years. He chartered it sight unseen the first time and has been back every winter for a month ever since. The two families are now close friends.

Boat swapping, like house swapping, has become a popular way of exploring new cruising areas in recent years. Two families, often living thousands of miles apart, exchange yachts, usually of equivalent size, for a few weeks. The exchanges are scheduled so that each family meets the other, is introduced to the other's boat, and remains on hand to take care of any problems. This is a fine way to sail in foreign waters, provided you are not afraid of arranging for a yacht sight unseen. Some friends of mine exchanged a Cal 34 in Santa Barbara, California, for a 35-footer in western Sweden. The arrangement worked out well. Both parties enjoyed an interesting, low-cost cruise in unfamiliar waters. Many such arrangements work through yacht clubs. Another useful contact is the Cruising Association, Ivory House, St. Katherine's Dock, London, E1 9AT, England, an international association of cruising people who sometimes know of yacht-swapping opportunities. I would not recommend a yacht swap for beginning charterers. Again, you are better off with a larger charter company.

Choosing your crew

Look at the faces of people as they unload their bags at the end of a week's charter. Is everyone smiling, drinking a final beer together, and obviously savoring the last moments of tropical bliss? Or is everyone going separate ways and not talking much? The body language of a newly returned crew speaks volumes for the success of a charter. The people you take along with you can make or break your vacation. Friends who are a social delight at home may soon pall at breakfast in the confines of a 44-footer. Their jokes may wear thin, their drinking habits aboard may differ greatly from yours. A crew of expert sailors may resent a beginner, who they think is not pulling his weight. Yes, the selection of your crew is probably the most important element of all.

What sort of people should you take along with you? The ideal, of course, is immediate family or people who have sailed with you for years. Many bareboaters return to the Caribbean year after year with the same small party of friends who enjoy each other's company, have common interests, and share expenses. Many people prefer to go in couples: husband and wife, boyfriend, girlfriend, whatever. In some ways this is even better, because you don't have to worry about other people and can have all the space and privacy in the world.

I met a blissful couple in the Virgin Islands quite recently, who were all by themselves on a 37-footer. We got into a discussion about anchors, which led to rum punches. Jean snuggled up to Mike as we talked. "What's so nice is that we can be absolutely alone and no one can call us. We don't have to talk to anyone else unless *we* want to," she said. It was no surprise to get a wedding announcement some months later!

Many charter crews are fascinating mixes of people from all walks of life. The rising cost of bareboating and a trend toward larger yachts have meant that crews have gotten larger, many of them share-expense arrangements between complete strangers. All too frequently, unexpected tensions arise. Some of the crew want to sail a great deal, others to drink ashore. One crewmember may be a fanatical diver, another a shell collector. The unfortunate skipper has to balance one person's wishes against another's for the whole cruise. Invariably, the crew returns home dissatisfied in varying degrees.

So choose your crew with special care. If you can afford it, take fewer rather than more people. You will have more space to move around in and fewer egos to pander to. Start by approaching sailing friends, people you know well, whose level of experience matches your own. You are then guaranteed a relatively uniform level of expectation and enjoyment. One of the nicest charter crews I ever met was in the Bahamas, four insurance adjusters who had raced together for a season and were cruising away from home for the first time.

Choose your crew with special care. If you can afford it, take fewer rather than more people. (Courtesy Yacht Cruising Association)

They were having a marvelous time. Breakfast each morning was at about 0900. Then they would sail hard for three or four hours, anchoring in mid-afternoon, "well before the sun crosses the yardarm," as one of them put it, spend some time exploring ashore, then socialize with other boats or take it easy. They called it the "drinking man's routine." It might not be everyone's idea of a charter, but they enjoyed it. The secret was that they all wanted to do the same things.

Most larger crews seem to include one or two more experienced sailors and a leavening of beginners. One good way to put together a group is to attach yourself to or organize a yacht club charter. A group of yacht club members puts together a group charter of, say, 10 boats, where everyone knows each other and buddy boats get together at intervals during the cruise. Such an arrangement can reduce the tensions that can erupt between complete strangers. If you are planning to take people you do not know, gather together a pool of potential charterers and ask them over for a drink to get acquainted. Then show them charts and photographs of the area, the yacht, and lay out exactly what you are planning to do—how much sailing, how many long passages, what you like to do ashore, and so on. Then

get everyone talking, find out what their expectations and experience are, and quietly observe the chemistry of the group. Be highly explicit about expenses and how they are to be shared, and what you expect the total cost of the vacation to be. Make it quite clear to everyone that you reserve the right to choose the people who go and that your decisions must be respected. Hopefully, this informal gathering will give you enough information to make intelligent choices.

Most of my crews, normally people I have known well, have worked out fine, partly because they have been adaptable individuals who are generally good at getting along with other folks. Many would-be charterers are eager to go along with a more experienced crew for the first time. I have found such people work out well, because they are eager to learn. I try to avoid mixing heavy drinkers and "good time" people out for a hit with the girls (or boys, for that matter) with quieter individuals who want to do some sailing, enjoy the scenery, and just relax. The latter may like to party occasionally, but this is not their whole lifestyle. Avid sailors and more leisured people who like to lie on beaches and snorkel all the time tend not to mix well, while serious divers are best advised to take a diving vacation. Another gulf divides serious sailors from more vacation-sailing types. I have been on wonderful charters with both groups, but have always been careful to avoid mingling the two, unless, of course, someone wants an introduction to more serious sailing. *Never forget that you are chartering not just to make a passage but to have a good time.* This makes crew selection unusually important.

It is astounding how strongly passions can flow on unhappy charters. I met Tom off the Bitter End, a bearded Iowan with long years of chartering behind him. He was sitting alone in the cockpit of his Morgan 41 one beautiful evening. Everyone else was ashore when I hailed him from our dinghy.

"Lovely evening," I said.

"Yeah, except for the lousy drunks I'm with," he said bitterly.

"Crew trouble?" I asked.

"My usual friends couldn't come this time, so I took these people I know through work. All they want to do is drink and bar hop. I came here to sail and enjoy peace and quiet. Thank God there are only two days left."

He returned to his brooding. Later we saw his crew propping up the bar. They were making a great deal of noise and eyeing the girls. We pitied Tom his lost vacation. It is so easy to make a mistake. But, with a little luck and some forethought, you should be able to return to the dock smiling, ready for that last nostalgic drink together before facing the real world.

9 Bareboats

Ten years ago, bareboats were still fairly hard to find. But everything has changed in recent years. The serious bareboater can find almost any type of yacht to fulfill any sailing fantasy. You can charter a Swan 41 in Corsica, a Gib Seas in the Aegean, an Endeavor 37 in Tahiti, and a Morgan 46 in the Virgins. Maine offers Bermuda 40s; Lake Superior, C&Cs; Southern California, Catalina 30s. If you look hard enough, you can probably charter almost any mass-produced yacht on the market today—somewhere. What should you look for in a charter yacht? Is there such a thing as the ideal bareboat? This chapter looks at some of the options and at some of the qualities of the ideal charter yacht.

The evolution of bareboat designs

In the early 1960s, such charter companies as were in business relied on a hodgepodge of vessels, many of them bought secondhand and reconditioned for bareboating. English charterers in particular used to offer bareboats ranging in size from 27 to 40 feet, all of them of wooden construction, most very conservatively rigged. The maintenance problems were complex, since every boat was different. One charter company I dealt with had 13 yachts, none of them of the same design, each described on a separate page of their brochure, which resembled a miniature Bible. It was hardly surprising that their boats were tired and suffering from very sporadic maintenance. But sometimes one could find a gem, like an English-built, Holman and Pye–designed Rustler 31 I once chartered for a cross-Channel cruise from the Solent to Brittany. She was an old racing boat that was kept in immaculate condition by her charterers. *Hustle-Bustle* sailed like a dream and had a sail inventory that was the envy of the private yachts tied alongside us in Guernsey. Such bareboats are few and far between, and, in these days of standardized designs and fiberglass construction, impractical to maintain in charter.

All this has changed as a result of fiberglass, aluminum alloy, and Dacron. Now the larger charter companies offer standardized fleets of robust fiberglass yachts of a size and complexity unimaginable even 20 years ago. The history of bareboating in the Caribbean shows how the business has evolved into a highly sophisticated arm of the tourist trade. Richard Avery of Saint Thomas was a charter skipper in the 1950s. He realized that many sailors did not need professional help, just a good boat to sail in. Today, Avery's Boatyard still charters some 20 yachts. The company flourishes because it caters to a specialized segment of the bareboat market—unpretentious sailors who want small, simply equipped, family yachts.

A larger charter company founded in the late 1960s introduced some revolutionary new concepts to the bareboat business. Caribbean Sailing Yachts (CSY) was organized by a group of New Jersey dentists and physicians, headed by John Van Ost, who liked to sail in the Caribbean during the winter. At the time, there were only about 20 bareboats in the entire Caribbean. CSY began by introducing the fleet concept to bareboating. They started with five Capri 30s that were operated on an experimental basis out of Essex, Connecticut, during the America's Cup year of 1967. They moved the boats to the British Virgin Islands in the fall. The company has been there ever since.

The business grew so fast that CSY thought up another new idea. They commissioned a new Alan Gurney design for a 39-footer, a center-cockpit 41-footer called the Carib 41. This was the first American production yacht with a center cockpit and separate cabins for two couples. This basic concept has influenced charter-boat design ever since. CSY took 26 of these boats in charter. But instead of buying them, they acted as the dealer, sold the boats to individual owners, then leased them back for a fixed period and for a regular monthly lease payment. CSY also assumed full responsibility for the maintenance of their new fleet.

Chartering caught on like wildfire during the 1970s, so much so that bareboating has become a primary industry in the British Virgins. Many companies large and small have followed CSY's lead, among them the Moorings, who started with a fleet of six Pearson 35s and five employees in 1969. Ginny and Charlie Cary and other partners pioneered another charter concept, that of maintaining a hotel at one's base, where clients could ease their way in and out of the workaday world. Today, the Moorings runs a full-service hotel and a complete maintenance base, with 80 boats in Tortola, as well as 200 employees in the Virgins alone. Their branch in Saint Lucia opened in 1981, while another 18 people service the Moorings office back in New Orleans.

CSY has expanded even more. They now operate over 100 yachts in charter at three different locations: the British Virgins, Saint Vincent in the Grenadines, and Roatan in the Bay Islands of Honduras. They grew as bareboats became more and more expensive and elaborate. Refrigerators, hot showers, Bimini covers, roller-furling gear, and all the luxuries became marketing essentials. Caribbean companies began to think more and more in terms of packaging and marketing, attracting a new clientele who wanted as much comfort and as little hassle on a sailing vacation as possible.

When CSY's Carib 41 leases expired, they realized that most production yachts did not meet their new requirements, nor were they built robustly enough to withstand the day in, day out wear and tear of bareboat chartering. The company wanted to keep maintenance costs on increasingly elaborate vessels down to a minimum. The only way they could do this was by insisting on top-quality yachts of their own specification. In the late 1970s, after three years of research and study and more than 10 years' hard-earned experience with bareboaters in all types of weather, they introduced their own line of yachts, the CSY-33, -37, and -44. So concerned were they with quality that they went into business constructing their own vessels.

Although CSY no longer builds its own designs, these three charter boats have been a brilliant success. Many of them can be found in the hands of long-distance cruising people as well. CSY's criteria for construction

Opposite: *I suppose one would describe the CSY-44 and CSY-37 as the grandmothers of all bareboating designs. Among the first vessels to be designed specifically for chartering, they have stood the test of very hard wear extremely well. CSYs are on charter in the Caribbean and South Pacific. The CSY-44 from aloft shows the spacious deck layout. Both the CSY-37 and 44 are cutters, a rig that subdivides the foretriangle into manageable areas. The center cockpit (normally covered with a Bimini top) provides incredible space for lounging, eating, and navigating, as well as ready access to the engine, an essential in charter boats. This aerial shot shows how many hatches ventilate the interior, a vital feature in tropical charter areas. A four-cylinder Perkins gives you over 6 knots under power and ample reserve for motor sailing. The accommodation is ideal for tropical chartering, with a huge aft cabin and a large forecabin providing privacy at both ends of the boat. I have known 10 people to sleep on these boats, but four to six is ideal. The large galley area is well ventilated and convenient to the cockpit, while the huge refrigerator/freezer area to starboard doubles as a chart table. A pilot house version with walk-through passage aft is also available. (Courtesy Caribbean Sailing Yachts)*

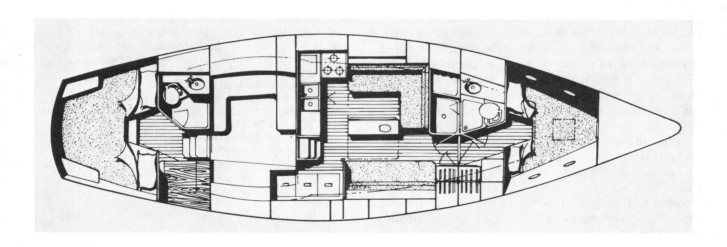

and design were absolutely uncompromising. The reason CSY went into the yacht-building business itself was because they wanted to control quality from the very beginning; quality, they realized, was the key to low maintenance on charter.

CSY's criteria for the ideal charter yacht make interesting reading. One concern was quality construction and low maintenance, a second that the boats be good-looking both inside and out. Their vessels had to be seakindly and sail well not only downwind but to windward, with a minimum of fuss and considerable stiffness. The rig had to be robust and very simple to operate, so that two people could sail the CSY-44 in strong winds if need be. CSYs were to be safe and comfortable to operate, anchor, and live aboard. The company chose the cutter rig to give good driving power at the bow and jiffy reefing to make reducing sail as easy as possible. They fitted a powerful diesel to drive the yachts through moderate chop with ease and designed huge water tanks and large fuel capacity to enable the boats to be largely self-sufficient for two-week charters. The result was heavy-displacement yachts that are perfect for tradewind sailing, even if they are a trifle slow to windward. Above all, CSYs are durable, utterly comfortable yachts that are ideal for tropical chartering.

The layout of each CSY design offers maximum privacy, yet provides ample ventilation and plenty of room for a crowd to eat, drink, or laze. The 44-footer has an enormous great cabin aft and a broad deck above that is nothing short of a private stateroom, complete with its own head and shower. The forward cabin provides a second private cabin, once again with access to a head of its own. A third couple can sleep in the main cabin. The 37-footer has a small aft cabin built into the port quarter and provides privacy for two couples. Both yachts boast of enormous galleys and huge refrigerators that have both deep-freeze and cool chambers. They are large enough to hold two weeks' frozen and fresh food and so well insulated that you just have to run the engine for an hour a day to keep the contents cold.

Ventilation is a primary concern in the tropics. The CSY-44 has no less than seven hatches and 18 opening ports, which, with the two companionways, assure a constant stream of fresh air through the boat. It does take a long time to batten the boat down for rough water sailing, however. All CSY designs have enormous cockpits with large storage lockers to hold diving gear, cockpit tables, life jackets, and all the other impedimenta of a leisurely charter. The cockpit on the 44-footer is no less than 7 feet square, providing not only comfortable seating but ready access to the engine room beneath.

Although no other charter companies have gone as far as to set up their own boatbuilding operation, and CSY itself is now out of the construction business, it's safe to say that their designs have exercised a profound influence on bareboat rig and layout throughout the industry. From the point of view of the charterers, the experiment with completely standardized yachts has been so successful that other companies have followed suit. Insofar as possible, spare parts are kept interchangeable among the different designs. Accurate maintenance schedules can be maintained, trends in gear failure spotted. So maintenance costs are kept to a minimum, overhead is lower, and the cost to both client and company is less than with a miscellaneous fleet.

We have dwelt on the CSY story at some length, because their designs epitomize the desirable qualities of a charter boat. Other large Caribbean companies like the Moorings and Stevens Yachts have now commissioned their own designs after using such production boats as Gulfstars, Morgans, and Petersons for some years. They have not gone as far as to build their own boats, but they have worked very closely with both designers and manufacturers to produce high-quality, low-maintenance vessels that will stand up to the rigors of the charter business. Companies of this size have considerable clout with the manufacturers as far as quality, inventory, and price are concerned, because they need large fleets of new yachts.

Opposite: *Stevens SC-47. The newer generation of bareboats is placing a much higher premium on performance. The Stephens 47 is one state-of-the-art version of this generation, a powerful cutter that is easily handled by a crew of four to six charterers. You sit in a center cockpit high above anything except the most persistent spray. The yacht is easily reefed and can be driven hard or just pottered along for days on end. Her 6-foot draft makes her ideal for the Caribbean or Pacific. A Ford Lehman auxiliary provides more than ample power. As with all Sparkman and Stevens yachts, the deck layout is well thought out and absolutely functional. A luxurious interior features a vast aft cabin with double and single berths, another stateroom forward, and ample space for a paid skipper. there are two heads, a large passageway galley under the cockpit, and more than adequate refrigerator/freezer space. What I like about this yacht is the minute attention to details like lockers, sinks, and so on. You could cruise an SC-47 anywhere. (Courtesy Stevens Yachts)*

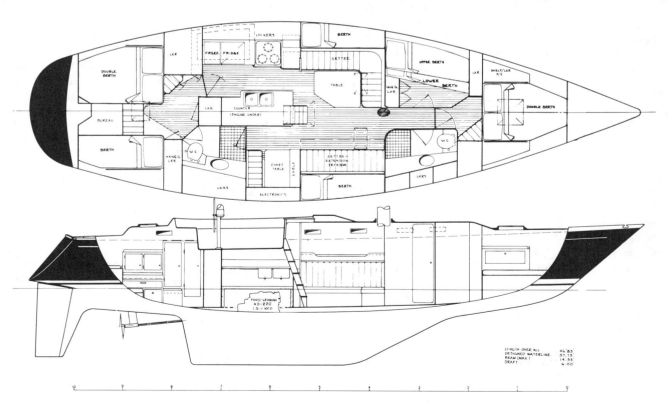

LENGTH OVER ALL   46'83'
DESIGNED WATERLINE   37.75'
BEAM (MAX.)   14.33'
DRAFT   6.00'

A few larger yacht brokerages maintain charter fleets consisting of yachts purchased by their clients, which are then put under charter management through the company. Sailboats Inc. of Wisconsin maintains a charter fleet of more than 200 Canadian-built C&C yachts on the Great Lakes, using its charter operation as a way of introducing people both to cruising and to yacht ownership. Under management operations like these, the company sells the owner a yacht, then manages it, paying a percentage of the charter earnings back to the purchaser (typically about 40 percent). Normally, the owner pays all maintenance costs. Management is fine if the company cares about its owners and clients, as some, like the Moorings and Sailboats, indeed do. But the arrangement can be very unsatisfactory for both buyer and charterer if the company uses management as a thinly disguised device for selling yachts and then does not follow through. This is where word-of-mouth referral is useful, for previous charterers will often report instances of poor maintenance to potential clients.

Stevens Yachts, based in Saint Lucia, Saint Martin, and in the Sea of Cortes, Mexico, offers two good examples of absolutely up-to-date charter designs. The Custom 40 and 47 are both Sparkman and Stephens designs, with a much higher performance potential than the CSY boats. They respond to an increasing desire on the part of some charterers for more performance, combined with sybaritic comfort below. Both are cutter-rigged, modified fin-keel yachts with center cockpits, roller-furling jibs, and accommodations for up to three couples. They compromise on water and fuel capacity and have somewhat smaller galleys than the CSY boats, but will appeal to many more experienced charterers.

Choosing your charter yacht

If you plan to charter in the Caribbean, you should resign yourself to bareboating in a larger yacht, somewhere between 37 and 50 feet long. Although some Saint Thomas companies do offer charter vessels between 30 and 35 feet, the trend is definitely toward larger boats. Anything above 50 feet will probably require a professional skipper. The companies prefer larger yachts because they are more profitable. Clients seem to prefer them, chartering as they do in groups of four to six or more to keep costs low. Also, the trend is definitely toward the larger and more luxurious, toward good living and gourmet food. Like every other type of packaged vacation, bareboating has come to be seen as part of the "good life."

While you can juggle some elements of your charter, particularly provisioning, you must reconcile yourself to a degree of standardization in the yachts available. Forget ULDBs, IOR racers, and that sleek 35-footer you saw racing around the buoys last month. Your bareboat will be a much more leisurely craft, but well suited for the sort of vacation cruise most people want.

Incidentally, it's interesting to note that a new generation of charter yachts that give better sailing performance is now coming into service. This is without a doubt due to the large number of repeat clients with considerable sailing experience and to a design trend toward faster cruising yachts.

Your choice of a bareboat depends entirely on the depth of your pocket, your experience, and the expectations of your crew. Above all, choose a boat that sails. Some mass-produced designs that are in common charter use are notorious for going sideways when sailing to windward. You may as well rent a motor yacht, for your sails will remain furled most of the time. It would be invidious to mention names, but beware of boats with very high freeboard, short ends, and low aspect-ratio rigs. Try to select a yacht with good hard-driving foresails that will carry you to windward in moderate chop.

Do not expect the sort of sail inventory you find on private yachts. Most Caribbean companies will give you a smallish genoa, tailored to moderate tradewind conditions. Every charterer is conservative about sails. The most liberal I know of in North America is Sailboats on Lake Superior, who supply a large genoa and one or two smaller jibs. But that's because the winds are predominantly below 10 knots during their charter season. A word of caution on sails: look at the specification in the charterer's leaflet and figure out if

Opposite: *Moorings 39. Another state-of-the-art charter yacht that originates from a Beneteau design. Again, this design stresses more performance than earlier charter boats. The Moorings 39 features a transom stern and plenty of deck space for sunbathing. With 5-foot draft, you can take her into even small coves, yet scurry for shelter under reefed main and partial jib when the wind pipes up. This is a yacht that will sail better than most of the competition and prove enjoyable even for the most hardened racing crew.*
The interior is subdivided into two double cabins at each end of the boat (personally, I would prefer the forward one). There are two heads, a well thought-out L-shaped galley, and saloon space for a six-person dinner. Unlike many charter yachts, the Moorings 39 has a light, airy interior accentuated by the emphasis on white surfaces. It gives a marvelously cool feeling. Many people ship aboard with six people, but I have a feeling that four would be ideal. A Moorings 43 is also available. (Courtesy The Moorings)

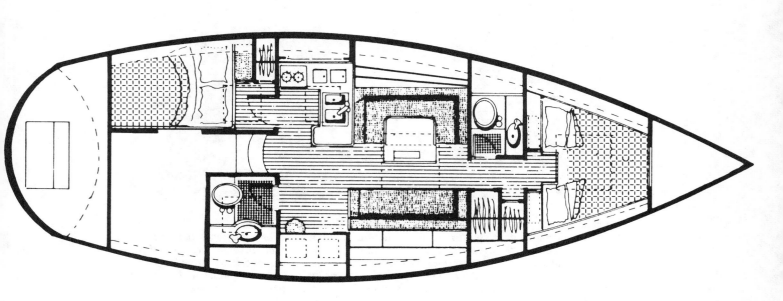

Catalina 30. This simple, family yacht is popular on the West Coast of North America. The sloop rig with its moderately high aspect main and roller-furling jib is ideal for a relatively inexperienced couple or a family. I like the center mainsheet and the spacious cockpit, in which you sleep if you wish. This yacht is notable for her tracking ability downwind and has an excellent cruising record in the arduous conditions of California's offshore islands. The interior is conventional, with two twin berths and a spacious U-shaped galley that is out of the way of cabin traffic. The navigation station is unusually spacious for a 30-footer. (Courtesy Catalina Yachts)

Preparations 91

the winches are of adequate size to handle the foresails.

Accommodations are almost as important as sailing performance on a bareboat. You can sleep six people on a 37-footer, but life will be a trifle claustrophobic. Most bareboats in the 39-to-45-foot range will accommodate three couples; some, like the Morgan 46 or CSY-44, as many as eight, if you enjoy sardine-like cruising. Look for designs that offer maximum privacy for all the couples in the crew. Are there private cabins for two or three couples? Or is one couple sailing away with four singles? In a crew of singles, do people have compatible cabin partners? If you want to cram as many people on board as possible to keep costs low, by all means do so. But unless this is the case, make privacy a primary criterion. Everyone will enjoy the charter much more.

Now take a look at the galley, refrigeration specifications, and storage capacity. A small capacity icebox or refrigerator may be fine for a week's charter in the Virgins, but it will be inadequate for a longer charter. Two toilets and showers are essential with a six-person crew. Two couples can make do with one, but two heads are still desirable. Fuel capacity is not all that important on most charters. The diesels on most bareboats are very economical, and you should be sailing most of the time. In any case, you are never far from a fill-up station in most places.

Most larger charter yachts have center-cockpit layouts. Indeed, this deck configuration has enjoyed greater popularity in recent years as a result of its suitability for tropical bareboating. In the tropics, choose a boat with a large comfortable cockpit and a solid cockpit table, because this is where you will spend most of your time. Check how many hatches and opening ports ventilate the cabin, so the breeze can blow through at night. Only the very largest and most luxurious yachts have air conditioning. Even in midwinter, you will need all the natural air conditioning you can get in the Caribbean and South Pacific. Cockpit size is less important in temperate waters, but it's still nice to be able to stretch out on passage.

Bareboat fleets in the U.S. and Europe seem to be less standardized. Most designs chartered in the U.S. are familiar enough to any regular reader of the major national sailing magazines. You can always obtain further information about them by consulting one of the annual directories produced by such journals as *Sail* or *Cruising World*. A European charter is a different matter. Few European fleets are standardized, most companies being little more than one- or two-person businesses operating with a range of vessels from about 27 to 40 feet. A recent issue of *Yachting World* revealed

a bewildering array of yachts: Maxis, Moodys, Rivals, Sabres, Sadlers, Westerlys. Unless you are a regular follower of the British yachting press, think of purchasing *Bristow's Yacht Charter Annual* (Navigator Publishing Company, Moorehouse, Kingston, Ringwood, Hampshire, England, about $12). This gives specifications of charter yachts not only in Europe, but all over the world. Fortunately, most European companies give a considerable amount of information about their boats in their brochures; rather more, in fact, than their American counterparts. Be warned that many European charter yachts are set up as much for passagemaking as they are for comfortable marina living. A design like a Rival 34, commonly in charter in British waters, is very much a passagemaking yacht—comfortable enough, but not a Caribbean-style charter boat.

Given the wide range of yacht designs in charter these days, you should have no trouble finding something to suit your tastes.

Equipment specifications

The days of stripped bareboats are long gone in the Caribbean and places like the South Pacific, where complete packaging of your trip is the rule. Most Caribbean companies boast that all you need provide is yourself and your crew. They are usually right, but you should always look through the equipment specifications very carefully. The Caribbean fleets operate with comprehensive, standardized inventory packages that go right down to knives, forks, and corkscrews. The yachts come with Bimini covers, cockpit cushions, a dinghy and outboard, basic navigational equipment, sometimes an AM/FM radio and stereo cassette—the little items that make the difference out on the water. The emergency gear will meet, sometimes exceed, U.S. Coast Guard requirements. Check that the charter fees include full water, propane, and fuel tanks. If you have to fill these, your charter costs will mount considerably.

European companies vary considerably in their specifications. Most will supply a full tank of diesel, but sometimes you pay for refills or top up the tank when you return. The safety gear is likely to be more comprehensive and will include deck harnesses, overboard lights, radar reflectors, and all the equipment needed to sail at night in rough weather. The navigational equipment will almost certainly include a radio direction finder, a much more comprehensive chart portfolio, as well as very detailed sailing directions, tide tables, and so on. You are certain to use most of it during your charter. The sail inventory will normally include several jibs and storm canvas, for many charter

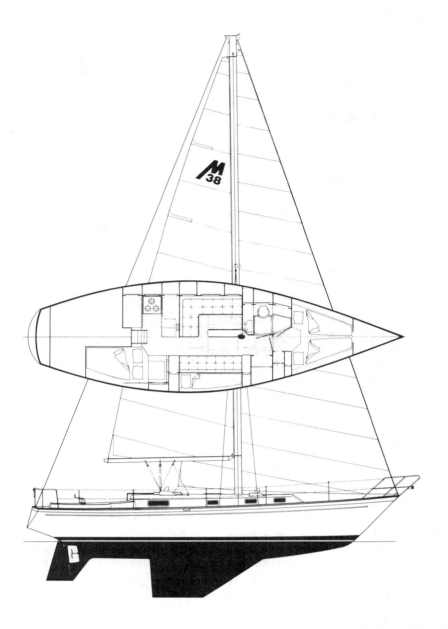

Morgan 38. A Brewer and Corey design with high aspect ratio main and high lift keel that gives unusually good light air performance. This is very much a sailing yacht, but one that is a popular charter design on the East Coast. The double berth aft doubles as a navigator's seat and is somewhat more cramped than the aft cabins on many Caribbean charter boats. The Morgan 38 would be a pleasant yacht for two couples to charter in a place like Florida or the Chesapeake. A 32-foot version provides much the same features, but less berth space. (Courtesy Morgan Marine)

yachts have been bought secondhand and put into the bareboat market or are managed for private owners. Very often, you will be supplied with an inflatable and oars rather than a fiberglass dinghy with an outboard, as is the rule in Caribbean waters. An outboard can sometimes be rented for an extra fee. With European and continental U.S. companies, be careful to check whether you should bring bedding and towels. While most Caribbean fleets provide these, some Old World charterers argue that this is your affair, for they have enough problems keeping the boats dry without worrying about laundry. Some charterers, like those in the Bay of Islands, New Zealand, offer bedding packages, which are well worth accepting.

The brochures will list an impressive array of standard equipment. The company will check out the inventory to you when you take off. Of course, it is one thing to have the equipment aboard and quite another for it to be in good working order. This is particularly true of first-aid kits, flashlights, and tool kits. Tool kits are the worst offenders. I have, on occasion, been reduced to tightening nuts on the engine with pliers and to using a pocket knife to tighten loose screws on the stove. Be sure to check these items out carefully. Ask for replacements if the kit is incomplete for even basic repairs. This is an area where European charterers may offer you more complete inventories, for they do not have the service boats that operate in Caribbean waters. You are basically on your own, so they assume that you will cope with most routine problems. It's important to discuss the tool kit with your charterer in some detail before setting off.

Charter companies vary infinitely in their attitudes toward spare parts carried aboard. Some Caribbean organizations boast that you need not carry a thing—they can reach you in two hours or less if a mechanical problem develops. Fine, but you do at least need spare flashlight bulbs and batteries and the like. Make sure they are aboard. The yacht may carry a few common spares aboard, especially engine belts and water-pump impellers, for these seem to fail on heavier yachts where the engines work hard with some regularity (the symptom is overheating). I would advise talking about spares with the company before you take off. Most Caribbean charterers will tell you to radio them before tackling anything but the most routine maintenance job, like checking the batteries. Follow their instructions.

Interestingly enough, almost no Caribbean companies send you out with spare shackles, small stuff, sail repair kits, or extra rope. Although I have never had rig trouble, other than small sail tears and some parting sheets, I find the lack of spares irritating at times. There are so many little things, like fraying halyards, that one can fix oneself in a few minutes with the right spares that I carry some of my own just in case, a precaution that has paid off again and again.

Some European vessels I have chartered have come equipped with everything necessary to tackle almost any routine and not-so-average repair job above and below decks, including a battery of spares that would allow you to cross an ocean, from fuel filters and gaskets to spare diesel injectors and halyards. But such inventories are few and far between, for spares deteriorate if not stowed properly on a hard-used boat. European companies are strong on spare shackles, cotter pins, and rigging materials, especially sail battens, because winds blow harder in their charter areas. Their engine spares are only a little more comprehensive and normally include filler funnels, spare oil, and filters, in case you have to refuel yourself in an area where the fuel is suspect.

Generally speaking, a bareboat anywhere will come equipped to do its job well within its own cruising area. Equipment specification is based on long experience of local conditions and clients' needs, as well as the extent to which you, the customer, are expected to be self-sufficient of the company during your cruise. The only items of equipment you should bring along are those that make you more comfortable aboard, in the broadest definition of the term.

The bareboater's ditty bag

I would define being comfortable aboard as protecting yourself from unnecessary frustration, whether this is caused by inadequate tools or by having to navigate without your favorite dividers. The wise charterer protects himself from unnecessary frustration by taking along a waterproof ditty bag containing some supplementary tools and spares for just such eventualities. A few extra items of safety equipment and navigation gear are also worth taking along. A small, well-organized holdall full of plastic bags or containers packed for peace of mind takes up minimal space and is easily stored in a convenient locker.

Here are some suggestions for your ditty bag.

Safety gear: Every charter company provides the basics—life jackets, horseshoe liferings, etc., but a few items can add to your safety margin.

● Safety harness. Though rough-weather passages are rare in the Caribbean, they can come on you unexpectedly more often on European charters. A familiar, well-tried harness is a great comfort when the roller jib jams or you need to furl the staysail. Some fleets do provide safety harnesses, but it is reassuring to have your own.

● Flashlight. Although some companies are very careful to supply working flashlights and a few insist you test them as part of the check-out process, it is surprising how many charter yachts are sent out without properly functioning torches. Sometimes the batteries are almost run down and no spares can be found. A light may fail to work when you are checking an anchor line on a dark rainy night in a squall or when an obstinately silent engine needs to be illuminated—as once happened to me in the middle of the Florida Straits in a thunderstorm. So it is far better to carry your old faithful and a set of spare batteries. In any case, an extra flashlight is always appreciated.

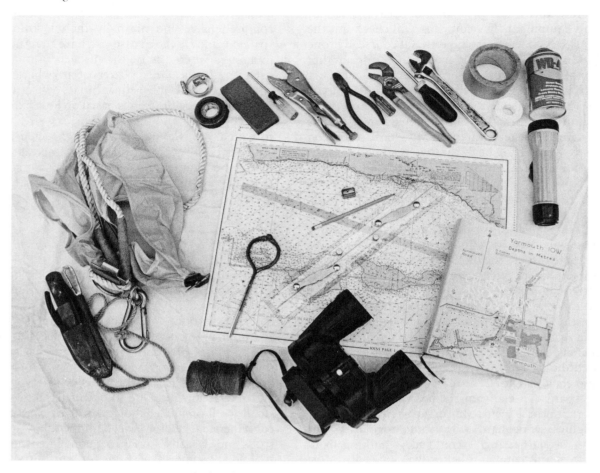

The bareboater's ditty bag. (Lesley Newhart)

Navigational equipment: Here I prefer my own equipment.

● Hand-bearing compass. A Minicompass or its equivalent is vital, especially in island areas where there are many confusing landmarks and submerged rocks. In the Bahamas and Grenadines, I have been thankful for a bearing compass when sudden rain-squalls obscured key landmarks at critical moments. It is at times like these that one grabs the company-supplied compass and finds that the prism is scratched. Far better to bring your own favorite instrument.

● Dividers, paper, pencil, pencil sharpener. It is remarkable how often one needs paper and pencil, even when one has forsworn them for the duration of the vacation. They can be used to jot down pilotage notes, to make shopping lists, to record scores in card games, or just to preserve those transitory moments of enlightenment that can come to you while on passage. The idea for a holdall came from such a moment of revelation. The note on a rum-stained scratch pad read,

"Where are *my* pliers! Bring a ditty bag." We had just been trying to tighten a loose bolt on the stove with a pair of rusty pincers. Why not pack a small pencil sharpener as well, also your own dividers? Most of those on charter yachts have been bent and spiked. Many seem to have been used to pierce the skins of roast potatoes.

● Binoculars are a matter of personal preference. I like to take my own; they are adjusted to my normal sight, the lenses are clean, not scratched, and I know that the crew will look after them. Many companies actually prefer you bring your own.

● Cruising guide and sailing directions. Every charter company provides sailing directions on board. Some send you them in advance, so you can plan your cruise ahead of time. Cruising guides vary infinitely in quality. Some are vague and incomplete; others are filled with advertising and outdated information; a few are brilliantly definitive accounts of complex cruising grounds. The best in the world come from England:

Adlard Coles's volumes on the English Channel are classics. It's well worth checking around to see what is available. For example, Donald Street's cruising guides to the Caribbean are rarely provided by charter companies, who favor cheaper directions (often filled with advertising). You are well advised to invest in the very best cruising guide available. At least, borrow or steal someone else's and make copies of key pages. Another useful investment for American and Caribbean charters: a Chart-Kit from the Better Boating Association, PO Box 407, Needham, MA 02192 (800-225-8317), if the area you plan to charter is covered by one.

Tools: The typical charter yacht tool kit contains a set of wrenches, a couple of screwdrivers, and some other items. Sometimes the tools are rusty and neglected. And invariably, the loose bolt that stops you cooking or works loose in the steering gear is the one for which there is no wrench in the kit. It's a good idea to take along some extra tools.

● Knife set. A knife, spike, and pliers holster set should be part of your kit anyhow, especially on a well-used charter yacht where rope ends are sometimes frayed, whippings come undone, and shackles are tight from neglect. But don't pack your knife in airline carry-on baggage. Who wants the reputation on board as the idiot who held up the boarding line at the airport?

● Sharpening stone. Have you ever tried to carve barbecued steak with charter-yacht kitchen knives? A few strokes of the sharpening stone will have them resembling cutlery again.

● Adjustable wrench. One or two small and medium-sized adjustable wrenches and a vice-grip will pay for themselves within the first two days, if nothing else for tightening slack lifelines. Smaller sizes are best, for it is invariably the lighter-weight wrenches that are missing from the tool kit.

● Screwdrivers. Take a Phillips and a conventional medium-sized screwdriver, also a small electrical one for those tricky jobs and set screws that fall out of cameras and binoculars.

A small hacksaw, wire cutters, and electrical pliers are desirable items, the latter if for nothing other than removing fish hooks from your catch. Electrical tape, a small can of WD-40, and two stainless steel hose clamps for seacocks and engine hoses complete the inventory. A roll of duct tape protects sails and clothing from cotter pins. You should carry some of the latter in a film can in the ditty bag as well. Add some rip-stop tape, sailmakers' thread and twine, and a couple of needles, and you are ready for most minor repairs from ripped sails to torn Bimini covers.

The inventory for your ditty bag can go on forever, limited only by your apprehension about the trip and the weight limits on the plane. Most other items are not essential, but do pack a can opener and corkscrew. All too often can openers sink, while corkscrews seem to be rare luxury items in the later days of a charter. A friend once anchored in a remote spot in the Tobago Cays in the Grenadines. The wine was produced, glasses polished. But alas, no corkscrew. Instead of serious drinking, a great deal of time was spent contemplating the sealed cork, which eventually was rammed into the bottle with a rusty screwdriver. So, a few hours spent preparing your holdall can take many of the day-to-day cares out of your charter. And it is always packed and ready to go when you decide to take off on your next dream trip.

10 Travel, Baggage, and Provisions

The worst part of any charter is often getting there. Finding out about discount airfares, car rental rates, package round-trip tickets, and long-term parking for your car can be worse than clawing to windward against the Gulf Stream. The problems may be compounded in Europe or the South Pacific by jet lag. Many charterers arrive at their yachts in a state of disoriented exhaustion, especially those who have driven long distances and then flown to their destination. I once spent 10 hours in the Saint Vincent airport with a group of charterers from South Dakota, who had driven all the way from Sioux Falls to Miami before boarding their plane to the Grenadines. Admittedly, they were all professional truck drivers, but even so.... They were facing the same drive at the other end. So do all you can to minimize your travel problems by seeking expert advice. (The pages on travel that follow are aimed at U.S. travelers, but the same basic principles apply in Europe.)

Making your travel plans

I doubt if many bareboaters are experts on airfare structures, unless, of course, they are professional travel agents. My first advice is to consult a travel agent and let him do all the work. It costs you no more and is far better than being on hold with the airlines.

The name of the game in European travel is cheap round-trip airfares. Most times, you will end up with an APEX fare, a discounted round-trip price that is good for between 90 and 180 days, depending on the country. Normally, you pay for these fares at least 21 days in advance. The rates vary spectacularly from season to season, with the highest rates during the peak summer tourist months. Since the best time to charter in Europe is in early summer or fall, you may be able to fly more cheaply during these months. When scheduling your flight times, allow at least two days at each end of the vacation to recover from jet lag and, if you are sailing at the end, for bad weather delays while afloat.

My second tip is to use the travel agents recommended by the charter company. Some of the larger ones like CSY or the Moorings either are associated with major travel agencies or own their own companies. They are specialists in Caribbean travel and have good connections with the numerous small airlines that service the lesser islands. I would not dream, for example, of making reservations for travel to Roatan in the Bay Islands except through Anchor Travel in Tenafly, New Jersey. They know the Honduran schedules intimately and monitor the changes all the time in ways that another more general agency can never do. This is one occasion when it is best to use the specialists and not your friendly neighborhood agent. The same applies for the South Pacific, where you should most certainly use the agents recommended by the charterers. Most American charter company agencies have toll-free numbers, so you can make reservations at no charge. They will also book you into hotels at, or close to, the charter base.

Bareboating vacations in the Caribbean and the South Pacific are becoming increasingly packaged, so that you may well get an inclusive quote for airfares, hotels when required, the boat, and provisioning, whether you come from Europe or North America. These packages are arranged with the airlines for use with the lowest possible airfares. On major trunk routes and itineraries that use jet airports down-island in the Caribbean, you may make out sensationally well, especially off season. Smaller commuter airlines have far less flexibility, so it may pay the thrifty charterer to charter from an island with a jetport.

I would advise you to sew up your travel arrangements at the same time as you make your charter reservations. The limited numbers of budget seats on popular long-distance hauls fill up long before the departure date. For instance, it's very difficult to get space between Los Angeles and Miami on days when cruise ships are leaving. Call up the recommended travel agent and give your cruise dates, the times when you want to arrive and depart from your home and the charter area. Make sure you give the agent the complete itinerary, not just the major trunk legs. It is sometimes harder to get space on small Caribbean airlines than it is on cross-country flights. The agent will either give you quotes and schedules at once or call you back in a few hours with bookings or options. It is well worth finding out the name of the agent you are speaking with, so that you can use the contact for future exchanges. It makes the whole process more personal and sometimes more efficient.

The travel agent will try and book you on the cheapest possible routing to keep your round-trip fares as low as possible. This policy can take you to some pretty bizarre places or have you flying much greater distances than you might expect. People fly from Ohio to Miami via New York, or from New York to Honduras via New Orleans, simply to save on airfares. A great deal of bareboat flying is done on "red-eye specials," especially if you are coming from the West Coast or the Northeast to the Virgins or Grenadines. If you do not want to fly to strange places or at night, tell the travel agent at once. It will cost you more, but some people think it is worth it. In some cases, everything is set up around the irregular schedules of small airlines in the Caribbean, so you may have to fly at strange hours simply to meet their departure time. Incidentally, expect a few hitches at small Caribbean airports. Some local airlines (I will mention no names, but any experienced Grenadines charterer will know who I mean) are notorious for their casual schedules and tardy departures. The travel agents do all they can to avoid putting you on them.

Once your bookings are made, you are well advised not to change them and to pay for them *at once*. You are then locked into the fare structure at the time of booking. If you pay later on, you may end up with a higher rate. Of course, if the fare goes down, the agent will issue your tickets at the lower rate, so you are protected all around. In any case, the travel agency will expect you to pay for your tickets by check or credit card 30 days before departure. They will then mail them to you well ahead of time.

If you have the time and can afford it, I would recommend resting up for at least one night in a hotel before taking over your boat. This gives you time to recover from jet lag, to get used to a slower pace, and to buy any last-minute goodies you might want over and above the provisions on the boat. For instance, you can often buy liquor more cheaply in Caribbean supermarkets than you can through the charterers. If you charter around Christmas, look out for spectacular liquor sales in the Virgins. A night ashore gives you time to check these things out at your leisure. Very often, the local cab drivers, especially in Tortola, will be mines of information about the cheapest food and drink. Again, the charterers' travel agents will be able to fill you in on the best places to stay. You can sometimes stay at their marinas, which is convenient, although the food is sometimes better in town.

One hint on travel arrangements: avoid making last-minute changes in your itinerary, for you will often lose out on super-saver fares and end up spending a great deal more. In particular, try to make your final choice of crew long before departure. Then everyone can take advantage of the same fare structure. If any member of the crew wants to go or come back a different way, give him the responsibility of working out details with the travel agency. It's his problem, not yours!

Many of the world's finest charter areas are so far from home that it is pointless to travel that distance just to bareboat. Australia and New Zealand are two such countries, while Europe offers endless possibilities for combining land and sea vacations. The notion of "adventure holidays" has taken hold in the South Pacific, where you can combine a week or so's chartering with some time traveling ashore. For example, charterers in New Zealand's Bay of Islands can prepay a rental car and motel rooms for as many days as they wish beyond their charter period and wrap up the entire vacation in a very attractive package indeed. The only way to book an "adventure" type of package is through a travel agent who specializes in such holidays and knows the bareboating scene as well. You'll find some specific recommendations in the South Pacific chapter below.

Europe is much more complicated, largely because everyone wants to do different things with his vacation time. Here you make your travel arrangements with your favorite agency and book your charter through a company in Europe or through a broker in the United States. Most European charter companies will want nothing to do with your travel. While some will meet your train or plane, in most cases it is up to you to get to their base. The planning of your charter will be circumscribed by disposable funds, the available excursion fares and their time limitations, and what you plan to do ashore. Usually, a European charter will be part of a longer vacation, in which case you can time it for the beginning or end of the trip, so that you can dump your sailing baggage somewhere while you tour on land. Personally, I prefer to take the charter at the end, because then I go to sea refreshed and thoroughly adjusted to European conditions. Hopefully, by the time you charter, grocery shopping and coping with foreign languages will no longer be a novelty. This will make your preparations a lot easier. Chartering at the end also allows you to turn in your rental car, if you have one. You can then go to the charter by train and cab and avoid the expense of car parking while you are at sea.

If you are going especially to charter, budget for a cruise that coincides more or less exactly with the cheapest airfare you can find. Normally, a 14-to-21-day excursion is about the lowest rate you will get, unless a price war is going on. If you are going chartering in Europe, or if you are a European planning to sail in North America, you will almost certainly find yourself flying during the intermediate or high seasons of the spring, summer, and fall months, when fewer cheap rates are available. You can sometimes get spectacular bargains by buying excursion tickets for summer in midwinter, when the airlines' marketing pitches are just beginning. When striking your bargain, allow at least two days at both ends of the charter to recover from jet lag and for any unavoidable delays at sea.

In addition, if you are going sailing, pay the extra to go on a scheduled airline rather than on standby or charter. Charter flights are especially chancy, for they can be rescheduled without warning. They may even be scheduled earlier than your original departure date and leave while you are still at sea. Sometimes they land you in cities like Amsterdam, far from your yacht. It may cost you more than the difference in fare from a scheduled airline to reach your charter point. So pay a little more and relax. It's one less thing to worry about.

Once you arrive in Europe, you are on your own. Most charterers will give you general directions to their bases, but will leave the travel details to you. If the marina is within easy reach of the airport or your hotel, take a cab. Many British charterers operate in small seaside towns that are fairly close to a major railroad station. Take the train to this point, then ask them to meet you, or take a cab. If the company is less accessible, and even if it is not, your best strategy may be to rent a car for a couple of days. This will allow you to arrive in good time, buy your provisions, and also explore the countryside for a few hours. For example, some of the finest pubs in Cornwall are to be found within a few miles of the charter company bases in Falmouth, England. There is no way to reach them without a car. Very often, the rental car will be cheaper than four or five rail tickets, cab fares, and other incidentals. You will often find a branch office of Hertz, Avis, or Godfrey Davis within easy reach of the charterer. Or, alternately, you can rent locally.

Whenever you are making travel arrangements to charter farther afield, I would advise spending a little more to make sure that things have less chance of going wrong. This does not mean going first or business class; small touches, like a comfortable hotel the first night in Europe or a rental car at the airport, make all the difference, especially if everyone is a little apprehensive about foreign waters.

A final point about foreign air travel. Most airlines require that you reconfirm air tickets within 72 hours of your return departure. Make sure you do this before you leave on your cruise, so that your tickets are still valid upon your return. The Caribbean companies will often do this for you, but farther afield you are once again on your own.

Another minor tip. When traveling from Europe, the continental United States, or Canada to the Caribbean, check your hold baggage only as far as the last major airport, like San Juan, Puerto Rico. Then check it onto the commuter separately. This reduces the risk of losing your baggage.

What should I take with me?

The answer is, of course, as little as possible. Take a careful look at other charterers when you arrive at a bareboat marina on a busy day. Their baggage is very revealing. Some parties arrive staggering under heavy suitcases and festooned with diving gear and fishing rods. They line up in rows to pass their impedimenta from dock to yacht until the decks are laden with a sea of half-opened baggage. In the end, there's not enough space, so they leave much of their gear ashore in the company's baggage room. It is amazing just how much even experienced charterers manage to bring along with them, when in fact all you need is a small holdall for each member of the crew and perhaps one extra bag for diving gear, tools, and reading materials. Some people going on Caribbean charters take along almost nothing except shorts, T-shirts, bathing suits, and suntan lotion. While you may not want to go to this extreme, be ruthless about keeping luggage to a minimum. Here are some pointers.

Baggage: However much baggage you bring along, pack it in soft holdalls and collapsible bags for easy storage. The Land's End company of Wisconsin produces a line of valises, garment bags, and airline holdalls that are perfect for a bareboater on the move. The ideal sailing duffel bag has a shoulder strap, several interior and exterior pockets for documents and valuables, and is made of durable canvas or PVC. The zippers are fabricated of tough plastic and sealed with a Velcro flap. You can even get waterproof holdalls if you want. Design your personal kit to fit into a bag no more than about 2 feet long.

Such a holdall should be all you need, except for a camera bag or a lightweight document case to carry reading material for the flight, passports, and so on.

Travel documents: Keep your airline tickets and travel documents in a special water-resistant wallet, preferably separate from your holdall. Although you can travel to some Caribbean islands with little more than personal identification or a birth certificate, I strongly urge that you obtain a passport. This takes all the uncertainties out of immigration procedures. Your passport is also excellent identification when you are cashing travelers' checks or dealing with officialdom in general. Visas are unnecessary nearly everywhere you will charter regularly, but the travel agent will advise you if one is required and even obtain it for you.

International certificates for vaccination against smallpox are anachronisms these days. You need not take one along, unless some temporary epidemic requires it. A driver's license is also useful, if you plan to rent a car. Also bring your medical insurance card along just in case.

Money: Take only a limited amount of cash for immediate expenses, say about $50. The balance should be in travelers' checks that can be cashed only against your signature. Keep the checks in one place and the supporting register in another, filling in details as you cash them. Travelers' checks can be stolen, and you will be out of money unless you can report the numbers of the stolen checks to a local office of the organization that issued them. I would strongly recommend you take American Express travelers' checks. They may cost you a commission fee ($2 per $100), but they are negotiable almost anywhere, and American Express has refund offices in nearly every country in the world. The last thing you want is problems with your money reserves.

How much cash will you need? That depends on your personal spending habits. You won't need much if you have opted for a total provisioning package and plan to eat all your meals aboard. Crews that spend a lot of time ashore and go from bar to bar and from restaurant to restaurant will need much larger sums. I normally allow about $100 per week on a fully provisioned charter, taking an extra $100 for emergencies. Take your major credit cards with you wherever you charter. They are accepted even in quite remote places. Some charter companies will accept them instead of cash for your security deposit, for your liquor and sundries account, or for purchases in their gift shop. Some can be used to get emergency cash as well.

Clothing: The essentials vary little from what you require at home, but plan on forgetting laundry during your charter. The size and scope of your charter wardrobe depend on the climate where you are bareboating. Wherever you go, the rule is simplicity and versatility. Here are the essentials for a tropical charter or for a summer cruise in North American waters:

- Underwear.
- Shorts.
- Bathing suits—at least two.
- T-shirts. At least two of these should be old ones that can be worn snorkeling. Figure on throwing them away at the end of the charter.
- Short-sleeve shirts or blouses. Take a couple of nicer, lightweight ones to wear ashore. The lighter the material the better, but avoid nylon or excessive polyester.
- Jeans or light slacks. You will need these when a cool wind blows in the evening or when dining ashore at better restaurants. I would advise taking light slacks rather than heavy jeans, although the latter can be invaluable when the mosquitoes are biting. The perfect long pants for both men and women are light cotton ones made of cheap cloth with a drawstring waist. They slip on over shorts or a bathing suit, protect you from sunburn, and keep the chill off your skin on warm evenings. I have sailed thousands of miles in such garments. They cost only a few dollars to make.
- Skirts. Lady crewmembers should pack one light skirt or pant suit to wear ashore. All the ladies I have sailed with recommend versatile, easily crushed outfits of skirts and pants that can be used in all sorts of combinations.
- Some form of light sweater will be useful on windy evenings.
- Sun hat. A sun hat, or at least a visor, is essential on tropical charters. Some people like the broad-brimmed canvas sailing hats beloved by Donald Street and other famous Caribbean sailors, but there is nothing wrong with the straw hats you can buy for a few dollars in the Bahamas and out-island. Just make sure that you attach a piece of line to the brim and pass it under your chin. Experienced charterers hang a piece of cloth from the aft brim to keep the sun off the back of their necks.
- Pareus. The pareu is my favorite item of tropical wear, a length of cheap cotton cloth that is wrapped and tied around the waist over a bathing suit. It is comfortable, versatile, and good-looking. All that's needed is a hemmed cloth that wraps a couple of times around the waist and hangs down to mid-calf. To my mind, this is the ultimate warm-weather garment. You can buy them overseas, but you can make your own with colorful fabric from your local sewing store.
- Sunglasses. Take good-quality Polaroid glasses with you and attach them around your neck with a stout string. Polaroid lenses relieve eye strain and are much better for eyeball navigation.
- Footwear. Bring a good pair of sandals. These are invaluable for walking ashore, much better than the ubiquitous flip-flops that fall apart at the slightest provocation. Invest in a leather pair with good walking soles. You will never regret it. A word of warning: crepe and plastic soles are lethal on fiberglass decks.
- Deck shoes are essential in rougher weather. Topsiders or the new Timberland boat shoes are a must for serious sailors. Occasional charterers can get away with cheap deck shoes from J.C. Penney's or Sears. Although you will probably go barefoot most of the time, at least take some rubber-soled shoes that can be worn on deck. A pair of antique sneakers is essential for snorkeling over coral and rocky bottoms. Plan on abandoning them at the end of the trip.
- Socks. Some people wear old ones to reduce blistering from snorkel fins. Take as few as possible. You will probably not use them.
- Foul-weather gear is entirely a matter of personal preference. Many Caribbean charters will go so smoothly that you will never need even a light anorak. But I have sailed on cruises in the Virgins where we wore foul-weather gear for days on end. On balance, you are best off taking a lightweight waterproof jacket. You are unlikely to need waterproof pants. Plan on wearing or carrying the jacket on the plane. It is often too bulky to pack in your holdall.
- Personal toiletries.
- Medications. Take along ample supplies of whatever medications have been prescribed for you. You cannot rely on obtaining them in many charter areas.
- Seasick pills. Many more people are enjoying sailing now that there are *prescription* seasick pills that really work. Although some unfortunate sufferers have problems whatever pills they take, most people achieve amazing results from the several prescription medications now on the market. On a recent Bahamas charter, I sailed with a novice crew who used the new behind-the-ear patch. Despite some very bumpy weather, no one was sick. In this day and age, it is foolish, indeed antisocial, not to obtain a prescription from your doctor. Some skippers of my acquaintance insist that you do so.
- Suntan lotion. Take several grades, from maximum screen protection down to conventional oil. If there is one item you should take on a tropical charter, this is it.
- Insect repellent. Another essential, especially in North American waters. The spray-can types are probably the best. Some coils are not a bad idea either.
- Plastic bags. Take a large plastic bag for dirty laundry and some smaller ones to keep watches and other delicate items dry.
- Camera and film. You should carry these with you

rather than packing them in your holdall. Take some plastic bags and silica gel to keep humidity from the camera, and remember to take some spare batteries along. Nothing is more frustrating than to have your camera run out of juice just at the most interesting moment of the cruise.

Armed with this inventory, you should be very comfortable on most tropical charters. Everything else, down to clothespins, is supplied by the charter company.

Packing for colder climates

The main difference between a tropical charter and a temperate northern European or North American charter is in the clothing and foul-weather gear you take along.

Your clothing should be versatile enough to make sailing in high summer conditions bearable, yet warm enough to protect you when the temperature dips into the 50s. Subtract such tropical items as pareus from your kit and add the following:
- Wool sweaters. Take one more than you think you will need. Pure wool is by far the best protection, because it stays warm even when it is wet. If you charter in Ireland, New Zealand, or Scotland, do not fail to buy yourself a thick sweater. It will last forever. The new nylon-bunting jackets are an excellent alternative— warm, lightweight garments that seal out the wind on the coldest days. I like the American Patagonia or Norwegian Helly-Hansen types best of all.
- Pendleton shirts or equivalent. Thick woolen shirts by Pendleton or other manufacturers are ideal for watchkeeping in northern summers. Try to find shirts with long tail flaps. They keep you warmer and drier in rough weather.
- Long pants. Again, take one more pair than you think you will need, and at least one pair of a heavier weight.
- Thermal underwear. Longjohns are ideal for night passages, even in midsummer. Take at least one pair along.
- A stocking cap, woolen gloves, and a warm scarf will make all the difference during a chilly watch at sea.
- Foul-weather gear. Take the very best outfit you can afford, preferably one with the safety harness and flotation built in. I have found the Henry Lloyd jacket and pants combinations superb even in the fiercest Bay of Biscay conditions. But they are expensive, and there are cheaper alternatives. Both pants and jacket are essential, the former with suspenders and a chest-high bib waist. The jacket should have a close-fitting hood; the wrists, close-fitting elastic. I prefer a detachable hood, for I find a good old-fashioned souwester of the type beloved by clipper skippers much better at keeping spray from going down my neck. Two or three lengths of old toweling at the throat will help, too. Do not skimp on foul-weather gear for chartering in European waters. Cheap outfits are a false economy.
- Good deck shoes are essential, as are rubber boots. Again, buy the very best. The knee-length Romikas are a superb lightweight design with drawstrings at the top. They have kept me dry in severe gales with water kicking all over the place. Wear a size too large over thick woolen socks so that you can kick them off in emergencies. Ankle boots are too short to keep seawater out effectively, even when you wear your foul-weather pants on top of them. Avoid the heavy Wellington boots worn by farmers. Their weight may be lethal if you fall overboard.

A little advance thought will mean that you will take along everything you need for your charter, yet still arrive with only a small holdall to worry about.

Provisioning

Let's face it, provisioning is a hassle, whichever way you look at it. There is nothing worse than arriving at your destination after an overnight flight to be confronted with hours of supermarket shopping and bag carrying before you can even begin to stow the food aboard. Fortunately, help is at hand. Now that large refrigerators are the rule, most Caribbean companies offer provisioning packages with a complete inventory of foodstuffs for each day of the charter, at a fixed per-day charge of between $15 and $20 (1984).

The original provisioning packages were standardized affairs—usually barbecued steak the first night, shish kebabs the second day, chicken the third, and so on. This standardization keeps prices low, because the companies buy in bulk and pass the savings on to the client.

Simpler packages still prevail in more remote areas like the Bay Islands or South Pacific, where everything, except perhaps fresh eggs and fruit, has to be imported. You will often find some interesting local products on your menu. The Bay Islands menus often feature local lobster tails and shrimp, while papayas are common on South Pacific cabin tables.

Basic packages may be the order of the day in remoter areas, but the Virgins and Grenadines are a different matter. Somehow, bareboating in these areas has become associated with gourmet living. So, inevitably, the charter companies vie with each other in providing the ultimate in good living. Here's a selection of options:

● No provisions at all. This means that you arrange your own. This is fine in the Virgins; indeed, charterers on Saint Thomas should plan on doing their own shopping. There are plenty of supermarkets in Tortola and Saint Thomas for the budget shopper. The Grenadines can be more chancy, but it is possible to stock up in some places.

● Self-provisioning. Here you check off items on a grocery list, write a check, and arrive to find the provisions you ordered on board. Some companies send you a list of basics, or even a basic package, which you can add to.

● Split provisioning. A standard provisioning package, with three evening meals omitted each week. This is for the benefit of those who plan to eat ashore several nights, a popular option in both the Virgins and Grenadines.

● Standard provisioning. This is the regular three-meal-a-day package chosen by 90 percent of all charterers and the best value. Some companies allow you to select the menus you want aboard; others, especially in more remote areas, give you a standard package of different meals.

● Gourmet menus. Here you pay for what you get, and you can get everything from New York steak, quiche, and stuffed quail to lobster tails and pate de foie gras. Some people like to travel this way, but you are probably better off purchasing a few gourmet items at a delicatessen or the charter company food store before leaving. The standard menus are a good value and very nutritious. Why spend more every meal?

● Diet packages and complete frozen dinners are available from some companies. You should ask for details if you want such provisioning options.

All these options have developed in response to competition among charter companies themselves and among provisioning organizations, especially in Tortola. You can buy literally any luxury food, even imported French pate and smoked salmon, from gourmet stores ashore. But beware: you are going to pay an enormous premium for such indulgences. It is possible to spend several hundred dollars on snacks, breakfasts, and lunches alone. I have enjoyed salmon mousse, pate, smoked oysters, and Beluga caviar on Virgins charters— all, I must say, provided by hospitable anchorage neighbors! I may be biased, but I prefer to take the normal provisioning package and go sailing. It is the cheapest way to feed a hungry crew in the long run. I don't go chartering to sweat under a load of full grocery bags. You can also pay for everything well ahead of time and avoid the bugbear of last-minute expenses. If you want the odd gourmet items, just buy them when you arrive.

When you choose a provisioning package, there's no need to bring any food with you, unless you need specific items that are unobtainable away from home. I always pack containers of garlic and chili powder, for I find most provisioning packages rather bland. I once dined with a skipper who brought along a glass jar of his own particularly potent barbecue sauce. Some people bring along their own cooking knives and a wider battery of spices. A good cook can concoct more than adequate meals from the abundant supplies provided. Why waste your time and money on something more elaborate, when you will probably barbecue most of your meals over the stern or cook on top of the stove rather than with the oven, which heats up the cabin?

Doris Colgate has written an excellent basic cookbook that should be in your baggage: *The Bareboat Gourmet* (New York: Offshore Sailing School, 1982). You can obtain this from the Dolphin Book Club.

Liquor is entirely a matter of personal preference. You can buy it at most Caribbean companies' marinas or at a nearby supermarket. Check prices, for it is sometimes cheaper to buy locally, especially in the British Virgins around Christmas, when price wars erupt in Tortola. Local beers, rums, and wines are usually much cheaper than your favorite U.S. variety, so this is the time to experiment with your palate. Purchase your duty-free allowances on European and Australasian charters; liquor is generally much more expensive in these areas. Every crew makes its own financial arrangements about liquor. Some prefer to split the cost equally, others to have everyone buy individually. Just make sure that you buy enough sodas, for you will probably drink more of them than you anticipate on hot days.

In Europe and North America, you should plan on doing your own shopping. Some companies will arrange for a local grocery to put your order aboard, but such service is rare. Normally, you just have to grit your teeth and go shopping. You can take a lot of the pain out of the process by making up menus and lists ahead of time. I normally plan on a good breakfast; a bread, cheese, and fruit lunch; and a more elaborate cooked dinner. While provisioning is more or less the same anywhere in the U.S. or Canada, European grocery shopping can be quite an adventure, not because there are no supermarkets (they are all over the place), but because of the language barrier. The best strategy is to buy nonperishable staples at the beginning of the cruise in order to reduce purchases of canned food, and to forage for fresh meat, vegetables, bread, and milk every day. European cooks prefer the freshest of ingredients, and you should follow their example. This strategy makes the initial shopping less burdensome and gives you the daily challenge of buying food in different places, often where no one speaks English.

Many cruising authors make a big deal out of shopping in strange places. There's really nothing to it, for many foods are the same the world over. Sign language works wonders, and animal noises will soon produce beef, pork, or lamb. Most labels can be deciphered without too much effort, although I once bought packaged Norwegian spring water in Denmark under the impression that it was milk. And it can be very frustrating to be confronted with German instructions on a can while a hungry crew drools for dinner. But the consolations are unending. There is nothing quite like fresh croissants and coffee for breakfast in a French port. You will find the crew competing to go to the bakery before breakfast just to savor the smell. Salad lunches of baguettes, pate, and nice smelly cheese washed down with vin ordinaire are guaranteed to send even the most jaundiced crew into afternoon ecstasy. The possibilities for gastronomic adventure are unending.

You will find that fresh meat and canned goods are more expensive in Europe, and in Scandinavia ruinously so. Like Europeans, you will end up shopping carefully and economically, keeping waste to a minimum and taking advantage of specials. Liquor prices vary greatly from country to country and are especially high in Great Britain and Scandinavia, where whiskey has the status of liquid gold. Plan to buy your full duty-free allowance on the plane when chartering in northern Europe. You will need every drop. The Mediterranean offers an infinite variety of wines and local brews. There you are better off taking potluck at every port.

When cruising in Europe, enjoy local fresh foods and make exploring them and the local cuisine part of the pleasure of unfamiliar waters. After all, what is better than enjoying Greek squid straight from the water or succulent New Zealand lamb in its homeland?

Lesley Newhart

PART III: CARIBBEAN CHARTERING

11 General Comments and the Virgins

"Have you chartered in the Grenadines?" I am asked every time I sail in the Virgins. And when you are bareboating in Belize or the Bay Islands, you'll be asked if you've sailed in other places. There's a constant debate about charter areas going on wherever you share an anchorage with others. One of the nice things about cruising is sailors' penchant for sharing navigational information over glasses of wine. Bareboaters do just the same, but with a twist: they exchange information not only about local anchorages, but about new areas and charter companies as well.

The chapters that follow take you on a brief journey around the bareboating world, to the Caribbean, North America, Europe, and the South Pacific, to charter areas you may never have heard of before. Every cruising ground has its own distinctive flavor, challenges, and dangers. You can charter in tropical paradises, rock dodge in chilly northern waters, idle along at 2 knots in the French canals, or anchor in the shadow of a Greek temple. I try to give you a general impression of each charter area. I do not list charter companies, because such directories are soon out of date and these chapters

were designed to withstand the test of time. You will find listings of charter companies in such well-known periodicals as *Cruising World* and *Sail*, both of which publish annual charter issues. Or you can consult Bristow's *Yacht Charter Annual* (Navigator Publishing Ltd., Ringwood, England).

Caribbean bareboating

The Caribbean is the most competitive charter market in the world. Its safe anchorages and warm tradewinds attract thousands of bareboaters every year, especially during the winter months. Many American and Canadian charterers gain their first experience in Caribbean waters. You will meet people from all over the world in the Virgins and Grenadines. I have shared anchorages with French and German bareboaters, with a group of Danish scientists, and with Englishmen on a package trip from Manchester. So this is the logical place to start our tour of prime bareboating locations.

A generation ago, you would have found but a

handful of bareboats in the Virgins, and even fewer in the Grenadines. Avery's Boatyard in Saint Thomas was one of the pioneers, catering to the northern sailor with a few weeks to spare for a winter vacation. Chartering was a strictly seasonal business in uncrowded waters. The boats were simple, refrigeration unknown. There was plenty of room for everyone. Then came the fiberglass yacht, the jetliner, and the package tour.

Now there are hundreds of bareboats throughout the Caribbean, most of them concentrated in the Virgins and Grenadines, to say nothing of a large crewed charter fleet as well. Bareboating has become big business, with standardized charter fleets, elaborate onshore facilities, and all the marketing and packaged-travel hype that goes with large-scale tourism. The prime cruising areas have become so crowded that finding an empty anchorage is practically impossible even in the off season. The charter season has grown to include every month of the year, even the hurricane season in late summer. Onshore facilities—restaurants, beach bars, dive shops, car rental operations, and so on—have expanded to meet the increased tourist traffic. Bareboating is the major tourist industry of the British Virgins and a major element in the Antigua, Saint Martin, Saint Vincent, and Saint Lucia economies. The facilities are now excellent and the choice of yachts unlimited. Above all, navigation is straightforward, especially in the Virgins, where most people charter for the first time.

The center of the charter business lies in the Lesser Antilles, a crescent of islands some 500 miles long that extends from Saint Thomas to Grenada. Practically every variety of tropical cruising can be found here, from sheltered passages between hilly islands to tough, open-water sailing among low-lying, sandy archipelagoes surrounded by hidden reefs. The Lower Antilles are famous for their consistently fine weather and for northeasterly trades that blow for weeks on end and act as natural air conditioning.

In fact, the direction of the trades varies slightly with the season. During the winter months, they blow mainly from the east-northeast to the east at speeds between 12 and 15 knots, although they can reach 25 to 30 knots for weeks on end. The best sailing months are probably just after the high charter season, between April and July. The trades blow softer, trending more to the east and southeast, and the weather is usually settled. Winter weather can be unpredictable, especially when a so-called easterly wave brings high winds and heavy rains to the islands. Any time the wind shifts to the north, you can expect a strong blow, but never anything that a well-found charter yacht cannot handle. The big mistake that many winter charterers make is to assume that the weather will be fine and settled during the precious days of their vacation. All too often it blows hard, or a period of rain settles over the islands. At least the temperature is bearable. You can still enjoy good, hard sailing, but you are unlikely to see much sunshine, and eyeball navigation is out of the question.

It can rain in the islands more or less any time, but a day of continuous rain anywhere in the Lesser Antilles is a rarity. Most of the precipitation falls in heavy, but usually short-lived, rainsqualls that move with the tradewinds. Many squalls sweep through during the afternoons. The clouds build ominously on the horizon and advance toward you, a mass of lowering grey. Often you can see the rain falling on the ocean as the squall builds and collapses, changes direction, and masks familiar landmarks. No one can predict just how much wind will come from such a squall. The strongest gusts often come from line squalls that hit just before the rain falls. I have known the wind to rise from a pleasant 10 knots to over 30 in the space of a minute, sat through torrential rainstorms that laid the wind completely flat, and blown out sails in 50-knot storms. The only defense against squalls is to make sure you are in deep water and to reduce sail before they hit you. At worst you will feel stupid, getting wet in a flat calm. There's never anything wrong with being prepared.

"What about hurricanes?" asked the nervous charterer at one Saint Vincent briefing I attended. This was in August, at the beginning of the hurricane season. "There hasn't been a hurricane here in years," replied the expert. "They normally pass north of us, so don't worry." A week later, we were snorkeling at Tobago Cays when a French yacht from Martinique called over to us. "There's a hurricane warning," they cried. We tuned in Barbados to learn that a hurricane had formed deep in the Atlantic, far to the east. During the next few days, the island early-warning system went on full alert. Hurricane David came nearer, but turned north just when tension had reached the breaking point. It was a close call.

Yes, hurricanes occur in the Caribbean, and they can strike when you are chartering. Theoretically, they can occur any month of the year, but most are concentrated in late July, August, and September, tapering off in October. These are the months when charter rates hit rock bottom and many charter companies offer two weeks for the price of one to keep their boats busy. Such rates are a bargain, if you are lucky and hit a spell of settled weather. But the trades frequently die, and you steam in a humid sweatbath that makes not only the cabin but also the cockpit a nightmare. However cheap the rates, avoid the hurricane months. Having been

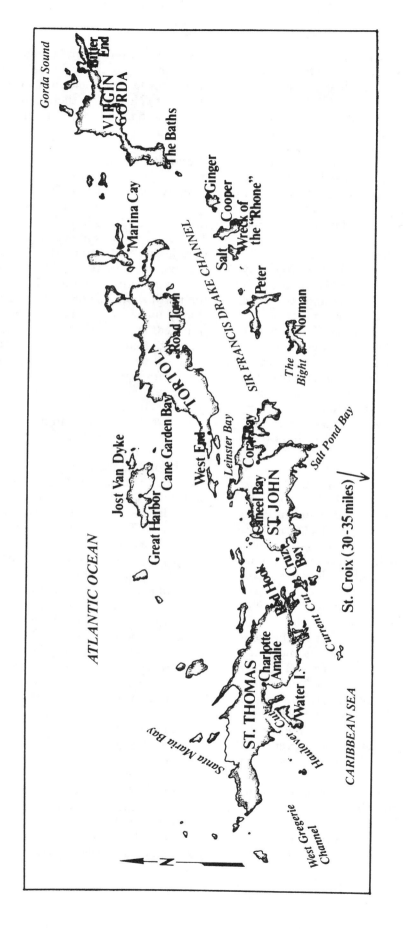

The Virgin Islands

through a serious hurricane warning, I assure you that it is no fun. Better to plan your vacation a few months earlier or in November, when things have settled down again.

While most chartering is concentrated in the Lesser Antilles, you can also bareboat in Belize and the Bay Islands off the Honduras mainland of Central America. Here the annual mean temperatures tend to be somewhat higher, and the humidity can be unbearable when the trades are down. In the Bay Islands, for example, there is only about 6.4 degrees' variation between summer and winter mean monthly temperatures—77.7 degrees in January and 84.1 in September, the warmest month. As elsewhere in the Caribbean, the big variable is the natural air conditioning offered by the wind. Belize and the Bay Islands are low-lying, with a rainfall averaging about 67 inches annually. The driest months are between March and September, but even then squalls may occur. Rainfalls of 6 inches or more a day are not uncommon in the wettest winter months. Occasional northers can sweep down on these areas during the winter, bringing southwesterly winds of up to 50 or 60 knots. The best time to charter these locations is probably during spring and early summer, say between April and July, when the chances of a norther are small and the trades are relatively predictable.

The time was when the Caribbean islands were inaccessible, way off the beaten track. All this has changed. The Virgins are easily reached through the Saint Thomas international airport. Or you can fly to Puerto Rico by jet and then go on by Air BVI to Tortola. Commuter airlines link the Lesser Antilles in a web of reliable and not-so-reliable flights. Tourism has become such big business that you can reach Antigua, Barbados, Martinique, or Saint Lucia by jet.

The adventure starts when you fly to the smaller islands. We once sat for 10 hours with six Sioux Falls truck drivers in the Saint Vincent airport until a well-known local airline decided to honor its published schedule after cancelling two flights in a row. The only consolation was the cheap rum and vodka we were taking home with us. Larger parties are probably better off with a private charter flight. The price may be high, but you will get there on time. Experiences like the one above are a good reason to use a travel agent versed in the ways of Caribbean airlines. They will know whom to avoid at all costs.

The Virgin Islands are universally regarded as the safest place for the beginning charterer. The qualifications needed to charter this area are less than those expected of people cruising down-island in the Grenadines or in Central America. Your best strategy is to start in the Virgins and to establish your credentials with a charter company there before trying one of their operations farther afield in the Caribbean. And if you are new to chartering, there is no better place to learn the ropes than in these warm and hospitable waters.

The Virgin Islands

Many experienced sailors rate the Virgins as the finest cruising ground in the world, way ahead of such places as the Grenadines, Tahiti, or the Greek Islands. They certainly rank high on my list, ever since I arrived there after a 24-day transatlantic passage from Madeira. We anchored in the Bight at Norman Island for a breakfast swim, then pulled into Cane Garden Bay on the north shore of Tortola for the first cold beers and rum punches in a month. The dreamy days that followed made one really appreciate this fabulous cruising ground. The Virgins have everything to offer: good sailing in sheltered waters, superb anchorages, excellent facilities ashore, and some of the finest snorkeling and diving in the world. Unfortunately, they are congested.

A Virgin Islands charter usually starts in Saint Thomas in the American Virgins or at Road Town in the BVI. Both are good places to begin, for an abundance of comfortable anchorages lie within an easy half-day's sail. Saint Thomas and Saint John lie at the southwest end of the Sir Francis Drake Channel, a great waterway that bisects the British Virgins. The mountainous scenery of Tortola dominates the north side of the channel, while a string of lesser islands—Norman, Peter, Ginger, Cooper, and Virgin Gorda—protect the southern limits. The channel ends in the treacherous reefs and shallows of Anegada Island, a graveyard for ships since the days of the Spanish conquistadors. Anegada is off limits to bareboaters, but Jost van Dyke Island, to the north of Tortola, certainly is not. The entire charter area is only about 35 miles long and 10 miles wide, with off-lying Saint Croix 35 miles farther south of Saint John to attract the more experienced bareboater. You can sample the Virgins in a week, but two weeks will enable you to explore most of the islands at leisure.

One reason the Virgins are so popular is that they are easy to reach by air; another, that the islands run east to west and protect the best sailing waters from the Atlantic swells that sweep down on the Lesser Antilles from thousands of miles away. So you can enjoy the trades in complete comfort. If the prevailing trades are up, you will find yourself beating to windward toward the more easterly islands. When you plan your charter,

Charlotte Amalie, St. Thomas (George Marley)

I recommend that you complete your windward work very early on in the cruise. A Saint Thomas boat could plan on a leisurely first day, stopping somewhere like Saint John or Caneel Bay for a comfortable evening. Then plan on an early start and make your windward mileage as fast as possible, pausing to clear customs at West End on Tortola. The trades often blow more gently in the morning hours, so with luck you can be well up the Sir Francis Drake Channel before windward work becomes uncomfortable. There are so many anchorages that you can stop for lunch almost anywhere on the way, too. It takes only about a half-day to tack from, say, Road Town to Virgin Gorda, so you should be anchored off your favorite anchorage in Gorda Sound by late afternoon, comfortable in the knowledge that everything is downwind from there on. I think it's particularly important for people with only a week in the islands to get their windward work out of the way. They will see much more if they do.

The Virgins are perfect for bareboaters who want a fairly civilized charter. There are dozens of restaurants and bars to choose from and any number of sheltered anchorages. This is a congested charter area, however, so you should take special care with your anchoring. Many favorite spots are deep-water berths, so plan on

laying plenty of scope and checking your anchor set with mask and snorkel. An ideal day in the Virgins starts with a leisurely swim and breakfast, then a short sail to a sandy beach. Take your lunch ashore in the dinghy, cook it over a driftwood fire, then explore before enjoying a nap and another short sail or some snorkeling. Finish the day with a rum punch or two and a barbecue over the stern, and you are in paradise. It may be difficult to leave. A timely warning here: please don't dump anything overboard or rip up the coral for souvenirs. Enough damage has been done already without our assisting in the further desecration of these lovely islands.

There are so many musts in the Virgins that it is difficult to know where to start, but here goes. I think the first priority is to enjoy some sailing. After all, the Virgins are a sailor's paradise. So plan on spending some afternoons sailing for the sheer pleasure of it, beating to windward in the sheltered waters of the channel, reaching from Tortola to Jost van Dyke as the soft trades massage your skin. You will never forget this sensual experience. I remember one afternoon in Saint John, when my crew decided to spend the afternoon shopping in Saint Thomas. As they took off on the ferry, I hoisted anchor and went off for an afternoon sail

Cruz Bay, St. John Island, American Virgin Islands, Tourist Authority (Courtesy Fritz Menle: Peter Martin Associates)

toward the Sir Francis Drake Channel. I raced other charter boats, short-tacked off the rocks, laughed aloud with sheer joy as the spray splashed me. It was heaven on earth—and my crew wondered why I was so cheerful that evening. Plan, too, on using your motor as little as possible if the trades are up. You'll have much more fun. But one golden rule in the Virgins: *Always use your engine when entering or leaving anchorages.* There is too much congestion to be a purist here—unless you're Donald Street, who doesn't have an engine anyhow and can sail a boat into anything.

Let's take a brief tour of the major islands and anchorages, starting in the American Virgins. The U.S. Government purchased them from the Danes in 1917, mainly for defense reasons. For many years before coming under civil rule, they were a naval base. I must confess that Saint Thomas is not one of my favorite islands. Charlotte Amalie, the capital, is a free port where up to five cruise ships may call in a day. It is a shopper's paradise where one can buy luxuries about as cheaply as possible. You can easily blow a whole vacation's budget in a few hours here. The town is crowded, hot, dirty, and dangerous after dark. Your best course of action is to collect your bareboat, stock up with provisions, and clear out, reserving perhaps half a day for boutique shopping. If you want to visit Charlotte Amalie and are chartering elsewhere, leave your boat in Saint John and take the ferry across. Those who do sail there will find that the harbor is large and completely sheltered. You can tie up to a marina, if there is any space, or anchor off among the many other cruising yachts in Long Bay or off Fredericksberg Point. Charlotte Amalie is a wonderful place to go yacht watching, for some of the crewed charter boats are magnificent antiques. Make sure you lock the boat if you go ashore.

The western end of Saint Thomas is not as interesting as other parts of the Virgins. The best access from Charlotte Amalie is through Haulover Cut, but be careful to dodge the seaplanes that land close by. There are a number of anchorages close to West Gregerie Channel, like Honeymoon (Druif) Bay, that are favorite spots with local sailors. The north coast has little to offer, except for Santa Maria Bay, which is a good summer anchorage. The only time I went in here, in May, there was no one else around. Red Hook Bay on the east side of Saint Thomas is the headquarters of a number of charter operations, including Caribbean Yacht Charters and La Vida, two of the larger companies operating in the Virgins. The deepest water is on the north side of the bay, while a full-service marina provides all facilities. The lagoon on the southeast coast is also an important charter base and full-service

marina, as well as being the best hurricane hole on the island.

If your charter begins in Saint Thomas, you are far better off making the effort to sail over to Saint John for your first night. The route from Charlotte Amalie or the lagoon takes you through Current Cut. The passage is straightforward, except for a 4-knot tide that flows strongest to the southwest. Pass on the east side of the light, where there is 23 feet, and use your motor, especially if you are fighting a headwind and foul tide. Running out of daylight? Anchor in Christmas Cove, just south of the cut. The most sheltered berths are on either side of Fish Cay between the cay and the shore.

Saint John is a lovely, relatively unspoiled island, much of it administered by the National Park Service. Plan to enjoy its many anchorages and to avoid Cruz Bay. The town itself is pleasant enough, but you have to anchor in the harbor, which is very congested. *The* time to visit Cruz Bay is over the Fourth of July weekend, carnival time for the town. This is very much a local affair, with stilt dancers, processions, and competitions. Join the crowd, and eat and drink at rock-bottom prices. Saint John's carnival is much more relaxed than those at Saint Thomas and Saint Croix, where there is stronger antipathy toward visitors. I know several crews who charter at carnival time every year.

There's an overabundance of good anchorages on the coasts of Saint John. The south coast is somewhat off the beaten track. The farther east you sail from Cruz Bay, the less developed the anchorages. I especially enjoy Salt Pond Bay, where I was once weatherbound for two nights in a strong norther. You can explore the National Park trails ashore and walk out to the summit of Ram Head. There is good snorkeling close inshore. Look out for the big reef in the entrance. You can pass on either side. The area known as Hurricane Hole on the southeast corner of the island is well worth exploring if you want privacy in high season. The fingerlike inlets into the mangroves offer complete protection in any weather. The anchorages tend to be buggy, but Coral Bay with its Moravian Mission and old sugar mill is well worth visiting. It is hard to believe that this was once the busiest harbor on Saint John, when sugar was everything to the islanders. The south coast is best visited in the winter, when the winds are steadily in the north.

It's surprising how many people stick to the more crowded north coast, starting with Caneel Bay, an open roadstead remarkable only for the plush resort of that name. It can be bumpy here. Most people anchor off to visit the resort, where a jacket and tie are needed for dinner. Far better to sail on a little to the unspoiled beauties of Francis Bay or, even better, Leinster Bay. Just make sure you keep north of the light that marks Johnson Reef. Francis tends to be buggy, so anchor some 200 yards offshore. Don't go ashore at night, you'll be eaten alive by insects. Leinster is another of my favorites. Enter, leaving Water Lemon Cay to port. You can anchor in at least four places, but I think the best is probably the eastern cove, often called Water Lemon Bay. Anchor close to shore, taking care to avoid the grass patches, and explore the old lime plantation ashore. Another lovely spot lies immediately southeast of Water Lemon Cay. I love this anchorage. There's always plenty of room.

Few charter companies forbid you to sail out to Saint Croix, but they tend to skim over it in their briefings. The 30-to-35-mile open-water passage is a very long day, something best left to more experienced charterers. The long sail is straightforward enough, provided you pick your weather. It's a reach both ways, and the landfall is a dead snip. Your best strategy is to take your departure from the east end of Saint John or Norman Island in the BVI (preferably the former, to save clearing customs at Saint Croix). Lay off a compass course, allowing for the current. Once you pick up the high ground of the island, steer for the saddle between the two hills east of Christiansted. As you approach, you'll pick up the houses of the town. Once you are close enough and still clear of the shallows, alter course for the eastern part of the city until the radio tower on Fort Louise Augusta bears 170 degrees magnetic. Close in, place this tower in the middle of the channel buoys, then follow sailing directions.

Christiansted is a fascinating town. Be sure to explore the old Dutch houses and to take a cab or rental car ride around the island. Buck Island is a fine daysail 4.5 miles northeast of Christiansted, a park with magnificent reefs. There are few other anchorages to appeal to charterers, but you will find less congestion here. Saint Croix is still an agricultural island, once famous for its cattle and sugar. Tourism, oil, and aluminum refining are now the major industries.

One final note about the American Virgins for visitors from the BVI. *Make sure that you clear customs at Cruz Bay before you anchor elsewhere.* You will be fined heavily if you are caught without clearance papers.

The same applies to the British Virgins. You can clear in at West End and Road Town on Tortola, at Jost van Dyke, or Virgin Gorda. Do this before you sail elsewhere. Again, the penalties for noncompliance are harsh. Don't take chances, and remember that it is a courtesy to wear a shirt or a blouse and shorts when clearing customs anywhere in the islands.

My favorite anchorages in the Sir Francis Drake Channel are all on the smaller islands. The south coast of Tortola has little to offer the bareboater. Road Town itself is best visited from a hotel at the beginning or end of your charter. West End is a pleasant enough anchorage, but there is little to see or do ashore. Most of the more accessible coves on the south coast are occupied by charter marinas, so you are best advised to spend time elsewhere.

Two or three relaxed days will take you through the anchorages on the southern islands. These are all within an easy sail of Tortola, but allow for some northwesterly to southeasterly current in the channel when crossing. This varies according to the tide and wind conditions. The Bight at Norman Island is probably one of the most visited anchorages in the Virgins, largely because it lies a comfortable distance from the major charter bases. It's a nice place to spend your first or last night. Norman is said to be the prototype for Robert Louis Stevenson's Treasure Island, but this may be apocryphal. The Bight is completely protected, with good holding ground in the northeast corner. Even on relatively calm days, a nice wind funnels through the anchorage to provide air conditioning. This is a congested berth, but a good place to meet fellow charterers if you are feeling sociable. Many's the time we have made new friends here and cruised with them for several days. The Bight is especially useful on windy days, for there is usually room to take shelter when other anchorages, like those on Peter Island, are full. The latter is not one of my favorites, especially since Great Harbor is deep, with only limited space for anchoring. Marina lovers may enjoy the resort in Sprat Bay, but a once comfortable anchorage is, to all intents and purposes, no longer available.

Salt Island is remarkable for its salt ponds and for the wreck of the RMS *Rhone*, which sank off the island in an 1876 hurricane. You can snorkel or dive on the wreck, anchoring close by for a few hours. The *Rhone* was at anchor taking on cargo and stores when a hurricane struck without warning. The captain managed to ride out the first part of the storm by running his engines at full speed. He weighed anchor during a lull and tried to reach open water. The wind came in again just as the *Rhone* was clearing the island. She was blown on the rocks and broke her back, with a loss of 125 lives. Divers will see more of the ship than snorkelers, but she is certainly worth a visit.

So are the Baths, a great jumble of huge granite boulders at the southwestern corner of Virgin Gorda. The piles of boulders form shady caverns and cool, crystal-clear, saltwater pools where one can bathe while

The Baths (Lesley Newhart)

the sun plays in intricate patterns on the cave walls. Plan on anchoring clear of the rocks, snorkeling a bit, and having lunch. Even on calm days a surge runs in here, so you should plan on overnighting elsewhere.

Virgin Gorda (Fat Virgin) is the second largest of the British Virgins. Both the Spaniards and the British mined copper here, but no miners have worked the deposits since 1867. Spanish Town, the only large settlement, was the capital of the BVI in the eighteenth century. Many charterers visit the Virgin Gorda Yacht Harbor to explore the island. Fine, if you like expensive resorts, but the discerning skipper will sail farther east to Gorda Sound, which lies at the eastern end of the Sir Francis Drake Channel. The best entrance is between Mosquito and Prickly Pear Islands. The channel is well marked, but you should beware of the shallows on the west side. Follow the markers, and eyeball the shallows carefully before you turn west toward Mosquito Island. Most bareboaters make a beeline for the anchorage off

the Bitter End Yacht Club, a restaurant that is famous throughout the Caribbean. There are at least three other restaurants in the area, however, and they all maintain high standards. Dinner ashore at one of these establishments is a must, partly because of the setting and the food, but also because you can meet fascinating people at the neighboring tables. Last time I ate at the Bitter End, we met a retired lawyer from Maine, a blueberry farmer, a restaurant owner, and a professional masseuse. You can make friends for life on a Virgins charter! There are excellent anchorages all around Gorda Sound, including Drake's and Leverick Bay, both of which have excellent restaurants and numerous snorkeling and diving possibilities. Gorda Sound is a good place to explore in bad weather, for its waters are sheltered in all but extreme conditions.

Gorda Sound should be an early stop on your itinerary so that you can sail downwind at your leisure to Marina Cay, Jost van Dyke, and the north side of

The Bight, Norman Island (George Marley)

Tortola. Marina Cay is a pleasant half-day's sail from Gorda Sound, a sheltered anchorage behind a reef and a small island where you can enjoy dinner ashore at another famous establishment. The nearby restaurant on Bellamy Cay in the middle of Trellis Bay on Beef Island is said to be excellent, too, but I have never been there. Beef Island is where Tortola-based charterers arrive by air. It got its name from the cattle grazed there by the early buccaneers. Until the road bridge was built, a small ferry took cattle and passengers from Beef Island to Tortola.

The north coast of Tortola is easily reached by one of two narrow cuts. The one between Great and Little Camanoe is probably the best, but be sure to go through on a clear day so you can see the reefs on either side, and look out for the strong current that can run through the channel. The north coast can be very bumpy indeed when the trades blow strongly during the winter. A passage downwind to Jost van Dyke is often uncomfortable under these conditions, and you should plan to sail there via the Sir Francis Drake Channel. Under normal conditions, the passage offers splendid mountain scenery. You will soon pick up the hills of Jost van Dyke (apparently a famous Dutch pirate) on the starboard bow. Shape your course to give them a fairly wide berth, so that you avoid low-lying Sandy Cay. Schedule your passage so that you have time to anchor in the lee of either Sandy or Green Cay, both of which are deserted tropical islands. Make sure you anchor properly in both places, for the swell can run in. Neither are good overnight stops. Indeed, it would be foolish to stay there when there are such good anchorages on the south coast of Jost van Dyke.

Until recently, most visitors to Jost van Dyke made a beeline for Great Harbor, which is a port of entry for the BVI. (Albert Chinnery, the customs officer, is a famous island personality.) The bareboaters' mecca was the Tamarind Club, otherwise known as Foxy's. But the last time I chartered from Tortola, Foxy's was closed. Fortunately, there are other alternatives, including three bar-restaurants in Little Harbor immediately to the east. As an anchorage, Little Harbor is to be preferred, but it gets very noisy when the bars turn their amplifiers up full blast and keep them that way until 0200. Ever tried Reggae Christmas music at 0130? This is where to find it in season. Lovers of peace and quiet may prefer to lie off Little Jost van Dyke in settled weather.

No Virgin Islands charter is complete without a visit to Cane Garden Bay, with its beautiful palm-lined beach and small settlement. There is the old Callwood distillery that still produces island rum the traditional way. You can buy their fiery product at the distillery itself, where the primitive manufacturing plant has to be seen to be believed. The product is rough, but I love it. Then there is Stanley Hodges' Welcome Bar and Restaurant, another must for charterers. A Stanley's T-shirt is a minor status symbol; his lobster, music, and rum punches are justly famous. There are other bars and restaurants here, but Stanley's is the most celebrated. Cane Garden Bay itself is a fine anchorage, well protected by an off-lying reef, except when the northerly swells roll in. Under such conditions, go to Jost van Dyke. Time your visit to Stanley's for the closing days of your cruise, planning a stop in Saint John or at one of the islands bordering the channel for your last night, so that you are within easy reach of home base the last morning.

The great thing about the Virgins is that they are compact enough to cater to both the most ambitious and the most timid charterers. All you have to do is to plan an itinerary that gets the windward work out of the way in the first few days. Then cruise downwind, pop a beer, and enjoy.

12   The Windward Islands, Honduras, and Belize

Sooner or later, most Virgin Islands charterers look farther afield and think of exploring other Caribbean cruising grounds. Until recently, you could bareboat only in the Windwards. The explosion in the charter business in the late 1970s has opened up many new areas. Let's explore three major charter grounds: the Windwards, the Bay Islands of Honduras, and Belize.

All three of these areas require somewhat more advanced skills than the Virgins. There is some open-water sailing, a good chance of strong winds and rough conditions, especially in the winter months, and greater navigational challenges around Tobago Cays in the Grenadines and off the barrier reefs of Roatan in the Bay Islands. But there is no reason why experienced Virgin Islands charterers cannot take off to any of these areas and enjoy themselves. It is simply that open-water sailing and reef navigation need more care and forethought than the Virgins' sheltered waters.

Saint Martin, Antigua, and Martinique

With the great expansion of bareboating in recent years, both the Virgins and the Windwards have become so congested in high season that small bareboat operations are opening up on islands like Antigua and Saint Martin. Charters around here are definitely for the more experienced bareboater. This is open-water sailing. The passages between these islands can be rough for beginning sailors. If you are a beginner and want to explore these waters, I recommend that you take one of the occasional delivery charters, when a major Virgins company wants to deliver boats south to Saint Lucia or Saint Vincent. These are one-way charters lasting between 10 days and three weeks, normally under the direction of an experienced skipper, that enable you to visit islands along the way. Watch the display advertisements in the major sailing publications for such opportunities.

Saint Martin, Saba, and Saint Eustatius lie some 75 miles east-southeast of Virgin Gorda. Once off the beaten track, they are now bareboated regularly. Stevens Yachts has recently opened a marina at Great Bay on Saint Martin, a good base for exploring these rugged unspoiled islands. Saint Martin is a political curiosity, an island owned half by the Dutch and half

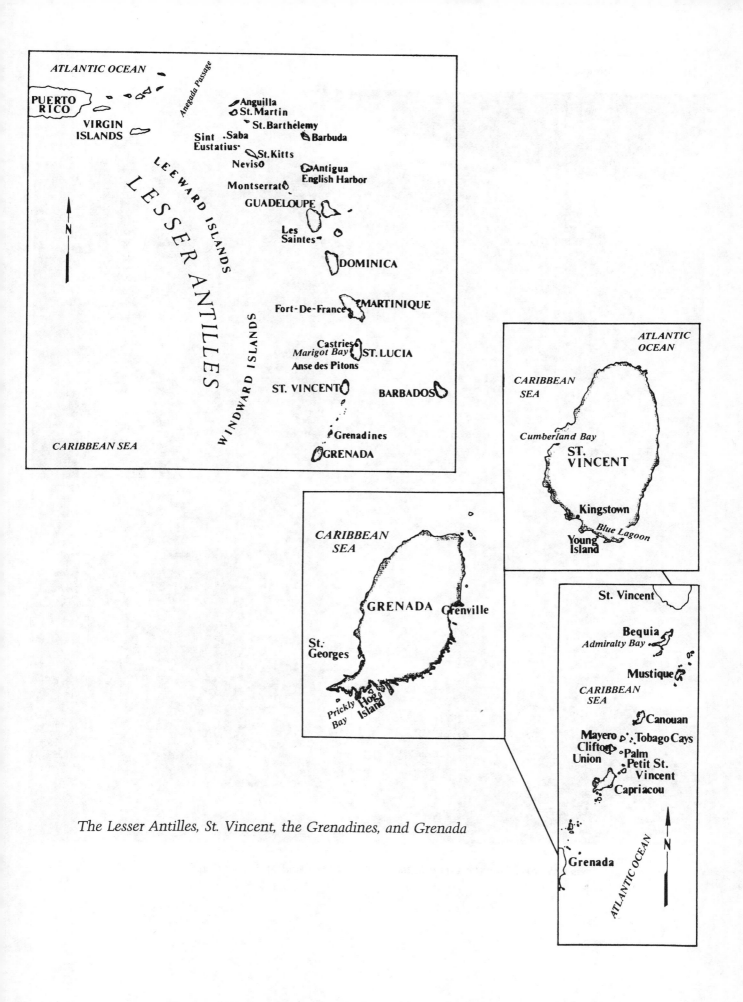

The Lesser Antilles, St. Vincent, the Grenadines, and Grenada

Saba: the road from the airport to the summit of the island (St. Martin Tourist Office)

by the French since 1648. Not that there are any frontiers, you just enjoy a delightful mixture of cultures. Marigot on the north coast is the main French town; Philipsburg, the Dutch port on the south. Both can be rolly when the swells are up, and you move from port to port depending on weather conditions. There are several good lunch anchorages off Saint Martin, but many charterers prefer to make the open-water passage to nearby Anguilla, a low-lying island with excellent snorkeling and a fine away-from-it-all feeling. The main port of entry is Road Harbor, where the best anchorage is in the northeast corner of the bay, out of the prevailing swell. There's a convenient small pier for dinghies and fishing boats. The little town of Sandy Ground lies about a mile uphill from the jetty. Not that there's much to do ashore except sunbathe and swim.

The Spaniards named the island Anguilla, "eel," for its wriggly shape. The sinuous coastline and its offshore islands make for several fine anchorages and some excellent snorkeling. Prickly Pear Cays and Seal Island reef are a two-to-three-hour sail northwest of Road Bay. The best anchorage lies on the west side of Prickly Pear North, but you can anchor almost anywhere in settled weather. The snorkeling conditions rival those at Tobago Cays in the Grenadines, but I would return to Road Bay for the night.

A charter in these waters can take you to Saint Barthelemy, known to everyone as Saint Barts, the ultimate free port. Gustavia is a charming town with massive stone architecture dating back to the Swedish occupation of the island in the late eighteenth century. The harbor is totally sheltered, but tends to be hot and sticky. There are other possibilities, too: Saint Eustatius, Statia, even Saint Kitts, but Saba is the most exciting attraction. Saba is a 3,800-foot rocky pinnacle that rises out of the ocean, with no natural harbors, only two swell-swept landings. About 1,000 people live on Saba, most of them in two settlements in and on the rim of an extinct volcanic crater. The villages are known appropriately as Bottom and Top. Do not even contemplate a visit unless the weather is very settled. You lie alongside a rugged pier that is tenable only in calm conditions. You'll need every fender in the ship and plenty of mooring lines. Best consult the charter company before making this stop.

Antigua has some unique attractions, among them English Harbor and windward reefs that enable one to cruise the east coast of the island in comfort. You can charter from Parham Bay and sail around to English Harbor. You must beat your way 9 miles into what was once Admiral Nelson's base. It is one of the unique experiences of Caribbean cruising. Anchor toward the north end of this congested hurricane hole. English Harbor has the great advantage of being an easy reach or run to almost any island in the Lesser Antilles. Small wonder it was a strategic naval base in the days of sail and is a major headquarters for crewed charter boats.

Take the time to explore the restored buildings and the fortifications on Shirley Heights. Meals ashore are fairly expensive here, but for what it's worth, the pizza is probably the best in the Caribbean. Beware of a drink called an Antigua Smile. I am still recovering from an overdose. Some competitive bareboaters charter a boat for Antigua Race Week each spring. This is a major racing event for sailors all over the world. Unless you are into crowds, high prices, and super congestion, best charter at another time of the year.

For some reason, most people explore English Harbor and little else on Antigua. This is a mistake, for there are many other sheltered coves and anchorages on this beautiful island. As Donald Street once wrote: "One of the thrills of a lifetime is to hold a booming reach along the lee shore of Antigua, rail down, over smooth, crystal clear water, the magnified terrain of the bottom slipping by below."

Should you decide to charter in Antigua, plan on a longer cruise, a minimum of 10 days, so that you can sail north to Saint Martin or 46 miles down from English Harbor to Guadeloupe with its spectacular cliffs and cloud-wreathed mountains. Clear into the poor fishing village of Deshaies and be sure to explore Bourg-des-Saintes on the Iles des Saintes off the southern end of Guadeloupe. This small resort town is restful and picturesque. It owes its prosperity to its popularity with local people. The anchorage off the island of Terre d'en Haut is one of the finest around, but somewhat tricky to enter. There's 9 feet in the channel, but keep close to the sand. Fort Napoleon is well preserved and the snorkeling is superb. If your boat has a nylon rode, be aware that most French yachts have all chain. They can anchor in closer quarters than you can because they will swing less. If in doubt, anchor well clear of others.

Some French-owned bareboat companies operate out of Martinique. I have no personal experience of these organizations. However, they tend to use Dufour or Beneteau yachts, which are excellent performers as well as being comfortable below. Several people I have spoken to have enjoyed themselves, so it might be worth exploring a Martinique charter if your French is sufficient to cope with boat check-out and provisioning. You can, of course, visit Martinique on a long charter from Saint Lucia or Saint Vincent, but most crews tend to head south to the Grenadines. A few companies offer one-way charters from Antigua or

*English Harbor, Antigua. Alas, this lovely spot
is usually congested. (Antigua Tourist Office)*

Martinique to the south, but you will probably pay a premium price for one.

Martinique is one of the largest islands in the Windwards, some 425 square miles. It is mountainous and lush, French-speaking and famous for its fine restaurants and excellent shopping. If you plan to sail to Martinique, purchase a set of the *French* charts for the island. They are by far the best and will guide you through the numerous small anchorages and reefs on the east coast, where the best sailing is to be found. Donald Street's *Cruising Guide* is excellent for these waters. Unlike some cruising guide authors, he has actually been there, not once, but many times. Fort-de-France is the best port of entry and a good base for exploring the east coast. Make a point of visiting the market when in town. It is extremely colorful. When sailing to the eastern shores, make sure you give the south coast a wide berth, for reefs extend up to a mile offshore in places. Mouillage de Sainte Anne is an excellent tradewind anchorage on the way.

The east coast of Martinique is not for the novice charterer. Take the French charts with you, consult the cruising guide at every turn, and eyeball carefully everywhere. This is an exposed shore until you sail behind the reefs, so exercise great caution when cruising these waters. On the positive side, they are a dinghy enthusiast's paradise. You can use the dink to find a way through reef passages with the lead and line. The coast is somewhat featureless, so you have to keep careful watch for buildings and other landmarks. Street is very good on these; he knows what it is to navigate with cruising guides that tell you all about facilities ashore and nothing about the landmarks to find the entrance. The towns of Francois and Havre du Robert are interesting and offer good eating. The anchorages away from civilization are even better, for you can lie in complete shelter in almost any conditions. I would rate the east coast of Martinique as one of the best places to practice eyeball navigation anywhere.

Terre-de-Haut, Iles des Saintes, Guadelupe. (Judy Gurovitz, Clement-Petrocik Company, New York)

Saint Lucia and Saint Vincent

The major Windward Islands charter operations are based on Saint Lucia and Saint Vincent. Saint Lucia lies between Martinique in the north and Saint Vincent in the south. It's a mountainous island, with an economy based on bananas, copra (dried white coconut meat), and tourism. The French first settled on Saint Lucia in 1652, but the island changed hands repeatedly for 160 years, until the British finally gained control at the end of the Napoleonic Wars in 1814. Since 1967, Saint Lucia has been an independent nation. The Moorings and Stevens Yachts maintain their charter headquarters on Marigot Bay and Gros Islet, respectively. Saint Lucia has the logistical advantage of direct jet service to the United States and elsewhere, obviating the necessity for an overnight stop in Barbados. But the cruising is more interesting in Martinique or farther south.

Few yachts visit the windward easterly shore, where there are few safe anchorages. Cruising the leeward coast is very straightforward, for the island is low enough not to blanket the wind most of the way. You must clear customs at Castries or Vieux Fort if you are going to Martinique or Saint Vincent. Castries is completely sheltered and well worth a visit if you like busy harbors and marinas. Many yachts anchor in Vigie Cove, where Saint Lucia Yacht Services are based. But look out for the Vieille Ville shoal in the entrance.

Many possible anchorages on the west coast are exposed in any swell, but Anse des Pitons is a must for any bareboat cruise in these waters. Some people consider this one of the most spectacular anchorages in the Caribbean, if not in the world. Gros and Petit Piton look like sugar-loaf mountains towering 2,000 feet above the ocean. It seems difficult to believe that you can anchor here, but a black sand beach backs a dramatic anchorage between the peaks. The problem is the 100-fathom line is only 400 yards from the shore, while you are still in over 30 feet a mere 200 yards out. The only way to anchor is to let go a stern anchor about 50 yards offshore, then ease into the beach, and secure a long bowline to a tree. A crewmember can literally jump off onto the beach, but you may be bothered by pestilential little boys who want to take your line. If the anchorage is crowded, as it often is, you had better enlist their help. Sometimes Anse des Pitons is so

Anse des Pitons, St. Lucia. (Hubertus Kanus, Photo Researchers, Inc.)

congested that you have to put out fenders to keep off your neighbors. Try to arrive early in the day, but do not miss this spectacular place.

The sail from Saint Lucia to Saint Vincent can be very bumpy indeed. It's a long day, even when the trades are blowing strongly. The west coast of Saint Vincent has little to offer you. Some charter companies discourage you from visiting Cumberland Bay, because the people are unfriendly and aggressive. Clear customs at Kingstown, then make a beeline for the sheltered anchorage at Young Island. A narrow and protected channel runs behind the island. You should plan to anchor on either side of the deepest part of the cut. Lay out plenty of scope, because the bottom is rock and coral, not the best of holding grounds. We had a superb dinner ashore on the island some years ago. The scenery is lush and tropical. Be sure to allow time for a dinghy ride out to Duvernette Island. Climb up to the eighteenth-century fort at its 200-foot summit. Incredible as it may seem, British sailors hauled the cannon to the top using only simple blocks and tackles and plenty of muscle power.

Caribbean Sailing Yachts has its headquarters at Blue Lagoon, close to Young Island. Many Grenadines charterers sail southward from here, for the best cruising waters lie south of Bequia. Going north is perfectly possible, of course, but you will need at least 10 days to do anything worthwhile. If you have the time, plan a day excursion to the summit of Soufriere, Saint Vincent's own volcano. The 4,048-foot mountain offers spectacular views. You reach to top by a well-marked trail through tropical forest from a point about 700 feet above sea level. Make sure you wear strong walking shoes.

The northern Grenadines

Most Saint Lucia and Saint Vincent charterers sail south to the Grenadines, the 65-mile string of islands from Saint Vincent in the north to Grenada in the south. These are lower-lying islands, covered with drier, cactus-like vegetation, extending south-southwest from Saint Vincent. The prevailing trades allow you to reach down-island and bring you close on the wind on the return journey. This is the major charter area in the Windwards, one that offers some of the finest snorkeling in the world. It's also one of the best sailing areas, too, for the winds blow steady and often strong. From December through April, the trades blow from the northeast to east-northeast at a constant 15 to 20 knots or even stronger. The summer trades are lighter,

veering more easterly and southeasterly from June to September. It can be very hot then. The best months for chartering are probably November and December and the late spring and early summer. Trades of 25 to 30 knots are common in late January and early February. Avoid the hurricane season (July to October), despite the attractive discounts given by the charter companies. There is so much to see in the Grenadines that two weeks is barely enough to enjoy just the Saint Vincent–controlled islands. Allow at least 10 days for your first charter in these waters. Incidentally, sail up and down the islands on their westerly, lee side. The open waters of the west coast of the Grenadines can be dangerous and very rough. In any case, there are few safe anchorages.

Most Saint Vincent charterers spend their first night at Bequia, only about 9 nautical miles from Blue Lagoon. The reach across the passage can be very bumpy, especially if the current is setting against the wind. Admiralty Bay at the southwest corner of the island is a world-famous haven and has been since the days of Nelson's ships-of-the-line and the New Bedford whalers of the nineteenth century. The entrance is straightforward enough, provided you keep clear of the Devil's Table on the north side of the bay. You'll find the anchorage crowded with yachts of every size and shape imaginable, from magnificent crewed charter boats to battered craft that have come all the way from Europe. The best anchorage is west of the church or, if the anchorage is crowded, off Princess Margaret Beach, well clear of Belmont Shoal. The settlement is full of life, especially when the ferries arrive. There are simple restaurants and the famous Whaleboner Inn. You can see local sailboats being built ashore. But you may be plagued with boat-borne hucksters, who constantly pester you with souvenirs, offer to do your laundry, or serenade you with local music. It's difficult to ignore them, but their ministrations can be a real nuisance. I have heard of cases where the solicitors became menacing, but have had nothing but courtesy myself. Make sure you pay a small boy to mind your dinghy at the public dock as you go ashore. If you don't, they will cast her adrift. But these minor inconveniences are a small price to pay for the interesting sights ashore.

No visit to Bequia is complete without an excursion to Friendship Bay and the islet of Petit Nevis off the south coast. Last time I was in Friendship Bay they were building a 50-foot sailboat on the shore. She was in frame and they were adding the planking. "Come back in a year for the jump-up when we launch her," cried the builder. Alas, we were unable to accept his invitation. The people living at Friendship on the west side of the bay are whalers. They hunt whales from

Admiralty Bay, Bequia. (Fritz Menle: Photo Researchers, Inc.)

open boats between January and April, pursuing them with harpoons under sail and oar, just as their ancestors did. We saw one of the boats, some 25 feet long, ballasted with heavy rocks that are moved from side to side depending on the tack. The whaleboats hunt in pairs. One harpoons the whale, while the other stands by. Twelve hundred feet of line snakes out over the bow, and the boat rides with the quarry, steered with a 30-foot oar. When the whale tires, they finish it off with long spears. The scene must be right out of *Moby Dick.* They butcher the whales on Petit Nevis. (You can anchor off the concrete ramp and shed where they winch the carcasses out of the water.) The whole village assists in the butchering; the meat is divided up between island families, while the blubber is reduced to oil in a huge iron pot. If you are near Petit Nevis when a kill is made and insist on seeing the butchering, be sure to get permission to watch.

Mustique is normally a short beat to the east, an island famous for its wealthy visitors, among them Princess Margaret, who owns property there. The best anchorage is Grand Bay, where you can anchor off the jetty in 12 feet or more. It can be uncomfortable from current surge; look out for Montezuma Shoal just over half a mile offshore of the entrance. There's not much to see ashore, but the snorkeling is excellent. If you anchor for lunch in the sandy bay off the Cheltenham Hotel at the northeast corner of the island, you can dinghy out to the wreck of the cruise ship *Antilles,* which ran aground and burnt inside the Pillories in January 1971. Fortunately, everyone was saved.

Most charterers head straight south from Bequia or Mustique for Union Island and Tobago Cays. Now's the time to be imaginative, especially if you like to get away from the crowd and to explore local life. Make a stop at Canouan. Charlestown Bay on the east side is easy to enter. Just line up the concrete markers shown in Wilensky's *Cruising Guide,* then turn northeast to the best anchorage in 18 to 20 feet at the northeast corner of the bay. The settlement is worth a stroll, and you will be visited by small boys offering lobster here. A young man may ask if you want a guide to take you snorkeling. Take him up on his offer if this is your passion, for the reefs on the east side of the island are among the most spectacular in the Grenadines. Your guide will take your yacht around to the anchorage on the south side of the island, then behind the reefs past Friendship Hill to a sheltered berth where there is all the snorkeling in the world. Although I have gone up this way on my own, it was a fairly taxing experience and I would recommend a guide. Look out for the currents around the reefs when snorkeling. One of the great advantages of Canouan is that it is less congested than Tobago Cays.

Ask most Grenadines charterers what the Grenadines are all about and they will immediately reply, "Mayreau Island and Tobago Cays." This is because of the fabulous snorkeling on the reefs. Salt Whistle Bay on Mayreau is a good picnic spot and an ideal base for exploring the reefs and beaches on this small island. You may need two anchors to counter occasional swells here. Be sure to explore the wreck of the British gunboat *Purana* that sank on the reef off Grand Col Point in 1902. Keep well clear of Catholic Rocks as you come south. From Mayreau to Tobago Cays is a but a short eyeball on a range that lines up the summit of Catholic Island on the north end of Petit Rameau (115 degrees true). This will carry you to a point where you can choose your anchorage in the Cays. There's another entrance from the south that carries 24 feet, but try this only when the sun is high and you can eyeball between the reefs. I think the sailing directions in Donald Street's *Guide* are about the best, but your charter company will give you further advice. This is an area where eyeballing is essential.

The Tobago Cays consist of four islands inside Horse Shoe Reef. They provide excellent shelter in most conditions. You can spend days here without being bored, especially if you are an avid underwater swimmer. Most boats seem to anchor off Baradal, protected only by the reef. This is a secure and convenient anchorage, even when the trades are blowing strongly. There is also plenty of room. I have seen as many as 30 yachts in here. You can also anchor in the narrow cut between Petit Rameau and Petit Bateau, lying to two anchors off the beach on the south side of the channel. The current runs strong, and you should choose another berth if there are more than a few yachts here. The wind can funnel strongly through the cut, but it is never bumpy. Wander ashore and admire the aloes. Collect shells on the beaches and, above all, snorkel. This is a place where you will use your dinghy for hours on end. Just make sure your anchor is well dug in and that you take the necessary precautions against the sun. I had to nurse a very sunburned crewmember after a day here. Another word of warning: beach your dinghy very carefully and drag her up above the water's edge. The current once swung my tender off Baradal beach and carried her away downwind. Fortunately, a French yacht caught it for me. Experienced gunkholers and divers will have a wonderful time at Tobago Cays, especially if they explore World's End Reef and Petit Tabac, which are seldom visited by charterers.

Palm Island, Petit Saint Vincent, and Union Island are part of the Saint Vincent Grenadines, the southernmost stop for many bareboaters in these enchanting waters. The first two are pleasant island resorts, the last well worth circumnavigating under sail. Most charterers end up anchoring in Clifton Harbor, where the reefs provide shelter even in strong winds. The entrance is straightforward enough in good visibility. Just be careful to stay outside the red markers that delineate the outer edge of the reef between Red Island and the entrance. The Grand de Coi reef, just over half a mile from the harbor, is very dangerous in bad light. The best place to anchor is off the resort hotel, where they have a pond full of sharks. Last time I was there, the food was excellent. You can buy basic provisions in Clifton and clear for Grenada at the customs house on the waterfront. There have been political tensions on the island, but these should not affect you. Clifton Harbor is often congested, so I sometimes anchor in the lee of Frigate Island 2 miles to the west. This is much quieter and bug-free. Take your dinghy and motor across the shallows to the village of Ashton, a poverty-stricken, straggling settlement remarkable for its preachers. The people were not effusive, but the place is well worth a visit.

Grenada

Grenada is settling down after an uneasy few years and charterers are more than welcome again. This is good news, for the island is a superlative cruising ground. A lot of the facilities that were discontinued during the socialist years are now open again and there is talk of major tourist investment in the air.

This attractive island is about 20 miles long and 12 miles wide, but the best cruising waters are on the southwestern coast. Plan your cruise to visit Saint George's first and clear customs there. After that you can go anywhere, but they will ask you for an itinerary. Be sure to clear in or out during normal working hours. There's an overtime charge for weekends. The passage south passes the hurricane hole at Carriacou, where I once caught dengue fever, then passes spectacular rocks like Kick 'em Jenny, Sail Rock, and London Bridge. Grenada itself should be approached along its leeward coast. The winds can be fluky with the high mountains, so you may be better off powering along close inshore so that you can enjoy the scenery. Halifax Harbor is a nice gunkhole along the way.

St. George's has a spectacular entrance that opens up at the very last moment, almost as you are upon it. The approach is in deep water, but look out for banana boats maneuvering near the freighter dock in the Careenage. Most visitors anchor in the lagoon south of the entrance or secure Mediterranean style at Grenada Yacht Services' facilites. Everyone warns you to lock up when you go ashore. The customs and immigration offices are nearby, on the west side of the lagoon. You will probably be accosted by small boys wanting to clean up, fetch, carry, or mind your boat. For peace of mind, you are best off hiring one for your stay. A short taxi ride will take you to the shopping area. The public market is well worth a visit, especially on Wednesdays and Saturdays. The fine Dutch-like architecture of the town amply repays leisurely exploration.

The south coast of Grenada ranks among the finest cruising grounds in the Caribbean. About the only place to rival it for convenient gunkholes is the equivalent coast of Roatan in the Bay Islands. Prickly Bay is a popular and convenient anchorage, but can be uncomfortable in the winter when the swell comes round the headland. Anchor off the Calabash Hotel in 10 feet or so. There is also a charter company operating here. Mount Hardman Bay, immediately to the west, requires some reef dodging. Watch the current in the entrance and follow the directions in Street or Wilensky very carefully. I think the anchorage just west of Hog Island is one of the best I have ever enjoyed. The easiest approach is to skirt the reefs off Mount Hardman Point, eyeballing your way to anchor in about 25 feet due west of the northern hill on Hog Island. Coming from seaward, eyeball your way through the reefs until the deeper water of the anchorage opens up to starboard. Wilensky gives detailed instructions. Hog Island is a great place for dinghy excursions. Explore the shallow channel into Clarke's Court Bay and snorkel the reefs off Hog Island itself. You can also anchor in a small cove on the east side of Hog Island.

Bay after enticing bay opens up as you sail along this unspoiled coast. Long peninsulas alternate with deep bays, reefs, and small islands. You could easily spend the whole of your charter in these few miles between Clarke's Court Bay and the town of Grenville halfway up the east coast. Most charterers go no further than Bacaye Harbor, having explored the secluded anchorages like Port Egmont. This is real eyeballing country, so you should be careful to enter and leave harbor with the sun in the right position so you can see the shallows. The coast beyond Bacaye is less frequented by yachts. On the whole, I would advise sailing straight to Grenville, for this is lee shore and strong currents set on to the coast. You can clear customs and sail north from here.

The Grenadines are such a superlative cruising ground that one could charter half a dozen times without seeing everything. The winds are predictable, the snorkeling superb. Plan on spending at least 10 days in the Windwards, making your way south fast, then

St. George's, Grenada. (Courtesy Karen Weines Escalera Associates)

anchorage hopping in leisurely stages as you make your way north toward base. The facilities ashore are adequate but not in the same league as those in the Virgins. But then who cares, when the winds blow steadily and the water are clear? Take the charter companies' provisioning package, a few bottles of rum, and cut the umbilical cord to shore. I guarantee you will return a second time.

The Bay Islands of Honduras

The first time I heard of the Bay Islands (Islas de la Bahia), I had to reach for an atlas to find out where they were. Their eight islands and 65 cays cover just under 92 square miles of land area 8 to 30 miles off the Honduras mainland. The largest island is Roatan, about 24 miles long, its north shore protected by one of the finest diving reefs in the world. And there are more superb anchorages per mile on the south coast of Roatan than almost anywhere else in the Caribbean. The other islands—Cayos Cochinos (Hog Islands), Guanaja, and Utila—all offer deserted anchorages and excellent snorkeling as well. The Bay Islands were settled by Maya Indians in prehistoric times, visited by Christopher Columbus, and used as a buccaneers' refuge in the seventeenth century. Black Caribs were

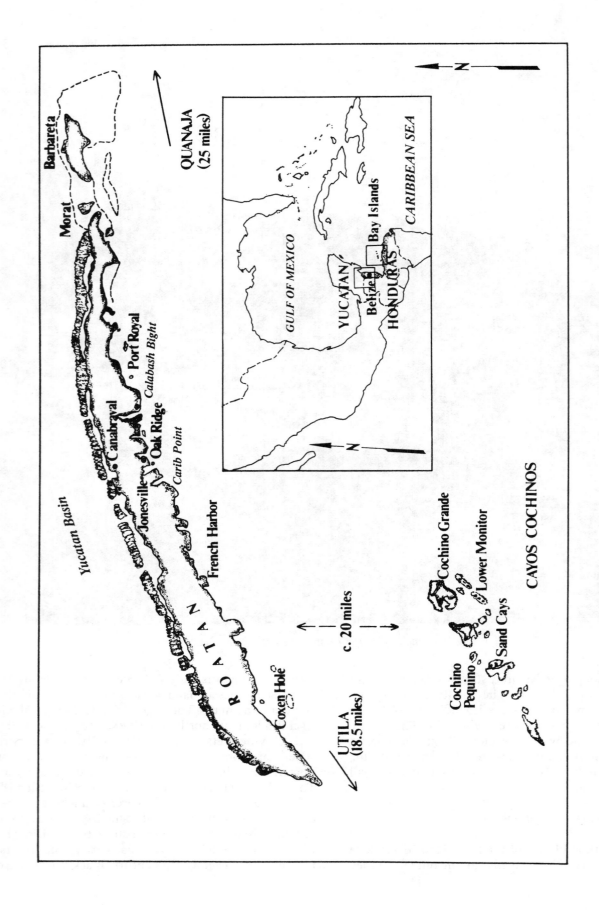

Roatán and Cayos Cochinos, Bay of Islands, Honduras

resettled here from Saint Vincent in 1797. Then white settlers from the Cayman Islands arrived in 1823, most of them settling in the Coxen Hole area, where they live today. The islands were annexed by Great Britain in 1850, but she was forced by the U.S. to hand them over to Honduras soon afterwards. The islanders cling proudly to their British traditions and speak English to this day. But the business of government is carried out in Spanish. The mainland authorities are doing all they can to acculturate the islands, but progress is slow.

The Bay Islands lie in the tradewind belt, so the winds blow regularly from the east between 10 and 15 knots. Normally the weather is fairly predictable, but between five and seven northers a year reach the Bay Islands, cold fronts that bring strong north winds and heavy rain. Hurricanes are very rare, but light winds and squalls are common in July and August. The very best time to cruise the Bay Islands is probably immediately after the hurricane season, in November and December, or in spring or early summer. We were down there in June. The weather was very hot when the trades were down, but delightful when they blew.

The Bay Islands are a unique charter area. Except for some private operators, only Caribbean Sailing Yachts runs a bareboat operation on Roatan. The anchorages are empty and you will enjoy the rare luxury of bay after beautiful bay all to yourself. There are effectively no facilities ashore, except for the occasional dive resort and the simplest of grocery stores in major settlements like Coxen Hole, French Harbor, and Oak Ridge. So if expensive resorts and fashionable boutiques are your delight, charter elsewhere. This is an area for those who love deserted cays and magnificent snorkeling, friendly people, and a mix of open-water cruising and gunkholing. Navigation is straightforward enough, providing you have previous eyeballing experience. You will tend to use your depth sounder here, for depths can shoal from over 100 feet to 25 within a few yards. Some of the islands, notably Roatan and Utila, are somewhat featureless near the coastline, and you may have some difficulty keeping track of your position. Unfortunately, the cruising guide does not pinpoint as many approach landmarks as one might wish. But everything usually goes smoothly if you tick off the anchorages and headlands as you go by.

The people who will rave the most about the Bay Islands are the divers. It is no coincidence that Caribbean Sailing Yachts is orienting more and more of its bareboat operation to what they call Sail 'n' Dive charters. You can charter a CSY-44 specially equipped with dive-tank racks and a diving platform. The company maintains a support boat that visits you regularly to recharge your air tanks and offer any assistance needed.

Even getting to the Bay Islands is quite an adventure. You fly to Honduras from Miami, New Orleans, or Houston, arriving at San Pedro Sula on the mainland. Then you change to an aged DC-3 that flies you to the dirt airstrip at Coxen Hole on Roatan. At the time we were there, they were carving away at a hillside, expanding the airfield to take jets. Your evening arrival on the island is a memorable experience. A crowd of small boys and officials meets the plane. You walk over to a tiny, wooden terminal building, clear customs and immigration, tip the child who carried your bags, and then board a battered bus for the ride to Brick Bay, where the bareboat operation is based. The airline schedules make it necessary for you to spend the night in the marina hotel before checking out your boat the next morning. Be thankful for the respite. Your flight from home will have taken most of the day.

I would plan a charter of at least 10 days, preferably two weeks, so that you can visit the outlying islands. This is an area where you must take the charter company's provisioning package, for supplies ashore are rudimentary at best. The package is convenient and varied. Ours included frozen lobster tails and local shrimp, as well as the usual steaks and chops. So all you need bring are your personal effects and charter kit. One word of advice: ask your physician for a prescription for antimalaria pills. Malaria is not unknown in the islands and it is better to be safe than sorry. Take insect repellent with you as well. You will need it if the trades are down and the air is still.

Planning a cruise in the Bay Islands is to be overwhelmed with possibilities. I would recommend making mileage to windward first. Spend a few days exploring the anchorages on the south coast of Roatan. This will enable you to get used to local conditions and to eyeballing the reefs. CSY recommends Dixon Cove as a first stop, but we thought it was one of the duller anchorages. We met some Ohio friends in Old French Harbor the first night. This landlocked cove is in the back streets of the French Harbor settlement. You anchor among the houses that perch on stilts over the shallows. Many of the dwellings are little more than wooden sheds with shutters instead of windows. Ramshackle piles and causeways lead over the water. We drank rum and watched the local scene. A man took potshots at fish in the shallows with a rifle. Women gossiped as their children played in the doorways. Each house had its own toilet perched over the water. Dugout canoes passed by, poled silently with one paddle, their occupants smiling softly as they passed. It was as if we were in another world.

French Harbor itself is a busy little settlement. Roatan prospers on shrimping, exporting millions of shrimp every year. The fleet was fitting out for the season while we were there, so French Harbor and other bays were bustling with the large steel fishing boats that spend weeks on end at sea. There are no paved roads, just a winding dirt highway that leads between brightly painted stilt houses and churches. Downtown consists of a dilapidated movie house, two restaurants, and the fish docks. Take the time to walk through the town. It is unlike anything in the Caribbean.

Some of the best south coast anchorages lie farther to windward, near Jonesville and Oak Ridge. The best bays are Carib and Calabash Bights, both of them quiet at night and removed from the bustle of the waterside settlements. I think Carib is the nicest of all. The water is clear, you can snorkel on the reefs, and you can explore with your dinghy to your heart's content. Calabash is just as attractive, except that people live around it and the water is murky. Look out for the narrow channel between the sandbanks in the middle of the bight. The channel is marked on its starboard side, but be careful to stay close to the stake. We watched another charter boat take three hours to get off the sandbank on the east side of the narrow channel.

Jonesville and Oak Ridge are a paradise for dinghy lovers. The islanders live mostly right on the water. Their front doors open onto the ocean and most travel is by boat. Over the centuries, the locals have developed a network of narrow canals that take you from Brick Bay all the way to Calabash Bight behind the reefs. We explored these canals with our outboard dinghy from both the Carib Bight and Calabash ends. The narrow waterways join each bay by tunneling through the mangrove swamps. A canopy of branches allows only mottled sunlight to penetrate to water level. The life of the settlements unfolds along the banks. Housewives hang out their washing, people go visiting in dugouts and narrow-planked boats with small inboard engines that hold a surprising number of passengers. There are even discos and bars that open on the canals. So a walk through town becomes a dinghy ride through people's backyards. Be sure to take a camera with you. The houses and their reflections are picturesque and unusual and the people, charming.

If you want to get your windward work out of the way first and the trades are up, take lunch in Port Royal, a huge bay with two wide entrance channels, once a buccaneer's refuge. You can dive on the wreck of a seventeenth-century ship here. Who knows, you might find another as well. Both Mr. Field Bay and Helene Harbor are good overnight spots. The Helene settlement is primitive but picturesque, while the main attraction of Mr. Field is Helene Creek—a narrow, mangrove-lined waterway that takes you through to the north coast in your dinghy. It's worth doing this if you do not have the time to explore the north shore in the yacht. Mr. Field should be attempted only in calmer weather with good subsurface visibility. There is 12 feet in the entrance, but some shallow patches, too.

Start early in the day if you plan to sail even farther east to Guanaja. You can anchor off the islands of Morat or Barbareta, but it is still 25 miles from the latter to an anchorage on Guanaja. The actual crossing is only 10 miles, but the islands are surrounded by coral reefs. Guanaja settlement itself is picturesque, crowded onto two small cays. This is a major shrimping port, teeming with watercraft. Best to anchor off just north of the Texaco fuel dock and explore the settlement from there. I would recommend a day visit, moving on into a quieter anchorage in Sandy Bay or El Bight for the night.

Most people visit Guanaja for the snorkeling and diving on the north coast. Don't try this area when a norther is blowing or the trades are strong. Waves can break across the passes through the reefs. The Soldado Channel has a 30-foot controlling depth, leading to the anchorage of that name, where you lie close inshore in the shallower water. This is where Christopher Columbus landed in 1502. He probably anchored outside the reef. In any case, he encountered Indians ashore and traded with them. A rather tacky monument commemorates the landing. I'd recommend a visit to Michael Rock, where the snorkeling is outstanding. The passage carries 40 feet and is straightforward once you have identified the rock, which lies inshore to the west of the cut.

Guanaja is a wonderful place for smooth-water sailing inside the reef. Do not try to visit it unless you have more than a week to play with. The island is a little out of the way and difficult of access against strong tradewinds.

Most charterers give Guanaja a miss and sail across from the south coast of Roatan to the Cayos Cochinos (Hog Islands), some 20 miles south of Coxen Hole. It's an easy reach with the prevailing trades, but Fagan's luck being what it is, we had calms and squalls the whole way. Cochino Grande is an easy landfall, for you can see the 469-foot peak miles away. The only safe overnight anchorage is under the lee of Pelican Point, in a sandy, reef-protected bay that reminds one of Cane Garden Bay on Tortola, except that Stanley's Bar is missing. Keep the north end of Cochino Pequeno in line with the north side of the red-roofed house behind the beach, and you will come right through the passage. A few people live on the island, which has a private dive resort. A retired American has built a magnificent boat-shaped house on the summit of a ridge overlooking the island. He enjoys magnificent views of the 8,000-foot peaks of the mainland and of the cays here, but it is a little too remote for me.

Cayos Cochinos is worth two or three days. You can eyeball your way up to several cays for snorkeling, among them Lower Monitor, where a seasonal fishing camp of thatched A-frame houses nestles among the palm trees. The fishermen will sometimes sell you lobster. "Buy-boats" from the mainland come over regularly to barter for their catch. The village is dotted with rusting deep freezes that hold nothing and have not worked for years. There is no electricity on the island. One wonders how they reached this remote spot and why. The fishing craft used by the villages are astonishingly simple. Most are crude dugouts, hollowed out with fire and adze from mahogany trees. The finest one we saw was an aged craft with mainsail and jib fabricated from construction plastic. Six fishermen piled into her and took off downwind. She moved with surprising speed. We had to run the outboard at full bore for some minutes to catch up with her. Wherever you sail in the Bay Islands, you will come across lonely dugouts, propelled by a single fisherman with unerring skill. They slip along silently and smoothly, even in choppy seas.

From Cayos Cochinos you have two options, an easy sail 35 miles downwind to Utila, or a reach round the west end of Roatan to the reefs and passages of the north coast. Most short-term charterers choose Roatan. The barrier reef extends most of the way along the coast, but there are several safe passages to the lagoons inside. However, you should avoid this area during winter storms and when the trades are blowing strongly. Your best port of call is Anthony's Cay Resort, a diving hotel that overlooks a sheltered waterway reached by a narrow pass from seaward. The entrance is tricky but well marked with plastic pipes. You anchor off the resort with two anchors, within easy reach of some of the finest snorkeling and diving in the world. Plan on spending at least two days here, if for no other reason than to enjoy the pina coladas at the resort bar. Big Bight's another safe passage, with magnificent snorkeling near the wreck of the Greek steamer *Syng*, cast up on the reef in 1903. The lagoon inside the reef reveals a spectrum of tropical colors. You can take your yacht as far west as Crawfish Rock settlement or anchor within a half-mile of the wreck. This is probably the best snorkeling in the islands.

Altogether, there are about six navigable passages on the north shore. However, CSY does not recommend all of them. You should follow the advice of the staff member who briefs you at the start of your cruise. The problem is not so much the passage itself, but identifying it from seaward. If you are short of time, go

Anchorage off Lower Monitor Cay, Cayos Cochinos, Bay Islands. (Lesley Newhart)

for Anthony's Cay and Big Bight. They will give you a sample of what the north coast has to offer. Unfortunately, we did not have time to explore Pollytilly Bight and the Black Carib settlement at Canabraval, which can be reached only by dinghy. Both are said by Wilensky and others to be well worth a visit.

Utila is 18.5 miles from the west end of Roatan, an easy sail in prevailing tradewind conditions. Be sure to allow enough time to beat or motor back, however. The island itself is 290 feet high and easily seen from a considerable distance. Just watch out for the east-setting current as you approach the island and shape your course accordingly. East Harbor is the only settlement on the main island, a semicircular bay that you can enter on a bearing of 020 degrees magnetic on the Methodist Church. You can walk through the entire settlement in half an hour. There's not much to see except for some interesting local architecture.

The reason everyone comes to Utila is for the snorkeling and diving off the southwestern corner of the island. Most people sail directly to Sucsuc and Pigeon Cays, two densely populated settlements linked by a wooden footbridge. The best anchorage is in the lee of Sucsuc Cay, reached via a narrow channel, marked with a red stake, that passes north of Diamond Cay. The inhabitants of both cays make their living from fishing. You will be offered guides here. I would strongly advise you to hire one. They know all the best places for snorkeling and diving and will more than earn their keep, apart from being very pleasant people.

Your guide will take you through the deep-water channel south of Pigeon Cay that leads to Middle Cay and the jumble of reefs and small islands that border the end of Utila. Be extremely careful, for much of the area is effectively uncharted. Wilensky's admirable chart is only a general guide to the area, as he himself admits. Keep someone at the bow all the time, do your eyeballing when the sun is high and behind you, and leave the boat anchored in deep water while you explore the shallows in your dinghy. I would allow at least three days for this wonderful area, more if you are a snorkeling and diving fanatic.

The Bay Islands are too far-flung to be explored in a mere week or 10 days. This is the place to go out on a longer charter, one that will enable you to explore places that few cruising people ever reach. As a bareboater, you can fly there in a few hours, as opposed to the months it would take in a yacht of your own.

Belize

Belize, formerly British Honduras, is a small country sandwiched between Mexico and Guatemala on the east side of the Yucatan. The coastline is tropical, low-lying, and protected by the second largest barrier reef in the world. Sail Belize operates a small bareboat fleet from Belize City that enables you to explore this unspoiled cruising area at your leisure. Like the Bay Islands, this is practically virgin cruising territory, yet easily accessible by jet from New Orleans or Miami, some 750 miles away.

This is a good place to charter if you want to combine sailing with archaeology, perhaps a tour of the Maya ruins in the Yucatan. You can spend a week or 10 days exploring sites in Mexico, then round off your trip with a week's charter in Belize. By taking a package tour to the Yucatan, you can substantially reduce the cost of the charter.

Belize itself was not settled until the seventeenth century, when it became a British buccaneers' haven and a major logging area. Many slaves were brought from Jamaica to work the forests. Despite constant Spanish efforts to take over the coast, the area was placed under British protection as British Honduras. It became internally self-governing in 1963. Controversy over the sovereignty of the area still continues. You may notice a garrison of British troops at the airport when you arrive. They are there because Guatemala claims Belize as its own. The threat may be real, but you need fear no warfare during your charter.

Like the Bay Islands, Belize is a diver's paradise, with hundreds of miles of unspoiled reefs and cays to explore. Also like the Bay Islands, there are few tourist facilities ashore, except for some simple restaurants and resorts near the village of Placencia at the southern end of the charter area. Few people live on the coast south of Belize City. You will encounter the occasional fisherman, but that's about it. Tourists are still a novelty on the coast, and you will be greeted courteously. The fishermen will speak what appears to be an unintelligible dialect but is in fact Creole. English is, however, understood and spoken in most places.

Belize is hot and low-lying, with a climate very much like that of the Bay Islands. Plan on chartering during late fall or spring, when the temperatures are cooler. The winters are fine, too, but there is the usual risk of northers, which can blow for several days on end. However, you are in more sheltered waters than the Bay Islands, so you should enjoy some magnificent smooth-water sailing and strong breezes. Belize is extremely hot from June to October, and I would avoid those hurricane-prone months, when the bugs are not to be believed. This being a remote tropical area, you will likely wear little more than shorts or a bathing suit. A pair of long pants, one thin sweater, and a long-sleeved shirt to deter bugs, and you are on your way. "Be sure to bring bug repellent," advised a much bitten charterer I met last June on a flight from Belize City to New Orleans. He had had a wonderful time, but had counted 150 bites on his wife one morning when she had forgotten to put on repellent at night.

The Belize charter area lies between the mainland and a long set of offshore reefs that keep the water smooth. You sail among mangrove cays and isolated islands that are not visited by human beings from one year to the next. Your charter limits extend from Belize City in the north to Placencia and Pompion Cay in the south. There's plenty to explore for those who like remote cays and sandy beaches. This is an area where eyeball navigation is vital, for the charts are somewhat unreliable and the bottom changes in some places. You have to take careful note of water colors and plan your day so that they are clearly visible. You will need clear, early-morning light and calm water to traverse the

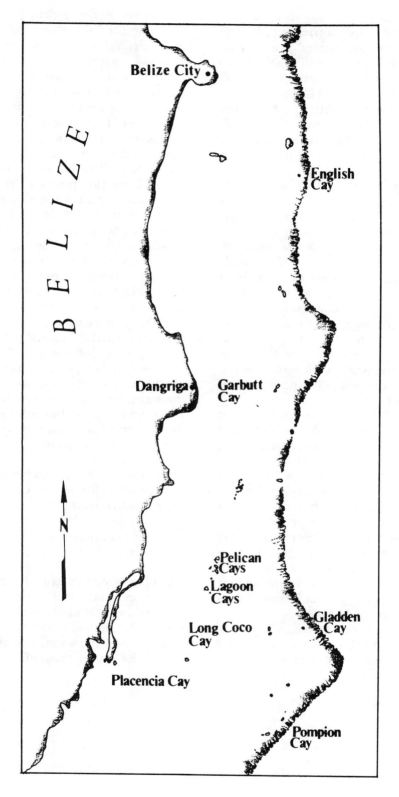

Belize

channels between the southern cays. For passage-making, you will find it decidedly easier to sail north through the reefs with the light behind you, so plan your itinerary accordingly. Planning will enable you to do your intricate pilotage when conditions are ideal. Water colors are unusually important in Belize, for the bottom can shoal fast and only differing blues and greens tell you exactly what the depths are. Coral heads are another hazard, especially when you are approaching the barrier reef. Your only protection is a sharp lookout from the bow.

At first glance, Belize seems unexciting, for the coast is featureless and low-lying. In fact, the area has a remote fascination of its own, for the numerous islands and the absence of landmarks make it easy for you to lose your way in what appears to be a maze of mangrove swamps. You should always keep the chart close beside you, so you can carefully note your exact position according to the few houses and other available landmarks. When close to the mainland, navigate from headland to headland. Offshore, count the cays, use the recommended courses given you by the charter company, and take special care locating the larger islands. A hand-bearing compass is vital here. Look out for mirages, too. They can magnify the height of islands, trees, and buildings.

A charter of a week to 10 days should be sufficient for most people in this area, allowing ample time to snorkel or dive. You will find yourself with some long sailing days, especially when making your way south. Most people spend their time south of the hamlet of Dangriga, about 30 miles south of Belize City, but you can easily plan shorter itineraries that take you on circuits through Pelican or Lagoon Cay, or even only as far south as Colson Cays. If you possibly can, get away from the muddy waters around Belize City and head south into clearer areas. I would plan a cruise that takes you south as rapidly as possible. You can be anchored at Placencia within three days, stopping at Garbutt Cay, a group of mangrove clusters on the way.

Placencia is a fishing village of about 350 souls, where you can eat ashore in three or four places and walk up the mile-long, 24-inch-wide sidewalk, the only paved track in the settlement. This quiet place makes its living off fishing and the occasional visitor, not much else. British Army personnel come down here for rest and recreation, so you may meet some other foreigners in the local resorts. Like everywhere in Belize, you will have to anchor off, but the advantage is that there are fewer bugs. The best anchorage near the village lies off Placencia Cay, but be sure to set your anchor well into the turtle grass on the bottom. You can buy a few provisions here, also seafood. This is the only significant village in the charter area.

There are two routes to the southern cays from here—one that takes you clear of all dangers or a more difficult transit north of Bugle Cay. The skipper will enjoy the passage much more by sailing as far south as possible in large hops, then using the favorable light to eyeball his way north from cay to cay on the tricky route. You have dozens of cays to choose from, most uninhabited, and more snorkeling opportunities than anyone can possibly ever exhaust. The highlights are Pompion in the extreme south; Gladden, which boasts of pretty coral and plenty of fish; and Long Coco, much used by local fishermen. There are plenty of fairly sheltered anchorages, but only Pelican Cay is safe in any wind. I would head for this berth if a norther threatens. Only one cay, South Water, is inhabited all year round. You can buy fish there upon occasion, and the settlement is a good stop before the all-day passage north to English Cay and the islands on the approach to Belize City.

Fortunately, the approaches to Belize City are easy to find, for the lighthouse on English Cay is the landmark for the main inbound shipping channel. I would advise that you not spend your last night here, for the anchorage is exposed. Better lie off Colson Cay to the south, although there is not much to see ashore.

No one would describe Belize as the most exciting charter area in the world. But it has a remote charm all its own, and it is ideal for those who like to get away from it all, snorkelers and divers who want to spend a lot of time in the water. You are really far away from everything among these unspoiled cays.

PART IV: NORTH AMERICA AND THE BAHAMAS

13 Florida Keys and the Bahamas

A description of all the bareboating opportunities available in North America is impossible. Even to summarize the major charter areas is difficult. "Ah yes," readers will say, "but you have forgotten Lake So-and-so or the fantastic services offered by X in Maine." Yes, of course I have, for no one can possibly charter everywhere, let alone visit every location where bareboats are to be found. All we can do is to sample some of the major charter areas in the United States and offshore in the Bahamas. This journey reflects my own experience, a great of deal of traveling on land, and conversations with charter operators and clients all over the country.

General charter conditions

Chartering in Canada and North America is nothing like the sort of big business that it is in the Caribbean, where charter operators offer large standardized fleets of yachts to an enormous clientele from all over the world. Few companies north of the Caribbean run standardized fleets. Chartering has evolved as a some- what casual, often seasonal, business in most places. Many charterers are little more than mom-and-pop operations offering a few privately owned yachts in peak season. Although many of these companies survive, a large number vanish quietly from the classified columns every year, so you need to be careful when making reservations.

Bareboating in North America is changing, however, for yacht brokers and manufacturers have realized that they are approaching saturation of the new-yacht market. Some brokers are moving into bareboat yacht management as a way of selling boats and of passing along tax advantages to their clients. This is likely to become a major trend in charter circles in the next decade, in response to both the rising costs of sailing and a rapidly expanding market for bareboating—as long as the tax laws continue to provide shelter for owners. Chartering one's yacht is never even slightly lucrative. It is the write-offs that make such a course of action attractive to high-income taxpayers. Once such protection is removed—and it may not last forever—the bareboating business will again undergo a rapid

metamorphosis. The tax laws governing Caribbean-based yachts have already been tightened, perhaps a sign of things to come on the domestic front. At present, however, small charter fleets are mushrooming all over North America.

As a client unconcerned with tax shelter, you can find extremely attractive yachts to charter, especially if you work with a company that specializes in a single range of yachts, say C&C, Morgan, or Pearson. You are likely to get a relatively new and clean boat, and the company will do all it can to serve you well. Why, you might buy a yacht one day, and it's in their best interest to provide you with a pleasant, leisurely sea trial of a vessel that you might like. Just be aware that brokers in the charter business are enduring the hassles of a bareboat operation as a way of selling new yachts to clients who do not plan to use them often.

Perhaps the people who benefit most from broker charters are beginners, for they can take advantage of a full range of services. For example, Sailboats Inc. of Superior, Wisconsin, has done a superb job of running a charter operation and brokerage for beginners. They offer everything from beginning instruction and charter certification to final sale of a boat, which the owner uses for a few weeks of the year and the company charters for the rest of the season—with obvious tax advantages to the owner. So you can either learn sailing and charter year after year, or buy a boat and enjoy both sailing and tax advantages. Many other companies are bound to follow Sailboats' lead in future years; indeed, some are already doing so.

Any legitimate company in the brokerage business that offers charter yachts as a means of selling boats should be very open about it. Most are. Beware, however, of the small brokerage that has a few yachts "in charter." Frequently, they take neither the charter business nor the maintenance of the vessel seriously. "Put the boat in charter," they say to the prospective owner. "The fees will take care of the maintenance, insurance, and slip fees—and look at the tax advantages." Given the wear and tear on the average charter boat, such claims are nonsense. A friend of mine chartered a 44-footer from a brokerage in Fort Lauderdale, Florida, for a trip to the Bahamas. It took him three precious charter days to sort out the problems on the boat. The toilet was broken, the diesel exhaust siphoned in saltwater, and the refrigerator was defective, just for a start. He had to threaten legal action to get a refund. Six vacations were ruined. Buyer beware! Shop around for a charter boat before you put down a deposit, and check references and track record carefully first. It is a good rule never to charter from a private owner unless you know him well. *Whatever you do,*

check the insurance policy on a managed boat or on one chartered from a private owner meticulously. In our ridiculously litigious society, you are asking for trouble if you rent a boat that does not have proper charter coverage, or one that is not Coast Guard safety equipped. Remember, too, that the agency fee for a privately owned charter boat is normally about 40 percent, so you have some room for bargaining, especially in the off season.

The choice of yachts available for bareboat charter in North America is unlimited, from tiny 21-foot trailer boats for inland waters to 50-footers in Florida. Skilled racing skippers will be able to charter an IOR ocean racer; expert cruising people, a vessel for a transatlantic crossing—if they can afford it. But what about us more common folk? As usual, your best source of information is the yachting magazines, especially the annual bareboating double issues put out by *Sail* and *Cruising World*. These are, of course, advertising and marketing devices, designed both to attract clients for companies and to give bareboat organizations a chance to peddle their services. Once you realize this, you can use these admirable directories as a first step in seeking information. As with Caribbean outfits, look for companies with the following features:
- More than six boats in charter.
- A track record extending back at least five or six years.
- Adequate maintenance facilities that specialize in service to charter yachts—at minimum a boatyard that sells and charters yachts.
- Up-to-date designs in charter and an inventory of relatively new boats.

There is such a variety of cruising grounds in North America that I suggest you make greater efforts to match the boat to local conditions than you would in the Caribbean. For example, I would be inclined to charter the Florida Keys, the inland waterways of northern Florida, or the San Juan Islands of the Pacific Northwest in a powerboat. Winds tend to be light, and the cruising ground rather spread out. Clearly, the best yachts for the Bahamas are shallow-draft craft drawing less than 4 feet, while a deep-draft vessel is ideal for Southern California waters. A smaller boat makes sense in the Apostle Islands of Lake Superior or a place like Lake Champlain, simply because distances are smaller and the water basically sheltered. I always take the time to find out what boats are popular in local waters and try to charter one of similar design. For example, I would love to charter a Bermuda 40 or a Hinckley in the Northeast, partly because I love the design and partly because I know that many experienced owners find them ideal for these waters. Just because a CSY-44 or a

Morgan 46 is ideal in the Virgins does not necessarily mean she is perfect for the Chesapeake Bay or the Gulf Islands off Vancouver Island.

North American charter areas are such that you can bareboat somewhere in any month of the year. I once met a man in the Virgins who spent two months a year chartering North America and the Caribbean. We met in Tortola in December. That year, he had spent a week in Southern California in April, two weeks in the Pacific Northwest in June, three weeks in Maine in early September ("the best of all," he said), and was rounding out the year with a brief charter in the British Virgins. Not everyone will go to such extremes, but it is nice to know the opportunities exist.

The pages that follow take us on a journey through some of the southern charter areas such as the Florida Keys, the Bahamas, and California waters. Then we continue the circuit, with visits to the Pacific Northwest, the Apostle Islands, the Chesapeake, and the Northeast. You can charter in all sorts of other places, too, like west Florida or the Sea of Cortes, even on lakes in Tennessee, but space restrictions force us to leave out many lovely places. One of the charms of North American chartering is that you have no idea what areas will open up next. The descriptions below will give you some idea of the riches that are available.

The Florida Keys

The Keys are America's tropical islands, stretching south and west in a long string from Miami for more than 120 miles. This is a well-developed cruising area with all the comforts of civilization close to hand. You can spend days, even weeks, exploring obscure channels and remote fishing grounds along the Keys in almost complete solitude. Or you can hop from resort to resort in air-conditioned luxury. There is something for everyone in the Keys, even an open-water passage to the Dry Tortugas, the westernmost point on the east coast of North America.

You can charter the Keys from Miami or Fort Lauderdale, or start from one of the charter bases down the islands at Marathon and elsewhere. These more southerly headquarters are better if you plan to cruise down to the Dry Tortugas. When choosing a yacht for this area, be sure to charter one with a draft of about 4.5 feet. Anything deeper is going to restrict your movements inside the Keys, and you will be barred from exploring many fine spots. If you like camping, you may prefer the versatility of a trailer yacht, which you can anchor in less than 3 feet of water. This will

guarantee that you get away from the crowd. Whatever size and draft of vessel you select, a powerful engine is essential, for the greatest delights of the Keys lie in narrow swatchways and sheltered pools where there is little room for sailing and eyeball pilotage is the order of the day.

By the standards of the Bahamas or Virgins, the Keys are well developed, with plenty of supermarkets and shoreside facilities at every turn. Some people stock up in Miami or Fort Lauderdale and take two or three weeks' provisions with them, others buy fresh food along the way. Either way, plenty of ice or a good refrigerator is essential. The bugs in Keys anchorages can be ferocious, so an emergency supply of netting and repellent will complement the screens on the boat. This is a charter area where the fishing is excellent and a dinghy makes all the difference, if possible one with a good outboard for those long trips into shallow water. The charter company should provide one. Be sure to check it over carefully before you leave. Don't do what I once did: take off with only one oarlock!

Even beginners will find Keys navigation relatively easy, provided they take along a Chart-Kit or the folding government charts that plot all the channels outside and inside the Keys. The Coast Guard has marked this area very well, so that you can navigate from mark to mark in complete safety. Just make sure that you check off the numbers, for the land is often low-lying and featureless, with only a few conspicuous buildings to help you find your way. I once wandered off the Hawk Channel into the shallows and ran hard aground when the wind came up, simply because I omitted to check the numbers on the channel beacons. In this low-lying area, it is very easy to become disoriented at some distance from land on either side of the Keys. But you should have no trouble if you keep a constant check on your position. Frank Papy's *Cruising Guide to the Florida Keys* (Publication Arts, Inc., Minnetonka, Minnesota) is revised regularly and provides excellent sketch maps of the main channels, anchorages, and resort areas.

You can cruise the Keys at any season, but the months from June to September are very hot and buggy, with a threat of hurricanes. The weather cools off around October 15, giving you two months of pleasant cruising. Winter fronts bring several days of cool temperatures and strong northerly to northwesterly winds followed by warmer southerlies. You can use these winds to your advantage, but plan an inside cruise rather than following the more exposed Atlantic side where you are fighting the Gulf Stream. The best cruising is between mid-February and late May, but you may still encounter unsettled weather, especially windy conditions in March.

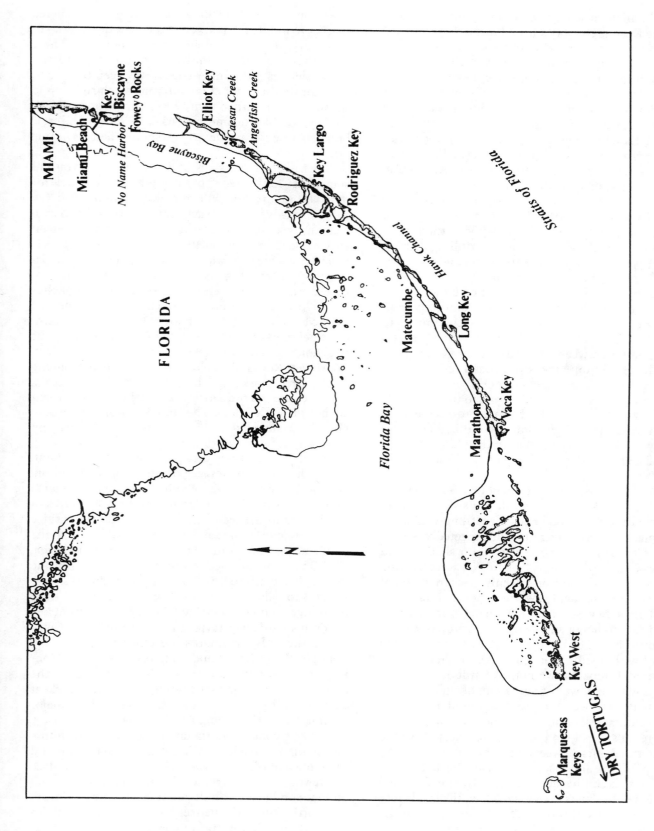

The Florida Keys

I would allow at least a week for a one-way cruise down the Keys, preferably a little longer. You can see a great deal in a two-week round trip. A 7-to-10-day charter from Marathon will allow you to cruise Key West and the Dry Tortugas in some detail.

The logical starting point for a Keys cruise, whether bound down the Gulf or Atlantic side, is No Name Harbor on the east side of Key Biscayne, a completely sheltered, though congested, anchorage with 9 feet in the midst of a state park. Many yachts lie up here before making a passage to the Bahamas or Key West. Depending on the weather, you can then decide whether to start on the Atlantic side or in more sheltered waters. The Atlantic route takes you out of the Biscayne Channel toward Fowey Rocks, then south through the wide Hawk Channel (controlling depth 9 feet) that passes between the barrier reef and the Keys. Hawk Channel is fine in normal conditions, but can be very bumpy in a northeasterly winter blow. Strong easterlies may have you rolling, but southerly conditions are very pleasant. Once you're committed to Hawk, it's difficult to cross to the inside route. Passages are few and far between, and currents run strongly in them. The Hawk route takes you past a series of low-lying keys to the narrow channels at Caesar or Angelfish Creek, where you can cross to the other side of the Keys. Caesar Creek channel provides a least depth of 9 feet (only 5 feet on the Gulf side) and is privately marked. You can cross to the Gulf side from here and anchor off the state park headquarters on Elliott Key.

The best and most sheltered anchorage is in a narrow cut between two keys to the south, but swinging room is restricted and the current runs very strongly. This is a tricky place to maneuver, for unexpectedly strong crosscurrents run from deep water into shallow, and you may go on the bottom really hard. We were fighting the current into the cut one evening, when a Miami boat ahead of us suddenly swung to port and ran hard aground in a few seconds. Fortunately, we had an anchor ready to let go and were able to stop ourselves from joining him. They were hard aground and listed to starboard with a strong current pushing them harder on the mud. It took us two hours of arduous kedging, towing, and dinghy work to get them off in the last of the twilight—and we nearly went aground ourselves a few minutes later. For all the hassles, we enjoyed our stay here: it's quiet and unspoiled, except for the outboard runabouts on weekends. There is not much to do except swim and fish. Angelfish Creek 5 miles farther south is another access channel on the Gulf side for shallow-draft boats drawing 4.5 feet, the last before Upper Matecumbe Key. You can anchor between the keys in up to 15 feet, but there is little to see.

As you sail south, picking your way from numbered marker to numbered marker, you will notice a series of lighthouse structures far away on the port side. These mark the outer limits of the barrier reef. Your port-hand marks delineate the inner edge of the reef. Be sure to keep inside them, for coral outcrops reach right up to the marks, as I learned to my cost a couple of years ago, when I grounded on one by marker 15. One of the crew broke her wrist as the wheel spun when we came off.

You will see more signs of development as you sail south past Key Largo. This is a major resort area for outboard sailors. You will spot offlying Rodriguez Key from a long way off. A yacht on passage to Key Largo can find good overnight shelter in calm weather on either side of the key, isolated from civilization. This is a marvelous place to wait up before going south on an early-morning passage, perhaps to meet a deadline back in Marathon. Shallower-draft vessels can take shelter in Largo Sound, entered through a narrow channel marked by flashing red buoy "2" north of Hawk Channel marker "35." There are several marinas, but the holding ground in the sound is poor. Both Rodriguez Key and Largo Sound are good stopping places after snorkeling the John Pennekamp Reef, a protected area on the barrier reef nearby, where you can anchor on settled days. The snorkeling and diving are not as spectacular as in parts of the Virgins and Bahamas, but still worth a day.

The Hawk Channel takes you past several excellent, quiet, sheltered anchorages on its way to Marathon. One of the best is Long Key Bight, where even a large sailboat drawing 6 feet or more can find shelter from southerlies in the lee of Highway 1. A bascule bridge with 50-foot clearance allows you to go through to the Gulf side on a major route to the west coast of Florida. The first time I sailed south from here, I became thoroughly confused by the lack of landmarks. The secret is to follow the breaks in the islands and to trace the bridges and viaducts that take Highway 1 from key to key. It's a little like navigating in parts of Scandinavia, where the only landmarks are church steeples. For example, Marathon stands out because of the conspicuous highrise on Vaca Key. This also marks the entrance to the channel leading to several bareboat charter facilities. Fortunately, the charts show major landmarks such as bridges and towers.

If you've come from the mainland and are running out of time, consider renting a car in Marathon and spending a day in Key West. This is also the last place where you can cross over to the Gulf side. I suggest you do so if you have the draft and it is blowing hard from the north. You can then enjoy a fast run south in smooth water. If you stay outside, plan on stopping at

Key West (John Launois)

Newfound Harbor. The entrance channel is straight-forward and just to the northwest of marker "50," taking you between low-lying islands to an anchorage or marina berth near Little Torch Key. Take your dinghy across to the ranger station on Big Pine Key and see the miniature deer that stand only 20 to 30 inches high. Once an endangered species, they are making a comeback in their protected environment.

Key West is a historic town, but also a typical tourist trap with a slightly raffish air. Behind the ardent commercialism is a charming old settlement, with its distinctive Conch architecture and exotic plants. Many of the clapboard houses have been restored, making the self-guided walking tour well worth the effort. There are the usual boutiques and artisans, plus dozens of seafood restaurants. This is the only place I know of that posts the time of sunset, the reason being that sunset watching is a local pastime. The party begins at least two hours before sundown in season. Every time I have sailed to Key West, I have had problems finding a berth. Frank Papy lists the major marinas. He strongly advises calling ahead on Channel 16 for a berth. You can anchor in the main entrance area of the harbor, but the anchorage is exposed to both weather and passing traffic. You can also anchor in Garrison Bay, but overhead wires inhibit its use by larger craft. Another popular anchorage is off the eastern shore of Wistaria Island. Perhaps you are best off shelling out the dollars for a marina slip, if one is available.

Most people prefer to use the outside passage to Key West, but a cruise down the inside can be even more fascinating, especially in a shallow-draft yacht. The controlling depth is an occasionally shaky 5 feet, which keeps out many larger vessels. Much of the inside bareboat traffic is in powerboats, whose shallow drafts enable them to stray from the deeper channels to anchor off remote keys. However, there is much to attract the sailor in these waters, too. The Gulf-side passage from Miami is entered by following a course of 193 degrees T from Biscayne Bay to markers "3" and "4" at Featherbed Bank. From there, you join a southerly course line that takes you down the inside of Elliott Key to the narrow, buoyed channel immediately north of Card Sound. You can cross over to the outside at Caesar or Angelfish Creeks. Personally, I prefer Caesar, for the channel is deeper and better marked. Look out for the currents. They run very strongly, sometimes across the sandbanks, so that you find yourself in shallow water in a few seconds. The Angelfish area is a good night stop. You can anchor in the mouth of the creek or in any of several side channels, where there is plenty of water. A Bahamian moor is essential, because the current runs strong and the swinging room is very limited. The first time I dropped anchor in Angelfish, I found myself enjoying dinner in the mangroves as the tide turned. It was not fun fighting the current and the mosquitoes to lay a second anchor to hold us in midstream. The many anchorages in this area are a comfortable day's passage from Biscayne Bay.

U.S. 1 crosses Little Card Sound toward the southern tip of Key Largo. The bridge gives you 65-foot clearance, so all but the largest charter yachts can pass. A lot of people stop at Alabama Jack's bar and restaurant, a yellow building near the east end of the bridge. You can anchor in about 5 feet off the establishment, where they can give you excellent advice on local fishing spots. It's a little noisy with the constant highway traffic. Barnes Sound lies ahead of you, with 7 feet controlling depth all the way to the entrance to Jewfish Creek on a course of 191 degrees T. The Largo Point entrance of the creek is a little hard to spot. However, you should be able to see the electrical overhead cables by the bridge at the south end. Steer for the easternmost mast and you should pick up marker "29" that marks the entrance. Jewfish itself is a narrow cut through mangrove swamps. Navigate with care! I almost disemboweled another yacht here, having underestimated the current that was flowing under my keel. The skipper was not amused. There are quite a few nice anchorages around here. I have anchored on the south side of Cross Key in complete shelter in northerly weather. You can do the same on the other side as well if the wind is blowing from the south. There is nothing ashore and the berth is quiet.

From Jewfish you cross Blackwater Sound, wend your way through Dusenbury Creek, across Tarpon Basin, and then through Grouper Creek. Stay within the channel markers and keep to starboard in the creeks. There is not a great deal of space. From Buttonwood Sound south, you are in more open water, with the keys close to starboard. The buoyed channel takes you across banks with 5 feet of water, through occasional narrow passes, like Cowpens Cut opposite Plantation Key. This is a routine passage, provided you keep a close watch on the marker numbers. Papy's *Guide* gives directions for the many resorts and quiet anchorages on the keys to port. He also describes the passes that will take you across to the Atlantic side. As far as anchoring is concerned, it is a matter of judging the best shelter for prevailing conditions and finding a deep enough spot. This part of the Keys is a mecca for bone fishermen. The bonefish lives in deep water and moves onto the flats to feed. It is here that the fisherman stalks them. First time around, you will need an expert guide, for the fish are wary and easily scared. Once hooked, bonefish fight ferociously and keep you on the run. This magnificent gamefish makes poor eating but wonderful sport.

Channel Five, just east of Long Key, is a good crossover if you want to venture outside for a while. You can see the radar domes and microwave tower on Long Key immediately west of the bridge for many miles on a clear day. By this time, you may realize that you do not have the time to visit the Dry Tortugas. Anchor in 7 feet or less off Grassy Key Sea School and take the seaplane. They'll fly you there and back, even provide the snorkeling gear, for a surprisingly modest cost—and children are half-price.

Many bareboat charterers start from Marathon on Vaca Key, where access to the Atlantic side is excellent. There are numerous marinas on the inside, but no crossover channel. It is here that you enter the Lower Keys, going through Big Spanish Channel between Little Pine and No Name Keys into the Gulf. Once you are out there, you are pretty well on your own until you reach Key West, the best access channels to the Lower Keys being on the Atlantic side. One anchorage is worth mentioning, a small cove in the waist of Bahia Honda Key that gives good shelter from southerly and easterly winds. Your passage south will take you some distance off the keys until you reach the entrance of Northwest Channel, which takes you into Key West. A bell buoy marks the approach to Northwest. You may have some trouble finding it, but once in the channel you should have no problems. Be sure to carry up-to-date charts of this area. The buoyage changes all the time.

The highlight of any charter in the Keys is a visit to the Marquesas Keys and the Dry Tortugas. If you have the time and the weather is settled, do everything you can to reach these destinations. You can reach Key West in two or three days of hard sailing. The Marquesas are low and mangrove-covered, but surrounded by interesting reefs. They lie about 24 miles west of Key West; the Dry Tortugas, some 50 miles farther on. There are no facilities in either of these areas, so stock up with food, ice, and water in Key West ahead of time. To visit either island group, pick your weather carefully and take your departure from 109-foot Sand Key Light southwest of Key West, leaving it well to starboard. Run from there in deep water down to Cosgrove Light. From there, run a course into Mooney Harbor Key in the Marquesas. Eyeball your way in carefully, there are coral heads. You can take 3 to 3.5 feet into the harbor through an entrance marked with privately maintained stakes, so deeper-draft yachts have to anchor off and dinghy into the creeks and diving spots. The southern entrance to Mooney Harbor is shoaled and should not be attempted. The only time I anchored in the Marquesas, we were eaten by bugs, but this was in a flat calm.

The Marquesas are a snorkeler's and diver's dream. Being a history buff, I prefer the Dry Tortugas, so named by the Spanish explorer Ponce de Leon, who found many large sea turtles there. Later sailors complained of the lack of fresh water, so they were labeled "dry." You reach them from the Marquesas by steering for Pulaski Shoal Light. The Rebecca Shoal Light, at mile 50, is a good check marker, and the radiobeacon on Loggerhead Key (286 kHz[OE]) will guide you in, if you have an RDF on board. Your first landfall will be East Key, which is higher than the other islands. This brings you up on the entrance to Southeast Channel, one of the two major routes into the islands. As you sail up Southeast, you'll spot Iowa Rock and its marker, with beacon "4" opposite. Steer between the two, then swing round to port toward Garden Key. The fort and lighthouse are conspicuous landmarks, as is the light on Loggerhead Key to the west.

Last time I was at Garden Key, we worked our way around the west end of the island, leaving beacon "6" to starboard and then taking the marked channel around the south end into the most commonly used anchorage between Garden and Bush Keys. The eastern channel between Bush and Garden Keys may be preferable on a first visit, however. Which berth you choose depends on the prevailing wind at the time of your visit. We checked in with the ranger at the pier, and he handed us instructions for anchoring as well as a copy of the rules and regulations. I have never been weatherbound here, but there seemed to be more than enough shelter for everyone in a norther, lying close inshore. The best strategy is to use your Garden Key anchorage as a base for sightseeing, fishing, and snorkeling. Fort Jefferson was built during the Civil War and is in a good state of preservation, while the underwater nature trail is well worth the time. Bird lovers will enjoy lying off Bush Key in a dinghy. Landing is prohibited, but the wildlife is abundant. Thousands of brown noddies and sooty terns nest here between April and August, the best time to view the sanctuary. We found the rangers extremely helpful. They knew the best places to snorkel and to fish. You can barbecue ashore if you feel so inclined— within designated areas.

The Dry Tortugas are quite far off the beaten track, so far off that the return passage can be very rough in bad weather. While Key West has a powerful radio beacon (332 kHz [FIS]), you are well advised to wait out frontal weather before sailing home. So watch the weather carefully and allow yourself enough time to return to base. Bear in mind the cardinal rule of bareboating: Always return your boat on time!

The Bahamas

The Bahamas lie just across the Straits of Florida from the American mainland, a tropical cruising paradise that has been a mecca to East Coast sailors for years. The islands form a 700-mile-long archipelago of low-lying cays and larger rocky islands surrounded by coral reefs and sandbanks. They extend from the waters off Florida to the very threshold of the Caribbean. Although deep-water channels separate the major cruising grounds in the Bahamas from one another, the real charm of chartering in these waters lies in the endless possibilities for gunkholing, eyeball navigation, and discovering new, completely sheltered anchorages. The water colors are brilliant hues of blue, dark green, and brown; the beaches are of the finest white sand. This is the cruising ground for those who seek solitude and love snorkeling, a place where you can escape from the world altogether. Beyond Nassau, there are no large cities and few settlements of even moderate size.

Christopher Columbus was the first westerner to visit the Bahamas. He made his landfall in the New World on San Salvador Island in 1492. At the time, the islands were inhabited by Lucayan Indians, who were soon deported to the mines and plantations of Hispaniola. The Bahamas were almost uninhabited until 1650, when the Eleutheran Adventurers tried to colonize them. They failed, and the islands became a haunt of buccaneers and pirates, who preyed on merchant ships headed through the Straits of Florida or the Windward Passage toward Europe. Although the pirates were eventually cleaned out, some isolated settlements still made their living by wrecking in the early years of this century. American Loyalists settled the islands at the end of the American War of Independence in 1789. Many of their descendants live in the islands to this day. The islanders enjoyed considerable prosperity during the Civil War, when Nassau was a major entrepot for Confederate blockade runners. Except for a brief flurry of activity during Prohibition, the islands were a quiet backwater until international tourism and the charter jet brought thousands of vacationers to Bahamian beaches and casinos in the 1960s. On July 10, 1973, the Bahamas became an independent nation after 300 years as a British possession. They are now heavily dependent on tourism for their livelihood. Cruising yachts are a major part of the tourist economy and, as such, are welcomed most places.

Most chartering visitors to the islands head for three major cruising grounds: Bimini and Grand Bahama, the Abacos, or the Exumas. The Exumas are easily reached from Nassau, but require at least two to three days of hard sailing from Florida. Although it is possible to bareboat in the Exumas, I would strongly recommend a first-time Bahamian charterer to head for Bimini or the Abacos, which are closer to the mainland.

Many American charterers pick up a yacht in Fort Lauderdale, Palm Beach, or Miami, then head across the Gulf Stream to the islands. This is fine if you plan to restrict your sailing to Grand Bahama or Bimini, which are just a long day's sail across the Straits of Florida. However, they are somewhat uneventful compared with the Abacos, where there are miles of islands and reefs to be explored. I strongly recommend the Abacos for your first charter in the Bahamas. There are major charter operations based on Marsh Harbor, and you can fly into the settlement from Florida several times a day. By spending a little extra, you can reach Miami or Fort Lauderdale overnight from, say, New York, Chicago, or Los Angeles, connect to an island flight, and board your yacht in the heart of the Abacos at noon. This not only saves you at least two to three days of sailing to and from the mainland, but puts you in the heart of a sheltered, all-weather cruising ground at little extra cost.

I have found that the companies operating in the Abacos are invariably efficient, courteous, and friendly. The larger companies' operations are run on the same lines as Caribbean charters, with standardized fleets and food packages. In contrast, most mainland bareboats are managed by yacht brokers and are privately owned. I have seen some that were complete wrecks and listened to too many horror stories of major defects and delays to be very confident of picking up a good boat on the mainland. If you can find a company that specializes in bareboating and meets the criteria in Chapter 8, fine. Otherwise, you are better off chartering from an experienced company in the islands. It is so much better to have a local base, especially in the popular winter months when strong northers make the Gulf Stream impassable for days on end.

In many respects, the Bahamas are a unique cruising ground. Their shallow waters and uncharted channels can make even experienced sailors nervous. A deep-water cruising friend of mine recently spent two months sailing the Bahamas. I met him in Bimini after 10 days. He sat me down with a beer and spoke in a hushed voice. "It's so *shallow*," he complained. "I can't get used to having less than 6 feet of water under my keel most of the time. It's incredible where people will go here." He seemed to be frightened by the lack of water under his keel. I was not surprised when he sailed off for the Caribbean a few weeks later and could imagine him settling back with a relaxed sigh as he sailed off the banks for the last time. In some ways, one can hardly blame him for being concerned. You can sail for weeks on end here with only 4 feet of water under your keel.

Yes, sailing in shallow waters can be unnerving at times, especially if you are used to rocky coasts and deep channels. You can reduce the strain somewhat by chartering a smaller yacht that draws between 4 and 5 feet, but the secret is to take it really easy for the first few days, until you have mastered the basics of eyeball navigation and overcome your natural fear of venturing in the shallows. After a while, you'll surprise yourself by going into narrow channels and behind reefs where there is barely enough water for the yacht to lie at low water. Cruising the Bahamas is an art, and eyeballing half the fun. Another secret is to take along the Bahamas Chart-Kit (Better Boating Association, Box 407, Needham, MA 02192, 800-225-8317), which gives you complete chart coverage of the islands. The *Yachtsman's Guide to the Bahamas* (Tropic Isle Publishers, Box 611141, North Miami, FL 33161) is an annual almanac with advertising that covers all the islands. Although the sailing directions contained therein are clear enough and the chartlets admirable, I have found the book sadly out of date on occasion—for an annual. The same publishers sell a series of sketch charts that are useful for eyeballing in the islands.

You can charter in the Bahamas most months of the year, but I would avoid the hurricane season from July to late October. Many northern sailors charter in the Abacos during the winter months. The winter weather pattern brings occasional outbreaks of cold, continental, high-pressure air that interfere with the normal easterly airflow across the islands. The wind shifts to northwesterly, then veers to northerly and northeasterly, sometimes bringing rain and blowing at velocities of up to 35 knots or more for several days. These northers can interrupt your sailing, even in sheltered waters, but are interspersed with day after day of fine weather when the wind settles in the southeast or northeast and blows between 5 and 15 knots. The last norther comes through in late April or May, when the summer weather pattern of easterly winds settles in for six months. The winds are lighter, between 5 and 12 knots, and calms are frequent. Thunderstorms are commonplace and temperatures can be sweltering. Occasional easterly waves, troughs of low pressure over tropical waters, interrupt the settled weather. The

Bimini Harbor from the air, entrance in foreground. (Bahamas Ministry of Tourism)

temperature rises, it is airless and very humid. These are the weather patterns that forecasters watch carefully, for some waves become tropical depressions and hurricanes. From the chartering point of view, I think the best months are April, May, and early June, when the incidence of northers is lower and warm summer weather is settling over the islands. Late June and early July can be still and sweltering. The last time I sailed in the Bahamas in late June, the midday temperature was 104 degrees in the shade, and there was no wind to boot —not my favorite cruising weather. You can enjoy many fine days in winter, but there's always a risk of a blustering norther that will keep you in port.

Many people go to Bimini or Grand Bahama on their first visit to the islands. You can see the sights with a week's charter from the mainland, sailing across the Gulf Stream from Fort Lauderdale or Miami. Many newcomers are nervous about this, for they worry about the strong current and the potentially difficult landfall on the low-lying islands. "Cross at night," advised my friends the first time I was bound for the Bahamas. "The winds are often calmer, and you can time your landfall for just after dawn." They were right. The crossing was easy, because we could use back bearings from mainland lights and pick up the island lights before daylight came. What I like to do on a Bimini charter is to take the first day easy, enjoying an afternoon sail down to No Name Harbor on Key Biscayne. Then, when the crew is fully relaxed and familiar with the boat, we take off across the Straits.

Having made the crossing many times, I feel confident making a day crossing. On a clear day, you will probably pick up Bimini or Grand Bahama about 5 miles off, but the advantage of arriving off Bimini just before dawn is that you should sight the conspicuous airport radio mast with its red flashing light quite some distance offshore. You can then pick up the low-lying island and white houses of the town at your leisure. A radio direction finder is an essential in these waters, for both Bimini and West End on Grand Bahama have powerful radiobeacons that can help you zero in on your destination from miles away. There are casual sailors who just follow the flight path of the seaplanes that land in Bimini Harbor, but I hope you are not among them.

No two sailors will ever agree on the amount of current you should allow for when crossing the Gulf Stream. The guides say 2.5 knots, but I have found that 1.5 knots can be more accurate. Much depends on wind conditions, on the angle at which you cross the Straits of Florida, and on the speed of your yacht. I would recommend using a figure of about 1.5 knots, but ask the charter staff what they advise and talk to people who have just crossed the stream. Monitor weather forecasts carefully and allow plenty of spare time in case a norther delays you in the islands.

Bimini is first and foremost a game-fishing town, but a somewhat raffish, charming, albeit rundown, weekend place as well. Many yachts call here on their way to Nassau across the banks. It's a fine place to lie up before returning to Florida, too. I love sailing into the crowded harbor, if only to enjoy a drink at the Compleat Angler and to watch the bustling life of the port. The entrance is easy, provided you negotiate the dogleg at the outer end of the channel carefully. Approaching from offshore, steer for the radio mast until the tower vanishes behind the trees behind the beach. Then select a point on the shore on the same bearing and eyeball your way inshore across the bar until you reach the deeper blue waters of the main channel. Bimini bar should never be attempted in strong onshore conditions. A deeper-draft charter yacht is best advised to arrive on a rising tide first time around.

As you approach the town, follow the deep water behind the shelter of North Bimini Island. The marinas and port quays will unfold on your port side. You can secure at several marinas—Brown's is nearest the entrance—but I prefer to move on upstream and anchor off the game-fishing resorts where the channel narrows. A strong tidal stream runs through the narrow cut, and you are likely to have company in the anchorage. A Bahamian moor is essential so that you take up the minimum space and swing easily with the tide. Look out, too, for mooring chains on the bottom. I have found the best place to anchor is about in midstream, well clear of the docks and of the seaplane landing area close to the sandbanks. It is somewhat disconcerting to watch a seaplane taking off straight at you, but he always lifts off in time.

Your first act must be to clear customs and immigration. The officials will come to your boat if you secure temporarily alongside, but you can often take your papers to their office on the high street. Check with your neighbors as to prevailing practice. You are then free to explore the town and to sail elsewhere in the islands. Bimini itself is just a small resort community. It offers numerous bars, a few T-shirt stores, and a multitude of churches. Plan to enjoy a drink, a meal, and a walk through the town away from the tourist quarter. The streets are narrow and populated with huge American cars and motor scooters. A game-fishing tournament was in progress last time I was there, so we watched the boats come in with fine cargoes of marlin that were hoisted one by one on the scales opposite our anchorage.

If you charter to Bimini, plan on spending a couple of days exploring the islands and reefs south of the island. You can anchor off Gun Cay or even visit Cat Cay marina, an affluent private resort. Gun Cay is easy to identify because of the conspicuous lighthouse on the south end of the island, marking the narrow passage onto the banks. You'll spot a battered wreck on your port side as you sail south from Bimini. This concrete ship went ashore during World War I and served as a club and rumrunner's storehouse in the 1920s, before being used as a target during World War II. The diving and spearfishing around the wreck are said to be excellent.

If you have the time, you can visit Grand Bahama as well, carrying the Gulf Stream up to West End or past Great Isaac light to the resorts on the south coast of the island. There is, however, little to see or do, unless you are interested in duty-free shopping or gambling at Freeport.

A charter from the mainland to Bimini will only serve to whet your appetite for chartering in these waters. At this point, you are ripe for the Abacos treatment, a charter where the waters are smooth, where you can sail from village to village and anchorage to anchorage in any reasonable weather, where the settlements are picturesque, clean, and friendly, and there's a wind blowing most of the time.

A privately owned yacht will have to sail all the way from West End to the Abacos across the Little Bahama Bank. This is a long, monotonous passage, which the charterer avoids by flying to the charter fleets at Marsh

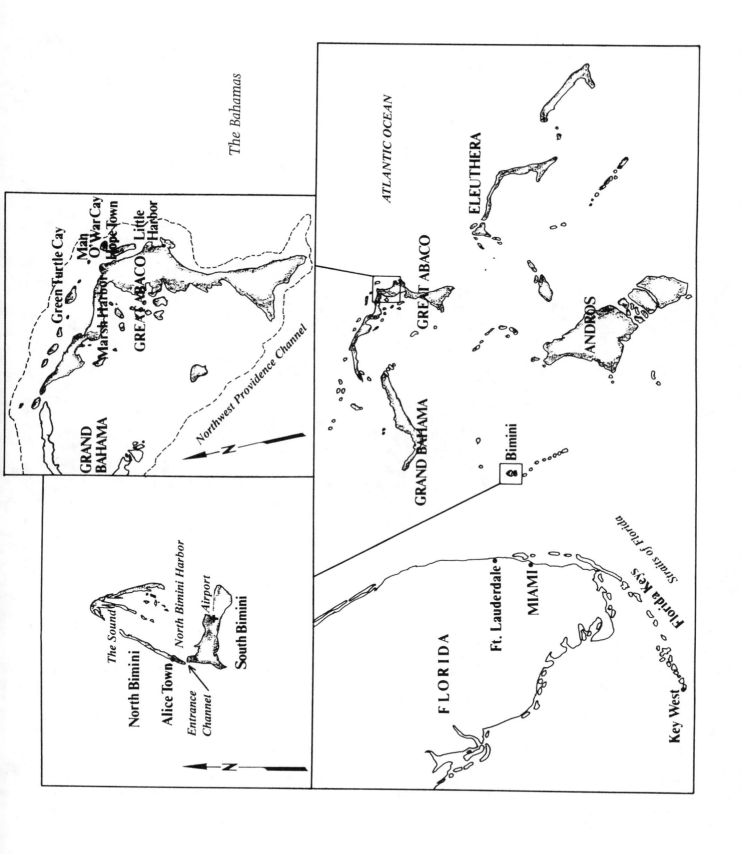

The Bahamas

Hope Town. (Bahamas Ministry of Tourism)

Harbor, in the heart of the Abacos. Many people just charter for a week here, but I would recommend at least 14 days if you can afford it—there is just so much to enjoy here. Marsh Harbor itself is easily accessible and completely sheltered. The deepest water is along the northern shore of the bight. The charter marinas are to be found at the sides and head of the bay. The town itself sprawls along the southern shore. Once prosperous from shipbuilding and sponging, Marsh Harbor suffered badly with the decline of sponge fishing. It is now the administrative and commercial hub of the Abacos, with several supermarkets and most supplies a sailor needs. Except for enjoying a drink and some conch burgers at the Conch Inn, there is really not a

great deal to detain you here, with so much good sailing at hand.

This is a charter area where every destination is within an easy day's sail or less of your last stop. It's also a place where the waters are smooth and the breezes constant, so you can sail just for the sheer joy of it. Last time I was off Marsh Harbor, I enjoyed an informal race to the death with another 40-footer. We tacked fiercely back and fro, going about only when the water was turning a dangerous light blue. He tacked under our stern, next tack we were under his. Each time we converged, buckets of water drenched the cockpit crews. The race ended abruptly a mile from the finish when we ran aground trying to sneak an advantage.

The shouts of triumph from our adversary ring in my ears to this day.

Your Abacos charter should be planned with several variables in mind: the prevailing wind direction and strength, how much you want to dive and snorkel, and how energetic you are feeling. You can spend a wonderful week without straying much more than 20 miles from Marsh Harbor, or venture as far north as Green Turtle Cay, exploring the excellent snorkeling around the northern cays. Nearby New Plymouth is a charming settlement that prospers on fishing and tropical fruit. Try to keep the schedule simple on your first visit to the Abacos, especially if you are unfamiliar with eyeball navigation.

Two places are musts in the Abacos: Hope Town and Man of War Cay. I would spend the firt day or so at Man of War. The entrance is narrow but straightforward with 6 feet at low tide. You can normally anchor without too much trouble. It's only about 5 miles from Marsh Harbor to the narrow entrance to Man of War, at the southeastern end of the island of that name. The approach is easy enough, provided you keep an eye out for the crosscurrents near the entrance. Once inside, you have two choices: bear to port and take the channel up to the main settlement, or anchor in the 12-foot eastern harbor to port. I would recommend following the channel up to the town and Albury's famous marina. However, the marina may be full and the moorings off the town, occupied. In that case, you can anchor in the eastern harbor, free of mooring chains and of the wake of passing motorboats. There's a narrow path that takes you to town in a few minutes.

Man of War is famous for its wooden boatbuilding industry. Even in this aluminum and fiberglass age, the local artisans still turn out fine runabouts and sailing dinghies that sail like witches. Many cruising sailors haul their boats here, even lay them up while they return home for a while. The settlement is spotlessly clean, like all Abacos villages, with brightly painted wooden clapboard houses joined by concrete walkways. The older wooden houses are especially attractive, while traditional boatbuilding buffs will drool over the sailing dinghies at the docks.

The second must is Hope Town on Elbow Cay, a completely sheltered harbor with a large red-and-white-striped lighthouse that can be spotted miles away. The approach from North Parrot Cay lies across a shallow bank with 6 to 7 feet on a course of about 150 degrees T. Many a yacht has gone aground by steering straight for the harbor entrance when still a considerable distance offshore. Turn parallel to the shore when you are as close as 100 yards off the old quarries on Elbow Cay. Then eyeball your way through the channel, giving a wide berth to the bar to starboard, passing inside of Eagle Rock on the white marks of the entrance range. Look out for the sharp turn to starboard close inshore, then find a clear anchorage in 12 to 18 feet in the harbor. Make sure, however, that your anchor is well dug into the grassy bottom. I have seen people drag here even in calm weather.

Hope Town is a charming place with the usual wooden houses and small stores. The real landmark is the lighthouse, which towers over the western side of the anchorage. You can climb to the top and admire the colorful view of the surrounding islands that unfolds from the top. The fishing around Elbow Cay is excellent, but I would advise you to retain a guide the first time. They really know the spots. We have enjoyed several good meals at the Hopetown Harbor Lodge and Abaco Inn over the years. Both require dinner reservations. The grouper, lobster, and conch are truly spectacular.

The Abacos are an area where the choice of quiet anchorages and beaches is almost endless. You will find the major settlements congested, but only a little imagination is needed to get away from the crowd, especially if you have chartered a shallow-draft vessel. Most charterers stay in the waters between Marsh Harbor and Green Turtle, where there are beaches and reefs galore. But I would think about heading south, perhaps even as far as Little Harbor. The trickiest part of the passage south lies through the Tilloo Cut, an 8-to-10-foot channel between shallow banks. Once clear of the cut and in Pelican Harbor, you can anchor off Sandy Cay and explore the fine coral reefs of the Land and Sea Park. This is superb dinghy country, but watch out for surge on windy days. Little Harbor lies at the southern end of Pelican Harbor. It's a fine place for shallow-draft yachts, with a comfortable 4.5 feet in the channel at high tide. You can anchor off the tiny settlement in the bay. A series of stakes and floats show you the way in. Plan on spending at least a day exploring and fishing with your dinghy near the anchorage. The "boiling holes" in the shallows near the rocky cays are great places for catching grouper and other species. You can snorkel and dive off Goule Cay nearby, but the main attraction is the Johnston family, who own Little Harbor. Randolph Johnston came to the island in 1950 in a Bahamian schooner. He made a living by chartering her at first, then became an artist full-time, building his own house and bronze foundry ashore. He, his wife, son, daughter-in-law, and grandchildren all live at Little Harbor, where they are gracious hosts to visitors. You can visit the foundry and purchase their work, and if you are lucky, you will hear three blasts on a conch horn that announce that Pete's

Pub is open. The pub is an old deckhouse from the schooner, converted into a bar that seats six people. Everyone in the anchorage is invited—and the home brew is guaranteed to put everyone in the mood.

If you like remote anchorages, sandy beaches, and fishing, you can do nothing better than charter the Abacos. It is a perfect place to try out sailing in tropical waters and to hone your skills at eyeball navigation.

14 The West Coast

Southern California

Bareboat chartering is still in its infancy in California. More's the pity, for the waters between Point Conception and the Mexican border offer a fascinating variety of cruising grounds. The charter area is very accessible from Los Angeles International Airport. A commuter airline, rental car, bus, or cab will take you to any of the base ports within a few minutes or hours. Once aboard, you can contemplate all kinds of cruises. Many people sail from marina to marina and enjoy fancy restaurants and the comforts of shore at every stop. They never use their anchors and hook their electrical system to the dock every night. The more adventurous charterer can take off for Catalina and the other offshore islands that lie within a easy day's sail of the mainland. While Catalina is somewhat developed, the northern islands let you see an unspoiled California, as the West of a century ago might have been. You can lie at anchor in quiet coves, watch sea lions sunning themselves on remote rocks, and fall asleep to the soothing lullaby of gently breaking surf on a sandy beach.

Southern California is a natural for major bare-boating operations, but the high cost of doing business and a shortage of slips have prevented the growth of large standardized fleets. There are several companies that manage a wide variety of yachts for private owners. They advertise both in the national yachting press and in local periodicals like the *Los Angeles Times*. You can also charter from a private individual, but I would not recommend doing so unless you live locally and have the time to look into the situation very carefully. The larger charter organizations in Southern California should check out well against the criteria in Part I; indeed, I have found some of them to have stricter check-out requirements than those of most Caribbean companies. One even requires a two-hour sea test before letting you off on your own.

Most of the bareboat yachts in this area are under management, so you have an almost infinite variety of choice. I would advise chartering a boat at least 27 feet LOA, preferably something in the 30-to-40-foot range. This will give you greater comfort at sea and a stable platform in island anchorages where the swell sometimes surges gently all night. The most common yachts in charter are typical family cruising designs with large cockpits and comfortable interiors: Cals, Catalinas, Ericsons, or Islanders. I find the Catalina range

155

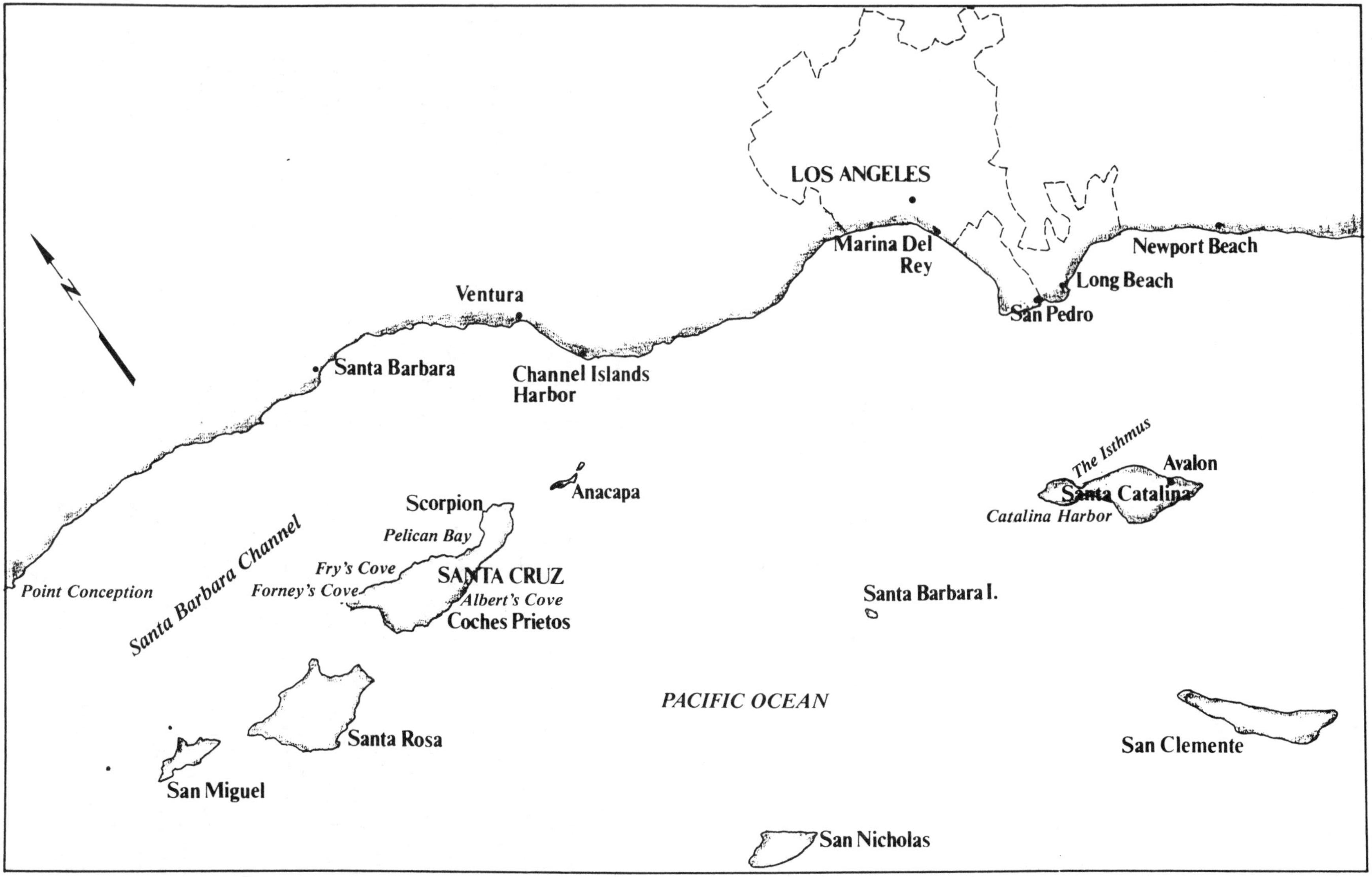

Newport Beach

Long Beach

San Pedro

San Clemente

Avalon

Santa Catalina

The Isthmus

Catalina Harbor

LOS ANGELES

Marina Del Rey

Santa Barbara I.

San Nicholas

PACIFIC OCEAN

Ventura

Channel Islands Harbor

Anacapa

Scorpion

Pelican Bay

SANTA CRUZ

Albert's Cove

Coches Prietos

Santa Barbara

Fry's Cove

Forney's Cove

Santa Rosa

Santa Barbara Channel

San Miguel

Point Conception

Southern California

especially comfortable under Southern California conditions. They are well laid out below and have a fine turn of speed at sea.

Southern California offers such a variety of cruising that you should make fairly specific plans before deciding where to charter from. When chartering south of Point Conception, you have a number of general cruise options:

• A port-to-port cruise in the Los Angeles area, from, say, Marina del Rey in the north to Newport Beach or San Diego in the south.

• A Catalina charter, departing from Marina del Rey, Newport Beach, or some other southern port.

• An offshore cruise to the northern Channel Islands such as Santa Cruz and Anacapa.

You can enjoy most of the pleasures of the southern ports or Catalina in the course of a week's charter. I would advise you to plan on picking up a yacht in Marina del Rey or Newport Beach for this type of cruise. A charter among the northern islands is another matter. If you charter from the Los Angeles area, it will take you at least an overnight passage to reach Santa Cruz Island, and that against the prevailing wind and swell. You will save time and money by chartering in the Channel Islands, Ventura, or Santa Barbara. Of these three ports, Santa Barbara is by far the most convenient for the islands, for you can reach over the Santa Barbara Channel in both directions and be out at the islands within four hours of leaving charter base. If you are unable to find out about charter opportunities in these communities, write or call the local Chamber of Commerce or Better Business Bureau, or order a copy of the *Pacific Boating Almanac* (Western Marine Enterprises, PO Box Q, Ventura, CA 93003).

The Southern California coast is famous for its serene and predictable weather. This is a year-round cruising ground, and you can sail in shirt sleeves during February off Los Angeles. However, the winter months can be dangerous offshore. A first-time charterer should plan on cruising between late April and early October when weather conditions off the coast are normally easygoing. The peak season for island cruising is between Memorial and Labor Days. I would do everything I could to avoid chartering during any long summer weekend. The islands are jammed with yachts all competing for the same small coves.

The prevailing winds blow up and down the Pacific coast, so you spend a great deal of time motoring to windward in these waters. Typically, the mornings are calm, with a moderate westerly wind of 10 to 15 knots filling in during the afternoon and dying down toward sunset. Most people plan their coastwise cruising with this wind pattern in mind. For example, if you are

chartering from San Diego and bound for Newport Beach or Catalina, you plan your windward passage-making for the night and early morning hours. Your "iron spinnaker" takes you to windward during the early days of your charter. You can then take your time riding the prevailing westerlies back to base.

This regular weather pattern is interrupted by winter storms, when low-pressure systems bring southeasterly winds and rain to the coast. These storms can reach 40 knots or more before the wind veers to the northwest and blows very strongly for a day or more. These post-frontal blows are especially hazardous near the islands, where they funnel south from Point Conception down offshore shorelines. The wind can be blowing at 30 knots close to the mainland and reach velocities of 60 knots at the islands on such a day. Fortunately, many island anchorages are sheltered from strong westerlies, so these are not the most hazardous conditions.

Ironically, the most dangerous times are those when the air is as clear as crystal and you can see for 50 miles, even in the smoggy Los Angeles Basin. This is when a high forms over the inland deserts. Fierce, dry winds blow down the mountain slopes and sweep over the Southern California coastline. Gusts of 60 to 70 miles an hour are not uncommon. These Santa Ana winds are truly devil gusts. They arrive without warning and turn the most sheltered island anchorages into a nightmare lee shore. No anchorage is immune from their blast. So the only place to be on these magnificently fine but lethal days is snug in a marina or back home. Still, many people ignore the telltale signs and venture offshore. In 1977, a large fleet of yachts was anchored at Santa Cruz enjoying a quiet Thanksgiving. The air was completely still, the atmosphere warm and dry. A slight north-easterly swell began to rock the boats at sunset. A few experienced sailors upped anchor and made for open water as the swells came in. The rest stayed. Half an hour later, the Santa Ana was blowing at 45 knots. More than 20 yachts dragged ashore that night. Fortunately, no one was drowned. Santa Anas are most common between September and February. The best charter months are normally Santa Ana–free. (You know when a Santa Ana is coming when radio announcers tell truckers to keep off Interstate 5!)

Navigationally, Southern California is a breeze. Waters are deep, there are few outlying dangers, and the approaches to anchorages are straightforward. There are three major hazards: fog, swell, and commercial or military activity.

Foggy conditions are a fact of life in Southern California, especially during the summer months. You soon get used to a diurnal cycle of fog and hazy sunshine. You wake up to a foggy morning, with

Off Catalina Island. (Elyse Mintey)

visibility restricted to a half-mile or so. As the morning wears on, the fog burns away and gives way to hazy sunshine. As the sun sets, the fog creeps in again until the next morning. The thickness of the fog depends on the inversion layers in the atmosphere. You can normally set out on passage under these conditions with the reasonable certainty that you will have ample visibility for your landfall. Just be careful to set an accurate compass course and to use your RDF or Loran if you have one aboard. Really dense fogs are uncommon. I have ventured out in such conditions, only to have to set a compass course to return to harbor 50 feet from the fairway buoy. Thick fogs rarely last very long, but it is suicidal to sail in them. If you are caught out in these ship-infested waters, keep out of shipping lanes, sound the correct fog signals, or anchor in shallow water.

Despite the moderate weather and sheltering effects of the islands, the Southern California coast is exposed to Pacific swells. These can reach 6 to 8 feet off the islands during the winter months, generated by intense storms far offshore. Summer charter conditions are normally much quieter, except when swells from tropical storms off Baja California roll into anchorages

and beaches much farther north. If such conditions are forecast, you can find shelter in anchorages on the mainland side of the major islands, but many roadsteads are untenable until the swells die down. Fortunately, tropical storms are tracked closely and you will normally have plenty of warning of hazardous swell conditions.

Southern California waters are heavily travelled by commercial shipping, not only deep-water freighters, but oil tenders and fishing boats as well. The Pacific Missile Range arcs out over the islands; oil platforms spring up almost daily in the Santa Barbara Channel and off Point Conception. All these activities affect your passagemaking, so you should keep a sharp lookout and ask the charter company about the regulations for crossing the Pacific Missile Range if you are bound for the islands from the Los Angeles area. As to ships and oil rigs, my best advice is to keep clear and resist the temptation to take a closer look.

For all these apparent hazards, Southern California is a superb charter area, especially for less experienced sailors. You don't have to worry about tides and currents, navigation is uncomplicated, and it is almost impossible to go aground. The hardest problem for most neophyte California charterers is anchoring at the islands. Most of the anchorages are so small that you will have to lay two anchors, bow and stern, both to keep you from swinging into your neighbors and to keep your bow into the slight surge that rolls into most coves even on calm days. No one here uses the Bahamian moor, preferring to lay out the bow anchor, then rowing out a second one astern with the dinghy. Some maestros drop the stern anchor from the yacht, pay out the line to twice the scope, drop the main anchor, then go astern and haul in the kedge. This is fine for experts, but you are better off leaving this for later in the cruise. California anchoring is no different from that practiced elsewhere: dig the anchor in well, lay ample scope, and choose your anchor spot carefully.

The mainland ports of Southern California are so well known that they require no detailed description here. If you plan a port-to-port cruise, I suggest that you make up a relatively firm itinerary and call ahead to see if you can get slip reservations, especially during the summer months. Many of the most popular marinas are perennially full. Some Southern California yacht clubs have private docks, which you can use if you are a member of a club with reciprocal privileges. Again, advance reservations are advisable.

Most people chartering from a Los Angeles or San Diego base will make a beeline for Catalina, an easy day's passage from the major marinas on the mainland. I am afraid that Catalina is not one of my favorites, largely because it is developed and the best coves are congested with privately owned moorings. However, you can have a great deal of fun at Avalon and the Isthmus. The passage from the mainland is very straightforward. If bound for the Isthmus, simply steer for the low saddle at the east end of the island, a course that will take you straight into the cove. Many people prefer to start at Avalon, so they look for the circular casino building at the harbor, which can be seen from many miles offshore. If only the peaks of the island are visible, steer for Blackjack peak with its conspicuous radio tower bearing a red flashing light. This course will bring you inshore just west of the harbor.

Avalon is a charming resort town, crowded with day tourists during the summer, but delightfully quiet in fall and winter. The harbor is easy to approach, the entrance lying just east of the casino building. A harbor boat will meet you as soon as you arrive and escort you to a visitor mooring, if one is available. Otherwise you will have to anchor outside and wait for a vacancy. The town is a wonderful run ashore, with fancy boutiques, picturesque narrow streets, interesting houses, and excellent restaurants. I would recommend stocking up here before moving on elsewhere.

After visiting Avalon, you can circumnavigate the island in either direction. I prefer to go clockwise, for I have found that the prevailing westerlies often blow less strongly on the south side. It's a comfortable day's passage along the south coast to Catalina Harbor, stopping for lunch at Little Harbor 3 miles to the east, a small cove with room for about 10 yachts to anchor. Catalina Harbor is a spectacular inlet, with space for about 300 boats to anchor clear of the moorings. The head of the harbor is shallow, so you should anchor under the west cliff in 25 to 30 feet. You can explore the Isthmus resort from here, purchasing a landing permit at the headquarters of the Cove and Camp Agency ashore.

Your next stop will be one of the coves that border the Isthmus area on the north coast of the island, exactly opposite Catalina Harbor. The western end of Catalina is steep-to. You can sail close inshore and enjoy the rugged cliff scenery. The Isthmus is a little trickier to approach than Catalina Harbor because of offlying rocks and reefs, but if you pass midway between Lion Head and the buoy marking Harbor Reefs, you'll have plenty of water. Unfortunately, the Isthmus coves are heavily congested with private moorings. You can normally pick one of these up if it is unoccupied, but plan on anchoring outside them or in the designated anchoring areas if the coves are busy. The trouble with Catalina for visitors is the number of highly organized moorings. There are very few safe, mooring-free anchorages if the wind pipes up. Fortunately, the weather is normally benign and seas smooth. Catalina sailors seem to consider anything that gives them some shelter from surge an acceptable anchorage—an unusual definition of a safe berth. The local cruising guides and chart kits will give you a wide choice of overnight anchorages on both coasts of Catalina.

No question, however, that the finest Southern California chartering is to be found in the Santa Barbara Channel area. The four channel islands—Anacapa, Santa Cruz, Santa Rosa, and San Miguel—offer every variety of anchorage and sailing condition you could wish for. Few charterers will visit the two northern islands. Santa Rosa and San Miguel are windswept and remote, and require lengthy windward passages to be reached. Your time is better spent savoring the delights of Santa Cruz Island, where you can anchor in a different cove every day for 10 days or more. To visit either Anacapa or Santa Cruz, charter at Channel Islands, Ventura, or Santa Barbara. The latter is probably the best base, for you can reach across to Santa Cruz Island in four hours or less on most days and avoid the half-day windward passage from the southern ports. The channel passage is easy enough on settled

Anchorage (Orizaba) on Santa Cruz Island. (Lesley Newhart)

days, but you should look out for strengthening winds in the last 7 miles before the island. This is Windy Lane, caused by winds funneling down the islands from Point Conception. On a typical summer's day, you can expect to tie down a reef or change down jibs in Windy Lane. In winds of over 30 knots in mid-channel, Windy Lane will have gusts of 40 to 60, so stay at home!

While Anacapa Island is a day excursion, with only two possible overnight anchorages, Santa Cruz can shelter you in almost any conditions. The north coast offers the best coves. First-time visitors normally head for Pelican Bay, once the site of a resort hotel frequented by the Hollywood stars of the twenties. Pelican is a spectacular anchorage bounded by precipitous cliffs where wildflowers bloom in spring. Up to 100 yachts can lie here during the summer months. Tuck yourself into the center of the cove and make sure your anchor catches hold—there's kelp and grass here. Pelican is not my favorite, partly because it is so crowded and also because a light easterly popple can roll in here and make the anchorage uncomfortable.

If you have a week or so to spend at Santa Cruz, you might prefer to go hard on the wind from Santa Barbara and sail for the western end of the island. Round the steep cliffs of West Point and spend the night in Forney's Cove. You lie behind some low-lying rocks in a shallow bay. The island slopes down to the shore here, and you walk on a brilliant carpet of wildflowers in spring. I disgraced myself on one visit by lying down on the blooms in a new shirt. It took months to get the vegetable dye off the back. This is a wild and desolate place, but it has the advantage of enabling you to sail downwind along either coast of the island. I would advise the north coast if you are short of time—there are more anchorages and more sights to see. Perhaps I should mention that everyone needs a landing permit to go ashore on Santa Cruz. The charter company will give you details.

Santa Cruz's north coast is made up of precipitous cliffs indented with a string of marvelous coves. Pass close inshore as you sail southward. There's 30 to 60 feet right at the foot of the cliffs. Caves penetrate deep into the rock; one of them, Painted Cave, is a favorite excursion for local yachts. You lie off the inconspicuous entrance and row your dinghy into a dark chamber. Your flashlights light up the deep cavern, in which dozens of sea lions have their home. They swim round your dinghy as you visit. The best time to visit Painted Cave is in the morning, when the wind is calm and swells are down. During the afternoon, you can run down to any of the famous coves to leeward: Cueva Valdez with its fine beach; Lady's, a tiny cove that holds up one or two yachts in complete shelter; Fry's, the most sheltered and comfortable of all, nestling between steep hillsides. And so on to Pelican, Prisoners', Scorpion, and a multitude of bays and inlets large and small. There are enough anchorages to keep the most fanatical cruising sailor happy, while the diving and snorkeling are excellent as well. You can browse over a good book, visit other yachts, walk ashore (with a permit), fish, or simply do nothing. This is California as it was a century ago. It is hard to believe that the bustling, industrialized mainland is only a half-day's sail away.

If you have time, visit the south coast anchorages as well. The most famous are Albert's and Coches Prietos, a pair of coves within a mile of one another midway along the island. Coches Prietos is especially beautiful, a fine semicircular sandy beach, with good walking and excellent shelter. Willows, a little further to windward, is another favorite, much frequented by fishermen in the 1920s, when permanent fishing camps were to be found in the major coves.

You could charter the Channel Islands again and again and never repeat your itinerary. Many people do indeed charter here year after year, enjoying a California that has long vanished on the mainland. With its predictable weather and safe anchorages, this is an ideal charter area for comparative beginners. Here the neophyte can get a taste of offshore sailing with minimum risk, before graduating to more advanced cruising grounds.

Northern California: The Bay area

The San Francisco Bay area enjoys a well-deserved reputation for strong winds and boisterous sailing. Perhaps this has discouraged bareboating, for chartering is very new to the bay. This is surprising, since both the bay itself and the Sacramento Delta that opens into it offer some fine sailing and excellent gunkholing. The rivers and channels of the delta are a world of their own, perhaps best explored in a houseboat chartered from Sacramento or Stockton. Chartering the delta under sail can be fun for a while, but you get tired of running one way and beating back or motoring the other (back to the bay). Unless you are into powerboating, you are better off sailing on the bay itself.

San Francisco Bay has a surface area of 420,000 square miles bounded by a huge metropolitan sprawl. Here the tides pull the water one way, the configurations of the coastline another. The Pacific weather and waters pour through the narrow defile of the Golden Gate. Sailing under the red span of the Golden Gate Bridge is a unique experience. I have drifted under the bridge with 5 knots of wind in thick fog, to find myself screaming along at 8 knots in bright sunshine a few moments later. Savor the moment of passing under the bridge. It really is the gateway to a continent.

This is a cruising ground for a short charter, even a long weekend to explore Angel Island or Sausalito. Equip yourself with a robust yacht, preferably a 30-to-40-footer, and plan for wet, hard sailing. It is possible to sail the bay the easy way, savoring the quiet morning hours and warm anchorages. But there are those charterers who cannot resist the call of the wild and windy. In the summer months, the afternoon westerlies funnel through the Golden Gate in a boisterous celebration of turbulent sailing that can teach you more about boathandling in a few hours than weeks on end puttering around Southern California or the Chesapeake. I sometimes go sailing in the bay simply to keep myself honest, my reactions in top fettle, and the rigging of my boat tuned for tough conditions. This is the place where I would charter to sail, sail, sail, a place where anchorages and marinas are secondary to enjoying the boat and the water. Of course, you can explore San Francisco itself and the boutiques of Sausalito or Berkeley. But charter here to spend long hours on the water, like the skipper of a 35-footer I anchored next to under the lee of Angel Island. He was a 50-year-old Chicago attorney, on the fourth day of a brief charter at the end of a business trip. His face was wind-burned, and his crew, three younger colleagues, were as lean and fit as he was. "Where have you been?" I asked, for they were to turn in the boat next morning. "Nowhere," replied the skipper with glee. "I do this every year when a case brings me out here. We sail our hearts out, so we don't forget what the ocean's like. Why stay at anchor when you have all this marvelous wind!" They were up at dawn the next morning and drifted away into the grey for a last run before the real

Aloha 34 in San Francisco Bay. This Canadian-built design is an easily handled charter boat for four to six people. It is popular in the Great Lakes area and can be chartered in the Bay. A lightweight four-cylinder diesel gives you 6 knots, but the yacht's overall performance in all weather conditions makes it especially suitable for small charter crews. Below, the galley and navigation station are especially well thought out.

world embraced them again. Enough said. Charter in the bay to sail and to celebrate the joys of strong winds and stout craft.

Pacific Northwest

Many people think of the Pacific Northwest as a place of fir trees, grey skies, and perennial rain. Yes, it can rain or drizzle for days on end, but much of the precipitation falls between November and March. Some sailors cruise year round in these waters, but the charter season is between May and October, when temperatures are warmer, reaching 90 degrees upon occasion. There is nothing like high summer in the Pacific Northwest—calm seas, brilliant blue skies, and day after day of light winds and peaceful anchorages. You may end up using your motor more than you like, but the environment offers so many compensations that it does not seem to matter. Some of the best cruising can be had in spring and fall. You may encounter some rain, but the crisp, clear days make up for the wet ones.

Most U.S. charterers bareboat out of Anacortes, a

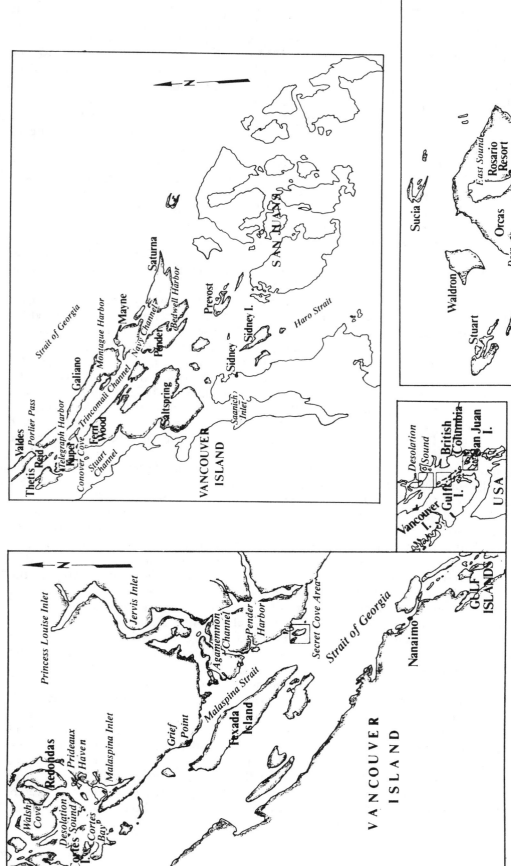

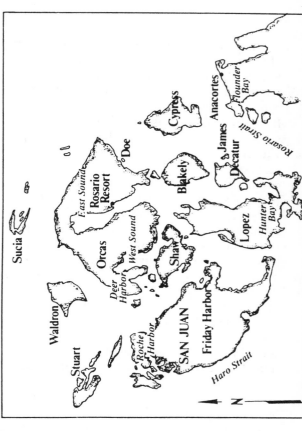

San Juan and Gulf Islands, with Desolation Sound

town of 7,000 people a little over an hour's drive north of Seattle. Anacortes is easy to reach. You can fly into Seattle-Tacoma Airport, rent a car there, and leave it at a rental office near your boat. The largest bareboat companies in the Northwest manage sizable charter fleets from Anacortes, many of them powerboats, for summer winds tend to be light here. You have an almost unlimited choice of sail or powerboats. There are Grand Banks and other well-known trawler designs, or you can charter sailboats ranging from a 28-foot San Juan to a Cal 46 or even larger. For this particular cruising ground, I would recommend a yacht in the 35-to-40-foot range with a powerful engine to get you to port in summer calms. All the charter boats come with a more or less standard inventory, but you are expected to bring your own bedding and do your own provisioning. Anacortes has several good supermarkets, so stocking up is a breeze.

Canadian charterers can base themselves on Vancouver Island, close to the magnificent anchorages of the Gulf Islands. Canadian fleets also contain a wide mix of yachts, but C&Cs tend to be the most common charter yachts here.

The Pacific Northwest climate is far from extreme, but there are marked seasons. Winter winds blow mainly from the southeast to southwest, often with considerable strength. Most of the annual rainfall occurs during the winter months, with gales blowing as often as four to six times a month. I would not recommend a newcomer's trying to charter during the winter. Better to wait for the more settled conditions between April and September. The summer winds are lighter and tend to blow from the southwest through northwest, around the Pacific high. As the mainland heats up, sea breezes are sucked into the Juan de Fuca Strait between Vancouver Island and the Olympia Peninsula. The normal settled weather pattern brings calms and light land breezes in the evening, night, and early morning hours. The sea breeze fills in during the morning and can reach about 15 knots, sometimes more, in the afternoon. A wind shift to the southeast normally portends rain and changeable weather. You will probably enjoy settled weather during a summer charter, with northwesterly breezes prevailing in the Gulf Islands, westerlies in the San Juans. You can get quite strong winds upon occasion, but are more likely to complain of light airs during the summer. Some of the best sailing of the year can be enjoyed during the spring—a bad time for clams, if you have a passion for seafood, but superb if you like anchorages to yourself and good hard sails from island to island. The high charter season in the Pacific Northwest is between Memorial and Labor Days, so I would try to cruise the

San Juans or Gulf Islands just before or after the crowded season. You may have stronger winds, but certainly fewer neighbors to contend with.

Whatever month you charter in the Northwest, you may encounter fog or rain. Fog is especially hazardous in these strongly tidal and well-traveled waters. Your only protection against fog is to remain at anchor when visibility is restricted. To attempt a crossing of, say, the Rosario Strait during a fog is to invite disaster. The fog often lifts during the afternoon, so you enjoy a few hours' clear visibility that takes you from port to port. Personally, I enjoy sailing in the rain, perhaps because it rains so rarely in my home waters. Whatever your preference, be sure to take along good foul-weather gear and rubber boots for those occasional rainy days. I have been lucky with mosquitoes in these waters, but everyone recommends that you take along repellent during the summer months. Insects are another reason I prefer to sail here in the spring or fall.

Anacortes is a superb base for a San Juan or Gulf Islands charter. Many charterers go even farther afield and cross the Strait of Georgia to Desolation Sound. The largest charter fleet is based on Flounder Bay at the north end of Burrows Bay, an ideal location for passagemaking across to the San Juans only a few miles away. You can see a great deal of the San Juans or Gulf Islands in a week, but will need a full two weeks to go all the way to Desolation Sound on mainland British Columbia. If you can manage it, take even longer. The extra days will make all the difference.

The most formidable part of a San Juans charter is the passage across Rosario Strait. It's only about 10 nautical miles across the strait, but there are complications. The first is the tides, which run strongly through the strait. You must shape your course to allow for the stream. In good visibility, you can steer for, say, James Island and adjust your course as you near the islands. On a first crossing, I would strongly advise you to stay on the mainland if there is any fog whatsoever. The Rosario Strait is no place to be caught out in thick fog, as a glance at the chart will tell you. There are not only rocks, but ships as well, the second major hazard of these waters. The Strait of Juan de Fuca Traffic Separation Scheme takes merchant ships through the middle of the strait in all weathers. Even on a clear day, you have to keep a weather eye out for ships, so that you can keep out of their way. All of this sounds very forbidding, but the passage is normally enjoyable and straightforward, provided you keep close tabs on where you are at all times. As you cross the strait, keep a sharp eye out for floating logs, a constant hazard in these waters. The most dangerous are "deadheads," water-logged tree trunks that have become separated from

Friday Harbor, San Juan Islands. (Steve Hilson)

logging rafts and float in a vertical position, with only their tips appearing above the water.

The San Juans are the sort of cruising ground that one returns to again and again. There are no less than 11 state parks in the islands, all of them accessible from your yacht. The Spencer Spit State Park is just over 10 miles from Anacortes, through the deep waters of the Thatcher Pass. You can anchor or pick up a mooring here, sheltered by the sand spit that extends out toward Frost Island. This is a busy place during the summer, but the saltwater lagoon trapped by the spit is a paradise for tiny marine animals. The park swarms with rabbits, which like playing in the moonlight, a memorable and extraordinary sight. Having spent the night here, you can sail out to the moorings and landing dock on the west side of James Island 3 miles away, right on the edge

of the Rosario Strait. The tidal streams run strong here, so an overnight stay can be bumpy. This is a place to enjoy a short hike among pines, with rabbits almost underfoot and a fine view over the islands and strait.

You will soon realize that a formal cruise plan makes no sense in these islands. There are literally dozens of anchorages within an hour's sail of your last stop, so why not plan to linger everywhere? However, I would recommend some longer passages in the first few days, so that you can putter on your way back instead of rushing the last few days. If you are bound farther afield to Victoria or the Gulf Islands, best do your mileage early in the charter, so that you have lots of short passages against the prevailing southwesterly winds. A good itinerary for longer charters would take you up to Doe Island Marine Park on the eastern shore of Orcas

Island, where you can anchor or moor near several small beaches joined by a trail. This puts you in a good position to take off for destinations like Sucia Island or Bedwell Harbor in the Gulf Islands the next day.

Most charterers make their way to Friday Harbor on San Juan Island very early on in their cruise. If you are Canada-bound or returning from Canadian waters, this is a port of entry in the islands, so you may have to stop anyway. Friday Harbor is busy, crowded, and often overrun with tourists. The town occupies the west side of the bay protected by Brown Island, on the west side of the San Juan Channel. Floats "B" and "F" are the visitor docks in the small craft harbor, but they are likely to be crowded in high season. Fortunately, there is an excellent anchorage in Park's Bay on Shaw Island across the San Juan Channel. So you can visit town for a few hours, then enjoy peace and quiet elsewhere. The harbor is straightforward of approach, but look out for the strong tidal streams when berthing. The University of Washington Oceanographic Laboratory is the big attraction here, for you can see all sorts of small creatures up close. A few hours spent enjoying the public displays will make you appreciate the more remote marine parks even more.

While some people circumnavigate San Juan Island for the fun of it, I would explore the more sheltered eastern shore and leave the other coast to the fishermen. Roche Harbor on the northwest coast is a popular resort with the locals. The entrance from the northeast is between Pearl and Henry Islands, leading to a land-locked haven with ample anchorage space in almost any weather. Narrow Mosquito Pass leads southwest from Roche Harbor to the west coast of San Juan Island, but is recommended only for those with local knowledge. Roche is an ideal place to spend several days, an excellent bad-weather refuge and a good stopping-off point for clearing to Canada.

Roche Harbor itself was once the site of the largest lime quarry west of the Mississippi. You can still see traces of the quarry operation. The village is now a tourist resort centered on the Hotel de Haro, built by John McMillin in 1886. The hotel is a superbly mellow hostelry, now a first-class resort. You can berth in a slip near the resort or anchor off in complete shelter in about 20 feet. Roche Harbor is a mass of flowers; the McMillin Mausoleum nearby is a strange symphony of columns, benches, and stone crypts. There are anchorages galore near Roche, too, among them Garrison Bay, where the British built a fort during a long simmering border dispute with the Americans that almost erupted in war when an American shot a British pig on the island in 1859. It was not until 1872 that the Emperor of Germany mediated the dispute and decreed that the Canada–U.S. border lay through the Haro Strait north of the San Juans. You can visit some of the original barracks and blockhouse buildings from the anchorage, but be careful about setting your anchor in the strong tidal streams.

Roche Harbor is a short sail away from Stuart Island, where two anchorages offer excellent shelter. Reid Harbor on the south side is an Underwater Marine Recreation Area that caters to divers. Be sure to enter Prevost Harbor by the western entrance. Once inside, the shelter is excellent and the clams are said to be outstanding. I enjoyed walking ashore here; you can look down on the island anchorages from higher ground.

Once you have visited Roche Harbor, you can either clear for Canada or steer northeast to the many anchorages of Orcas Island, a mountainous, wooded island whose southern coast is deeply indented. A comfortable itinerary takes you through the islands that protect the western entrance of Harney Channel and into West Sound. You can lie alongside at West Sound village or anchor off, but I prefer to explore the nooks and crannies on the west side of the sound. There are islands with gruesome names: Skull, Victim, even Massacre Bay, all memories of Haida Indian slave wars of past centuries. This is one of those places where you can have an island all to yourself and anchor off in complete solitude. Deer Harbor, immediately to the west of West Sound, can be reached through the narrow Pole Pass inside Crane Island. Deer is very popular in the summer, with 30 feet close to shore at the head of the bay. In both these sounds, look out for brisk westerlies funneling up the bay in the afternoon. This by no means exhausts the anchorages on Orcas, since the whole of East Sound, with its several resorts, lies just a short distance east through Harney Channel. Many charterers speak highly of Rosario Resort on the east side of the sound. You need to call ahead if you want a mooring or reservations for dinner. The resort was once an estate, run from a mansion with thick concrete walls. The evening pipe organ concert in the library is not to be missed.

The San Juans cruising ground has something for just about anyone. If you have the time, for example, plan on sailing through President Channel to Sucia and Matia Islands, both state parks with fascinating rock formations and wildlife. Matia is a wildlife preserve, with fine-weather anchorages off the western end. But I would plan to spend the night in Fossil or Echo Bay on the east side of Sucia in westerly weather. You can pick up a mooring or lie off the beach in about 25 feet (sand) in Echo, choosing a different place every time you visit.

Be careful of local currents that can set you onto the rocks around here. The quiet bays of Sucia were once hideaways for smugglers carrying Chinese laborers, opium, and other contraband between Canada and the United States. If you like cod or rockfish, this is a good place to catch them.

Most first-time charterers to the San Juans never leave the islands, but it is very easy to visit Canadian waters, provided you follow the correct (and straightforward) customs procedures at both ends. Your charter company will brief you on the regulations. Many people head for Victoria and spend several days savoring its varied delights, among them the British Columbia Provincial Museum, which is surely among the best in the world. Do not miss the totem poles and the Indian exhibits. Except for constant ferry and steamer traffic, Victoria is easy to approach, so we will pass it by here and head for the Gulf Islands, which extend from the northern side of the Haro Strait as far north as Nanaimo in the lee of Vancouver Island.

The Gulf Islands offer an almost unlimited choice of anchorages for the charterer. The best anchorages are to be found in the coves where government docks are provided for the use of local residents and fishermen. You can lie alongside these docks if your draft will permit, but the most popular coves tend to be crowded in high season and you may have to anchor off. Try to avoid those anchorages that are exposed to ferry wash from the steamers that pass to and from Vancouver to such ports as Swartz Bay and Nanaimo, otherwise you will roll and toss all day. The tides run strongly in the narrower passes, and you should try to navigate these as close to slack water as possible. The offshore islands are especially interesting, despite the scarcity of anchorages, for you can hike for miles along the shore and enjoy magnificent views across the Strait of Georgia. Plan to take along large-scale topographic maps of the major islands with you. You can obtain these from the British Columbia Provincial Government Map Sales Office, Room 111, 553 Superior Street, Victoria, B.C., Canada.

Sailing conditions are very similar to those in the San Juans, with the exception that there will be more north in the winds in the summer months. It can be very calm here in late summer, so you may find yourself motoring many miles. A dinghy is essential in these waters, for many fascinating bays are not accessible to deep-draft yachts.

The southernmost Gulf Islands are considered by many people to be the most beautiful of the entire archipelago. They are still sparsely populated, with occasional farmhouses and only a few major resorts. You must clear customs at Bedwell Harbor Resort on South Pender Island, which is a good base for exploring the neighboring islands. This is where you should buy your fishing license, too. My favorite southern island is Saturna, named after the Spanish ship *Saturnina* in 1791. Hundreds of yachts descend on Saturna Beach south of Breezy Bay every July 1 for the annual Dominion Day lamb barbecue. Join the party if you are in the islands at the right time. I also enjoy exploring the anchorages between Mayne and Saturna Islands, especially Irish Bay on Samuel Island, where you can lie comfortably in 20 feet in the southeast corner. The tidal streams run at speeds of up to 5 knots around here, so be careful and play your tides.

Most of the marinas serving the greater Victoria area are to be found in the Tsehum Harbor area, on the Saanich Peninsula of Vancouver Island. Some Canadian charter companies operate from these ports, but American charterers are probably better off heading farther north into the islands. It would be foolish to suggest possible itineraries. Rather, it is a question of finding several suitable bases and exploring the areas around them. If you enter at Bedwell, I would suggest sailing north along the outer islands, then turning south to explore the waters close to Vancouver Island. There is no particular logic for doing this; indeed, the charm of this cruising ground is that you can just follow your nose.

Bound north from Mayne Island through Navy Channel, you should avoid Active Pass, where the tides can run at 8 knots during springs and the ferry and ship traffic is unceasing. Many people stop at Montague Harbor Marine Park on the inside of Galiano Island. The bay in which the park lies is sheltered by Parker Island, but is very busy with ferries and motorboats during the summer. There is a small marina and anchorage off the park and in two small coves at the north end of Parker Island, which are quieter. I think you may be better off in the superb sheltered anchorage in Glenthorne Passage on the west side of Prevost Island, but enter from the north end—the western pass is too shallow. This is a quiet spot, far from commercial marinas and ferry traffic, but you will probably have neighbors in high season.

After a night at Glenthorne, prepare for a longer day, as you sail through the wide Trincomali Channel to Telegraph Harbor, regarded by many sailors as the safest anchorage in the Gulf Islands. Kuper and Thetis Islands, named after a British frigate and her captain, lie opposite Porlier Pass, where spring tides run at 9 knots through a rock-infested passage between the outer islands. Kuper is an Indian reservation, with a conspicuous school building complete with aluminum cupola that you can see from a long distance off when

Montague Island, Gulf Islands, B.C. (Steve Hilson)

approaching Telegraph Harbor. The harbor is entered through a dredged boat channel and offers completely sheltered anchorage as well as two marinas. However, it can become very crowded during July and August, in which case you may be better off anchoring in any one of the fine-weather anchorages within easy reach.

You can sail all the way up to Nanaimo or beyond if you wish, but most Gulf Islands charterers will probably turn around in this area and head back south by a different route. Parts of Saltspring Island are well worth exploring. Saltspring is the largest Gulf Island and was first settled by blacks escaping from slavery in the U.S. during the 1850s. Most of them settled at Fernwood on the east coast, just south of Wallace Island, where you can find a superb anchorage in Conover Cove in 30 feet or more. Most visitors to Saltspring spend a night at Ganges, a small town named after the last sailing ship-of-the-line, where several marinas are to be found. Alternately, sail down Stuart Channel on the west side of Saltspring, stopping off to explore Booth Inlet and Maple Bay, where you can

swim off the beach. This is a busy place, and you are better off going down to Sidney Spit Marine Park off the island of that name. Only the early birds will find a vacant mooring here or off the town. Fortunately, the summer months are very calm here, so you can probably anchor off safely. From either Ganges or Sidney you are a day and a half from Anacortes through the San Juans, but remember you have to clear customs at Roche or Friday Harbor.

More and more charterers take the time to sail north to Desolation Sound on the British Columbia mainland. You will cover quite a lot of miles on this charter, so you should allow three weeks under sail, at least two in a powerboat. The effort is worth it. Desolation Sound is surrounded by 10,000-foot mountains. In 1973 the Provincial Government created a large marine park on the west side of the sound that extends from Prideaux Haven to the Gifford Peninsula. The charter companies that allow you to sail to Desolation recommend that you spend some time planning your cruise before you arrive. Here are some suggestions as to itinerary. Sail

Princess Louise Inlet, B.C. (Bill Berssen, Pacific Boating Almanac)

hard the first three days, stopping at, say, the Sucia Islands the first night, then clearing into Canada at Bedwell Resort before sailing on to Nanaimo that evening. Here I would spend the night in the marina and stock up on fuel, water, and provisions. Day three should take you across the Strait of Georgia, a 25-mile passage to the Secret Cove area. Local experts say that you are best off crossing in the early morning before the wind kicks up. The tides in the strait can attain speeds of 3 knots, but the winds will probably be from the northwest and stronger in the afternoons. Whatever you do, monitor the weather forecasts carefully. The Strait of Georgia is no place to be in a gale.

Now you can slow down and explore the mainland. Take your time, for this is some of the most scenic cruising you will ever come across. Secret Cove is really several different coves, with a number of marinas. I prefer to anchor off Smuggler Cove Marine Park at the north end of Welcome Passage, where there is excellent shelter in almost any weather. Just look out for the reefs at the entrance. The next days, when you run up the Agamemnon Channel to Egmont and then on to Princess Louise Inlet, are real highlights. Egmont offers marina accommodations or a government float, but most importantly fuel, since the passage to Princess Louise Inlet is 40 miles each way. The Sechelt Rapids are an extraordinary sight, especially when the current is flowing most strongly. You can walk to them from Egmont. The passage inland is one of the most spectacular sailboat rides I have ever taken. The scenery is fjordlike, with Jervis Inlet divided into three reaches, each named after a member of the British royal family. You have to time this passage carefully to arrive off Malibu Rapids at the entrance to Princess Louise Inlet at or near slack water. A large-scale chart is essential, but the passage is simple enough unless there are white-water overfalls. The marine park at the head of Princess Louise is 4 miles from the narrows. You anchor at the foot of the 120-foot waterfall, whose roaring mesmerizes you in the calm of evening. Of course, there's a trail ashore so you can explore the falls more closely.

This is only the beginning. A couple of long days will take you back the way you came and out into the strait through Jervis Inlet. After a night at Grief Point Resort or the government docks at Westview, you pass through the Copeland Islands and round the Malaspina Peninsula. On a clear day, the mountains open up in front of you, ringing Desolation Sound in snow-capped magnificence. The large-scale chart of Malaspina Inlet will take you into sheltered waters and the anchorage at Grace Harbor or Isabel Cove on the east side of the inlet. This is a fine place for oyster lovers.

The next few days will be scenic magic. The Prideaux Haven area is a jigsaw puzzle of islands, anchorages, and unspoiled corners. You can anchor in many places, provided you allow for the tidal range. Melanie and Laura Coves are the most popular. The water temperatures are unusually warm here, partly because of shallow waters and partly because the islands prevent the warmer waters of the strait from mingling with the chilly ones of the Pacific, so you may swim in comfort. I would allow two to three days for exploring the Redonda and Cortes Island areas. Walsh Cove, on the west shore of the Waddington Channel, which separates the Redondas, is a fine anchorage. All you do is find a convenient "notch" in the edge of the cove, anchor, and take a line ashore. There are literally dozens of anchorages in this general area. You can find complete solitude or join a crowd of yachts, explore in your dinghy, fish, or just admire the scenery. Cortes Bay, at the south end of the island of that name, is a good stop on your way out of the sound. You can buy fuel and provisions here, before taking off down the coast to Pender Harbor or some other convenient jumping-off point for Vancouver Island. You can, of course, sail direct to Nanaimo from Desolation Sound, but there are 70 miles to cover. The passage home to Anacortes will take you back through the Gulf Islands and San Juans in two or three days. The landfall on the Gulf Islands can be tricky in bad visibility. You may be better off heading for Nanaimo before sailing inside the islands.

Some people call the Pacific Northwest the "Maine" of the Pacific. Some heretics even say they prefer it to those northeastern waters. You can spend a lifetime here without even scratching the surface of this charter area. The spectacular scenery alone beggars description.

15 Lake Superior

Although the Great Lakes are a major sailing area, bareboating is still a relative newcomer to these waters. This is partly because of a short sailing season and also because cruising has only recently become a popular sport in the Midwest. The aggressive marketing campaigns of Caribbean charter companies have opened many prospective sailors' eyes to cruising near home. So things are changing in the 1980s. Every season sees a new company or two starting up a small fleet on one side or the other of the lakes, so you should be able to find something to sail in many large harbors. Rather than be comprehensive in my coverage of all these opportunities, I focus on Lake Superior, where the largest and most successful bareboat fleets are to be found. Since the Midwest has a large population of neophyte sailors, these operations cater to everyone from experts to complete beginners.

The Apostle Islands

If I were asked for the perfect charter area for complete beginners, I would recommend the remote and hauntingly beautiful Apostle Islands of Lake Superior above all others. "Lake Superior," most potential charterers may shrug. "Isn't the lake too cold?" Yes, the Chippewa Indians' Big Sea Water does indeed have a reputation for winter gales and ferocious thunder squalls, but most of the bad weather falls between October and April. The summer months are so pleasant that the Apostles have become a major charter area for Midwesterners. They are also home waters for the largest bareboat fleet in U.S. waters.

You may have to consult a map to find out where the Apostles are, for they are far off the beaten track. The 22 low, forested islands lie off the southern shore of Lake Superior and were named after the Apostles by early French trappers. Once the site of prosperous fishing and lumber industries, they are now a quiet vacation backwater where people come to camp, fish, cross-country ski, and increasingly to sail.

Most people drive from the airport at Minneapolis-St. Paul to Lake Superior. The drive north through rolling farm country to the Duluth area takes about three hours. Your yacht will be based at either Superior,

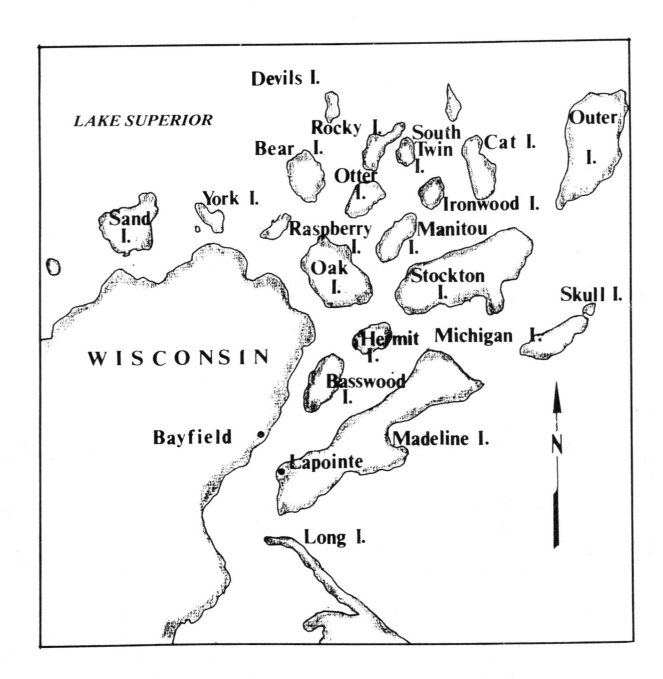

Apostle Islands, Lake Superior

Wisconsin, or at the small town of Bayfield along the lakeshore to the east. Organized sailing is relatively new here; chartering is even newer, a phenomenon of the last decade or so. You will have to look closely in the charter columns of the sailing magazines to find out about companies operating on Lake Superior. They advertise more in Midwest newspapers and local markets.

Lake Superior chartering was the brainchild of a yacht broker named Jack Culley, who now operates one of the largest bareboat companies in North America. Culley realized long ago that the short sailing season on Lake Superior makes owning a sailboat an expensive proposition. So he made the charter option a major element in his brokerage business, placing his clients' yachts in charter so that they could enjoy substantial tax advantages. The new yachts are supplied with a comprehensive standard inventory and are managed by the company on a percentage basis. Since the owners are also clients, there are obvious incentives for the company and the owners to keep the boats in immaculate condition. And immaculate they are. This is due in part to a freshwater environment and lighter use, but also to meticulous maintenance schedules.

At the same time he started a charter operation, Culley studied his potential charter market. He found that most of his clients would come from major metropolitan areas like Chicago, Milwaukee, and Minneapolis, people with an interest in sailing who had never had the chance to go out on a big boat before. So Sailboats Inc. developed a complete certification program to qualify these beginners for chartering. Their basic certification course of eight hours' classroom instruction and two days' actual sailing is one of the best I have ever seen. That it works well seems unquestionable. The company has few accidents on its record and an impressive roster of repeat clients and satisfied owners who began as complete beginners. Dick Caswell, the vice-president in charge of training, told me that the secret was a highly structured curriculum that emphasizes boathandling and anchoring, and rigorous instructor certification. The company also offers a sophisticated advanced cruising curriculum that involves a 100-mile overnight passage across the lake to Isle Royale National Park in Canada.

The advantages of Sailboats' charter system—it is nothing less than that—are obvious. Newcomers to cruising can take a basic course attuned to the local charter area, then go off on their own in sheltered waters, returning again and again until their skills are sufficient for them to graduate to more advanced areas like the Virgins. The advantages to the company are obvious. They can draw on a far wider market of

prospective charterers than most companies, monitor their qualifications as they become more expert, and maybe one day sell them a yacht. Many of Sailboats' customers are repeat charterers, so the concept obviously works. The company has expanded. Sailboats now maintains charter fleets of Canadian-built C&Cs at Superior, Bayfield, and Marinette, Wisconsin, on Lake Michigan's Green Bay. They have recently expanded in a modest way into Florida, maintaining a small operation at Longboat Key on the west coast. Without question, this company is riding the wave of the bareboat future. The same concept is bound to expand into other charter areas.

You can charter from the marinas at Superior, Wisconsin, close to Duluth, but it will take you a day or more to sail to the Apostles. It's more fun to drive 60 miles east and base yourself on Bayfield, a pretty little lakeside town close to the Apostle Islands National Lakeshore, where most Lake Superior sailors congregate. Bayfield was a prosperous lumber, quarry, and fishing town in the 1880s, but has slumbered quietly for most of this century. It is now enjoying a mild resurgence as a tourist resort and artists' colony. But the attractions for sailors are the modern refuge harbor and the tree-covered islands lying close offshore.

Lake Superior is one of the largest bodies of fresh water in the world and, for all practical purposes, must be treated like open ocean. The waters are cold, and the weather can be extremely changeable. Sometimes these changes can be spotted in advance, when dark clouds or a squall line appears to windward. At other times, the wind will strengthen out of a clear sky and you can easily be caught unawares. Generally, however, summer weather on Lake Superior is calm and predictable. Northeasterly winds prevail between May and August, with morning calms building to an average of 10 to 12 knots in the afternoons and dying away at sunset. The winds are so reliable around here that the charter companies equip their boats with lightweight genoas, something rare in my experience. You will use the genoa most of the time. A 40-year plot of storm occurrences shows a negligible percentage hitting the Apostles during the summer months, so you are almost certain to have fine weather, except for the occasional thunderstorm and some early morning fog. You can monitor weather conditions by listening to the marine weather reports for western Lake Superior, but be aware that local conditions in the Apostles may be considerably different. The National Park Service headquarters in Bayfield may also be able to give you up-to-date local weather information.

The peak charter season in the Apostles is between Memorial and Labor Days. These are the months of

Charter fleet at Bayfield. (Lesley Newhart)

light winds and calm conditions. I chartered the Apostle Islands in mid-September, after the summer rush. The weather was ideal: not too hot, not too cold, with a slight crispness in the air that spoke of fall. We had rain and some strong winds, but no mosquitoes and plenty of space to anchor. This may be the best time of all to charter in the Apostles. Although people sail here into October, a late fall charter is probably a gamble in terms of the weather.

Sailboats Inc.'s fleet is made up entirely of C&Cs, performance yachts that sail unusually fast for charter boats. I think they are ideal for Great Lake conditions. They track well in light air, are seakindly and extremely comfortable below. Other designs are available from competing companies, if you prefer them, but the C&C has the great merit of being fast in moderate to light air. Most charterers ship out on a yacht in the 30-foot range here. This size is ideal for local conditions, enabling you to come alongside island docks, anchor in relatively shallow water, and yet sail well in prevailing conditions. We chartered a 27-footer, which was superb for two people, but a little small for a family.

The most important thing to realize about Lake Superior is that the lake waters are very cold, even at the end of the summer. Whether you fall overboard or merely get wet, remember that the water and wind will cool your body temperature fast. Hypothermia will kill you in 55-degree water in two hours or so, even if you are wearing a life jacket. So take plenty of warm clothes, even in the height of summer, and practice your man-overboard drills. Otherwise, take the normal sailing gear for a warm-weather charter. Don't forget to pack some mosquito repellent. The bugs can be savage in the Apostles during the warm months.

The Apostle Islands are so close together that any sort of formal cruise plan is a complete waste of time. I would spend the first couple of days sailing through the islands getting a general feel for the environment. Our first day was a still, grey afternoon. We drifted away from Bayfield through the West Channel, which took us from the cozy harbor past Basswood Island and close to the densely forested shores of Oak Island. The highest of the islands, Oak is covered with dense hardwood forests that were logged during the nineteenth and early twentieth centuries. Two hundred years ago, Oak Island was the lair of a notorious but short-lived band of pirates who named themselves the Twelve Apostles. Today, the Park Service maintains a dock, campsite, and trails on the island. You can anchor close offshore and explore the forests.

The wind strengthened slightly as we sailed north toward the outer limits of the islands. Grey clouds and brilliant blues alternated as we pursued our course from tree-lined shore to ice-carved cliff. The Apostles are a compact cruising ground that can be sailed from one end to the other in the course of a day. We tacked between a jigsaw of islets, sighted Devil's Island with its remote lighthouse—the northernmost point of land in Wisconsin—and raced two other C&Cs eastward to the pier off South Twin Island, a favorite stopping place for Apostle charterers. This is a charming place for hiking, birdwatching (the loons are famous here), or simply swimming and talking to your neighbors. We found ourselves secured alongside delightful neighbors, families from Minneapolis who were taking a last-minute vacation before winter set in.

The wind came in from the west next morning, so we cleared out in a hurry and headed southeast to the fine anchorage on the south side of Stockton Island. We beat to our anchorage against a steadily increasing wind, found shelter under the cliffs near the pier, and explored ashore. People have lived on Stockton Island during the summers for more than 3,000 years, fishing for trout and gathering blueberries in season. Today, it is a popular camping area, with fine nature trails that lead through majestic pines and birches. We made our way over a carpet of forest flowers and through shrubs, the light filtering through the trees, sun and clouds far overhead. If you are lucky, you will sometimes see sandhill cranes, ducks, and geese, even an occasional pike in a quiet landlocked pond. We had the forest all to ourselves, and the only sound was the constant swishing of the branches in the strengthening wind.

This anchorage can be bumpy when the westerlies blow in the fall. But you can find excellent shelter under the lee of Presque Isle Point in smooth water off a long sandy beach. This is a marvelous place to explore in the evening, a landscape of dunes, conifers, and thick forest. When we woke up here, there was a slight arctic bite in the air. In mid-September, winter was not far away in these northern latitudes.

In the Apostles, you never have to sail more than a few hours in any direction. Perhaps your longest sail will come when you explore Sand Island, at the western end of the Apostles. This is a low-lying island, with a wonderful carpet of wildflowers and moss. A pioneer village once flourished here, but it fell into decay when the fishing industry declined early in this century. The Sand Island lighthouse was first lit in September 1881 and is famous mainly because of the wreck of the 3,100-ton steamer *Sevona*, which broke up in mountainous seas a mile and a half northeast of the light in 1905. You can moor to the Park Service pier in East Bay or anchor off. It is also possible to lie on the other side of the island, but look out for submerged boulders.

From Sand Island, I would take passage west to explore the mainland shore. This is trickier than it sounds, for a sandbank links the island with the mainland, with depths of 5 to 30 feet. Use your depth sounder to traverse the shallows before heading inshore to the Apostle Islands National Lakeshore headquarters in Little Sand Bay. Here you can explore Hokenson Fishing Dock, the beginnings of an exhibit on Lake Superior fisheries, including a small museum. National Park Service personnel give tours of the museum several times during the day. I don't know that I would overnight here or at the Squaw Bay caves 3.5 miles southwest of Little Sand Bay, still on the mainland. Better to dock at the village of Cornucopia, 4 miles farther on, where you can eat cheaply ashore. The Squaw Bay caves extend along some 2 miles of the shoreline, some of the caverns carved up to 60 feet into the sandstone cliffs. You can visit some of them in your dinghy on a calm day. Although the water is deep inshore, post a lookout on the bows when feeling your way close to land.

No visit to the Apostles is complete without a sail to Madeline Island, the largest of the Apostles. Madeline is outside the Apostle Islands Park and is privately owned. We sailed there the morning after a front had gone through, bringing strong westerlies in its train. The seas had smoothed, the breeze dropped to a fluky 10 knots. It was now that our C&C came into its own, moving effortlessly to windward along the western shore of Madeline Island under a cloudless sky. The 15-mile passage to the marina at the southwest corner of the island took a mere three and a half hours against the wind. It was a pleasure to sail a charter yacht that was not only in immaculate condition and impeccably maintained, but also carried an inventory of jibs for charterers to play with. And how nice not to have to fuss with roller-furling jibs when the wind blew up! There is a small settlement on Madeline Island. La Pointe is a resort-retirement community with a handful of stores and boutiques, a museum, and a ferry landing. You can take your car across to the island on the ferry during the summer. Winter visitors drive their vehicles across the ice all the way from the mainland.

We were lucky enough to be able to look down on this charter area from a private plane. A cold front was advancing toward the islands as we took off from the Madeline Island airstrip. The scudding overcast brought somber shadows to the forests below us. The blue waters of the morning had given way to lowering greys and blacks that made us feel winter was on its way. We saw the Apostles as something special—a hospitable cruising ground still a part of the wilderness. If you are tired of congested anchorages and huge marinas, take a charter in the Apostle Islands. And if you are a beginner, this is *the* place to learn the skills and delights of bareboating.

16 The East Coast: The Chesapeake, the Northeast, and Maine

Chesapeake Bay

Chesapeake Bay is North America's largest bay, with a shoreline that extends over 6,000 miles at high water. One of the most celebrated cruising grounds in the United States, it has the great advantage of being readily accessible by air, road, and rail, so that you can plan a short charter here with ease. But try to plan at least a couple of weeks in these waters—they have a fascination all their own.

"The country is not mountainous not yet low but such pleasant plaine, hills and fertile valleyes, one prettily crossing on other...," wrote Captain John Smith in 1608. "The waters, Isles, and shoales are full of safe harbours for ships of warre or marchandise, for boats of all sortes, for transportation or fishing," he added. Today, he would have to add yachts as well, for the Chesapeake's innumerable snug harbors and gunkholes cast a spell on the cruising sailor. At first glance, the Chesapeake looks like an uninterrupted body of water. Then you notice a large creek, follow it, come upon a smaller one, thread your way through mudflats,

and discover the snuggest coves and swatchways imaginable around every corner. Even cruising guide authors, the most persistent of anchorage searchers, give up when they come to the Chesapeake. One of them quotes an early cruising man, who remarked that the bay was like the deck plan of an octopus. The opportunities for bareboating on this remarkable stretch of water are absolutely unlimited. You could spend a lifetime chartering here and still have more to discover—around the next bend.

The Chesapeake extends about 170 miles from its Atlantic entrance between Capes Charles and Henry to the Delaware Canal. At least 40 rivers drain into the bay, most of them navigable. You approach important seaports like Baltimore or Norfolk through the Chesapeake and visit Washington, D.C., by cruising up the Potomac. This is an area of great cities and major industrial parks, of highrises and suburbia, too. But it is also farms and villages, swamp and tree-lined shore, where people still wrest a living from the ocean. Even today, you can see sailing skipjacks, crabbing skiffs, bugeyes, sailing canoes, and push boats, for this is

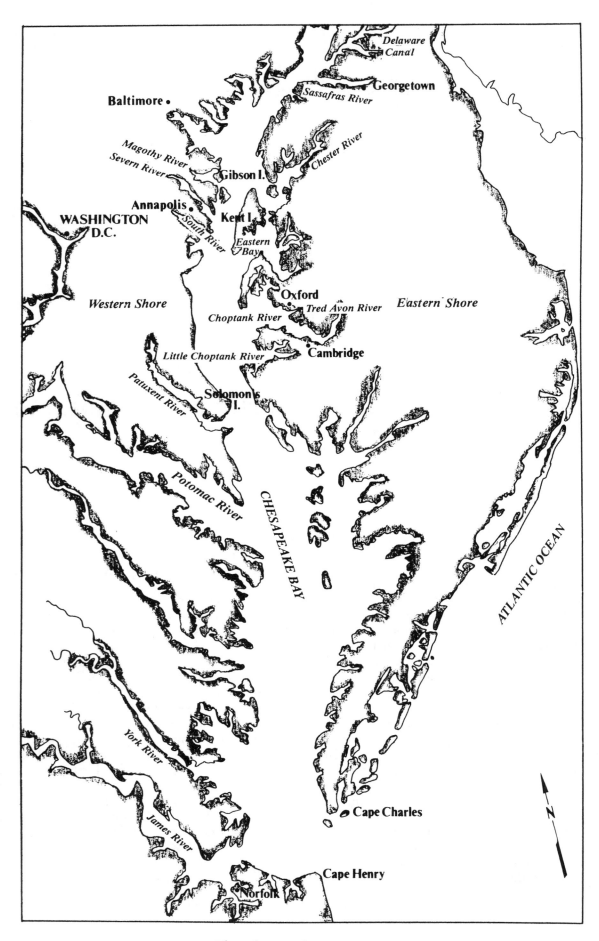

The Chesapeake

where oysters are still gathered under sail. Many tidewater people still make their living by farming, taking to the waters of the bay during the crabbing, oyster, and fishing seasons.

Bareboating is a new industry on the Chesapeake and therefore still relatively undeveloped. As with most charter fleets in the United States, the Chesapeake's yachts are individually owned and managed by a charterer. The major fleets are based on four Chesapeake ports: Annapolis, Georgetown, Norfolk, and Oxford. You can sometimes charter a yacht from an individual in these and other cities, but use caution. Be sure to check insurance coverage and the condition of the vessel before signing anything. Better to stick with the larger companies, who will be glad to give you bank references and the names of clients you can talk with.

The chartering season on the Chesapeake extends from April to October, somewhat longer than in the Northeast. "The summer is hot as in Spaine," wrote Captain John Smith nearly four centuries ago. "The winter colde as in France or England. The heat of sommer is in June July and August, but commonly the coole breeses assuage the vehemencie of the heat." The main disadvantage of a summer cruise on the Chesapeake is the heat from June to August, when the prevailing winds are from the south and calms are frequent, especially at night. You can nonetheless encounter vicious, late-afternoon thunderstorms, with winds sometimes reaching 60 knots or more for brief periods. I vastly prefer sailing the Chesapeake between mid-April and mid-June, and after September 15. The winds balance out between the northern and southern quadrants, there are few mosquitoes or flies, and you will find less congestion in popular anchorages. The fall is perhaps the best of all, with the reds and oranges of the changing leaves matching the brilliant autumn sunsets as you lie quietly at anchor in a deserted creek. However, if you prefer hot weather, by all means charter in the height of summer. Despite the heat and mosquitoes, the Chesapeake is delightful throughout the season, for the experienced skipper will soon learn how to anchor in narrow creeks where afternoon winds blow and to find cool places away from the stifling land.

Like the Bahamas, the Chesapeake is a shallow-water cruising ground. Many people believe that you spend all your time bumping from shoal to shoal. Nothing could be farther from the truth. There are at least 200 harbors and anchorages where you can berth a yacht with 6-foot draft. You have to ship out in a vessel drawing 3 or 4 feet to open up a significantly larger number of anchorages—and that will often limit you to a powerboat. The fact remains that even the most experienced sailors go aground in the Chesapeake more frequently than they do elsewhere. With so many tempting creeks, outlying shoals, and dredged channels, the chances for contact with the putty are legion. In many instances, all you have to do is push yourself off with a boathook or jump overboard and shove. These are waters like the east coast of England, where my venerable cruising friend always sails with a sounding pole aboard. A quick trip to the local lumberyard and a few moments with a felt pen will give you a navigational device that can be infinitely more valuable than any electronic depth sounder. Leave it behind at the end of the charter and the next skipper will bless you.

The Chesapeake charter companies offer a wide range of bareboats, ranging in size from 40 feet or more down to the mid-20-foot range. I suspect that the best size for these waters is about 30 to 35 feet, sufficiently large for comfortable sailing in open water, yet small enough to squeeze into narrow channels and anchorages. A large, airy cockpit and galley are essential in the hot summer months. As in the Apostle Islands, I enjoy the Chesapeake most with a small crew, perhaps just a couple. This is an intimate cruising ground, where you can drop out of sight for days on end, following your nose from creek to creek, occasionally emerging to eat dinner ashore or to buy provisions. My Chesapeake experiences have always been this way. When I want to party, I go to the Virgin Islands.

Planning a Chesapeake cruise is a nightmare the first time around, because there is so much to see and not enough time to savor it all. My advice is to plan several charters in these waters, changing charter base each time. People speak in terms of the Eastern and Western Shores, but you can zigzag between them and plan your cruise so that you rarely have to beat against the prevailing winds. A charter of a week to 10 days will allow you to cover quite a lot of ground, but I would work out only the most general of objectives ahead of time. Then study the prevailing weather conditions and shape your daily passages accordingly. For example, you might plan a cruise from Annapolis on the Western Shore to Oxford and Cambridge and the Choptank River on the Eastern. How do you get to the Choptank and back without a single mile of windward work? The answer is to play each day's passage by ear, zigzagging on your way and easing off to a convenient anchorage if the wind comes ahead or blows too strongly. Where else can you find a choice of anchorages and safe ports that allows you to cruise this way?

Long before you embark, make a wise investment

Annapolis is normally crowded, but well worth visiting for the charming old town and the Naval Academy. (Brian M. Fagan)

and buy William T. Stone and Fessenden S. Blanchard's *A Cruising Guide to the Chesapeake* (New York: Dodd, Mead, 1978). These gentlemen know the bay backward and forward; their sailing directions should never be far from your hands.

I think that the best base for a Chesapeake charter is Annapolis on the upper Western Shore. You are only a few hours' sailing from the best cruising waters of the Eastern Shore, a mere 14 miles to Gibson Island, one of the major yachting centers on the bay. The scenic and gunkholing delights of the Severn, South, and West Rivers are within easy reach. You could spend a busy week and never stray much more than 15 miles from base.

Annapolis itself is a crowded but charming historic town with narrow Colonial streets, home of the Naval Academy. Do not miss the Maryland State House, where George Washington surrendered his commission after the Continental Congress of 1784. The historic waterfront is being restored. While waiting for your charter boat, make a point of exploring the eighteenth-century Custom House and the City Dock on Market Square at the bottom of Main Street. You may complain about the crowded yacht facilities at Annapolis, but remember that the explosion in sailing has led to the revival of Annapolis's maritime past and to extensive historic preservation in town.

If you plan to stay on the Western Shore, try to spend your first day on the Severn River upstream of the town, for this is one of the finest rivers for upstream exploration in the entire bay. The shores are wooded and mostly unspoiled, while Round Bay, only 5 miles upstream, lets you enjoy open-water sailing in complete comfort even when it's blowing merry hell on the Chesapeake. Three blasts will open the bridge just above the Annapolis Yacht Club, except during rush hours. Motor through, set sail, and take your pick of the creeks that line the river, especially on the southwest shore. I prefer to make a beeline for Round Bay, where I spend some time getting used to the yacht before snuggling down for the night in Clements or Brewer Creek. Brewer is especially snug, which may make it stifling in hot weather.

South River lies just south of Annapolis and flows at such an angle that you can reach up and down it during the prevailing summer southerlies. This is a place to explore on weekdays; the river is very busy on weekends. The scenery is enjoyable, but the creeks that lie on both banks are the real attraction. My favorites are Church and Crab on the north bank, despite a rash of building in recent years. Both are easy to reach from the river, provided you navigate around the shoals at the entrance. There's a perfect 10-foot anchorage just inside Crab, in a small cove that opens up to port as you enter. If you're gregarious, join the crowd in Glebe Creek on the southwestern bank. Personally, I prefer more solitude.

You can cruise farther south on the upper Western Shore to explore Rhode or West Rivers and to eat some seafood at Galesville. But if you are heading south and are relatively short of time, do not miss the Patuxent River and Solomons Island. It's a comfortable day's passage south to the conspicuous high bluffs at the Patuxent mouth, with navigable waters for at least 40 miles upstream. Of course, if you want to break the journey, you can always slip across to the Choptank on the way. Solomons Island protects the Patuxent entrance—a low, flat islet connected to the mainland by a causeway. This is a busy little place, with well-equipped marinas and a great deal of summer traffic. You can usually anchor off or tie up to a slip to provision or enjoy a meal at Bowens Inn, but I would recommend moving across to Mill Creek for the night. This is the other arm of the harbor opposite the village. Thread your way up the channel past Olivet, hugging that shore until you can turn into any one of a number of completely sheltered anchorages. The cruising guide describes a number of quiet coves up the Patuxent. St. Laurence on the north shore of the river is one of the best, although it is being developed rapidly.

Many Annapolis charterers will head north from base to explore Gibson Island and the Magothy River. Gibson Harbor is a sailor's paradise, an attractive, completely sheltered place run by the Gibson Island Club, the parent organization of the Gibson Island Yacht Squadron. The entrance is intricate, but well marked. Once through the entrance channel, shape a course to pass east of the lighted beacon off the east end of Dobbins Island. Then alter course for the lighted beacons that show the harbor entrance. Privately maintained markers lead into the inner harbor. This is usually crowded, guest moorings are few, and you will probably end up anchoring in the cove immediately to starboard of the entrance. This is a marvelous, unspoiled base for exploring the Magothy creeks. Again, rely on the cruising guide for the best spots. One of my favorites is Forked Creek on the south shore, with about 5 feet in the entrance (it's deeper inside). Cattail Creek on the same shore is especially attractive and completely sheltered, but look out for the shoal off Focal Point.

Georgetown on the Sassafras River on the upper Eastern Shore offers some charter opportunities. Like Oxford on the Choptank, it's a good base for a 7-to-10-day cruise through the highlights of the Eastern Shore. You can explore the waters around Annapolis from here, too. The Sassafras was one of the many Chesapeake rivers explored by the formidable Captain John Smith in 1607–1609. There is a monument to him close to the town, which is located on a fine natural harbor within easy reach of Wilmington and Philadelphia. Many Chesapeake sailors regard the Sassafras as one of the bay's finest rivers, with attractive wooded scenery and opportunities to try out your gunkholing skills in Turner Creek 3 or 4 miles up the river.

The Chester River is a favorite destination for some Georgetown charterers. If you like exploring rivers, you have 26 miles of it here, as well as Queenstown, a pretty, unspoiled town with fine old houses. You can anchor off the town in complete shelter to obtain provisions before exploring farther upstream. The cruising guide will give you any number of options for the night. An interesting circular charter itinerary can take you as far south as the Chester River and across the bay to Annapolis, working your way up the Western Shore on the way home.

The Choptank first came to my notice when I read James Michener's blockbuster about the bay. It was no surprise to discover that it was a favorite cruising destination on the Chesapeake. The waters between the entrance and the city of Cambridge are among the best cruising on the bay. Although you can sail 45 miles up the river, the low-lying scenery above Cambridge is barely worth it. Most charterers come to the Choptank from Annapolis, reaching across the bay both ways. You can, however, bareboat from Oxford, a famous Colonial

Yacht under spinnaker: Light breeze on a Chesapeake afternoon. (Brian M. Fagan)

seaport before the American Revolution. This friendly, unspoiled town is, however, relatively inaccessible except by automobile off Interstate 50, 11 miles away. If you are visiting the port, plan on anchoring in Town Creek as far away from the congestion as you can.

Anyone chartering from Oxford should spend several days in the waters of the Choptank before sailing elsewhere. I would start by exploring the waters of the Tred Avon River that flows past Oxford, perhaps a good place to shake down before venturing farther afield. The scenery is less spectacular than that on, say, the Severn, but the cruising guide lists no less than eight anchorages in the 9 miles above Oxford. After one or two nights upstream, why not explore the creeks on the north shore of the Choptank, close to a proliferation of fine coves and anchorages protected by Tilghman Island. The cruising guide describes these fine spots in some detail, but don't miss Dun Cove, where you can lie in secluded shelter. The northern branch of the cove has 8 feet—once you have navigated through the shoals at the entrance. This is a favorite spot for yacht club cruises, and I would go elsewhere if a meet is in progress.

Cambridge lies on the south shore of the Choptank, the largest city on the river, but less appealing than Oxford to sailing folk because of the shallow water and commercial activity in Cambridge Creek itself. Most discerning charterers settle for Island Creek close to the entrance to the Tred Avon. There is 5 feet in the entrance, but the creek itself offers no less than four sheltered anchorages. La Trappe Creek just to the south is even more attractive for those who are nervous about shallow water. The entrance is marked by a conspicuous, black-lighted beacon that can be seen from some distance away. You can anchor behind a sandy spit to port of the entrance in 7 feet, or settle down in Saw Mill Cove, about halfway up the creek. Much of the shore is high and wooded. Best of all, your anchorage is an easy 4-mile walk from the stores in Cambridge.

Most Chesapeake chartering activity takes place in the upper bay, between the Choptank and Patuxent Rivers. It is possible to charter out of Norfolk, Virginia, where you can explore the James River and other historic waters. But for a first-time charter in these waters, I would recommend Annapolis or one of the other cozy charter bases up-bay.

The Northeast

The coastal waters between Long Island Sound and the Canadian border offer a bewildering array of charter vacations, mostly through small companies that manage a handful of yachts for absentee owners. Some of these boats are to be found in the Northeast in high season, in the Chesapeake in the fall, and as far south as Florida or the Caribbean during the winter months. The choice of vessels available for charter is quite extraordinary—everything from wonderfully finished Hinckleys to Taiwan-built 35-footers, standard fiberglass yachts of every size and shape, even cat ketches and tiny shoal cruisers. The choice of yachts is matched by the choice of cruising grounds, from gunkholing in deserted Maine bays to exploring the classic ports of Connecticut and Massachusetts. We can touch on only a few highlights here.

I must confess that I have never bareboated in these waters myself. But I have daysailed from several Connecticut ports and visited many of the places frequented by cruising people in these waters from the land, chart in hand. So this account relies heavily on the experience of others and on my notions of what a fun charter in these waters should be.

The first problem in chartering the Northeast is to

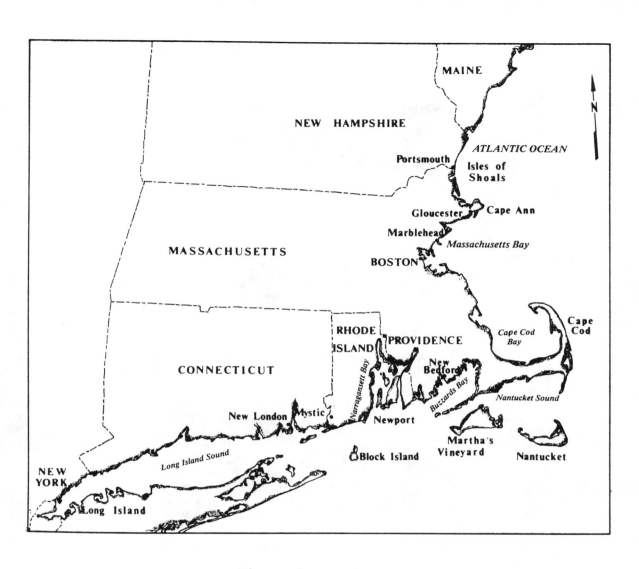

The Northeast and Maine

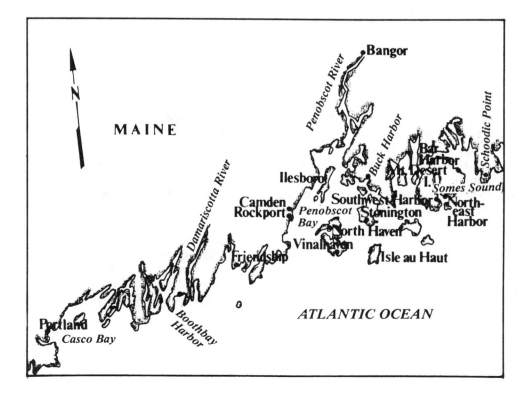

The center-cockpit layout Pearson 395 gives privacy for two couples, with the galley tucked away on one side of the companionway. This common East Coast charter design is exceptionally easy to sail, especially when equipped with a roller furling jib. The four-cylinder power unit gives ample performance under power.

know where to start and how to find a competent charter company. The many brochures I obtained all promised a clean, well-maintained yacht, fully equipped with all safety gear, some even with bed linens. The best seemed to come from charter operations attached to boatyards or yacht brokerages. At least two of the companies I contacted about insurance were somewhat evasive. Closer inquiries revealed they were run by individuals on a part-time basis. The charter business being seasonal in these waters, some people are tempted to operate charters in a casual way. Apparently, demand exceeds supply, so they seem to get away with it, season after season. I would steer clear of such operations and of private individuals operating on their own. Ignore phrases like "owner-maintained," "deluxe," and "avoid high overhead." If you want to charter from an individual, check the yacht out ahead of time and insist

on reviewing the insurance policy down to the fine print. Of course there are some superb individually owned yachts for charter, but I am afraid that the majority of owners are in it for the tax deduction and are less concerned with the client's interests. So stick with the established and the well-known.

Where to charter? The choice is vast. You can bareboat from the Connecticut ports on the north shore of Long Island Sound, explore Martha's Vineyard and Nantucket. Here you will encounter a great deal of calm, humid weather and chronic congestion in high summer, but the afternoon southwesters can be refreshing. There are relatively few charter opportunities in the Boston area, although you can sometimes bareboat from Marblehead. These are historic waters, redolent of the early days of yachting, but crowded. Many of the ports, such as Manchester, are

Marblehead. (Courtesy Thomas Naylor)

packed in the summer. Yachts are moored and tied up everywhere, and you often have to lie outside. I was complaining about the congestion one day while rowing around Marblehead in a friend's dinghy. "Look at it this way," he said gently. "Just think of the incredible yacht watching. After all, yacht watching, like girl watching, is an addiction. Why not indulge your vice?" Places like Mystic, Gloucester, and Marblehead are a paradise for anyone with this addiction. Why not indulge yourself with a brief charter, preferably during a northeaster when everyone huddles in port? At least borrow a dinghy and explore. I have heard of people chartering in Connecticut and Massachusetts so that they can race in such events as Marblehead Race Week in late July each year. This is a type of bareboating unlikely to appeal to most readers of this book, so we will pass on.

Unless you have compelling social reasons to do otherwise, plan your Northeast charter in Maine. There is less congestion, the choice of anchorages and ports is far more appealing, and the sailing and navigation are a wonderful challenge. These idyllic cruising grounds start just north of Cape Elizabeth, where the coast trends more to the east. Long, rocky headlands extend far into the Atlantic, their ledges projecting far offshore underwater. The deep bays between them are protected by forested, rock-girt islands that break the force of great Atlantic swells. Sheltered anchorage after sheltered anchorage lies behind these natural fortifications. So far, the Maine coast has escaped much of the suburbanization of the more southerly coast. Marinas are few and far between, even rented moorings are scarce as you sail northeast. This is still an unspoiled, although occasionally congested, cruising ground. If you liked chartering in the Pacific Northwest, the Apostle Islands, or Scandinavia, you will love Maine. I make no apologies for sending the potential charterer in the Northeast to these waters.

The Maine sailing season lasts from late April or May through October. The weather will be cooler and more unpredictable in spring and fall, but you will enjoy many clear days and crisp nights in deserted anchorages. The prevailing summer winds are from the southwest, depending on the position of the Azores High and on a branch of the cool Labrador Current that runs close inshore near the heated land. Nights and early mornings will be calm and often humid, but a daily southwester will fill in as the land heats up, reaching a velocity of between 10 to 15 knots in many places. Locally, the wind can blow considerably stronger, especially in places where heated islands disturb the even flow of the breeze over open water. This can be a major advantage when you are bound westward along the coast; it may pay you to beat through the islands, enjoying a pleasant breeze when yachts in the open Atlantic are becalmed.

This stable summer weather pattern is occasionally interrupted by cyclonic disturbances that bring clouds, then clearing skies, and a brisk northwester that blows from a clear sky. I have stood at Bar Harbor and watched people reveling in this wind close offshore, ducking between the islands and setting off on fine passages to the west, covering several days' mileage in one day. Northwesters can last several days, but sometimes blow out about midday. Several times each summer, an easterly will fill in, sometimes with clear skies, but more often with thick clouds, rain, and winds of over 20 knots. Easterlies can pose much more of a hazard in spring and fall. Hurricanes rarely reach this far north, but if one is approaching, you'll have plenty of warning to find shelter.

The major hazard and frustration of Maine chartering is fog, which becomes more prevalent the farther you sail to the east. Maine fogs are formed as saturated warm air from offshore meets colder, churned-up tidal waters inshore. The saturated air turns into thick droplets and you have fog. Fog can cling to the coastline for a week or more, especially at the head of bays and behind the islands. On sunny days, the fog will burn off close to the land and in the lee of islands but linger elsewhere, closing in again during the evening. This pattern can last for days on end; you may be unlucky enough to have restricted visibility for your entire charter.

Your best chance of avoiding fog is to charter in early summer or fall. The second half of July and August can be the foggiest, but even then you can avoid some of it by cruising close inshore and avoiding the offlying islands. At times, the visibility will be zero, and you can do nothing but stay in port. But at others, you can navigate safely from port to port provided you have a reliable compass and a depth sounder. Few bareboats have radar or Loran, but both make fog navigation much easier. Most people will rely on compass courses and their wristwatches to calculate the time between markers in thick weather. This is one of the cruising grounds where your watch is essential, not only for tides, but also for speed-time problems. Fortunately, the major sea marks and principal dangers are conspicuous. Beware, however, if you cruise off the beaten track, for even today there are many unmarked dangers and unexpected shoals that do not appear on the large-scale chart. As in Sweden, navigation here is a matter of having a strong sense of horizontal direction and of knowing exactly where you are on the chart at all times. If you charter during the summer months, come prepared to sail in fog. Otherwise you may never leave port. If you are a first-time visitor, it may pay you to hire a skipper for a couple of days.

Maine waters are strongly tidal, with the velocities of tides and currents increasing as you sail east. The tide runs east on the ebb, west on the flood, setting in and out of the coastal bays in many places to such an extent that you have to allow for a cross-set when bound up or down the coast. The tide tables will give you the times of high and low tides, but be aware that local conditions such as topography and strong winds can affect these times and the range.

Your charterer should provide you with a Chart-Kit or complete set of charts for the charter area, together with a set of tide tables. *Eldridge Tide and Pilot Book* (Robert Eldridge White, 51 Commercial Wharf, Boston, MA 02110) is indispensable. Roger F. Duncan and John P. Ware's *A Cruising Guide to the New England Coast* (New York: Dodd, Mead, 1983) is excellent. I would buy a copy ahead of time for cruise planning.

Bareboats are scattered throughout Maine, but most of them are headquartered on Boothbay Harbor or Penobscot Bay. Boothbay Harbor is somewhat more accessible from Logan Airport, Boston, where most out-of-state charterers will land, but a lot of people prefer to drive the extra miles to more northern ports. Boothbay Harbor itself is a large, well-protected harbor, a good place to start a charter. The entrance between the islands is simple to follow and a good introduction to Maine navigation. The Cuckolds light has a powerful horn in fog and a brilliant light at night, so you should be able to find your way home in most reasonable conditions. Boothbay itself is very much a tourist town, with excellent motels where you can spend the night before boarding your yacht. Some of the most attractive cruising on the Maine coast lies within easy reach. You should be able to venture as far as Schoodic Point in a two-week charter, provided the weather cooperates.

The charter area between Boothbay Harbor and Schoodic Point is a favorite with many cruising people

Camden, Maine. (Brian M. Fagan)

from all over the world. The coastline is well protected by islands, there are many harbors and sheltered anchorages, the fishing is excellent. You can moor in crowded harbors or explore uninhabited islands. The choice of destination is infinite. Fog can be a problem in summer, but you soon learn to navigate from buoy to buoy on compass courses or to spot the darkening loom of an island a short distance ahead. Screaming gulls on the rocks, the smell of spruce trees, even the swish of breakers on the shore, all are telltale signs of land. Maine is lobster country, its waters strewn with traps, most of them laid in shallow rocky water. If you come upon a trap in the fog, proceed with care, for it may signal hazardous waters. Here, as elsewhere, it pays to stop and listen. You have run your distance and a buoy or island does not appear. You stop the engine and the sound of diesel and ship's way dies down. Listen for birds or breakers, for the wind whispering in trees, for a horn, a bell. It's surprising what clues you can pick up. Try a sounding, or simply anchor and wait for the fog to lift a trifle. Maine is a place of magical fogs that drift in and out and lift without warning. Very often, the lees of islands will be fog-free, while the rest of the coastline is mantled with white gloom. Fog is part of the mystique

of chartering in these waters. You soon learn to live with it.

Exploring Maine waters is a never-ending process. A charterer with limited time faces agonizing choices. Is it best to sail through Penobscot Bay for a quick once-over, or to concentrate on an area like Mount Desert Island and sail only a few miles all charter? This is a matter of individual choice. All I can do is to make some suggestions. Ideally, your first charter in Maine waters should be a carefully planned combination of passage-making and rock hopping. One possible itinerary would take you from Boothbay Harbor to explore the Damariscotta River for a couple of days. You can carry 6-foot draft for at least 15 miles upstream. On foggy days, hug the west bank and you may find a beautiful summer's day upstream. There are anchorages galore above East Boothbay, many of them described in Duncan and Ware's *Cruising Guide*. Chart 314 gives you all the information you need to anchor off the village of Damariscotta on a muddy bottom. "Hang a bucket over the stern to help lying with the tide," remarks the *Cruising Guide* succinctly. But "don't forget to take it in in the morning."

From a snug anchorage in the Damariscotta River, I

would recommend making a longer passage past the forked rocks of Pemaquid Point to Penobscot Bay. There are some charming places like Round Pond and Friendship for those with time to spare, but you may be better off visiting them on the way home. Friendship is a peaceful anchorage well worth visiting, the home of the Friendship sloops, magnificent gaff-rigged vessels. If the passage proves too long, you can always stop at Port Clyde, a large convenient harbor, but with little to offer ashore.

A good route first time through Penobscot will take you through the Muscle Ridge Channel to Owls Head Bay, an inside route that is to be preferred to the rough waters offshore. There are plenty of good anchorages along the way, too, especially Home Harbor, where you shelter between several islands in about 16 feet, sounding your way out of the tide for a good night's sleep. Those in need of supplies might spend a night in Rockland, where every facility is to be found. But it's a commercial port, with the noise and bustle that that implies.

The Muscle Ridge Channel leads into the western reaches of Penobscot Bay, where you should find a summer fair wind eastbound. The waters are sheltered, the scenery pretty, but the sailing somewhat uninspired. This is the way to go when the fog lies thick offshore. Fortunately, there are plenty of fine harbors and anchorages to amuse you. Rockport is a charming little port, with a pier and good anchorage. You can eat ashore and buy supplies, but I would keep clear on Friday nights when the cruise schooners from nearby Camden spend their last night partying in the bay. There are interesting boatyards ashore, but not as much to see as there is in Camden.

Camden is one of those places where I would like to live one day. Its fine Victorian houses overlook a cozy harbor busy with yachts and "windjammer" schooners in the cruise trade. Camden was once an important port for granite, lime, fish, and ice exports, but now flourishes from tourism. Its streets are crowded with day trippers and boutiques. You can eat well, even expensively, here. The trouble with Camden is that the anchorage is murderously crowded and often rolly, for a chop can enter the bay all summer. There are some moorings, but they are normally taken. You are better off anchoring elsewhere and visiting Camden by land. It is the perfect place to explore when fogbound somewhere else.

From Camden, this cruise would take you to somewhere like Gilkey Harbor, a large protected harbor at Islesboro. You can lie in any of several coves, some with moorings. Warren Island nearby is a state park, with cook-out facilities and three guest moorings.

Some people leave here to explore the Penobscot River as far upstream as Winterport, a delightful sail between wooded banks, if there is fog in the bay. Best to carry the tide upstream with an afternoon wind behind you. Sometimes you can pick up a northerly to carry you down in the morning. Most yachts bypass this part of the bay and sail from Islesboro across to Bucks Harbor, a well-protected anchorage behind Harbor Island, at the northwest end of Eggemoggin Reach. Best to anchor in the cove to the east of the main harbor, where it is quieter, even when the windjammer cruises come in. There is a store ashore where you can buy snowballs (yes, snowballs) in July! The owner collects them in winter and keeps them in his freezer.

You can sail down Eggemoggin Reach between Deer Isle and the mainland and reach Bass Harbor at the south end of Mount Desert Island in an easy daysail. The Casco Passage on the way is safe for deep-draft yachts and is well marked. Be warned that the tides run strongly in these waters.

If you sail east along this route, you can return through the offshore islands that protect Penobscot Bay from the Atlantic. Just in case some readers want to take this way east, we describe it from west to east. You simply reverse the route coming west. The island passage passes through Fox Island Thorofare between North Haven and Vinalhaven Islands. Here there are several musts, among them Pulpit Harbor, a popular well-protected harbor on North Haven Island. Pulpit is hard to identify on a hazy day, and you may sail past. In that case, look out for the large house with gables on each end high on the shore. Work back the way you came close to the shore, and you will wonder how you ever missed the place. The usual anchorage lies in the mouth of the cove, but there are no facilities except a water hose and a telephone at a wharf near the head of the cove.

The Fox Island Thorofare is deep, the shortest route from the western bay to the eastern half of the bay. The passage is easy in clear weather, but apt to be hazardous in thick conditions because of the constant traffic. There are several anchorages off the passage, among them North Haven, where you can stop for supplies simply by anchoring off the town and going ashore before moving on to another anchorage nearby. The thorofare is where short-time charterers may be forced to retrace their steps. You have to turn back here, promising your crew you'll return soon.

Vinalhaven Island is worth a day or two, if you have the time. Armed with your copy of Duncan and Ware, you could spend more than a week in these waters. Carvers Harbor is the most popular destination, a lobstering and fishing village on the southern coast of the island. The entrance is extremely hazardous in stormy weather. The tides run strongly and fog can be a problem, too. It is best to visit Carvers Harbor on a fine clear day when you can pick out the leading mark—Heron Neck Light. This is a difficult place to anchor, for the bottom is soft mud and grass. You are better off finding a mooring or lying alongside the wharf if there is space. Carvers Harbor is very much a fishing town, a refreshing change from the many tourist towns on this coast. You can catch a plane to Boston from the island airstrip a mile and a half from the harbor. Vinalhaven has several other anchorages and a well-known Outward Bound school.

The most direct route across east Penobscot Bay will take you north of Mark Island and then through the well-marked channel between Deer Isle and the islands to the south. Many charterers stop for a night at Stonington, at the southern end of Deer Isle, a fishing town with an excellent anchorage off the harbor quays. As with Vinalhaven, the Deer Isle quarries were once very prosperous. The Stonington quarries provided the granite for the Museum of Fine Arts in Boston. The town is now home to one of the most successful fisheries cooperatives in Maine.

If you have the time and the weather is clear, go south to Isle au Haut. Once privately owned, much of the island is now part of the Acadia National Park. High and wooded, Isle au Haut was named by the great French explorer Samuel Champlain in 1604. There are several anchorages. The best for visitors is the Isle au Haut Thorofare at the northwest corner of the island. Steer for Kimball Rock west of Kimball Head, then use the light on Robinson Point to enter the thorofare. You can anchor out of the tide on the Kimball Island side, then dinghy ashore to visit the white church and the store, owned by a cooperative of summer visitors. The ranger station is nearby.

From Stonington, your easterly route takes you across Jericho Bay through York Narrows, and then on to Mount Desert Island, probably the ultimate destination of any Maine charterer. Many people charter from Hinckley's in Southwest Harbor or from other companies working out of Bass Barbor, thereby saving the long passage down east from Boothbay Harbor. Mount Desert (the "island of barren mountains") was named by Samuel Champlain and has a long and colorful history. Champlain's name for the island is apt, for the peaks shine brightly in the afternoon sun as you sail toward the island from Penobscot Bay. You can anchor in dozens of sheltered tidal coves, explore the only fjord on the Atlantic coast of the United States, and walk for miles on National Park trails. If you really want to see the coast, take a cab to the summit of Cadillac Mountain at sunset and survey Penobscot Bay and the islands. Although the tourist industry has discovered Mount Desert, you can get away from the trippers without too much trouble.

Most bareboaters will arrive at or be based on the harbors that open into Great Harbor, the confluence of the Eastern and Western Ways and Somes Sound, Mount Desert's fjord. This is a good place to shake down a newly chartered yacht. Both the ways are well marked, but the tides run strongly through them. A few charter yachts operate out of Bass Harbor, where there are two marinas, but the harbor can be rolly in southerly conditions, which makes it less crowded than Southwest or Northeast Harbors in the peak months. Southwest is famous for its association with the Hinckley boatyard, which turns out probably the finest production yachts built in the United States. The entrance is easy, but the main harbor is very crowded with ferries and fishing boats; visiting yachts are low on the totem pole. You may be able to anchor off Manset on the south side of the harbor near Hinckley's or off one of the wharfs nearer the town. On the whole, Northeast Harbor across the water is a better place to visit. Access is easy, the harbor sheltered. There are several marinas, moorings are plentiful, and everything you could possibly need is readily available ashore. If you find there are too many gift shops and boutiques, there is one consolation—you can eat very well ashore here.

The main reason for visiting either of these harbors is to sail with the flood tide up Somes Sound. At first, the mountains rise almost sheer from the waters of the fjord, then they ease back from the shore as you enter the well-marked channel into Somes Harbor itself. Anchor off and dinghy to the public landing. The tiny settlement is graced with fine old houses in a peaceful setting. This is one of my favorite places on the Maine coast.

I think you are better off exploring Somes Sound and some of the outlying anchorages in Frenchman Bay than going to Bar Harbor on the east coast of the island. Bar Harbor was once a glittering resort town, where steam yachts anchored and elegant, aristocratic families spent the summer in imposing mansions overlooking the bay. All this is gone now, most of it destroyed by fire in 1947. Bar Harbor was not my favorite, despite an extremely friendly and helpful harbormaster, who showed us to a mooring west of the town pier. But supplies are easy to find, and the harbor is well situated as a base for more leisurely exploration of Frenchman Bay or as a starting-off point for yachts bound still farther east. Bar Harbor is worth a couple of hours before you sail across the bay to Winter Harbor, where there are three comfortable anchorages.

Mount Desert and Frenchman Bay are likely to be the easternmost destination for most Maine charterers. Of course, it is possible to sail all the way to Nova Scotia, but you are better off exploring Penobscot Bay first.

Once past Schoodic Point, you leave the world of organized yachting and enter a new one of cold waters, fast-running tides, and uninhabited islands. This is certainly a cruising ground for the experienced charterer, but it provides the very incentive you need to return down east again on a longer, more ambitious cruise.

PART V: EUROPE

17 General Comments and Scandinavia

There will be times when the lure of tropical islands and soft tradewinds will pall and you will think of chartering in more temperate climates. Europe will spring to mind at once, but many people will hesitate, either because of the expense or because of the problems that have to be overcome at long distance. At first glance, the prospect *is* somewhat daunting. You're thousands of miles away from the charter area; no one packages the travel, yacht, and provisioning for you; and you know nothing about local conditions. Do not be discouraged! Organizing a European bareboat cruise is surprisingly straightforward, provided you use common sense and do your homework ahead of time. And the expense can be relatively modest, if you take advantage of cheap excursion fares and off-season rates. The pages that follow give some suggestions for arranging a charter in Europe, then examine some of the seductive cruising grounds that await the adventurous charterer.

Planning for a European charter

European bareboating is very different from the intensely marketed and packaged Caribbean scene. Here you are on your own, dealing for the most part with small owner-operated companies with low overheads and a bewildering variety of boats. You will also have a far wider range of yachts to choose from, from Swan 44s to 25-footers. The choice of cruising grounds can be downright confusing for the beginner.

Most first-time European charterers make a beeline for Greece, partly because the weather's warm and partly because it is such a spectacular place. But why join the crowd when there are so many other places to sail? Corsica, Sardinia, and the French Riviera are attractive alternatives. The Balearics are a charterer's paradise. Island hopping in Scandinavia is a must for Maine lovers, while southwest Ireland, western Scotland, and the English Channel coasts offer great varieties of scenery and sailing. Too cold? You may encounter tropical weather in northern Europe during the summer. Agreed, you may sail in rainy, windy weather for weeks on end, but the sunny days make it all worthwhile.

Perhaps the hardest thing is finding out what each cruising ground is like. Start by deciding in general terms which area you would like to explore—for example, the English Channel or the Greek islands. Next, order one or two general charts of that area from your local chart agent's catalog (or write to the Defense Mapping Agency in Washington, D.C.). At the same time, send for brochures from charter companies operating in that general area. You will find their advertisements in major European periodicals like *Yachting Monthly* or *Yachting World*, available in many large marine bookstores. You'll find comprehensive listings each month, many of them for small, highly reputable companies that do not have the large promotion budgets of Caribbean organizations. Send a letter to each one that interests you even slightly.

Your charts will probably arrive at the same time as the first brochures. Start with the charter company literature. Then eliminate all those companies that reply by surface mail. They are either not interested in your business or not used to dealing with charterers from far away. The last thing you want is a breakdown in communications. If you are thinking about chartering in Britain, you might write to the Yacht Charter Association, 60 Silver Dale, New Milton, BH25 7DE, England. They will send you a list of member companies who adhere to their safety standards. Be sure to gather as many leaflets as you can, so that you can comparison shop and get an idea of what yachts and possible charter bases are open to you.

If you are still serious about chartering in Europe at this point, it's time for the homework that will make all the difference later on. Look over the leaflets carefully and establish in your mind what the charter limits of your chosen areas are. Then turn to your chart, measure off some distances and decide how far you want to travel during your charter. Make a list of the places that are essential for your itinerary. For example, no sane charterer departing from Piraeus near Athens with 10 days ahead of him would want to miss Sounion and Hydra. Next, delve more deeply into local conditions. What are the prevailing winds? What are the best months to charter? What about tides, currents, and special hazards? What design of available yacht is best suited to your purposes and these conditions? Try to find someone who has sailed in the area before. Fellow yacht club members are often helpful—if you belong to a club, that is!

This is the point at which you start acquiring local cruising guides and perhaps more detailed charts from foreign suppliers or their U.S. agents. There are, for example, Admiralty and French government chart agents in the U.S. Locally compiled charts are much better than American copies. By the same token, you would use U.S. government's charts for California waters. The best source for European cruising guides in this country, other than marine bookstores, is the Dolphin Book Club, Camp Hill, PA 17012. They send out a list of those they have in stock with their monthly bulletins. You can order cruising guides direct from Britain by writing J.D. Potter Ltd., 145 The Minories, London EC3 1NH, England. They are also Admiralty chart agents and will supply you with a portfolio for anywhere in the world. If you are planning a cruise in northern Europe, I would recommend that you obtain a current edition of *Reed's Nautical Almanac*. This encyclopedic publication contains tide tables for European waters as far south as Gibraltar and a mine of information on such esoteric subjects as radio frequencies, buoyage, radiobeacons, and major lighthouses. It's well worth keeping for future reference, even when the tide tables are out of date. You can always reread the pages and pages of instructional material when weatherbound or on anchor watch.

Reed's and the sailing directions will give you a general impression of the cruising area you have chosen. For example, a cruise from the Solent area of southern England to the Channel Islands and back means playing the tides that sweep east and west through the Channel. When departing for France from, say, Lymington in the Solent, you want to carry a favorable tide past the Needles and would certainly prefer to lee bow a west-going stream if hard on the wind for Braye Harbor, Alderney. *Reed's* will enable you to plan the outlines of your cruise ahead of time. Does it pay you to putter around the first afternoon of your charter, perhaps eating dinner in the comfort of Studland Bay before setting off for France? Most certainly it does, if you want to time your arrival at the entrance of the Alderney Race for the beginning of the ebb. Too early a departure time could keep you jilling around in open water off Alderney for several hours. Familiarize yourself with prevailing weather patterns, the times of weather forecasts, and the forecast zones. The more advance preparation you do, the better off you will be. Quite apart from anything else, European charterers tend to be more casual about navigational briefing, since most of their charterers have local sailing experience. Best be well prepared, so that you can ask specific questions at briefing time. Remember that you will probably be taking over a totally unfamiliar design of yacht, so the less you have to worry about cruise planning at the last minute, the better.

One of the best ways to learn about European cruising areas is to subscribe to a British yachting magazine for a few months and to read the cruising stories that appear in their pages. *Yachting Monthly* is probably best, for it is heavily oriented toward cruising. Avoid the yarns of circumnavigators who make their living writing books and articles. They tend to write "wish you were here" travelogues that are light on seamanship and conditions and heavy on places and people. You are after information and insights from amateur sailors who know their local cruising areas intimately. If you plan several European charters, you might consider joining the Cruising Association, Ivory House, St. Katherine's Dock, London E1 9AT, England. They issue an invaluable bulletin crammed with useful information, book reviews, and accounts of members' cruises. They also publish the *CA Handbook*, a compendium of port and anchorage information that covers most of northern Europe. This "Bible" is very compressed and much codified, but well worth the price. Most of the Cruising Association's activities are of local interest only—membership meets and winter lectures—but overseas members can join for a surprisingly modest cost. Their headquarters at St. Katherine's Dock is a delightful place; their library, superb; and their cruising files, of incalculable value. If you are a member, make a point of calling there before your charter starts.

The Royal Cruising Club is a highly exclusive organization with membership by invitation only. However, they publish annual *Roving Commissions*, gathering members' reports of cruises that include many classic cruising grounds worldwide. You will find articles by the likes of Arthur Beiser and Eric Hiscock alongside pieces by vastly experienced, but less well known sailors who know their home waters extremely well. I have found *Roving Commissions* invaluable when planning my charters far afield. You can obtain them from J.D. Potter or R.C.C. Press, 4 Coval Lane, London SW14, England (about $12 a volume).

Choosing a charter company

First, make your plans very far in advance. The European season is much shorter than the Caribbean's. Regular clients will make sure to book for the following year at least six to nine months ahead of time, and repeat customers are the bread and butter of any self-respecting company's business. So make reservations well ahead.

Your choice of charter company should be made even more carefully than in the Caribbean. I would suggest the following criteria in addition to those listed in Chapter 8:

- The company should have been in business a minimum of five years.
- Its yachts should include several newer ones, of proven design, known to you or to friends of yours.
- The company should, if possible, be one owned by an individual or a small group of individuals. Avoid charter agencies that offer yachts on behalf of many different private owners. You may well find the boats scattered all over the place and poorly maintained.
- The company should be prepared to supply bank references and the names of previous clients to contact (go for American clients if they have any, you can call and talk to them in person).
- The company's brochure should include a complete list of equipment on board its yachts. Check that it includes more than adequate safety gear—safety regulations are not as strict as those in the United States.

Of course, there are exceptions, but why invite disaster when you don't have to? Go for a company that has a proven track record and is serious about upkeep schedules. Experienced charterers can tell which they are from their brochures. If you're chartering in Britain, stick with companies that are members of the Yacht Charter Association.

Travel, provisions, and timing

The length of your charter depends on your other overseas plans and on the area you want to visit. Many people combine a 7-to-10-day charter with a land vacation in several European countries. For any European charter, I would allow about two weeks, even longer in areas like Greece or the Baltic where there is so much to see. The longer time will also enable you to spend a few days getting used to local conditions before going farther afield. Even if the locals speak the same language, all sorts of things are different: provisioning is a challenge, the weather pattern is unfamiliar, even the anchoring conditions and tides are alien to you. Give yourself time to adjust.

Chartering in Europe means taking a chance on the

weather. You may have magnificent northeasterly weather in April, tropical heat in June, and Indian summer in early October. Or it may rain for weeks on end. Such unpredictability is one of the charms of northern European cruising. Then there are the crowds, which reach their height during the vacation months of July and August. The best times for a northern European or Mediterranean charter are during spring and early summer or early fall. You may well have good luck with the weather—early June often brings fine, settled weather, for example. The risk of bad weather rises sharply in mid to late September, when the equinoctial gales can play havoc with your plans. However, by going slightly off season, you'll avoid the biggest crowds and the highest prices. You can also take advantage of lower season rates on the airlines. Organize your charter with the following variables in mind:

• Your overall plans for a European trip. For example, do you want to spend three weeks touring ashore, then two afloat? One of the best trips I ever took involved a three-week charter on a 27-footer in Denmark, two weeks on a French canal boat, and 10 days ashore in Spain.
• Airline fare structures. Which excursion rate is the most attractive: 14–21 days, 45 days, or more? Do you have to shorten or extend the trip to accommodate time limits or particular travel days? (Be aware that some European companies insist on Saturday-to-Saturday charters in high season.)
• Travel discounts. Are there major discounts that you can use, tickets that you pay for in advance at substantial savings? It may, for example, pay you to buy your tickets in February to take advantage of temporary low fares.
• The best months for chartering in the area of your choice.

The airline arrangements are best made with your favorite travel agent. APEX, Super Saver, excursion fare, whatever—the rates and restrictions are so confusing and change so often that you have to rely on an expert to get the cheapest rates for you. Buy a round-trip ticket to the European capital nearest your charter base, then plan on renting a car. This is probably better than arriving by train, for it will enable you to buy provisions and run around doing errands as you take over the yacht. Besides, it's fun to drive in a new country. Remember that air travel within Europe is often very expensive. You can sometimes pick up local bargains once you have arrived in, say, London or Amsterdam. For example, if you are chartering in Greece, there may

be advantages in taking a package tour fare from London to Athens and buying it in Europe. The flotilla companies are especially aggressive about this. They will send you information with their brochures. Look out for the fine print, however. You may end up with a package that is totally unsuitable for your needs.

All the European companies I have dealt with assume that you will do your own provisioning. Some will give your advance order to a local supermarket that will deliver or have it ready for you to collect, and you should ask if this service is available. For all the fuss that is made about it, provisioning in any European country is pretty much the same as at home. The languages may be different, the supermarkets smaller, and the weights in kilos, but people still have to eat. Shopping for groceries is part of the fun of a European charter. Sign language is a powerful communicator and often hilariously funny. You may end up with the wrong item, but you'll have fun acquiring it. Each charter area has its own peculiarities. Here are some general pointers to help you:
• Buy simple and buy fresh. European fruits, vegetables, and bread are at their best fresh from the store. Plan on going for staples every day.
• Plan a solid breakfast, a picnic lunch, and a more elaborate dinner. The evenings are long in northern Europe and dinner is a major event of the day. Lunches are my favorite European meals, for you can enjoy various cheeses, wines, and sausages with delectable bread for weeks without getting bored. Barbecuing is not commonly a sailor's pastime in Europe.
• Long-life milk is one of the great boons of European chartering. You can keep it unrefrigerated for weeks. It is practically unobtainable in the United States.
• Food prices in Europe are about the same as they are in the U.S., although meat and canned goods tend to be more expensive. To reduce waste, I recommend that you keep your stock of provisions to a minimum, buying frequently along the way. Most European yachts do not have refrigerators, so you'll probably end up doing that anyway. No need to bring any foodstuffs with you. You may develop a craving for Mexican food, real hamburgers, or genuine American pizza, but the local foods will prove more interesting.
• Liquor can be astronomically expensive, especially in Scandinavia. Plan on bringing your duty-free allowance with you on the plane. European wines are moderate in price, so experiment to your heart's content. European beers are outstanding; beer drinkers will soon feel quite at home.
• Bring your own prescription drugs, suntan lotions, and film from home. Film is especially expensive in most European countries.

● For planning purposes, assume that the charterer will provide nothing except bedding, linens, and cleaning materials. With provisioning, you are on your own.

Organizing a European charter may seem a formidable task, but in reality it is not much worse than arranging a packaged Caribbean cruise—and far more fun to put together. Study the charter area carefully, develop a cruise plan, make your bookings and travel arrangements well ahead of time, and you should have the trip of a lifetime.

As I pointed out in Chapter 10, good foul-weather gear and warm clothing are essential on any northern European charter—and you will need waterproof jackets and trousers in the Mediterranean as well.

Let's visit a few of the best bareboating areas in Europe, starting with Scandinavia, which offers some of the most challenging cruising grounds of all.

Chartering in Scandinavia

Yes, I know I am biased, but Denmark and Sweden are my favorite cruising grounds. I am unrepentant. There is something special about charter areas where the sun does not set until 2300 and rises again in the small hours of the morning. Hardly any Americans visit these enchanted cruising grounds. More's the pity, for the variety of sailing and places to visit is unending.

My first Scandinavian charter was in Denmark. We flew by SAS to Copenhagen, explored the city and its famous Tivoli Gardens and Stroget, the shopping street, for a couple of days, then took over a Nicholson 35 for a longer charter through the southern archipelago. The Nicholson is a British-built fast cruiser rarely seen in North America, a magnificently weatherly boat that is ideal for four people. Our charter was in late June, at the beginning of the high season that starts around midsummer. I'd recommend that you charter this area between May and early September, by which time the nights can become chilly and the weather less settled. The only problem is that everyone else agrees with you and tries to make maximum use of the short season. So you will probably find considerable congestion in the Danish archipelago. The islands lie close to northern Germany. Hundreds of German yachts venture north each summer, their lockers crammed with cheap liquor. They raft up in the tiny Danish harbors, but are almost invariably hospitable and friendly.

We were not prepared for provisioning expenses. There was a modern supermarket close to the harbor, but the food prices sent us into shock. They can be as much as 40 percent higher than in the United States. Meat is very expensive, liquor astronomical. Plan to bring as much duty-free with you as you can. We ate simply and well, relying rather heavily on pork chops and meatballs. Don't plan on eating out much, unless you are very wealthy. But do try the local eels, they are out of this world. The pastries are, of course, outstanding, and no Danish sailor would be seen on the water without Carlsburg beer, one of the best lagers in the world.

The best cruising in Denmark is in the southern archipelago. If you have two to three weeks, you might try circumnavigating Zealand and Funen. Plan a clockwise cruise, southward form Copenhagen, through the Storstrammen past Vordingborg, then north-about Langeland to Svendborg. The Little Bight offers beautifully wooded scenery. The narrows are spectacular; the best harbor is Middelfart, on the Funen side. The rest of the circumnavigation will mean some longer passages, to the interesting village of Sejero and across the Great Belt to the industrial city of Odense, the birthplace of Hans Christian Andersen. This, the third largest city in Denmark, is well worth a visit. Explore the Isefjord from Nykobing, entered through a dredged channel. Plan on making the 40-mile passage from the Isefjord to Helsingor (Shakespeare's Elsinore) in one hop. The only intervening harbor is Gilleleje, a useful stopping place if you do not mind the company of others. Last time I was there, you could walk from one side of the inner basin to the other on people's decks. A visit to Kronborg Castle at Helsingor should be compulsory for all hands. Find a berth in the harbor north of the castle, but be warned it will be crowded. The sail south from Helsingor through the sound is an interesting experience, but look out for the ferries that charge across the straits at full speed.

Ferries are a major hazard in Scandinavia—they give way to no one. Approach major harbors with caution, just in case a ferry is entering or leaving. In my more paranoid moments, I suspect that there is an International Society of Ferry Skippers, which gangs together so that at least one of its members enters or leaves the harbor as I approach.

The circumnavigation is a fairly hefty undertaking. You can spend two less ambitious weeks among the low-lying, wooded islands of the south, savoring the scenery, quiet villages, and tortuous channels. Most of the sailing is in quiet water, so you can sail even when the wind blows strongly and the Baltic is kicking up. A good itinerary is south form Copenhagen to somewhere

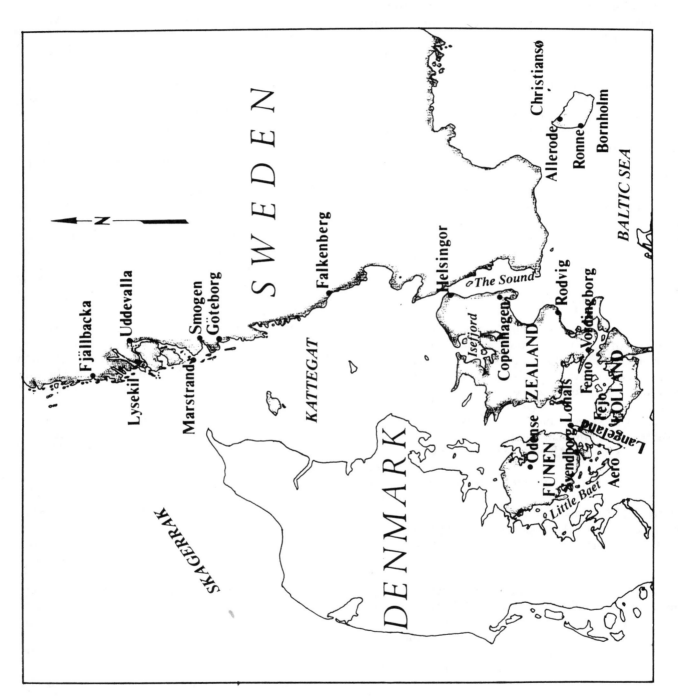

Denmark, western Sweden, and Bornholm

like Rodvig, then through the Storstrammen to visit the castle at Vordingborg. Use the north harbor where there's 2 meters. The channels east of the town are narrow. Follow the markers very closely. I hope you do not meet the round-Zealand race fleet in the narrowest part of the channel, as we did. To cap it all, we were beating, while they were under spinnakers. It was a calm sunny day, so we anchored at the edge of the channel and watched them drift by.

Once clear of Vordingborg, visit the islands of Fejo and Femo off the north coast of Lolland. The Danish charts, readily obtainable in Copenhagen, will show you the narrow channels that lead through the mudbanks into the tiny harbors. Fejo is one of my favorites, a minute haven with, of all things, showers for visitors. A lovely restored Baltic trader shared this spot with us. She was too large to moor in the harbor, so she anchored off. Here, as everywhere in Denmark, a polite official arrived to collect harbor dues. These are high by others' standards, but you cannot begrudge the fees. The Danes maintain their harbors beautifully, and there are dozens for them to look after and for you to choose from.

Langeland on the west side of the Great Bight has little to offer, but spend a night at Lohals at the north end of the island before entering the most famous part of the archipelago south of Funen. Sail up the Svendborg Channel to the pleasant town of that name. The approach is intricate but well buoyed; the scenery, pastoral and rewarding. If you are lucky, you will see the Danish royal yacht moored off the town. Make a point of visiting the picturesque village of Tröense on the east side of the channel. Old sea captains' houses line narrow cobbled streets, and there is a fascinating maritime museum. Tröense is where we consumed large quantities of eels on the recommendation of Danish friends.

Aero Island, some 20 miles south and west of Svendborg, is the most popular port of call with German sailors from Kiel and other spots just across the water from Denmark. You can sail there through deep-water channels or take the gunkholer's route through small islands and mudflats that brings you out at the harbor of Marstal. This is fun, provided you stick to the channel. This can be an interesting experience when beating against the prevailing southwesterly winds. Do not make the mistake I did of trying to sail straight for the Marstal entrance from the end of the channel. It took half an hour to get off.

Marstal is a beautiful town with a superb old ship museum that is a paradise for modelers. The town itself is picturesque and well worth a couple of days, but the berths at the south end of the harbor are usually crowded with German yachts. Our neighbors were two

well-oiled German gentlemen in a Folkboat taking a brief vacation from their families. We fraternized over one of their numerous bottles of schnapps. The party lasted until an advanced hour, while our hosts reminisced about World War II. "Ach, it was a good war!" cried one of them. He was going to Leningrad with his family the following week. "Only got within 10 kilometers during the war," he added, laughing. English friends with us were horrified!

There are weeks of cruising in the islands and channels around Aero. A leisurely cruise can take you to the showpiece town of Aeroskobing, then to the islands at the entrance of the Little Belt. The nice thing is that you can retrace your steps along a quite different route without any effort.

We were more ambitious in the Nicholson 35. Having 10 days ahead of us, we decided to make a long passage to the most outlying Danish islands, Bornholm and Christiansö. The journey is straightforward enough, provided you keep clear of East German territorial waters. The direct course from the southern tip of Langeland to Rönne, the capital of Bornholm, takes you fairly close to the patrolled areas, and you worry about currents. They say the East Germans will confiscate your yacht and make you eat fish heads and oatmeal porridge. Closer to Sweden than to Denmark, Bornholm is a wooded island some 120 nautical miles across the Baltic from the Danish archipelago. The open waters of the Baltic have been friendly both times I have made the passage, but this inland sea can be rough. It is notorious for its sudden summer storms and short, steep seas. Monitor the forecasts carefully and make other plans if it is blowing.

Bornholm is a farming and tourist island that is far off the beaten track for Americans. You will make landfall at Rönne, a pleasant town with a large artificial harbor. This is a good place to be weatherbound. Ernest Gann wrote memorable and evocative descriptions of a fall gale here in his *Sirens of the Sea*, a must for all serious cruising sailors. If the weather's fine, explore the town, buy provisions, and sail along the coast to one of the tiny havens that make Bornholm so fascinating. We spent a night in Vang, an artificial refuge with a right-angle entrance so tiny that we had to warp the Nicholson around inside end-for-end before we could leave. From here we explored the great castle at the northern end of the island, then spent a night at Alleröde in another minute harbor whose entrance off the beach was only some 20 feet across. This was where the harbormaster charged us less because we were Americans. Go for a walk inland and enjoy the view to the island of Christiansö, 12 miles away, shimmering in the evening light.

Christiansö is a magical place—actually a group of

Maxi 108. The Maxi designs are the most popular charter boats in Scandinavia and are widely used in flotilla fleets, especially in Yugoslavia. Designed by Pelle Peterson, they can stand up to the tough weather conditions sometimes experienced in Danish and Swedish waters. The 100 series are larger yachts, with powerful engines, center cockpits, and aft cabins that make them ideal for family charter parties. The Maxi 84 (not illustrated here) is a 28-footer, which sleeps four in comfort. This is an ideal beginner's yacht, especially when equipped with a roller furling jib. The raised deck makes for ample headroom below and plenty of sunbathing space on deck. (Courtesy Maxibatarna, Goteborg, Sweden)

islands, only two of which are inhabited. An arm of the sea runs between these two, forming a narrow harbor at either end of which a yacht can take shelter. A footbridge connects the two islands. Most visitors use the southern arm, where you can lie alongside under the shadow of the circular fortress, now a lighthouse, with walls 6 feet thick. Christiansø was a base for pirates until the Danes succeeded in throwing them out. Today, Christiansø is a quiet artists' and fishermen's colony. Plan to explore in the early morning or evening, for the island is invaded by tourists during the middle of the day. Most inhabitants stay at home during these hours.

There is not much to do on Christiansø except to walk around the island and admire the rocks, pine trees, and ponds so thick with water lilies they look like meadows. So few people live on Christiansø that the lighthouse keeper is chief of police, pilot, customs officer, and magistrate. This is without exception the ultimate bareboat destination.

One word of advice if you bareboat these waters. Allow plenty of time for the return journey, as you may be delayed on your passage back to the sound by bad weather.

Sweden offers two superb and quite different cruising grounds. The west coast is a land of windswept rocks and narrow channels winding through a glacial landscape. Small fishing villages with brightly colored houses cling to rocky hillsides. There are few trees. Those that survive the relentless onslaught of the westerlies are gnarled and whipped into strange shapes. The east coast is green and wooded, a peaceful archipelago of dark narrow channels and still anchorages surrounded by conifers and tumbling rocks. On the west coast, the open sea is always close at hand, but in the east you can sail for weeks in still waters and sheltered channels even on the roughest days. Swedes are water-crazy. There are more recreational boats per capita here than in anywhere in the world. The Swedish Cruising Club has over 24,000 members. Charterers and sailors from other lands are always welcome.

Bareboating companies are few and far between in Sweden. All are small operations with only a few yachts. The Swedish National Tourist Board, 345 Fifth Avenue, New York, NY 10024, should be able to supply you with an up-to-date list of them. Most companies offer Pele Petersen Maxis, which are ideal for these waters. You may also be offered a Hallberg-Rassy design, another excellent choice. The Swedish summer vacation season begins in mid-June about a week before Midsummer, the celebration of the summer solstice, and ends in late August, when everything seems to shut down for winter. While you can charter in May or early September, the weather is likely to be cooler and sometimes downright unpleasant. Better to plan on chartering in the high season here.

Sweden in high summer is glorious—as long as the sun is shining. The days are long, the evenings golden with a glowing light that permeates everything. I remember being anchored in a tiny sheltered pool some 30 miles south of Stockholm on one such evening. We ate dinner in the cockpit and sat for hours watching the golden light filter through the trees. The air was completely still. Children's voices carried across the water. The summer homes on the eastern shore shone with a deep russet red long after the sun had set. It was as if the twilight were never going to end. But there were other days when the wind blew and the grey clouds scurried over the low islands, and we needed woolen caps, long pants, sweaters, and foul-weather gear. You are very far north here, so you should be prepared for cold weather, even in midsummer.

You can charter the west coast of Sweden from Denmark, but you will have an 80-mile passage from Helsingor to Falkenberg near the southern end of the archipelago. The best strategy is to find a company near Goteborg, Sweden's second city with a large international airport. Then you are in the heart of the islands, with no passagemaking before you start gunkholing. The best and most accessible cruising for bareboaters with limited time is between Goteborg and Fjallbacka. There are more islands than you could possibly explore. The charter operator will supply you with a portfolio of local charts bound in a large folder so that you can flip from sheet to sheet as you make your way through the skerries. Each chart covers about 5 miles and records every marker, literally every rock. Even with these remarkable aids, you can easily get lost. At least as far north as the fishing village of Smogen, I would recommend that you stick to the main channels until you are familiar with the buoyage system (System A cardinal and lateral buoyage, like the rest of Europe) and with the peculiar problems of navigating among islands that all look alike. The hardest problem is maintaining a sense of direction. An English engineering friend of mine taught me the best way. "Think horizontally, in at least three directions. Think about the relationship of each island to the others, then look for this relationship on the chart. It's just like reading an architectural plan." Once mastered, Swedish navigation is a snap, provided you always know where you are to within less than a quarter-mile!

The western archipelago has few towns. One of the first you will come to is Smogen, a place that most Goteborg sailors visit at least once a year, so it is always crowded. The fishing-village-turned-tourist-trap nestles along the sides of a deep inlet where yachts moor in rows. You can walk along a boutique-lined boardwalk and meet sailors from all over Europe. Be sure to take the narrow and spectacular bypass canal as you go north. There's barely enough room for a single boat. The best route north lies through the Sotenkanalen, an artificial inside passage that keeps you away from the open sea. The next, and most famous, settlement is Marstrand, a major yachting center with an island castle. You lie stern-to the quay here, with plenty of company. This is a tourist spot, but a marvelous place to see fine old Colin Archer yachts, some of them converted pilot vessels. The town is colorful and spotless. If you like open-water sailing, plan to sail out to the Vaderoarna, the desolate Weather Islands that lie 10 miles off the mainland. The government maintains a network of *gasthamnar* (guest harbors), where there are toilets, showers, and garbage disposal facilities as well as shelter in rough weather. They will charge you between $5 and $10 a night to use them, but plan to use several during your cruise, including the one on the Weather Islands.

The waters between the islands are generally smooth and ideal for leisurely chartering. (Swedish National Tourist Office)

Marstrand is where I would sail inland, taking a long detour up spectacular inshore passages to Uddevalla, around Orust, and out toward the Skagerrak at Lysekil. You will enjoy forest and cliffs, completely sheltered anchorages, and some fine sailing. Sail as much as you can; the water is generally deep in the channels and the wind will give you all manner of different lifts. You never know what is in store next. One day you will explore cul-de-sacs and narrow side waterways, mooring all by yourself; the next, you'll be in a crowded harbor.

Anchoring in Sweden is never a problem. For once, there are more safe anchorages than yachts. You can anchor off if you wish—this is sometimes advisable when there are mosquitoes. Or do as the Swedes do. Find a cleft in the rocks, lay out a stern anchor, and ease your bow into the rocks. You just tie your bowlines to convenient rock outcrops, and there you are. A dinghy is unnecessary. You may share the anchorage with some other yachts, each tied into its own cleft, but there's plenty of room for everyone. This is where you may meet some local sailors. If you do, pick their brains. They will tell you about magnificent gunkholes that no visitor would ever find. A Norwegian couple befriended us near Fjallbacka and sent us to places where the locals were astounded to find Americans. As in every other cruising ground, the best places are often off the beaten track. Incidentally, the Swedes are meticulous about garbage. Be as fastidious with beer cans and other debris ashore as they are.

The islands are so entrancing that one is tempted to sail on and on, right up to the Norwegian border and beyond. Be firm and turn back in good time! You will be able to savor the ground you have already covered or to return by a different route. The prevailing winds are from the southwest, so you are likely to sail north faster than you will sail on your return to the south. Not that the headwinds are a problem—distances between anchorages are short and there is always sheltered water. Most charterers will probably turn south around Fjallbacka, which will give them time to explore the myriad islands near Lysekil.

The west coast is for those who like windy skerries and desolate landscape. The east offers other less dramatic charms. Your charter company will be based within easy reach of Stockholm, perhaps on the outskirts of the city itself. You can sail right into the center of the city to visit the *Vasa*, the restored seventeenth-century warship that was raised in one piece from the harbor. In the summer, the islands themselves are crowded with vacationers; the channels, a constant parade of yachts old and new. Many are smaller craft, beautifully maintained Folkboats and gaff-rigged, lapstrake-planked traditional craft. Then there are fiberglass Maxis, Hallberg-Rassys, and Norlin racing boats, even the occasional Swans. Children play in inflatables and sail Optimist dinghies. Never have I met such courteous sailors.

You can do a great deal in a week here, but try for two, so that you an explore the archipelago both north and south of Stockholm. The greatest crowds are near Sandhamn, where the Royal Swedish Yacht Club is based. Avoid their crowded docks and anchor in a nearby cove. Here again, the charts are meticulous and on a very large scale. If anything, navigation is harder on the east coast on account of the trees and low topography. Just be sure to avoid the restricted areas on the chart, defense zones where foreigners are outlawed. The east coast is island cruising at its very best. There are occasional small villages where you can buy provisions—as in Denmark, the prices are astronomical by U.S. standards. But this is an area where anchorage recommendations are useless. Go forth and find your own: the choice is infinite, the only limit is your imagination.

Once you are used to the area, make a point of leaving the bustle of the main channels and explore little swatchways and bays where only a few summer homes are to be found. It was here that we met some Swedish friends, who still send me Christmas cards. They saw us anchor and came to find out where we were from because they had relatives in the United States. We drank Scotch, visited their tiny wooden cabin high above the anchorage. They gave us fresh pike for breakfast. Later we rowed out to the boat by the light of a shimmering full moon. The taste of the pike lingers to this day. So does the memory of this rock-girt bay, down a minor channel. We were the only yacht for miles, in a northern paradise unlike any place we had cruised before.

18 Britain and Ireland

The British Isles offer a wider variety of cruising conditions than anywhere else in Europe. There's something for everyone. Gunkholers will find heaven among the rivers and estuaries of the Essex and Suffolk coast. The English Channel offers fast-running tides and the pastoral beauty of the West Country or the iron-bound coasts of Brittany and the Channel Islands. Southwest Ireland and western Scotland are rugged cruising grounds with incomparable scenery and open-water sailing. Once you've discovered the charms of these cruising grounds, I guarantee you'll return.

Dozens of small charter companies operate in Britain and a handful in Ireland. You will find their display advertisements in *Yachting Monthly* and *Yachting World*. Bareboating is often referred to as "self-steer" in British circles. Most charter companies are small operations offering fleets of half a dozen boats or so. If you are chartering for the first time, select a company that is a member of the Yacht Charter Association. Their members equip their boats with safety equipment up to the association's stringent criteria and carry approved insurance.

The choice of yachts is almost bewildering. For a first-time charter, I would recommend a party of no more than four people and a yacht with a maximum size of 35 feet. Why? Because European harbors tend to be crowded and smaller than American marinas, and a smaller yacht is preferable if you are not used to local conditions. Four people aboard a 32-to-35-footer will have plenty of room to move around, yet there'll be enough watchkeepers for the occasional longer passages.

Four or five designs seem to dominate British charter fleets, all of them sturdily built yachts. Rival 34s and 38s are robust cruising boats that do well in the Channel and Scotland. Readers of American magazines will be familiar with Dufours, Moodys, Nicholsons, and Westerlys, all of them available in sizes between 39 and 26 feet. You will find occasional exotica like Frers 44s, Swan 371s, and so on, but my advice is to stick with less flamboyant designs, where you know what you are getting into. I would not recommend taking a vessel smaller than 29 feet or so on your first British charter. Above all, do not be tempted to charter from a private

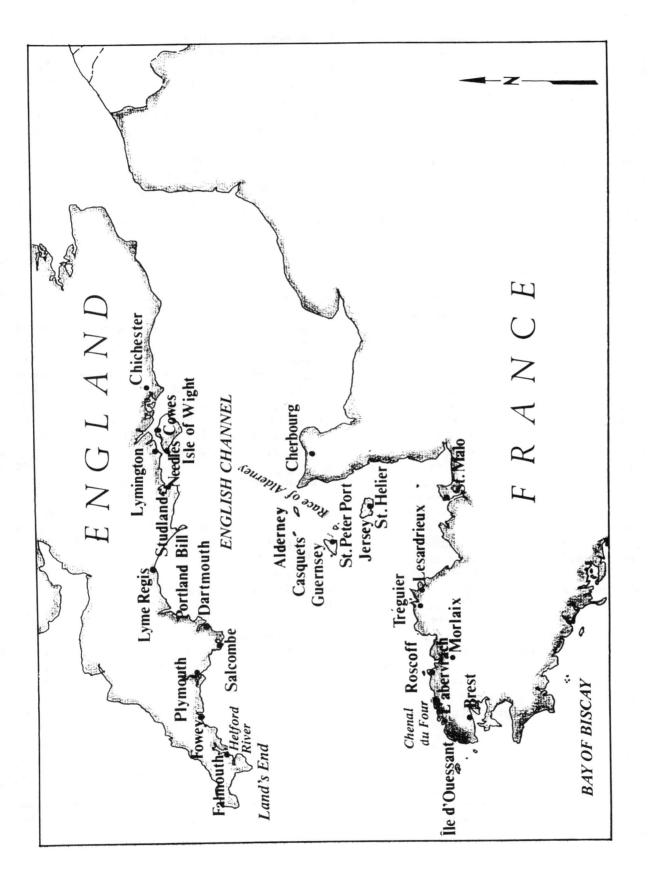

The English Channel and Brittany

owner, unless you are negotiating a boat swap. You have no guarantee of proper maintenance or adequate insurance. Wait until you are familiar with local conditions and have some good contacts before entering such a risky arrangement.

People sail in Britain all year round, but the charter season lasts from April through early October, with a somewhat shorter period, perhaps May to September, in Scotland. Chartering in April can be chancy. I once had spray freezing on deck on a spring trip. We were sailing in the snow in weather so cold that the shrouds were encased in ice. Needless to say, we spent most of our time in the pub drinking hot toddies! But there are those clear spring days when the northeasterlies blow day after day, bringing promise of summer. So you pays your money and you takes your choice, as they say! July, August, and the first week of September are high season. The weather *can* be more predictable, but there are crowds everywhere, especially during the school holidays between mid-July and mid-September. On the whole, I would plan a charter in late May or June, or early September. I have had good luck in June most times, with more than a few days of sunny warm weather and moderate breezes. The crowds are thinner, and the chances of gales are about even with high season. Mid to late September can be chancy, for the equinoctial gales of early fall can be vicious and you could be weatherbound for several days.

In spite of my being born there, I don't think British weather is that bad. True, the summers can be wet and windy, but they can be glorious as well. No one who has sailed in western Scotland during high summer will ever forget it. Britain and Ireland enjoy an oceanic climate, affected by the position of the Azores High in mid-Atlantic. Most of the year, a steady procession of lows passes over the British Isles, bringing periods of rain and strong winds to Europe. The most settled weather comes when an anticyclone settles over northern Europe. Winds will be calm, and the days warm and sunny for days, sometimes weeks, on end. But most of the time you can expect fast-moving, sometimes unpredictable weather in these charter areas. Only twice have I chartered in British waters and not worn foul-weather gear. In both cases, an anticyclone was hovering over northern Europe and there was no wind.

The secret is to monitor the BBC weather forecasts with sedulous care. You will find that your neighbors in harbor or at anchor will pass around gale warnings and more routine forecasts willingly. The shipping forecasts consist of a summary of the weather map, station by station predictions, and reports of current weather conditions. You can put these together every three to six hours to keep a panorama of changing weather in front of you. The forecast areas are given on a loose card in *Reed's Nautical Almanac*, which is bound to be on board. Your yacht should have a radio receiver on board. Be aware that wind speeds are usually given on the Beaufort Scale instead of knots and that gale warnings are broadcast as soon as they are received. (Incidentally, the commercial-free BBC radio programs are an enjoyable part of a British charter, provided you can tolerate constant record request programs.)

You can bareboat in four major areas of Britain and Ireland: the English Channel, southwest Ireland, western Scotland, and the east coast of England. Each has a special charm of its own.

English Channel chartering

Most English Channel charter operations are based on the Solent, the stretch of tidal water that separates the Isle of Wight from Hampshire. Another group of companies operates to the west, in Devon and Cornwall. Both areas are easily accessible from London by rail.

On the whole, I would advise taking your first English Channel charter from the Solent. There are plenty of interesting, if congested, harbors to explore on the English side, and the cross-Channel passage is only about 60 miles. If you are unfamiliar with fast-running tides, you might choose to spend a couple of days in the sheltered waters of the Solent before venturing farther afield. Cowes, Lymington, and Yarmouth are all worth a visit, and you can play with the tides to your heart's content. Most Solent charter companies are based on the Hamble River, Lymington, or Chichester at the east end of the Solent. If the tides and weather forecast are favorable, you can leave any of these ports on the first of the afternoon ebb, carry the outgoing tide through the Needles and clear of the Isle of Wight during daylight, and cross to France during the night hours. On days like these, plan on arriving early in the day and doing your provisioning while the charter operator completes work on your boat. You can then check out, store your provisions, and time your departure with the first of the ebb.

Most local charterers make a beeline for France and the Channel Islands, where liquor is cheap and the cuisine more interesting. Cherbourg is a favorite weekend run for Solent sailors, a good place for stocking up on duty-free liquor. Personally, I would avoid it. The marinas are crowded and noisy and the city has little to offer except a huge commercial harbor. Much better to sail straight to the Channel Islands from

Beaulieu River on the Solent, a favorite port of call for English charterers. (Brian M. Fagan)

the Solent, where you will have dozens of fine harbors and anchorages within easy reach, all for a few hours' extra sailing.

The first thing you should do upon arrival at the charter base is to get an update on the weather forecast. If the forecast is unsettled or a front is passing through, plan a short sail the first afternoon. For instance, I once arrived for a Solent charter to find a front due in 24 hours. So, on the charter company's recommendation, we took an easy daysail west to Studland Bay, a delightful anchorage near the entrance of Poole Harbor, and lay there in complete comfort while the rain and gale-force winds from the front passed through the next morning. There was a sandy beach and a fine pub ashore, where we met some new friends also bound for the Channel Islands, with whom we later cruised in company. You will have to anchor quite a distance out to allow for low tide, but France is only a long daysail away. Incidentally, check customs clearance regulations with your charterer ahead of time.

The classic Channel Islands charter itinerary takes you from the Solent (or Studland, for that matter) through the Alderney Race to Saint Peter Port in Guernsey. Then you spend a few days in the islands before sailing to St.-Malo in Normandy or setting course southwest to the Brittany coast. I would allow

two to three weeks for leisured exploration of these fascinating waters and make allowance for possible delays on the return leg if conditions are unsettled. Your cruise plans should depend on the weather. The prevailing winds are westerlies, so you are best off harbor hopping on the way west and sailing back to base in long legs. If the breeze settles in the north or east, sail as far west as you want to go early on in the cruise, so you can carry prevailing westerlies back (this is, of course, assuming that the winds change back soon). Under northeasterly conditions, I would recommend that you plan a landfall at somewhere like Roscoff on the Brittany coast, timing your arrival for the last hours of darkness. This will enable you to pick up the major coastal lights while still offshore. You can then shape your course to allow for stronger tidal streams closer inshore.

Make no mistake about it, the English Channel is no place to take liberties with the weather. Watch your weather forecasts and expect rapid changes in wind and sea. In some respects, visibility is more important than wind strength. If the weather is foggy, stay in port, for the hundreds of ships that traverse the Channel every day make no allowance for reduced visibility. Sometimes the Channel weather will be hazy for days on end. Better change your plans and stay on the English side—

the Channel Islands and Brittany are no place to be in a fog with strong tides under your keel. Shipping is an even greater hazard than the weather, even on clear days. Thousands of ships pass through the Channel every month, not only small coasters but huge supertankers and ocean liners. They pass in an endless procession along official separation zones that you must cross at the correct angle. Be sure to ask the charter company about the current regulations and *keep out of the way* of all ships. You are an idiot if you insist on your rights in these congested waters.

Most charterers use the Alderney Race route to the Channel Islands, the narrow waterway that separates the island of Alderney from the French mainland, where tidal streams can run up to 9 knots at spring tides. The race is easy to pass in settled weather, but you must time your arrival off the fast-running race for the ebb south and west toward the islands of Guernsey or Jersey. Wind-against-tide conditions here are downright dangerous in any breeze at all. Fortunately, you can divert for Braye Harbor in Alderney if you miss your tide, a huge roadstead sheltered from westerlies by a vast, eighteenth-century breakwater. Braye is usually crowded, but tuck in behind the breakwater as far as you can. Alderney is a fascinating, unspoiled island, a German stronghold in World War II. Take time to wander through the streets and admire the magnificent cats that sun themselves in local gardens.

Alderney is where you will experience the awesome range of Channel Island tides for the first time. The landscape is transformed in a few hours. At high water, the water laps the rocky shoreline and you step ashore from your dinghy at the top of the harbor steps. Six hours later, you gaze down into a deep hole. The water has vanished, the harbor is much smaller, and your dinghy would be hanging from its painter if you didn't know better. Estuaries become streams, isolated rocks become rocky islands. Your life is regulated not only by weather forecasts, but by tides. Every time you anchor, you have to lay out ample scope for high water, yet allow sufficient depth under your keel for low tide. Experienced Channel sailors are especially careful during spring tides. If you run aground at high-water springs, you may have to wait a month before you get off. Be sure you know how to calculate the depth of water under your keel at low water. You'll need this calculation every time you charter in Channel waters.

The art of Channel Islands and Brittany cruising is to play your tides. Let's assume you are bound from Braye to Saint Peter Port on Guernsey through the Swinge Channel at the western end of Alderney. This takes you through a narrow, rock-girt passage inside the Casquets lighthouse. Of course, you can pass outside in deep water, but what self-respecting sailor wouldn't take a short cut to save hours at sea? The weather is fine, the wind out of the northeast. Sailing directions will tell you when to enter the channel to carry a favorable south-going stream (2 to 2½ hours after local high water). As always in this area, let the tides work for you. Once you are through the Swinge, the approach to Saint Peter Port is simple, through the well-marked Great Russel Channel, which is more than 2 miles wide.

Nearly everyone who visits the Channel Islands spends a night or two at Saint Peter Port, the major port for Guernsey. The congestion can be terrible, especially if you want to berth in Victoria Marina. The tides being what they are, you can only pass into the basin for six hours or so on the high side of half tide. Many visitors moor to the large buoys reserved for yachts in the outer pool. You will be cheek by jowl with boats from all over Europe, with your anchor out forward and your stern tied to the buoys. The bumping and confusion increase on busy weekends. In August, many people anchor outside.

There is always something going on at Saint Peter Port, a major tourist spot. Ferries come and go, freighters load vegetables, tourists crowd excursion boats for France or Sark. The streets of the town are always bustling with shoppers in the famous duty-free shops. Be sure to visit Castle Cornet, which overlooks the harbor, and see the historical museum. For what it's worth, I have always found good Chinese food here. The daily ferries and frequent flights make this an admirable place to change crews if need be.

Jersey is easy to approach from Guernsey, but the entrance to Saint Helier Harbor, while well-marked, requires careful pilotage. This commercial port welcomes visitors, but look out for fast-moving coaster traffic. One yacht marina lies immediately to the south of the entrance, another near Albert Pier. The town is crowded, touristy, and cheerful, with excellent stores. You can tour this pretty island by bicycle, bus, or cab. Make time to explore Gorey Castle on the east coast, a superb fortress overlooking a wide bay and small harbor that dries out at low tide. Most charter companies prefer that you not take their yachts into drying harbors, so you should plan to visit Gorey by land.

The diminutive island of Sark is a kingdom of its own, a place that lives in a quieter era. Motor vehicles are outlawed; there are few telephones. You must visit Sark. Its high cliffs and green meadows are a spectacular sight on quiet summer days. You can anchor in various coves, but expect to lay out a large amount of scope to accommodate the huge tidal range. The three harbors on the island are tiny and much frequented by tourist boats. You can anchor off any of them in quiet weather

St. Peter Port, Guernsey, Channel Islands. Truly an advanced charter area for American sailors. (British Tourist Authority)

and row in. My favorite is Havre Gosselin, where the harbor nestles under high cliffs and you walk through a tunnel to the interior of the island. There is a quiet, pastoral charm about Sark that defies description. You could easily spend a week exploring the many nooks and crannies around its shores.

Malcolm Robson's *Channel Islands Pilot* or David Jefferson's *Brittany and Channel Islands Cruising Guide* will give you an almost inexhaustible supply of anchorages to explore in this wonderful cruising ground. Be warned, however, that some of them are distinctly adventurous. Follow sailing directions precisely and play your tides right. Above all, monitor the weather forecasts and do not venture far from the major harbors when gale warnings are in effect. Stay in port during foggy conditions, for tidal streams are unpredictable and you will soon be lost. If you are caught out, try to anchor in shallower water until the weather clears.

You can see a great deal of the Channel Islands in a week's charter, and a well-timed passage from, say, Saint Peter Port through the Alderney Race to the Solent will take you less than a long day if the winds are favorable. Better, however, to charter for two weeks and explore the adjacent French coast as well.

If you want to visit France and have limited time, choose St.-Malo over Cherbourg. The latter is a large commercial port; St.-Malo, a pleasant old town with a restored walled quarter where the eating is good. The Chenal de la Grand Porte is well marked and easy to follow, provided you use the tides. Time your arrival for near high tide to gain access to the yacht marina at St. Servan on the starboard side just before the commercial harbor. Personally, I prefer the pontoons in the Bassin Vauban under the walls of the old city, which you enter through a lock three hours either side of high tide. There you are close to everything. This is a good place from which to explore the island fortress-town of Mont-St.-Michel on a day excursion, for it is, to all intents and purposes, inaccessible by yacht.

The Brittany coast is nearby to the west, a wilderness of deep estuaries, tumbling rocks, and fast-running tides. This is my favorite part of France—dour, grey, unpredictable, and fascinating. While you can sail west from St.-Malo, the prevailing southwesterlies will give you a dead beat, so you are probably better off sailing from Saint Peter Port or Saint Helier to the estuary villages of Lesardrieux or Treguier, a passage of about 50 miles. Time your sail so as to arrive off the somewhat featureless Brittany coast just before dawn. You can then use the lights to shape your course to either estuary. The tides run strong here, so make sure you enter the estuaries on the flood and look out for strong cross-streams that can carry you close to the rocks.

Lesardrieux is a pretty Breton village lying at the head of the Trieux River. First time, enter by the Grand Chenal, your sailing directions close to hand, for the stone towers, beacons, and lights are downright confusing until you get used to the buoyage system. The large-scale plan in the pilot book is essential. The rising tide will carry you past La Croix light and green, wooded shores to the marina at Lesardrieux. There are several places in the river where you can anchor, but look out for the fast-running streams. The estuary will seem enormous at high tide, but it shrinks dramatically on the ebb. Lesardrieux is a stone-built village with a central marketplace. Make sure you enjoy the crepes!

Treguier is even prettier, for the estuary is narrower. The entrance is 3 nautical miles west of Les Heaux, the rock shelf off the Trieux estuary. First time, best take the Grand Passe entrance, which is accessible in almost any weather. The channel is well marked, but look out for cross-streams. Once you are past La Corne beacon, the estuary narrows to a buoyed river channel passing through beautifully wooded countryside. Treguier is a charming little place with a marketplace and old stone houses. You can secure at the marina or anchor off in the river. Whatever you do, lay plenty of scope or tie up your boat securely. The streams run strong. Treguier has excellent restaurants.

Life on the Brittany coast is dictated by the tides. The ebb carries you west, the flood east. Roscoff is about as far west as you will be able to go on a two-week charter, even if you bypass the Channel Islands. There are several attractive ports and anchorages between Treguier and Roscoff, among them Perros and Tregastal. But my favorite is Morlaix, especially if you want an adventurous excursion up a narrow tidal river. Start your passage from Roscoff, a pretty little town that is a ferry port for Plymouth-bound steamers. You will have to dry out against a quay, but this is easy enough, provided you cant the yacht in toward the wall and the terms of your charter permit this. Time your arrival off the entrance to the Morlaix River for an hour before high water. That way you will avoid the strongest stream and have plenty of water to traverse the 3¾-mile twisting channel up to Morlaix lock, which opens for about an hour and a half either side of high tide. You then berth at pontoons right in the middle of town, under the shadow of a high, nineteenth-century railroad bridge.

Morlaix is a town of steps and old houses, with excellent creperies and restaurants, a superb place to be weatherbound. There are even showers on the quay. If this is your farthest point west and you have time, try renting a car and exploring the obscure villages and estuaries west of Roscoff from the land. Antique buffs will have a wonderful time in this part of Brittany.

Many stores carry stocks of antique Breton shutters that make fine fireplace mantles—if you have the space to carry one aboard.

With the prevailing westerlies, you should have no trouble making the Solent in comfortable time. If the winds are consistently in the east, you are better off visiting the Roscoff area at the beginning of your cruise. At worst you will have headwinds on your way to the Channel Islands; at best—and this never happens to me—the winds will veer to the west and you'll sail downwind both ways.

A cross-Channel charter from the Solent provides a great variety of weather and cruising conditions and can be strongly recommended for a first-time European adventure.

Western Channel charters

Many charterers elect to sail west from the Solent, to explore the classic cruising grounds of England's West Country. This can be a tough trip, because the prevailing westerlies make it a windward ride all the way and there's a long passage west across Lyme Bay to be faced. I think you are better off chartering in the west, at such ports as Plymouth or my favorite, Falmouth. The West Country is my favorite part of Britain, but I am biased, for I learned to sail there. Dorset is soft and rounded; Devon, red-cliffed; Cornwall, harsh and rock-bound, with more austere towns. Devon and Cornwall offer such famous estuaries as Dartmouth and Salcombe, picturesque villages like Fowey and Saint Mawes, and all the facilities of Falmouth and Plymouth. The big problem is congestion, so I would recommend a May, June, or September charter in these waters.

Falmouth is a logical charter base, because it is sheltered by the Lizard and within easy reach of numerous attractive ports to the east. A two-week charter will give you ample time to explore the ports between Torquay in Devon and Falmouth itself. Although the tides run less strongly than on the Brittany side, you should take them into account when planning your cruise. If the winds are out of the west, plan to sail east as fast as possible, then harbor hop back to the west against the wind.

Wherever you are bound, be sure to make your first stop the Helford River just west of Falmouth, a rural estuary accessible at all stages of the tide. Anchor or moor off Helford village, explore the river by dinghy, and drink at the pub, a truly memorable watering hole.

Rival 34. This is the epitome of the classic British cruising yacht and an ideal charter boat in the unpredictable waters of northern Europe. Fast and weatherly, the Rival has excellent windward performance and is exceptionally dry in rough weather. (Courtesy Rival Yachts)

Bound up-channel, stay at least a mile offshore to avoid outlying dangers, much more in rough weather. Your first stop will probably be Fowey, a charming fishing town in a deep estuary, with the disadvantage that anchoring room in Wideman's Pool opposite the town is very limited. The Royal Fowey Yacht Club is especially hospitable to American yachts and sometimes has visitors' moorings. Plymouth is a major city and worth a visit only for its imposing harbor and the opportunities for exploring the estuary with its naval dockyard. There are several marinas and other berthing opportunities, but I cannot imagine anyone spending much time here. Far better to sail on to Salcombe or Dartmouth, where commercial traffic is at a minimum. Salcombe is notorious for its estuary bar, which is very dangerous on an ebb tide in strong onshore conditions. Make your entry in quiet weather, and try to find a visitors' mooring off the town. The alternative is to anchor in the Bag or farther upstream clear of the moorings. Like all West Country ports, Salcombe is crowded during the season. But there is much to see in the winding streets of the town. Dinghy enthusiasts will have a wonderful time exploring the river upstream of Salcombe. You can go as far as Kingsbridge on the top of the tide.

Dartmouth lies to the east of Start Point, one of the major headlands between Land's End and the Solent. Give the point a very wide berth (safe distance is 4 miles), to avoid the tidal races off the rocks. Pass well outside the Skerries bank and identify Dartmouth entrance from the Mew Stone, which lies immediately to the east of the entrance. Use your engine to enter the river, for the high cliffs blanket the wind. Most of the town lies on the west wide of the river, and there are several marinas to choose from. You can also anchor, but look out for the mooring chains. This is an attractive, bustling place, famous for the Royal Naval College that overlooks the river. Take time to explore Dartmoor and Exeter by car or bus. Exeter Cathedral is one of the most distinguished in England, and the Maritime Museum is full of fascinating workboats from a century ago.

Falmouth also offers other charter options for the more experienced sailor. You can sail cross-Channel to western Brittany, to the barren coast west of Roscoff. The principal attractions are L'Abervrac'h and the ports on the northeast coast of the Bay of Biscay, accessible through the Chenal du Four. This is not an area for the beginner, for the tides run fast, the weather can be unpredictable, and the pilotage is tricky. Like Treguier farther east, L'Abervrac'h is an estuary town, with a relatively easy landfall on Isle Vierge light, 3 miles east. Make sure you arrive off the coast at dawn in time to pick up the flashes. First time you cross this way, I would advise a stop at L'Abervrac'h to take the uncertainty out of the landfall before going around the corner.

The northwest corner of France is notorious for its winter gales, fogs, and fast-running tides. This is a dour, rock-bound coast that fortunately has been well traveled by expert cruising sailors who have charted every nook and cranny for you. You can actually visit the dreaded island of Ushant itself on fine days. I intend to do so one day—if the weather is right.

Adlard Coles and A.N. Black's *North Biscay Pilot* gives detailed sailing directions for the Chenal du Four, the rock-lined passage that takes small craft inside Ushant. The Chenal is easy on a fine clear day with the tide under you, and leads not only to the great naval port of Brest, but to plenty of picturesque ports and anchorages, among them Camaret, Douarnenez, Morgat, and Concarneau. The farther south you sail, the better the weather, especially beyond Point Penmarch, at which point you are well inside south Biscay. You can spend weeks exploring mainland ports, offshore islands, and quiet country estuaries. This used to be a totally unspoiled area, but is now crowded with French yachts. You can actually charter from ports like La Rochelle, but the language difficulties may keep many English-speakers from doing so. Many of the well-established anchorages and ports where you once tied up with the fishing boats now boast of small marinas. In other places, you will find yourself cheek by jowl with dozens of other yachts, many of them of diminutive size. Make sure you have enough water under your keel at low water in these crowded harbors, and expect to use Mediterranean mooring techniques here, dropping an anchor over the bow and lying stern-to the quay. Northwest Brittany is a wonderful cruising ground, but needs three weeks for a thorough exploration. Few Americans venture to this beautiful area.

It is possible to pick up a bareboat in Falmouth and to sail to southwest Ireland, following part of the Fastnet Race course. This is a superb passagemaking cruise, provided the weather is settled. The 1979 Fastnet showed just how dangerous conditions can get off Land's End. You should allow three weeks for an Irish charter based on Cornwall, for you may well be delayed on passage. It's as well to assume that you will sail from Falmouth nonstop to, say, Bantry Bay. There are no all-weather ports in between. Expect the charter company to check out your skills pretty thoroughly if you want to set off on this passage. You can, of course, pick up a yacht in Ireland itself, saving both time and money, but the open-water passage around Land's End is an interesting experience.

I think one of the ultimate charters is a cruise from Falmouth across the Bay of Biscay to northern Spain and back. It is possible to make this trip on a bareboat from a Falmouth company, provided you have the necessary open-water experience. Make no mistake, this can be a tough one, for the bay is notoriously stormy and unpredictable. You should allow two weeks for a leisurely Spanish cruise. I promise you an unforgettable experience. You have a number of passage options. One is to take off nonstop for northwest Spain, passing 20 miles outside Ushant at the northwest corner of France and making a landfall on Cape Ortegal. This is what you should do if the winds are in the north. You will be down in Spain within three days, with all the time in the world to explore the fascinating estuaries and ports between Bayona and Ribadeo on the north coast. You'll have so much time in hand you'll be able to come back via northwest Brittany instead of returning nonstop. It's not so much the navigation as the weather and shipping that are hazards on this charter. The major ports and headlands are well marked with lights and long-range radiobeacons. Cynics say you can sail to Spain by following the major shipping lanes across the bay from Ushant to Cape Ortegal.

If the winds are in the west, cross to L'Abervrac'h, then traverse the Chenal du Four and coast as far south as the Isles de Groix or La Rochelle. This shortens your Biscay crossing considerably, especially if you head for San Sebastian, a busy but colorful city at the eastern end of Basque country. You can then visit the ports of the north Spanish coast, ending up at Bayona ready (hopefully) for a fast nonstop ride home with the prevailing westerlies behind you. Robin Brandon's *South Biscay Pilot* gives full details of this beautiful, friendly coast. The people are courteous, the seafood superb, and every village and town different. This is an area where the locals still live from fishing and yachts are always welcome. Again, this region is little visited by Americans. You will find mainly British and French yachts here—and no bareboaters.

The best months for Spain are between May and early September, when the weather is often settled for long periods of time. But you can have bad weather at any time, and you should be prepared with adequate foul-weather gear and seasick pills. If you encounter a gale at sea, heave-to and sit it out, but be careful to do so well outside the shipping lanes. The Biscay shipping lanes are the equivalent of a Los Angeles freeway, so keep well clear, even in fine weather.

This cruise is one of those special trips that you make only once or twice in a lifetime. It offers the bareboater every challenge from open-water passagemaking to intricate navigation, fine scenery, and interesting sights ashore as well.

Southwest Ireland

Only a few small companies offer bareboats in Ireland, but these are of high quality, run by charterers of long experience. You can charter from Bantry Bay or Schull in the southwest, or from Galway, where you can explore Connemara and the Aran Islands. Both are superb cruising grounds, with wonderful sheltered anchorages, deep water, ample opportunities for sailing on the open Atlantic, and all the variety of weather that an oceanic, northern-latitude climate offers. You can reach these charter areas by flying into Dublin, then taking a train to Galway or Cork, or by renting a car. Do come prepared for changeable weather, for the winds can blow hard and it rains all months of the year. The weather can be cool in the summer, but is never cold. The best months to charter are probably May through July, or early September, leaving the high season to the locals.

Most people automatically associate Ireland with boisterous pubs and Irish good cheer. They are right, for the people are sociable and delightful. A cruise that takes you from village social center to village social center can be very enjoyable. But take time for long walks ashore and explore as far afield as you can. Another nice touch in Ireland: there are all sorts of little shops where you can rent a bicycle for nominal sums to explore the countryside when you need a change from the ocean. This is an area where boning up on the sailing directions ahead of time will be well rewarded. Take the trouble to acquire the Irish Cruising Club's *Sailing Directions for the South and West Coasts of Ireland*, which can be purchased from Mrs. J. Guinness, Censure House, Bailey, Co. Dublin, Ireland (£15 in 1983). They will take you into all sorts of beautiful and unspoiled places.

Southwest Ireland is worth at least two leisured weeks. Head for Bantry Bay for your first charter, a 20-mile-long sound once described as being large enough to house all the navies of Europe. A charter fleet is based in Bantry Harbor, itself of little interest. But you should spend at least a couple of days exploring its quiet northern shores, sheltered by 6-mile-long Bere Island, with the best anchorage in Lawrence Cove on the northeast corner. This is the site of a Glenans sailing school, a clone of the French school of the same name in Brittany. The small village of Rerrin is home to Brendan Murphy's pub. It acquires quite an international flavor during the summer, when Glenans is in operation. Adrigole Harbour is another recommended stop on the north shore, but the shoals in the bay need careful attention as you come to anchor. Some charterers anchor in Glengarriff Harbour, a famous tourist spot with a celebrated botanic garden on nearby Garinish Island. Be warned that the ferry boatmen are rapacious—take your own dinghy in the quiet hours!

You might want to stop in Castletown's Bere Haven harbor while deciding where to go next. The harbor is a major fishing port, but yachts can usually find a berth, especially in high summer when the fishing boats are up north. The harbormaster is especially helpful. The town is a typical, old-fashioned Irish place with superb pubs. If the industrialized scenery bothers you, anchor in Dunboy Bay, close to the entrance of the harbor. There's heavy seaweed in the bay, but you can anchor comfortably within 100 yards of a ruined Victorian mansion burnt by the IRA in 1921.

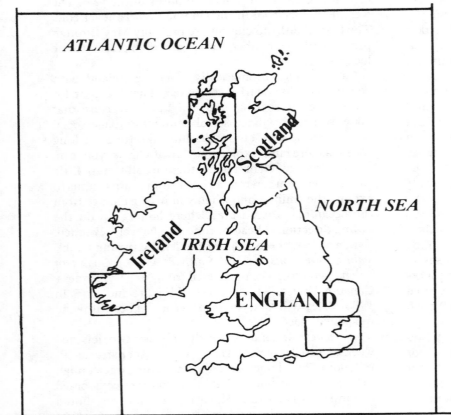

Southwest Ireland

Bantry Bay. (Courtesy Bord Fáilte–Irish Tourist Board)

Once clear of Bantry Bay, you can sail either east or west, depending on weather conditions and the time available. On the face of it, the green, iron-bound coast looks very inhospitable. But you are never more than about a two-hour sail from a safe harbor or sheltered anchorage. There are few hazards and you can sail close inshore. Just keep an eye out for lobsterpots and salmon drift nets, marked either by inconspicuous buoys or fishing boats. The salmon nets are a menace on foggy days. If you come across one, call up the fisherman on the VHF if you have one. If you do run over a net, try to keep the boat at 90 degrees to it. Nine times out of ten, you'll bounce across quickly without fouling the propeller. The tidal streams are weaker than in Brittany, but can run strongly off major headlands like Mizen Head near Crookhaven. Keep well offshore in places like these.

A westward charter could take you as far as the mouth of the Shannon River, or to the Blasket and Aran Islands. If you have less time to spare, explore the deeply indented coast between Bantry and Valentia Harbor. My absolute favorite spot is the Kenmare estuary, the next great bay to the west beyond Bantry. This is still a lonely place, with completely sheltered harbors among green mountains, a place where you can catch the essence of the Irish countryside. You round

Gull Rock, then head up the estuary to your choice of three fine, sheltered harbors. Sneem on the north shore is a small haven, where you can anchor in about 12 feet. You pass between Sherky and Pigeon Islands until you can pick up the conspicuous Parknasilla Hotel that leads you to an anchorage close to the pier. It's 2 miles to the village, but you can reach it by dinghy on the flood tide. Killmakilloge is farther up the bay on the south side, a sheltered inlet that offers no less than three anchorages, only one of them, Bunaw, a village with supplies. The sailing directions will take you around the islands and submerged rocks off these unspoiled anchorages, or into Ardgroom, where more provisions and a castle are to be found. Kenmare is so lovely you may be tempted to spend all your charter there.

Portmagee and Valentia farther to the north and west are not so attractive, Portmagee on account of its dangerous entrance in strong winds. Valentia is an all-weather port, and there are several sheltered anchorages inside the bay. The channel up to Cahirciveen offers the only access to a town with comprehensive supplies. This means crossing the Doulas or Cahir Bars and following a set of rather inconspicuous leading lights up to an anchorage in the fast-running current off the town. I found it more fun to explore Kenmare, then to head east to the coast between Bantry and Cork.

Heading east, you must give the tidal race off Mizen Head a wide berth out to sea. The tides can run at 4 knots here and the overfalls are savage in heavy weather. Crookhaven lies up a deep inlet tucked behind Mizen Head, a completely sheltered place in any wind. This used to be a busy fishing port, a place where Australian-bound windjammers would lie up for last-minute instructions. Then the fishing declined and the village went to sleep. Only summer visitors liven up the place now. There's one store and two pubs. You can anchor off the village or find shelter behind Granny or Rock Islands if the weather pipes up. I loved the 5-mile walk along the coast to Mizen Head with its pink and white sandstone cliffs.

If the winds are from the east, I would make a beeline for Rosbrin or Schull, both fine natural harbors where you can find shelter in most conditions. Rosbrin is guarded by the ruins of a fourteenth-century castle built by a chieftain named O'Mahony. You can walk ashore through countryside literally ablaze with flowers. Schull is still a fishing port, a fine refuge except in southerly gales. You can anchor off or lie alongside a

Opposite: *Beacon Point, Baltimore Harbor. (John Watney)*

fishing boat while exploring the small village. Tommy Newton's is the place where the fishermen drink. Both these anchorages are excellent places from which to sail out to the Fastnet Rock. The Fastnet is famous for the tough Admiral's Cup yacht race that rounds it every other August. Even in the height of summer the weather can be savage here, as the racers found to their cost in 1979, when 17 people lost their lives in a fierce gale. The present lighthouse was built in 1903 and replaces an earlier structure erected in 1854. In calm conditions, you can go quite close inshore.

You could spend weeks exploring the coastline between Baltimore and Cork. Most people linger for a few days in the sheltered waters of Baltimore Harbor, exploring the many islands that lie close by. The entrance is easy to find. Just look for Lot's Wife, a large white beacon on the eastern side that is conspicuous in any weather. You can berth at the New Quay in the harbor or anchor off Sherkin Island. Clear Island, about halfway to the Fastnet, is well worth visiting (by ferry, if you want to save time). The island is especially interesting as an outpost of Gaelic culture. Clear Islanders were once skillful pilots, who brought transatlantic sailing ships into Cork in almost any weather.

Once east of Baltimore, you begin to enter less frequented waters. You'll always find a few yachts in the main harbors, but there are anchorages galore awaiting discovery in the indented coast, especially between Glandore and Kinsale. Castletownshend and Glandore are musts. The narrow Castletownshend estuary leads to a quiet anchorage about a small, unspoiled village, once a bastion of Anglo-Irish land-owners and still the site of Mary Ann's Bar, one of the oldest pubs in Ireland. Glandore is a picture-postcard place with wooded hills and painted cottages forming a backdrop to the tiny harbor. In quiet weather, the anchorage off the village is like a millpond, but it turns vicious in a strong southerly. You can find shelter round the corner off the drab village of Union Hall. Getting away from the crowd is easy in settled weather. Just sail along the coast and find a sheltered anchorage in the many long bays that indent the thinly populated sheep country.

Kinsale is about as far east as most charterers will probably get, an all-weather entrance leading to a charming town of narrow streets and old houses. This is a popular spot for yachts, boasting of a small marina. Kinsale also has a reputation as *the* gastronomic center of Ireland. You can feast in any one of a dozen or so gourmet establishments or simply enjoy delicious fish and chips on the quayside, as I did. Many sailors come here to admire the architecture and to wander through

Glandore Harbor, Cork. (John Watney)

the Norman church, the Mall, and to admire the restored almshouses and other buildings in the town.

Many people consider southern Ireland the finest cruising ground in Europe, but my advice is to charter there soon. The shadow of the developer is beginning to fall across this delectable coast as new marina schemes spread slowly westward from Cork. This is one of the few places where you can still anchor in complete solitude, even in mid-August. Long may it stay that way!

Western Scotland

"To experience western Scotland in high summer is to experience paradise," cried one of my sailing friends when we started talking about chartering in the north. He's right. Like Sweden, Scotland is magical during those few weeks of the year when an anticyclone settles over the North Sea. Blue skies, purple heather, the murmur of bees in the flowers—this is wild country and scenery beyond peer. Even on gloomy, rainy days, western Scotland is alluring, the mountains hiding in caps of lowering mist, land and ocean a symphony of greys. Then there are the smells—the odors of rocks and mud exposed at low tide, the smoky aroma of smoldering peat, the lingering aftertaste of local whiskey. This is a special place to sail. More and more people are discovering the delights of a charter in these waters, most of them British or European sailors. Precious few Americans bareboat in Scotland.

There are at least 35 charter companies operating in western Scotland, offering everything from 40-footers to small motor cruisers. You will find their advertisements in the British yachting press and a listing of all major companies in the Scottish Highlands and Development Board's annual water sport guide, *On the Water* (Bridge House, 27 Bank St., Inverness IVI 1QR, Scotland), an admirable publication that will give you enough data to narrow down prospective cruising grounds and potential charter fleets.

Like Scandinavia, Scotland is farther north than most European charter areas. You can get bad weather any

Western Scotland

month of the year, but many locals claim that you have a better chance of settled conditions from late May through late June. I would strongly advise chartering either early in the season before prices rise for the busy months, or in early September. Many local charterers go out in March when the boats are heavily discounted, but that's a little chilly for me. Even in summer, the nights can be cool, so you should come prepared. Pack your foul-weather gear and boots, but splurge on a local wool sweater. They are some of the best in the world.

The charter company will provide you with Admiralty charts and a cruising guide, probably a copy of the *Clyde Cruising Club Sailing Directions*. This is an invaluable guide to hundreds of ports and anchorages, compiled by local cruising people with generations of experience on the coast. They will brief you on the tides, which have ranges as extreme as 18 feet. The streams can run hard and strong, too, especially in narrow channels like Kyle Rhea near Skye. You have to be careful about depths when anchoring, too, so the sort of calculations you use in Brittany or Maine are needed here. Anchoring is easy enough, except that you can encounter seaweed or rock-infested bottoms. Fortunately, most anchorages are well sheltered and uncongested even during the summer, so you should come to no harm. You can lie alongside harbor quays, too, but be sure to ask permission first.

The finest chartering is probably to be found between the Oban area in the south to Kyle of Lochalsh in the north. A cruise in these waters will give you a sampling of the best of western Scotland and a chance to visit the islands of Mull and Skye, among the most beautiful in Europe. Several charter companies are based in the Oban region, a convenient rail stop that brings you to the heart of the islands. Your boat may be based at Oban itself or at a marina somewhere like Loch Melfort. Wherever you board, you are only a short sail from the Firth of Lorne and Mull. A marvelous first-night stop lies at the north end of Seil Island, 8 miles southwest of Oban, a sheltered lagoon named Puilladobhrain (pronounced "pulldoran"), strongly recommended in the *Clyde Cruising Club Directions*. If you are lucky, you'll sail into this calm place on a grey day, when the steep rocks and black silhouettes of the islands and mountains give a mysterious feeling to the landscape. The experience is unforgettable.

From Puilladobhrain you can circumnavigate Mull. In fine weather, I'd sail south to the south end of the island and visit the small island of Iona, the site of one of the earliest Christian communities in northern Europe. There's a good day anchorage off the island, which is an easy distance from an excellent anchorage at Loch na Lathaich 4 miles away. You can anchor at the head of the loch or sail farther north to Gometra, a perfectly protected harbor where you anchor off some cottages in about 20 feet. Look out for weed on the bottom. Fingal's Cave, immortalized by Felix Mendelssohn's overture, is only a short distance away on the island of Staffa. Unfortunately, you can only visit this place in the calmest of weather.

The Sound of Mull on the northeast side is a more protected route to Tobermory, the largest settlement on the island. The tides can run up to 3 knots here, but the dangers are well marked. Tobermory itself is a small town with steamer service to the mainland. The entrance to the bay is wide and safe and you can anchor off the pier. This is a good place to buy provisions and stretch your legs ashore, but I would plan on spending the night in Lochaline, 10 miles southeast of Tobermory on the mainland side. This gentle, misty place is very sheltered, but the tide runs hard in the entrance. The best anchorage is east of the entrance near the small village inside. These are just a few of the possibilities around Mull. You can spend days exploring Loch Linnhe and the lochs and islets on either side of the Firth of Lorne without ever retracing your footsteps.

Folklore has it that Ardnamurchan Point, the westernmost extremity of the Scottish mainland, separates the cruising men from the boys. You can have a wonderful charter without venturing into the open waters beyond the point, but a cruise north to Skye offers no special problems in good weather. Large swells can run off Ardnamurchan in westerly weather, but you will be comfortable enough if you pass at least a mile offshore. From there you can hug the mainland or visit the offshore islands of Eigg and Rum. The former offers somewhat better anchorage, at the southeast end of the island. From Eigg, it's a short hop to the wild and desolate southwest coast of Skye. This is very much a coast for the expert, for people fascinated by dour landscape and deep lochs. You can lie in places like Loch Scavaig, near the magnificent scenery of the Cuillin Hills. Scavaig is definitely a fair-weather anchorage, exposed to the southwest. Even in quiet weather, savage gusts will sweep down on your anchorage, causing the yacht to veer all over the place. You're best off taking some lines ashore.

Much better to take the narrow sound that separates Skye from the mainland. Provided you follow the charts carefully and play your tides, you should have no difficulty reaching the multitude of sheltered anchorages between the town of Portree on Skye and Lochcarron. Just look out for sudden wind shifts in the deep lochs. You'll often find quite different conditions outside. Acairseid Mohr (Gaelic for "large harbor") is a

Portree, Isle of Skye. (Richard Dibon–Smith, Photo Researchers, Inc.)

much used (and misnamed) anchorage on the island of Rona close to Portree. Use care entering, for there are plenty of rocks in the entrance. There's some nice walking ashore. I prefer to lie here rather than in Portree, a busy little town in the season, with tourists, steamers, and several hotels. You can buy supplies there before setting off again into the wilds.

Rather than going farther north along the steep coasts of Skye, you may have better luck with good anchorages by working your way back to the mainland. Just play your tides in the narrow passages between the islands and you should enjoy some fine sailing. As to anchorages, there's Fladday off the island of Raasay, close to Portree, a snug anchorage where only a few yachts can lie. Or linger among the desolate coves of the Crowlin Islands, where your only companions may be hundreds of seals. You'll find softer scenery in Loch Alsh, where you can lie in a tiny bay close to Eilean Dolan castle, surrounded by green hills and soft light.

The number of quiet, unspoiled places is almost unending. And nearly everywhere, you can walk ashore, climb hills, or simply sit on a rock and contemplate scenery untouched by industrial civilization. This has got to be one of the finest places to cruise on earth!

A two-to-three-week charter based on the Oban area should give you enough time to visit both Mull and Skye. You can, of course, charter twice, once near Oban, and then later from somewhere farther north like the rail head at Stromeferry on Lochcarron, but I doubt if you will save much time. There are charter boats scattered all along the coast, even as far north as Ullapool, from which you can explore the Summer Isles or even the Hebrides. But I would leave these stormy waters for a later highland charter. There's more than enough to enjoy around Mull and Skye or farther south.

The Essex and Suffolk Rivers

Like most British-born cruising people, I was brought up with the stories of Arthur Ransome. In my later years, I read the cruising yarns of Maurice Griffiths and a marvelously old-fashioned yachtsman-author named Francis B. Cooke, who in the 1920s and 1930s wrote the equivalent of Eric Hiscock's cruising bibles. These men sailed the rivers of Essex and Suffolk in the days when cruising yachts were few and far between and you could buy a 25-foot yacht for well under $500. Not only did they sail, they wrote as well, about a series of tidal estuaries flowing through a countryside little changed from a century or more ago. They wrote of quiet anchorages, gentle mists, and sluicing tides, of lumpy passages between sandbanks and of sudden gales in estuary mouths. Theirs was a quieter cruising world, but the rivers themselves remain unchanged. There are 10 rivers with more than 300 miles of navigable water flowing into the North Sea between Kent and Suffolk, a distance of no more than 45 miles. This is a cruising ground of meandering rivers and tidal creeks, of mudflats and gravel banks that extend miles offshore into the shallow, stormy North Sea. If you charter in these waters, you'll spend your time waiting for tides, pushing your way into narrow swatchways, and gunkholing to your heart's content. If you want to test your pilotage skills, your ability with compass, chart, and lead and line, this is the place to do it. Best of all, the east coast rivers are a short distance from London, so you can see a great deal of lovely countryside in a few short days of bareboating.

The east coast rivers are a highly distinctive cruising ground. Apart from the tides, mudflats, and creeks, the featureless topography often means that you must have a three-dimensional eye to work out your exact position. There are hundreds of beacons and buoys. Even a simple passage from, say, the Blackwater River to the Orwell requires careful planning, so that you carry the ebb down the one estuary and the flood up the next. There are times when you will anchor offshore in the shelter of an exposed sandbank at low tide to wait out an adverse wind or to catch a tide. The weather can change rapidly. Even a moderate breeze blowing against the tide can bring a short, sharp chop that tortures even the most hardened stomach. But even on gale warning days, you can sail far inland in quiet waters or wander ashore through medieval and Tudor houses or country churches set in a timeless landscape. The east coast rivers are the domain of the putterer and the gunkholer, for purists who go sailing in shallow-draft yachts with a marked pole as a sounder. Humorist P.G. Wodehouse used to refer to his short stories as "snorts between the solid orgies." I would describe these delectable cruising grounds as a bareboating snort of the same type, the sort of long weekend experience that you will never forget.

Although the villages and towns of Essex and Suffolk are too far from London for daily commuters, their ports and anchorages are becoming more and more congested with yachts. Places like Burnham and Brightlingsea live off yacht racing, boatbuilding, and yacht maintenance, and there's often little space to move, even in the spring. But there's plenty of room away from the main ports and anchorages, in remoter archipelagoes like the Walton Backwaters, or in the upper reaches of the Orwell. Even if the anchorages are crowded, there are plenty of compensations, not least of them the finely restored working boats. With luck, you'll see a Thames barge under sail or a converted oyster smack working her way into the Colne. As late as 1900, there were still 2,000 barges in the coastal trade, carrying fertilizer, coal, and other cargoes to and from London. Now there are about 50 under sail, most of them in charter work.

The charter companies in this area cater almost entirely to local sailors and tailor their service accordingly. Most of the yachts are in the 25-to-35-foot range, and I would try for one about 28 feet for the first time. The relatively shallow draft and small size of such a yacht go well with local conditions. The best charter base is probably Maldon at the head of the Blackwater. Apart from anything else, it's a gorgeous place, with Thames barges lying alongside the town quay. You can catch the first of the ebb down the river, lie for the night in Bradwell Creek marina near the mouth of the river, then sail with the tide up the coast to the Orwell or south to the major yachting center at Burnham. Personally, I prefer the Orwell and the Walton Backwaters every time. The scenery is infinitely more beautiful.

A passage to the Orwell means a sail up the Wallet, a sandbank-protected, deep-water channel past Clacton and around the corner into the Orwell between the ferry ports of Harwich and Felixstowe. These busy harbors offer nothing to the bareboater, so you should sail on upstream to the old barge village at Pin Mill, a tiny hamlet nestling among the trees on the south side of the river. Unfortunately, Pin Mill, with its famous sixteenth-century Butt and Oyster pub, is much congested with moorings. You are probably better off securing at Woolverstone marina, then walking a mile downstream through green meadows and oak groves to the village. This is where Thames barge races are held every year. If you are lucky enough to visit on race day, you'll enjoy an unforgettable sight: 15 or more barges

Eastern England

Right: *English Channel waters are tidal, and many harbors are dry at low water. (Lesley Newhart)*

Below: *Lyme Regis, Dorset, an occasional port of call for charter yachts. The harbor dries at low water, so you have to anchor off, or lie alongside the quay wall at its outer end, canting your boat in towards the pier with a line to the spreaders. (Lesley Newhart)*

Above: *Malden Waterfront, with Thames barges. The church is a famous cruiser's landmark. (Brian M. Fagan)*
Left: *Pin Mill, Suffolk. The famous Butt and Oyster pub in the background. This has been a favorite stop for Thames barges for centuries. (Brian M. Fagan)*

with tan sails and bluff bows jockeying for the start as competitively as the most fanatical ocean racers.

If you have only a few days, explore Pin Mill, then ease down river and take the marked channel past the end of Pye Sand and into the Walton Backwaters. This is a world of reeds and narrow creeks, many of them little more than salty dribbles at low water. You can lie among the islands in any weather, surrounded by whispering reeds and mudflats where curlews whistle and herons feed. Your dinghy will take you into remote channels where a larger yacht can never penetrate, into one of the last swampy wildernesses in England. Only a few farmers live here; the rest is still untouched, a haven for wildlife and for sailors.

Last time I lay under the lee of Horsey Island was on a rainy evening in June. The misty skies cleared at about 1800, leaving a shimmering silver light on the still water. An aged wooden sloop ghosted into the anchor, one older man aboard. He dropped the jib, scandalized the gaff main, a maneuver I hadn't seen since my teenage years, and came to anchor just inshore of us. Later we talked through a magnificent sunset. He was a retired civil servant who had owned the same boat for nearly 30 years. Every June, he spent two weeks puttering around the Backwaters, leaving his wife at home. "My time of rebirth," he murmured. "My father brought me here when I was 12. I've tried to come back every year since." We talked till midnight and beyond about birds and boats, of passages that were triumphs and of others that were not, of quiet anchorages and boisterous ports, of tides caught and tides missed. Some of the magic of this special place rubbed off onto me that evening.

From Walton, it's just a short distance back to base. If you have more time, you can explore the Deben, the Stour, the Crouch, or any number of the other estuaries and muddy creeks that make this such a distinctive cruising ground. The charm of chartering in the British Isles is the sheer variety of cruising available—and the east coast rivers make up just a small part of it.

19 Mediterranean Bareboating: Corsica and Sardinia

"A kind of radiance, like that of the sun or moon, lit up the high roofed halls of the great king.... The interior of the well-built mansion was guarded by golden doors hung on posts of silver which sprang from the bronze threshold.... On either side stood gold and silver dogs ... to keep watch over the palace of the golden hearted Alcinous and serve him as immortal sentries never doomed to age." Thus did the Greek poet Homer describe a Bronze Age palace in the Ionian Islands of more than 3,500 years ago. His writings, and those of others, still captivate the imagination. Fortunately for us romantics, the Mediterranean is now familiar bareboating ground. Many people even take their first European cruise there. It's a good choice. The waters are warm, the weather relatively predictable, the people friendly, and the sightseeing opportunities nothing short of incredible. Where else can you have an ancient ruin to yourself and visit a monastery little changed since the eleventh century? Where else can you spend the night in a haunted anchorage, or hobnob with the jet set? Sooner or later, every serious cruising sailor ends up in the Mediterranean. The lure of these historic waters is irresistible.

General chartering conditions

Bareboating is a relatively recent phenomenon in the Mediterranean and is still much less organized than it is in the Caribbean. The greatest expansion has been in flotilla fleets, in sailing vacations that are packaged with cheap airfares to form a low-budget holiday for families in northern Europe. You can flotilla cruise in Yugoslavia, Greece, Turkey, and the south of France, even in areas that were recently inaccessible to all but the most experienced cruising sailors. Bareboating, as opposed to flotilla chartering, is still in the hands of small companies with just a handful of vessels, most of them between 30 and 45 feet. Many are British or French owned, but some countries, especially Greece and Spain, place severe restrictions on foreign ownership and control of charter companies operating in their waters. Greece, in particular, has rigid ownership requirements, so you are certain to be dealing with a local organization there.

The largest Mediterranean charter markets are among northern European sailors, so these companies' advertising efforts are concentrated in Old World

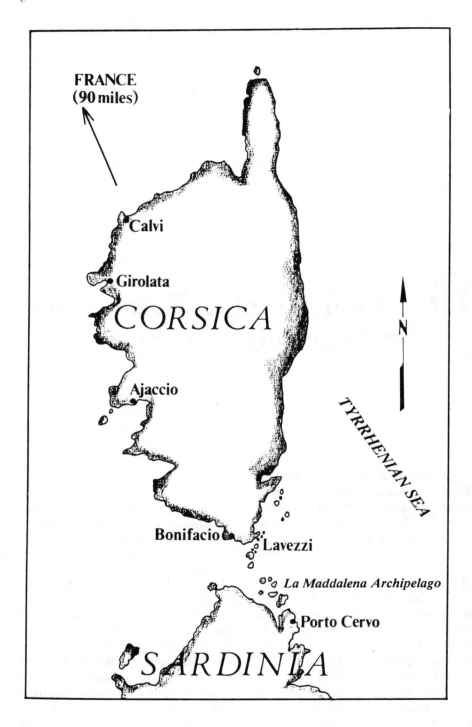

Corsica and Sardinia

journals. Relatively few of them cater to American clients, although you are certainly welcome to charter with them. As with a northern charter, get a few copies of European sailing periodicals to obtain the widest perspective on charter opportunities. A few American organizations act as agents for European charter companies, especially those operating in Greece. Be sure to check out the credentials of the company on the ground before signing up, insist on referrals to previous clients, and extract guarantees that you will actually set sail on the boat that you reserve.

The Mediterranean offers such a variety of bareboating opportunities that it is hard to know where to begin. Chartering is a seasonal business with relatively primitive facilities in most places. The European holiday season is surprisingly short. High season is only about two months long, with the charter "window" extending about six weeks on either side of mid-June to late August. The use factors are probably too low and the seasons too short to attract the sort of highly standardized charter operations found in the Caribbean and South Pacific, where 20-week seasons are not uncommon. You can charter a yacht from a small company in almost any major Mediterranean sailing area. People charter in the south of France, in Corsica and Sardinia, Spain, the Balearics, Yugoslavia, Greece, and Turkey. But the major charter areas are still from the south of France south to northern Sardinia and the Greek islands. I would definitely advise a first charter in one of these areas, simply because facilities are better. If you have the slightest doubt about your ability to handle Mediterranean conditions, go on a flotilla cruise the first time (Chapter 2). They are set up with a nice balance of cruising in company and independent sailing that suits novices and relative experts alike. And it's comforting to know that the flotilla staff is close at hand if you do run into trouble.

Cruising people have a strange ambivalence about the Mediterranean. They find that they spend hours motoring in flat calms—calms interspersed with days of fighting 35-knot headwinds. My own experience bears this out. Time and time again, I have started out on passage on a beautiful calm day. The sea is as flat as a millpond. Then a finger of breeze snakes across the water. An hour later, it's blowing at 30 knots and you're heavily reefed down. Astonishingly vicious, steep-sided waves appear from nowhere and toss you around like a cork. Even Homer's heroic mariners complained about the stormy Mediterranean. This is no place to be careless or cavalier about open water. Contrary to popular belief, too, Mediterranean winters can be savage. Icy north winds can blow over the Aegean for days on end during the winter. The south of France is beset with hurricane-strength *mistrals* during the winter and even very occasionally in summer. It is not until one sails offshore in winter that one realizes just how rough the Mediterranean can be. I was once at sea in a midwinter gale in a 9,000-ton tank-landing ship off Algeria. The seas were so rough they caused the deck to flex and ripple. True, the ship was built for a single cross-Channel trip on D-day, but the effects of the gale were awesome. Bareboating is definitely a summer pastime in these waters.

For all these warnings, summer sailing conditions are normally very agreeable. The best months are probably May, June, and July in Corsica and Sardinia, when the northwesterly winds are normally light to moderate. There is sometimes a period of bad weather in early August, while early September can be delightful. The Ionian Islands enjoy generally moderate conditions throughout the summer, but the Aegean is beset with the famous *meltemis* between June and early September, summer northerlies that can blow at over 30 knots day after day. Fortunately, there are good local forecasts in each of the major charter areas. Your company will give you details.

In many respects, Mediterranean chartering is the same as in northern Europe—you are on your own. Provisioning is your responsibility, but there are plenty of supermarkets and food stores in major ports and small towns. Bring all medications and film with you. Sunglasses and a sun hat are essential, otherwise bring what you would take to the Caribbean plus some slightly heavier sweaters for chilly nights. You can dive and snorkel, but the underwater scenery is nothing on the Caribbean. Plan on enjoying the sights ashore more than those underwater.

Wherever you charter in the Mediterranean, you are going to use your engine far more than in the Caribbean. In settled weather, the mornings are often calm, with a light breeze filling in during the afternoons and dying at sundown. You are probably best advised to motor to windward in the calm mornings and at night, planning your windward work for as early in the charter as possible. This will allow you to take your time coming home. Even during prolonged periods of calm weather, strong winds can rise almost without warning. The winds can strengthen from 10 to 35 knots within a half hour. In some ways the Mediterranean is like Southern California, where people learn the subtle signs of changing weather over years of cruising. It's difficult for a short-term charterer to recognize such phenomena on the basis of a few weeks' experience. So monitor forecasts carefully, and watch for these basic signs of changing weather:

Beneteau 13.50. A German Frers designed 44-footer that is coming into charter in the Mediterranean and West Indies. She features a large flush deck and easily handled inboard rig (most charter versions do not have spinnakers). The large cockpit is ideal for Mediterranean cruising. Four to six people can charter in luxury, with a huge aft stateroom, another one forward, and a saloon that will swallow up a dozen visitors. The Beneteau 13.50 has an exceptionally well thought out galley. (Courtesy Beneteau (USA))

● Waves rolling into an anchorage on a calm day can presage a strong wind.

● Hazy conditions often mean settled weather, while hard outlines to shorelines and distant mountain peaks may signal strong winds on their way or blowing off the land.

● Veil clouds tumbling off ridges and peaks are often a sign of strong winds.

● A line of pearly haze at the foot of distant land may sometimes mean that strong winds are blowing there.

● Extreme dry conditions and high temperatures may be a sign that strong, local downslope winds may develop.

● Hot air rising off the land during the day can sometimes kill wind at sea, but the breeze will return in the cooler hours of evening and night.

● Cumulonimbus thunderheads over the land and dark rain clouds can mean squalls in the offing.

With experience, you will learn to identify signs of changing Mediterranean weather for yourself.

Most modern Mediterranean charter boats are well equipped with two anchors, a gangplank, full safety gear, and a roller-furling jib, more than adequate equipment for the sailing you are likely to encounter during your vacation. The main challenges to your seamanship come in boisterous weather, at anchor, and in port.

The greatest hazard in the Mediterranean is not so much strong winds, but the short, steep seas that kick up within a few hours. The motion from many Mediterranean storms makes you feel as if you were being twisted around by a corkscrew. Conditions tend to be worse in shallower water, so even if the winds are not excessive, exercise extreme caution on account of waves. I have seen seas in the aftermath of a day's 35-knot blow that jibed you all standing even in a moderate wind, simply because the ship was hurled about by waves moving in all directions. The entire crew, even people with hardened stomachs, were rendered helpless with nausea in a few short minutes. If in doubt, staying in port is a good idea. And if you are caught out and have plenty of sea room, heave-to and wait out the storm. Most summer blows are short-lived, so they should not delay you long. Generally speaking, it is hopeless to try fighting headwinds and steep seas. Better to bear off to an alternate destination slightly downwind or to wait for more settled weather. Most of the time, however, summer weather is pleasant and predictable, even if the winds blow hard sometimes.

The most popular Mediterranean anchorages and ports are invariable congested in high season. Fortunately, there are plenty of viable alternatives, many of them pleasant anchorages not mentioned by the cruising guides. I met one elderly English cruising man in the Ionian Islands in a trim, heavy-displacement cutter, who spent every summer in the Mediterranean. When I praised Denham's admirable guide, he chuckled drily.

"Yes, dear boy, it's splendid. But do you know the best guide of all?" he asked.

"Is there something better?" I asked in surprise.

He reached over to the shelf by his chart table and took down a battered, thick, blue-cloth volume. It looked dull and dry.

"Admiralty sailing directions," he said proudly. "The boys who compiled these in the nineteenth century did all their surveying in small cutters and whalers. You can guarantee that they knew where to get their heads down when it blew. The trouble is that they're gutting the *Pilots* now and this edition's going out of print. Only large ships use them, and the cost's too high. This is an old edition, a real treasure. Never sail without it. If you have any sense, you'll try and pick one up before they're all gone. You'll find the Victorians recorded things that modern cruising guides haven't even thought about. They were *real* sailors."

Three months later, I managed to track down the volumes of the *Mediterranean Pilot* in a London bookstore. My English acquaintance was right. Time and time again, they have taken me into obscure, sheltered bays a few miles away from the port where everyone was holing up. On one occasion, for example, a strong southerly came up unexpectedly off the west coast of Corsica. Thanks to the Admiralty *Pilot*, we were able to duck into a gorgeous cove that was completely empty. We were weatherbound there for two days, while boats in a nearby harbor dragged all over the place because there was not enough space for everyone to anchor. But the *Pilots* can lead you astray as well. The old survey officers were tough birds, who thought nothing of lying in exposed roadsteads that are far too bumpy for effete twentieth-century sailors.

You will find yourself lying to a single anchor in most larger Mediterranean anchorages. I would recommend not laying a second one unless you have to because of restricted swinging room. Given the unpredictable winds in many places, you are best off allowing the yacht to swing. You may experience stronger winds in Mediterranean anchorages than you have ever met elsewhere, perhaps downslope winds that hurl dust and spume at you horizontally, while the noise blanks out all other sounds. Best to be mentally prepared for such conditions, when you just hunker down, lay out maximum scope, and set an anchor watch. Most times, the winds tend to die down without notice in the middle of the night, so you should get some undisturbed rest. Check the bottom carefully, for grass is common in many Mediterranean anchorages. Be absolutely sure that the anchor is well snubbed in, even on the calmest evenings, and lay out as much scope as you can. You'll almost certainly stay where you are and sleep better anyway. Most people who drag in this part of the world have not anchored properly in the first place.

Marinas are springing up all over the Mediterranean as yachting explodes as a major tourist industry. My advice is to avoid them like poison unless you want water, fuel, or other necessities, or are feeling extravagant. Most are astronomically expensive, and, in any case, you may find yourself mooring Mediterranean-style with few more facilities than you would find in a normal harbor. They are really designed for larger luxury yachts that cannot exist without an umbilical cord to land. A few, like those in the Piraeus, the south of France, and Porto Cervo in Sardinia, are well worth a sail-through or a visit from the land just to admire the incredible yachts and the outrageously expensive boutiques. Where else but in the Mediterranean will you have yachts to which fresh flowers are delivered every day? The real charm of the Mediterranean lies in its ancient ports and deserted anchorages, not in modern-day developers' efforts to improve on centuries-old facilities.

Most ports will ask you to secure stern-to a crowded quay. This can be a hazardous maneuver for people used to going alongside in comfortable marinas. A great deal depends on your abilities at steering your boat astern and on the way you lay out the bow anchor that keeps you off the quay. Here are some suggestions:

● First, select the spot where you want to secure, preferably one where there is plenty of space between neighbors. Make sure there's enough water alongside.

Decide where you will let go your anchor (allow for as much scope as possible), judge the probable effects of the wind on your maneuvers, and prepare the anchor for letting go. Two stern lines should be coiled ready on the stern. If you have a dinghy, send a crewmember ashore to take your lines.

● When everything is ready, make another pass, drop the bow anchor, *and make sure it is snubbed in hard* by motoring astern toward the quay. Build up enough way so that you snub in properly and can maneuver precisely astern.

● Now approach the quay, throwing lines ashore or to your dinghy oarsmen as soon as possible. Land the windward line first, secure it to the dock, and pull in *from the yacht*, using cockpit winches if necessary. With luck, there will be people on the dock ready to help you. If not, approach close enough for crewmembers to take lines ashore, then haul off.

● Once secured, adjust your lines to keep the rudder clear of the wall and bottom, and lay out your gangplank over the stern. Hang fenders over both topsides to keep off aggressive neighbors.

Everyone seems to moor stern-to, but I prefer to come in bow first, partly because I have better control when approaching the quay, and also because there's much more privacy in the cockpit. Your rudder is also safe from the wall. Purists may argue that you can pull out from the wall faster when the wind comes onshore, by going ahead and hauling in on the windlass. Maybe, but a well-laid stern anchor has always served me well. I have had to leave the seawall at Mykonos in an emergency when a 35-knot wind came up in minutes, threatening to blow the yacht onto a concrete wall. We simply brought the stern anchor line to a genoa winch, cranked hard, went full astern, and were off in seconds.

You will find that most ports reserve a section for yachts, although Yugoslav harbors are still relatively uncongested and much more flexible about where you secure alongside. Try to avoid commercial ports or quays. They are invariably filthy, although coaster skippers are sometimes delighted to swap paperbacks. Most harbor officials are courtesy itself, provided you are cooperative in return. So are fishermen, but realize that they may leave at odd hours of the night. Best to inquire ahead of time if they plan to depart before dawn. Otherwise, they will courteously and firmly bang on the cabin roof at some ungodly hour.

There are so many different areas where you can charter in the Mediterranean that it is difficult to know where to begin. Instead of covering a great many areas in sketchy outline, I decided that I would concentrate on a couple, both well-known cruising grounds where excellent yachts are readily available. Yes, you can charter in Yugoslavia and enjoy the sights of Dubrovnik, Split, and the Gulf of Kotor, or sail in unspoiled Turkish waters, or from resort to resort in the Balearics. But I think your first bareboat charter is best taken in either the Tyrrhenian Sea or in Greek waters.

A Tyrrhenian charter

The Tyrrhenian Sea is the name the Greeks gave to the waters that lap the west coast of Italy between the Tuscan Islands in the north and Sicily in the south, as well as Corsica and Sardinia. This historic body of water offers so many unspoiled anchorages and fascinating ports that one wonders why so many people make a beeline for congested Greece. The summer weather tends to be more settled and agreeable than in the Aegean, with light to moderate northwesterly winds predominating. Occasional stronger winds blow, and you may have local thunderstorms with gale-force squalls at times. Otherwise things are pretty quiet, except for occasional *libeccio*s that blow from the southwest and make many normally sheltered anchorages exposed nightmares. If you are unlucky or are early or late in the season, you may encounter a *mistral*, the fierce northwesterly wind that comes in like a lion from the Gulf of Lions. The wind raises great swells that fan out toward Corsica and the Balearics, although the islands' mountains often lift the gale up from the ocean. You are most unlikely to encounter a *mistral* during high season, but if one is predicted stay in port.

You can charter these waters from a number of locations, among them the south of France or Porto Cervo marina in northeast Sardinia. Bareboating is well established in the south of France. The French Tourist Bureau will gladly send you information on companies, yachts, and facilities. There are also a handful of English companies operating on the French Riviera, about the best of them being Robin Brandon Charters based on Port Grimaud. Some people simply cruise along the French coast, sampling the cuisine and visiting the opulent ports and tourist spots of the mainland. There is no point in describing these well-known waters here. Even more fascinating and less well known delights await you offshore in Corsica and Sardinia. Be warned, however, that you need at least two weeks, preferably three, to cover the 400-odd miles needed for a successful round-trip cruise.

The ancient port of Calvi on Corsica is only about 90 nautical miles from Nice and is your best port of entry.

The passage is straightforward in settled weather. On no account set out if there is a *mistral* forecast. Time your passage both ways to arrive about dawn, so you can use lighthouses for your landfall. Dense haze often mantles the Corsican coast during the hot summer months, but lifts slightly at dawn. You sometimes see high mountain peaks hovering in the sky when the shore is still invisible. Fortunately, the French government maintains a powerful radiobeacon on Revellata Point near Calvi, which will guide you in to your destination. This is one of the few places in the Mediterranean where you may encounter a pod of large sperm whales blowing peacefully close offshore.

Corsica is a dramatically beautiful island with 9,000-foot mountains, whose slopes are covered with *maquis*, a form of chaparral vegetation that has given its name to local patriotic resistance movements for more than two centuries. In Roman times, Corsica was a poor country whose inhabitants made their living by "brigandage more savage than wild animals." The Genoese controlled Corsica for a long time, to be followed by the French, who have administered the island for most of the past two centuries. Corsica is famous as the birthplace of Napoleon, although he left at the age of 21 and never returned. It is also celebrated for its associations with British Admiral Lord Nelson, whose ships used its superb west coast ports. The island was returned to France at the end of the Napoleonic Wars, so you do not have to clear customs at Calvi.

Calvi is an attractive sheltered port protected by an imposing thirteenth-century Genoese citadel. The town has stayed small and many of the old buildings remain. Nelson besieged the fortifications in 1794, landing 24-pound batteries to bombard the town. The French surrendered with honor after a month's siege. The port is crowded with French and Italian yachts during the summer, many of them very aggressive about finding a place to secure at the dock. You can anchor off in good shelter, provided you keep clear of the steamer berth. I enjoyed good meals here and obtained fine fresh vegetables from the morning market.

At this point, you should weigh time, weather, and your plans very carefully. Do you plan to visit Sardinia or not? If so, and you want to go as far south as Bonifacio, and if the winds are in the north, make a long passage of it and get right down to the southern extremities of the charter area. You can then take your time, coming home against the prevailing winds in short hops, rather than in one giant slog. When making your decisions, be careful to allow enough time for the homeward crossing from Calvi, giving yourself at least a day's leeway in case of bad weather.

The west coast of Corsica is not only spectacularly beautiful, but blessed with superb anchorages an easy daysail or less apart. Denham recommends that you cruise this coast in June or July, when the weather is most settled. He is probably right, for I have encountered sudden gales here later in the summer. During these months, you can shelter in several inlets between Calvi and the Gulf of Girolata. Pilotage can be tricky in the prevailing haze. Fortunately, the coast is dotted with the ubiquitous Genoese watch towers that were part of the coastal defense system as late as the Napoleonic Wars. They are often a sign that a viable trading anchorage once lay nearby. So is the fortress guarding Girolata Bay, a tiny cove with protection for about 15 yachts in northerly weather. This was once a pirate's lair, where fleets of fast galleys once lay. Girolata is a tiny hamlet so remote that it has to be provisioned by sea. The beaches are good for swimming, so many French yachts congregate here during the summer.

Ajaccio is the capital of Corsica, with a well-protected, all-weather port, excellent restaurants, and good shops. Yachts secure to the eastern quay, but you may find quite a crowd. This is where Napoleon was born; his birthplace in the old quarter of the town is now a museum. The town, with its fine gardens and avenues, has been a winter and spring resort for over a century. Ajaccio is a good place to rent a car to explore the interior, but you will need strong nerves—the local drivers have a death wish. I wouldn't spend too long here, however, for much more attractive ports and anchorages lie on the southwest coast of Corsica, a day's sail farther south. You can pause at Propriano or Port Tizzano, but the highlight is the landlocked harbor of Bonifacio, with an entrance so narrow and inconspicuous you can easily miss it. Only the massed houses on the cliffs reveal the presence of the town.

Sailing into Bonifacio is quite an experience, for the steep cliffs press in as you motor into the calm harbor. The massive walls of the medieval fortress-village look down on you. The fortress itself is garrisoned and off limits, but the thirteenth-century churches inside can be visited. One of them, Sainte Marie Majeure, has special water cisterns designed to capture rainwater during long seiges. Be sure to walk around the citadel and along the heights, where houses are perched over the ocean. This place was impregnable and has always been an important secure port. Unfortunately, the port is very congested, and you may have trouble finding a place to lie safely. Persist—the town is well worth it.

Bonifacio is the northern limit of the best cruising area in Corsica and Sardinia. There are plenty of anchorages and sandy beaches you can enjoy on settled

Bonifacio, Corsica: photograph taken before the explosion of cruising in recent years. (French National Tourist Office)

days. We talked to several French yachts, some of them regulars, and they gave us some valuable tips.

"Be sure to visit Lavezzi," said one skipper. "It's haunted."

"How come?" one of my companions asked.

"I'm telling you, it's haunted," said the Frenchman. "Look, I am going there. Why don't you follow me and let me know later if you think I'm right."

That was challenge enough, so we drifted south toward two isolated islands off the southern tip of Corsica, Cavallo and Lavezzi itself. Lavezzi is little more than a jumble of rounded and wind-scoured rocks, the anchorage nestling among the boulders, overlooked by a pyramid-like memorial to 750 seamen and sailors lost when the French frigate *Semillant* was cast ashore here during a *mistral* in February 1855. All but two members of her crew perished, and are buried in cemeteries behind the beach. Only the captain could be identified by the rescuers—by his uniform. We followed the Frenchman east past some outlying rocks into the most

gorgeous anchorage imaginable, a calm lagoon with a sandy beach completely sheltered against the north wind. We were not alone. There were 20 other yachts anchored bow and stern in the bay. We swam and drank wine, scrambled over the cyclopean rocks, and visited the rusting memorial to the *Semillant*'s men. It was a quiet evening, with a spectacular sunset. Then, at twilight, the sound began—a faint wailing and shrilling, as of men in distress. The seagulls' shrilling went on for an eerie hour before silence fell. The anchorage was completely silent. You knew that everyone was listening, looking for ghosts. Next morning, we rowed over to the Frenchman and admitted that Lavezzi was indeed haunted.

You can spend days exploring these islands. The waters are clear, so you can eyeball in and out of small coves between the reefs. Look out for the local rodents. They think nothing of swimming out to your boat and strolling up the anchor line. We chased one enterprising rat off. He was quite unconcerned, took a superb swallow dive off the stern, and swam over to our neighbor.

The east coast of Corsica has less to offer and can be hazardous from squalls sweeping off the mountains. I recommend that you explore the La Maddalena archipelago at the northeast corner of nearby Sardinia instead, then return the way you came.

The Strait of Bonifacio separates Lavezzi from Sardinia, an easy passage in settled weather, although the winds can blow with considerable force through the channels, even in the summer. There's generally more wind in the La Maddalena archipelago than there is farther north, due to the funneling effects of the two large islands. To quote an early edition of the *Mediterranean Pilot*: "...all sorts of vessels can go through without fear, although the sea is sometimes very high here with a prodigious roaring." Bound south from Lavezzi, plan on taking the South Channel between the Maddalena Islands and Sardinia itself. You can enter Italy at La Maddalena, securing in Cala Gavetta to the western quay. This is a small commercial and naval town with good shops and markets, and a fine starting point for exploring the seven islands of the archipelago. The three northern ones are barren and have little to offer except some sheltered, desolate anchorages. Caprera is about the same size as La Maddalena and is joined to it by a causeway. The Italian statesman Garibaldi made it his home in exile until his death in 1882. His flat-roofed house, named Cala Bianca, is now a fascinating museum a short cab ride from La Maddalena.

There are plenty of attractive anchorages in the archipelago, especially for history buffs who want to trace Nelson's maneuvers as he came to anchorage in the Agincourt Strait, the enclosed waters between Sardinia and Santo Stefano Island. The strait was surveyed by the warship of that name in 1802, then used as a base for the British blockade of Toulon in the south of France. Nelson beat his entire fleet into this anchorage in foul weather under double-reefed topsails the following year, an extraordinary feat of seamanship in heavy warships with minimal windward ability. "It is evident, my Lord, that Providence protects you," remarked one admiral with justice to Nelson some months later. When Nelson's ships left Agincourt Strait for the last time in January 1805, they set out on the long journey that ultimately led to the Battle of Trafalgar 11 months later. It's great fun to spend a few days following Nelson's tracks through these sheltered waters. Denham's book is an admirable guide.

You are now on the Costa Smeralda, a stretch of spectacularly beautiful Sardinian coast, much of which is owned by the Aga Khan. For what it's worth, at least one James Bond movie has been shot on this coast. Small wonder—Bond would approve of the lifestyle around here! The Aga Khan headed a consortium that developed the world-famous resort and yacht harbor at Porto Cervo, one of the plushest and most expensive marinas in the world. The marina lies in a deep inlet just south of Cap Ferro and can be entered in all weather and at night. You will probably be met by an inflatable boat that will direct you to a berth in the marina at the head of the inlet. Porto Cervo is so expensive that you will probably want to stay for one or two nights at most. I would recommend that you make an exception to your anti-marina rule this time, simply for the experience and to see the sleek motor yachts that vacation here. They are quite unbelievable. Even a 45-footer is a mere minnow here. The shopping complex is labyrinthine, very expensive, and somehow incongruous in this wild landscape of rocks and mountains. Buy your provisions elsewhere and plan on eating aboard. Otherwise, you'll be bankrupted in a few hours.

On the whole, the Costa Smeralda has been developed very tastefully. There are unspoiled and surprisingly uncongested anchorages within a short distance. I doubt, however, if any charter yacht will go south of the ferry port at Olbia or Tavolara Island. Olbia is a convenient place to pick up and drop crew, if you so desire. I believe that you can bareboat from Porto Cervo itself, but have been unable to obtain details of the yachts or companies operating them. It would certainly be an attractive short cruise in the midst of spectacular scenery. But there's little ashore except for jet-setters and inquisitive package tourists.

By this time, you will be about 200 miles away from charter base, and even the hardiest charter skipper should be thinking of turning around and retracing his steps, visiting some of the ports and anchorages he missed the first time around. Such is the variety of scenery and places to visit that you will have no objection to returning the way you came. These are wild and rugged islands that may well beckon you for a return charter one day.

20 Greece

Greece is a magical place for sailing—brown hills, blue water, and clear skies with sharp-edged clouds when the summer *meltemi*s blow. The houses of Aegean villages glisten in the sun, their brightly painted shutters set off against brilliant white walls. Double-ended, multicolored fishing boats cluster in tiny harbors virtually unchanged since the Middle Ages. In April, spring flowers turn the countryside into a blaze of color. This is the land of the Olympian gods: of Aeolus, the god of wind, whose gales blow furiously from the north; of Zeus, the cloud gatherer, whose lowering thunderheads menace from distant mountaintops. The Greeks themselves are gregarious, turbulent people, who welcome tourists and sailors alike with open arms. You can anchor in the shadow of a Classical temple, explore islands barely touched by industrial civilization, dance until dawn in waterfront tavernas, or spend the night in deserted coves with only the wind and bleating goats for company. All this and much more is within a short bareboating distance of Athens or Corfu. Greece is one of the great cruising grounds of the world, not so much because of the

sailing, which can be stormy, frustrating, and at times downright uncomfortable, but because there is so much to do ashore.

Until recently, bareboats were few and far between in the Aegean and Ionian. Those that were available were in the hands of private owners, some of them frankly villainous. Then came flotilla cruising, a form of organized bareboating that flourishes in the Ionian Islands, in the northeastern Peloponnese, and in Turkey. Independent sailing was not far behind, and you can find plenty of boats for charter these days. The Greek government has strict laws for charter boats, which must be at least 51 percent locally owned. So the bareboat fleets in their waters are at least nominally under local control. Although some companies do work through brokers in the United States who advertise in major sailing magazines, I would be inclined to explore the opportunities available through English agencies as well. Any edition of *Yachting Monthly* or *Yachting World* will give you their addresses and an idea of the kinds of yachts that are available.

Once you locate a suitable charter broker or com-

236

TURKEY

GREECE

Thessaloníki

Khalkidhikí

Mt. Athos

Préveza

CORFU
IONIAN
ISLANDS
Levkás

CEPHALONIA
Ithaca

Zákinthos

IONIAN SEA

AEGEAN SEA

SPORADES

EVVOIA

PELOPONNESUS

Gulf of Corinth

ATHENS
Aegina
Sounion
Epidhavros
Návplion
Póros
Spétsai
Hydra
Saronic Gulf

Monemvasía

Kéa
Síros
Kíthnos
Sífnos
Sérifos

Tínos
Mikonos
Délos
Rínia

Náxos

Thera

SEA OF CRETE

Iráklion
CRETE

DODECANESE

RHODES

Greece and the Aegean

←N

pany, check it out very carefully. There can be a world of difference between what is promised through the mails and what you actually find in Athens when you arrive. If you have the slightest doubt about the reputation of a broker, look elsewhere. The stakes are too high to do anything else. Your best guide is previous clients. You should insist on referrals before putting down a deposit. Also ask more questions than usual: How many boats does the charter company operate? Are they berthed together? What are their long-range maintenance plans? How do they handle breakdowns on remote islands? Does the company guarantee you the yacht you choose, or reserve the right to substitute another at the last minute? What are their refund policies? The best guarantee for satisfaction is to use a well-established U.S. broker who is familiar with the local companies. Marina conditions near Athens being what they are, you'll probably find that the charter company office is in town, while their yachts are scattered among several harbors near the Piraeus. Get some information on local facilities ahead of time.

All of this sounds very forbidding, but should not be, provided you ask the right questions ahead of time and do your homework. You have a wide choice of vessels to work with and the selection expands every year. You can find magnificent Swans, or Dufours, Gin Fizzes, Pearsons, Westerlys, Maxis, and other well-known American or European designs for us more common folk. In selecting a yacht, be aware that 20-mile open-water passages are commonplace in the Aegean. I would charter something in the 35-foot range in these waters. You will be a lot more comfortable if the wind pipes up. The equipment inventories for most yachts are pretty good, but you should check through the lockers carefully before setting out. Adequate anchor gear and mooring ropes are particularly important. You'll need two anchors, at least four docklines, and plenty of fenders.

Neither the Aegean nor the Ionian Seas are charter areas for complete beginners, so you should measure your experience carefully against local conditions ahead of time. It's advisable to obtain a letter from a sailing school you have attended, your local yacht club commodore, or someone with whom you have sailed, certifying that you are competent to handle a yacht in the size range you are chartering. This letter should specify some of your qualifications. You need more than basic navigational and seamanship skills in Greece, especially some experience of strong winds, open-water sailing, and anchor drills in rough conditions. A couple of Caribbean charters, one of them in the Grenadines, should give you adequate preparation to keep out of trouble. If you are nervous about

chartering in strange waters, arrange for a skipper to accompany you. Everyone I have spoken to has had wonderful luck with them. They know the best restaurants, the best anchorages, and local weather conditions. However, you should be aware that Greek law makes you responsible for the vessel whether or not a skipper is aboard.

There is so much to see and do in Greek waters that I would plan on at least two weeks aboard. Many charterers come unprepared for the long distances between Aegean islands. You should allow more time than you think necessary. You are certain to encounter some strong winds that may keep you weatherbound for a day or more. Many port captains will not allow you to leave if the wind blows more than about Beaufort Force 6. So budget plenty of time and enjoy a relaxed and challenging charter.

A Greek charter costs several thousand dollars, not so much because of the cost of the yacht, which is moderate, or because of provisions, which are cheap and abundant, but because of the long air flight. Your best option is an APEX fare from New York, which will land you in Athens in about 13 hours. Olympic Airways, the Greek national airline, usually seems to have the most attractive prices, although their flights are almost always full. Most of the passengers seem to smoke, which can make your life uncomfortable. With a 21-day trip, you can combine your charter with some land travel.

The cheapest way to charter in Greece is to go on a flotilla cruise. There are several companies and different areas to choose from—the Ionian, the northern Peloponnese, and the Halkidiki area of northern Greece. Some of these flotilla vacations are astoundingly good value. American charterers can probably save quite a bundle by flying to London, then taking a package that includes airfare and all charter costs from Britain. You will find all the reputable companies advertising regularly in *Yachting Monthly* and *Yachting World*. Nearly everyone I know who has been on one of these charters has enjoyed both the places and the people they met. This is a very good way for virtual beginners to charter in Greece, especially if you plan to combine sailing with touring ashore.

Opinions differ as to the best time to charter in Greece. Theoretically, you can sail year round, but I would not recommend the late fall and winter. Icy north winds can blow for days, and you will never be out of sweaters and foul-weather gear. Greece is very crowded during the high season between mid-June and early September. This is when the *meltemi* blows, the strong north-northeasterly wind that brings rough seas and hard squalls to the Aegean Islands. The winds funnel down island channels and off the mountains without warning, so a Force 4 wind in the open sea can be Force 7 or more in a narrow channel. There are plenty of secure anchorages, but the screaming wind may be a constant companion, making dinghy travel well nigh impossible. My favorite months are April and May, or the early summer. Then there are the halcyon days between early September and late October, when the crowds have thinned out and the air is still warm. The winds tend to be lighter, the weather more settled. These periods also have the advantage of lower-season airfares.

Should one charter the Aegean or Ionian first? Anyone interested in archaeology or Classical Greece should make a beeline for the Aegean, where ancient ruins abound. The Ionian has no major sites to offer, but an abundance of peaceful beaches and small fishing villages, as well as sheltered sailing waters that escape the *meltemi*s of summer. A good compromise would be a charter in the Ionian and an archaeological excursion on land from Athens.

Whether you charter the Aegean or the Ionian, you will almost certainly land in Athens if coming from the United States. Plan on spending a couple of days in the capital, both to adjust to jet lag and to see the Parthenon and the ruins of Delphi. The Parthenon, like the Pyramids, is one of the great wonders of antiquity and worth traveling across the world to see. But surprisingly large numbers of people miss Delphi, the site of the most celebrated oracle of antiquity. The major tourist agencies run daily bus excursions to Delphi, so you can sleep off your jet lag on your way to and from the site. Delphi is fascinating, even if you are no archaeologist. For centuries, the ancient Greeks adorned this famous hillside with shrines and temples, erecting superb armories where trophies won in battle and at the games were displayed. Everything is ruined now, but you can wander for hours among the blocks of marble and abandoned columns, trying to imagine what it was once like. High above the valley lie the silent amphitheater and the stadium, as if waiting to welcome the jostling crowds at festival time. Last time I was there, a shower had just laid down the dust. The ancient flagstones glistened as a great rainbow arched over the Gulf of Corinth to the south. Just for a moment you could savor a Greece long vanished, a country that was civilized while most of the world was still illiterate. If nothing else, Delphi will give you a good idea of what to expect at places like Epidavros and Delos during your charter.

Most Aegean charters start from the Piraeus, the port suburb of Athens, while Ionian charterers fly into the lovely island of Corfu off the west coast. Plan on taking a cab to your boat in Athens, even if she is out at an outlying marina. Even if your boat is elsewhere, do take a trip out to Zea marina in the Piraeus, where the *really* big yachts berth. They defy description. Some have their own helicopters; shipboard sports cars are commonplace.

Corfu is accessible by air from Athens or from other European capitals. You can also take a car ferry from Brindisi near the toe of Italy that will drop you in Corfu on its way to the Greek mainland.

In Greece, as elsewhere in Europe, you should plan on doing your own provisioning. Such self-sufficient chartering is fun. Test your ingenuity at shopping in a foreign language when you try to find something like ice. It's just like cruising on your own. There are plenty of supermarkets and small food stores that can supply every reasonable day-to-day need, even on the less developed islands. Most charterers seem to eat breakfast and lunch aboard, then enjoy dinner ashore. Eating out in Greece is a wonderful experience. Most tavernas have unpretentious decors, but are so hospitable and friendly that you feel part of the family. Admittedly, there are tourist restaurants, but one of the joys of Greece is that everyone tends to eat and drink in the same places, so you really meet the locals. There are thousands of Greek-Americans who have retired to their homeland with their social security. They love meeting Americans, and such encounters can lead to all sorts of fun: dancing until the small hours, a visit with local families, the sampling of a new and unfamiliar dish. Life in most Greek ports revolves around the waterfront and the tavernas. Make the most of the opportunity! The main disadvantage is the menus, which tend to be prosaic. They normally run to shish kebabs, chops, local fish, and salads with goat cheese. You can often enjoy the pleasant Greek custom of choosing your food from dishes on the stove in the kitchen. The cost of eating ashore, except in tourist traps, is minimal by American standards. Even in 1983 you could enjoy a multi-course meal with wine for between $6 and $8 a head. The bill-of-fare gets monotonous after a while, but it's rare to be confronted with a really bad meal.

Shopping for breakfast and lunch will take only a few minutes, for the local cheeses and cold meats are excellent. Only fresh vegetables can be in short supply on some of the smaller islands, although the local tomatoes are superb. Count on eating a lot of tomato salads topped with feta cheese, small fish, and the inevitable pork chops. Everything is cooked in olive oil, which is alien to some palates, but one gets used to it. My foul-weather gear still bears the olive oil stains of several memorable Greek trips. You should have no trouble in communicating with storekeepers. Many of them have a smattering of English, and every village boasts of a Greek-American on vacation from New Jersey. Greek wines are very pleasant. The most famous is retsina, a resin-flavored wine that is the vin ordinaire of Greece. This is an acquired taste. Perhaps you should visit a Greek restaurant before leaving home to test the vintages. The unresinated Domestika reds and whites are pleasing alternatives. Best buy your wines in bottles rather than experimenting with varieties from the barrel in local wine stores. They are often rough, even fiery, resembling the vinegar sold at the same locations.

Although Greece is a tourist country (with a special tourist police force), you are better off bringing your prescription medicines, film, and reading matter with you. Make sure everyone has seasick pills and foul-weather gear, for Aegean seas can become extremely nasty within a few minutes. This is the only place I have ever sailed where the seas came from every corner of the compass—all at once.

Aegean chartering: The Peloponnese and Cyclades

You could spend a year chartering from Athens and see only a fraction of the Aegean Islands. However, with two or three weeks available, you can explore a surprisingly wide range of anchorages and ports within easy reach of the capital. There are some musts—Sounion, Mykonos, Hydra, and Epidavros—but a great deal depends on the prevailing winds at the time of your charter.

This is an area where cruise planning is essential, so purchase a cruising guide well in advance. The best are H.M. Denham's *The Aegean* (New York: W.W. Norton, 1975), a brilliant combination of intelligent sailing directions and Greek mythology, and Rod Heikell's *Greek Waters Pilot* (London: Imray, Laurie, Norie & Wilson Ltd., 1982), which explores every corner of Greece in superb detail. Read what they have to say about prevailing winds and plan accordingly. Most times, you will be sailing in prevailing northerlies, so I would suggest you make your circuit eastbound. Your route depends on weather conditions in the open Aegean. Most charterers on 7-to-10-day charters stick close to the mainland and visit the Saronic Gulf, where the winds blow less strongly during high season. But there is nothing to stop you visiting the islands, provided you plan for strong winds and allow time for possible weather delays in the islands. If you do go to the Cyclades, count on a couple of longer passages—one out to Mykonos, the other back to the mainland.

Both may involve some night sailing. The strongest winds seem to fill in during the morning and moderate around sundown. But this is no invariable rule, for the summer *meltemi* can blow for days on end. You will probably fare better by timing your passages for early morning and late afternoon. Night passages are entirely possible, for there are few outlying dangers. Most islands are unlit, so navigate with care and try to time landfalls for daytime.

The Cyclades

Eastbound to the Cyclades, make Sounion your first anchorage. It's an easy daysail from the Piraeus. You anchor in hard sand in a sheltered bay under the glistening white Temple of Poseidon on the headland that guards the entrance to the Saronic Gulf. Twelve fifth-century B.C. Doric columns still stand, glazed with sea salt. You can watch the sunset and gaze over a panorama of islands from here, search for the English poet Lord Byron's name carved on one of the columns. The temple has been a sailor's landmark for centuries and is now a mecca for camera-toting Japanese tourists. However, their buses leave soon after sunset and you will have this enchanted place to yourself.

Unless you are in a hurry, I would stop at the island of Kea, a short sail into the Aegean east from Sounion. You sail through a narrow entrance into a large bay, once an important nineteenth-century coaling station for British warships. The quays of both hamlets are somewhat exposed to northerlies and often crowded, but it's well worth landing to explore the mountain village (*chora*) in the center of the island. You can take a bus up to the settlement with its Venetian fort, but you will have to walk through the narrow streets, where even the garbage is collected by mule. I was at Kea during a fall gale, so we huddled up to a quayside restaurant owner's oven and drank retsina while our dinners cooked. What had been a refuge from rough seas turned out to be a cozy, friendly place, a little off the beaten track for many charterers.

Your next stop will probably be Mykonos, the most famous island in the Cyclades. The passage from Kea is over 50 nautical miles. Leave very early in the day, because night sailing is forbidden by most charter companies. The most direct route takes you past Yioura and the southern shores of mountainous Tinos. Mykonos is easy to approach. An island of no importance in ancient times, it owes its present-day prosperity to the thousands of tourists who flock to nearby Delos, one of the great oracles of the ancient world. Unfortunately, the picturesque harbor is very crowded during high summer and can be very rough in strong northerly winds, this despite the new northern breakwater. In such conditions, you may be better off anchoring in the sheltered bay at the southwest corner of the island, tucking the boat up toward the head of the cove, where the sandy bottom shallows gradually. It's a half-hour walk into town, but the scenery is interesting.

Mykonos is a cruise-ship port and a tourist trap, with prices to match. The town is a charming melange of whitewashed houses, some with colored doors. The windmills with canvas sails are a famous tourist attraction. You can easily get lost in the winding streets of Mykonos, where there are more boutiques and tavernas per head than anywhere in Greece. You can find the same tourist items cheaper on other islands, but the cosmopolitan life along the waterfront attracts people from all over the world in high season. I would visit, eat, and then leave to sail across to Delos.

Delos and its neighbor Rhinia lie across the strait from Mykonos. Legend tells us Delos was the birthplace of the twin deities Apollo and Artemis, a once-floating island given to their mother Leto by a sympathetic Zeus. It has been a holy place since at least the eighth century B.C. and was purified by the Athenian tyrant Pisistratus in 540 B.C. The island was held to be defiled if anyone was born or died there, so the pregnant and dying were ferried across to Rhinia close by. Today, Delos is deserted except for tourists and ruins, but in 88 B.C. more than 20,000 people lived on the island, which is only 3 miles long and a mile across. They were massacred in that year by an Athenian ally. The monuments were plundered by the Venetians and others in later centuries, but there is still a great deal to see.

The island has a small haven, used mostly by the cruise-ship tenders and excursion boats that arrive from Mykonos. You can wander to your heart's content through the Terrace of the Lions, about all that remains of the oracle and its shrines. The Hellenistic city nearby is more spectacular. Explore it on the way to the summit of Mount Kinthos, where you can look out over the encircling islands. It was here that I met a somewhat harassed Massachusetts surgeon and his wife gazing out over the landscape. They greeted me as I arrived at the top.

"Hi! Are you on the cruise, too?"

I told them I was on my own.

"Have you ever seen a view like this?" asked the wife. "Everything seems so old and unchanging. How I wish we had the time to explore the whole island."

It turned out they were taking a five-day cruise between two medical conventions in Germany. As we talked, a distant horn summoned them back to the ship's tender.

"Here we go again," complained the doctor. "There's always a schedule." He packed up his camera bag. "By the way, how did you get here from Mykonos?"

I pointed to my charter boat anchored off the quay. "Under sail," I replied. "We'll spend the night, then go on to Santorini."

The doctor and his wife didn't say much, but I could see that they were envious. It is nice to be able to pace oneself through places like Delos without worrying about other people's schedules.

The Cyclades are so named because the inner islands of the archipelago form a circle around this holy place. Here you can savor antiquity, enjoy the romance of ruins, and really feel the touch of history. It is not difficult to imagine the bustling streets and market-places of the ancient city, the chants of worshipers at the greatest shrine in the Aegean. I may seem to have a thing about ruins, perhaps because I am an archaeologist by profession. But it is the temples and ruins, not just the tavernas and spectacular cruising, that make Greece such a special place. Savor them to the full!

If the weather really comes on to blow, slip away from Delos and make your way to the anchorage on the south side of Mykonos or to one of the deserted bays on the eastern side of Rhinia, not that this desolate island has much to offer beyond deserted fields. Allow at least a day for Delos. You will never regret it.

I doubt if you will have the time to venture much farther out into the Aegean. In any case, there are ample cruising riches at hand in the Cyclades. Paros is an attractive island with a safe, if crowded, harbor and a charming old town with fine churches, while Naxos is more commercial. Siros is capital of the Cyclades and was once an important commercial port. There is still some industrial activity in the port of Ermoupolis, but the harbor is lively and full of Aegean craft of all kinds. The town square is amusing on Sunday evenings, when the band plays and everyone takes the air. This island has excellent beaches. Everywhere in these islands, plan on securing stern-to the quay, Mediterranean style.

Some more adventurous charterers with plenty of time will sail south from Paros or Naxos to Santorini, the volcanic island reputed to be the site of the lost civilization of Atlantis. They even make Atlantis wine on the island. Santorini is one of the most fascinating bareboat destinations imaginable. The center of the island blew up in about 1450 B.C., sending huge tidal

Hydra. (National Tourist Organization of Greece)

waves south toward Crete and North Africa. Clouds of volcanic ash covered parts of Crete to a depth of a foot or more. The explosion may have started the decline of the Minoan civilization that ruled over much of the Aegean at the time. Experts believe that folk memories of this catastrophic event may have passed into history as the legend of a civilization that vanished under the ocean. Was Santorini actually Atlantis and the lost

civilization that of the Minoans? We shall never know, but it is fun to speculate about one of the great myths of history.

You can see abundant traces of the great explosion and the eruptions that preceded it if you sail into the deep waters of the vast crater that was once the center of the island. Santorini is now a series of islands, the largest of which lies to the east. The village perches on the top of ashy cliffs looking out toward the moonlike landscape of the active volcanic cone in the center of the flooded crater. Although there is a harbor on the east side of the island, *the* most spectacular place to lie in calm weather is at the foot of the town, with your stern toward the quay below the town. The cruise ships lie to mooring buoys close offshore. The brooding cliffs tower high above you, casting deep shadows on moonlit nights. A zigzag mule path winds up the precipitous hillside. Dozens of tourists ride precariously up this cobbled road on muleback (I think it's more fun to walk) and explore the narrow streets of the picturesque village on the summit. The anchorage is at its best on still nights, when the water is dark and you feel as if you are at the bottom of a deep hole. A faint smell of dust and mule dung drifts on the night wind, while the moon shimmers on the water and the smoke plume from the volcano drifts across the sky. This is one of the most memorable ports I have ever visited.

The highlight of Santorini is the buried Minoan village of Akrotiri on the south side of the island. Take a cab to this spectacular archaeological site buried under several feet of fine volcanic ash. Akrotiri was abandoned as earthquakes rocked the island. The archaeologists have uncovered its narrow streets and empty houses still standing two stories high, complete with storage pots, wall paintings, and other furnishings. The village bears a remarkable resemblance to some of the more remote island settlements of today. This archaeological site gives you an even more vivid impression of Minoan civilization than the Palace of Knossos on Crete itself, 70 miles to the south.

The passage back from the Cyclades to the mainland is best undertaken from Paros or Naxos. It is over a 100-mile sail to the Peloponnese, broken up by an overnight stop at Sifnos or Serifos on the way. Sifnos offers good shelter in the port of Kamares and is famous for its olive oil and pottery. Make a point of visiting the old island capital of Castro, the architecture is superb. Serifos is a high island, with a fascinating mountain village in the interior. The island is alleged to be the site of the cave of the legendary Cyclops blinded by Odysseus.

The Saronic Gulf and eastern Peloponnese

If you opt to stay closer to the mainland, you will probably sail across to the Peloponnese from Athens and down the eastern coast to Hydra, the most likely landfall for a returning island charterer. So we will explore this general area from this starting point. The eastern Peloponnese offers a multitude of fine ports and anchorages. Your only constraint is going to be time. I suggest a landfall on Hydra, a long bare island that was once the home of adventurous merchants during the Napoleonic Wars. The town and harbor lie on the west coast, facing the mainland. You will see little until you are just outside the narrow entrance, when the horseshoe bay opens up between the cliffs. Yachts moor bow- or stern-to the offshore breakwater, leaving the quays for commercial traffic. Hydra is invariably crowded during the summer months. You are best advised to time your arrival for the morning hours, when many yachts have left and newcomers have yet to arrive. You are almost certain to meet a flotilla cruise here. Try to arrive before they take up all the available quay space. If the wind is blowing strongly, drop your stern anchor well out in the middle of the harbor and nose your way to the quay with plenty of power to maintain control of the bow. When the quay is full, you can usually lie between two other yachts, with your bow some distance from shore. Choose larger neighbors if you can, it's easier to get ashore.

Hydra is a picturesque town with no motor vehicles, full of tall, handsome merchants' houses built in the early nineteenth century. Each was once a self-contained world, with its own water cistern, bakery, and storerooms, strong enough to withstand a siege. One of them is now a historical museum. The town is colorful, cramped, and full of good restaurants. This is the only place where I have eaten accompanied by 24 cats. Hydra's felines are famous among sailors the length and breadth of the Aegean. Apparently, they flourish during the summer and starve in the winter. Our British neighbor at the restaurant was a vastly entertaining raconteur, who spent his evening hurling persistent cats from his lap. For some reason they adored him.

I think this is my favorite Greek port, a place where you can watch the ebb and flow of local life. The quays bustle with life early in the mornings, when the local coasters arrive with wine, furniture, and other necessities. They pump the wine from the boats to the tavernas with a long hose and a water pump, or you can buy your supplies from the boat by the bottle or bucket. You'll see mules staggering under floral couches, a building contractor counting cement bags, boxes of detergent with familiar American names. Fishermen unload their catch and mend their nets, black-clad widows buy vegetables in the cool of the morning. Meanwhile, old men gossip in the warming sun, children listen wide-eyed to stories of a world outside. The same scene is repeated at every small port in the Aegean where the

Santorini. ((National Tourist Organization of Greece)

caiques (coasters) with their bluff bows operate. They come in all colors, shapes, conditions, and sizes. Once they operated under sail, but now they are diesel-powered. Caiques are still one of the main commercial lifelines between the islands and the mainland. Many have been in the same families for generations. This is the Hydra of the Greeks. It's not until later that the tourists emerge and the cruise ships arrive.

If you have the time, sail from Hydra to Spetsae a short distance away. This is a lively island, a favorite summer holiday resort for Athenians. But I would rate it a lower priority than Navplion, the small town at the head of the Gulf of Argolis, where the inevitable Venetian fort broods over the town. The main reason for going to Navplion is to take a bus or cab ride to the Mycenaean fortresses at Mycenae and Tiryns. The Mycenaeans once ruled over the Plain of Argos and traded the length and breadth of the Aegean between 1700 and 1200 B.C. Mycenae is where the great German archaeologist, Heinrich Schliemann, discovered a series of gold-decorated skeletons in the 1880s.

These he claimed were the graves of great Homeric heroes like Agamemnon. Later researchers have proved him wrong, for the burials were deposited long before Homer's time. The view from the ruins of the fortified palaces is spectacular, and you can explore a huge, dome-shaped beehive tomb nearby.

Your return passage to Athens will probably take you through the narrow channel between the island of Poros and the mainland. The current runs strongly here, but pilotage is straightforward. Poros is a naval training center, but a pretty town much visited by weekenders from Athens. It's worth a lunch stop before you sail on to Epidavros, where you must spend a half-day to visit the famous amphitheater nearby. The port is small and cramped, and you may be better off anchoring in the sandy bay by the town, especially if a flotilla cruise is in town. The amphitheater is a fairly long cab ride from the harbor, but worth every drachma of the ride. You climb up the steep tiers of stone benches and gaze down at the circular stage far below you. When I was there, a man was reciting Euripides's stanzas from the center of the stage. You could hear every syllable in the top row, even when he whispered. You could close your eyes and imagine the crowded theater leaning forward to catch the hero's tragic words, when the games were celebrated and playwright vied against playwright for the coveted olive wreath.

Epidavros is just a short distance from the Piraeus. If you have time, spend your last night at Aegina, only a few miles away from your base. Anchor on the east side of the island at Agia Marina and climb up to the beautiful fifth-century Doric Temple of Aphaia high on a hilltop overlooking the ocean. Try to time your visit for sunset, for the ancient columns gleam reddish gold in the setting sunlight and the entire landscape is bathed in a serene glow that makes you feel that the goddess is nearby. It's a wonderful place to savor the unique atmosphere of the Aegean Islands for the last time.

Most Aegean bareboating activity is confined to the mainland and the Cyclades. But this by no means exhausts the possibilities. You can flotilla cruise in the Halkidiki area of northern Greece, a charter that will take you to the monasteries of Mount Athos (no women allowed) and to Thessaloniki, where you can see Philip of Macedon's fabulous gold treasure in the museum. This is a little visited area of the Aegean, at its best in September. Incidentally, Halkidiki flotilla fleets actually give a prize for the cleanest yacht at the end of the trip—surely the strangest trophy ever awarded.

If you have time after your charter, allow some days to explore Greece by land. Do fly or take a ferry to Heraklion and explore Crete, ancient home of the Minoans. Visit the Palace of Knossos and take a trip through the mountain villages. These are little changed from a century ago. Then there's Rhodes, the Turkish coast, and the Sporades far to the north. Turkey is just opening up to bareboating and flotilla cruising, and the coast is still largely unspoiled. I hope to charter there one day.

Ionian Islands

The Ionian Islands are where flotilla chartering first began, for their sheltered waters and gentler winds are ideal for smaller yachts and inexperienced skippers. The cheapest way to see these islands is to go on such a cruise. There are several bareboat companies operating near Corfu, an attractive island with fine eighteenth-century buildings and the magnificent Church of Saint Spyridon (1589), its patron saint. Corfu was under British protection in the early nineteenth century and

was governed by a series of highly eccentric commissioners, one of whom introduced cricket to the island, where it is still played to this day. There is so much to see here that I suggest you spend a couple of days exploring ashore before taking off on your charter. English is spoken widely, and the island has everything from good restaurants to an imposing Venetian fortress.

As in the rest of Greece, you need a good guide book to get the most out of your time ashore. Two essential publications for a sailor in these islands are Arthur Foss, *The Ionian Islands: Zachynthos to Corfu* (London: Faber and Faber, 1969), and H.M. Denham's classic sailing directions, *The Ionian Islands to Rhodes: A Sea-Guide* (New York: W.W. Norton, 1972). The Ionian Islands were the homeland of the legendary Odysseus. Be sure to take an English translation of Homer's *Odyssey* with you on the charter. E.V. Rieu's Pelican translation is by far the best and is available on Corfu. I have vivid memories of sitting in the cockpit at anchor off Ithaca, drinking wine and listening to the story of Odysseus' homecoming read aloud in the twilight. Homer is a wonderful guide to these romantic islands. There are no signs of the great heroes now, but it is fascinating to imagine and to dream.

Most of the flotilla charters start from the commercial port of Prevesa or from Levkas, well south of Corfu. These ports are close to the sheltered waters between the Ionian Islands and the mainland. Levkas is mountainous, its west coast barren, the east green and fertile. The island is separated from the mainland by a narrow canal originally dug by the Corinthians in 640 B.C. and guarded at its northern end by an imposing medieval fortress. The fort can be seen a long distance off, but you may have a few anxious moments when sailing fast toward it, for the canal entrance is low-lying and hard to spot from offshore. You can motor through and spend the night at Nidri (Port Vliko), a major flotilla headquarters, where you can anchor off the beach. You are now at the northern frontier of Odysseus' ancient kingdom. He ruled from the lovely island of Ithaca, a day's sail to the south. But before sailing there, pause among the islands just east of Levkas and spend a night in the narrow wooded inlet at Sivota on the south shore of Levkas. The winding entrance to the bay ends in a circular, natural harbor that is still unspoiled.

Port Vathi is Ithaca's major port, tucked away at the head of a deep inlet that branches off from a large bay. You secure to the quays and will lie comfortably unless a strong northerly brings in a sharp popple. Port Vathi is a busy little town, not one of my favorite stops in the Ionian, but at least I managed to get a haircut here. I looked as if I had been scalped. The Homeric palace is said to be an hour's drive away at Stavros. The view is superb.

Ithaca was a strategic island because it had anchorages on all four coasts. Polis on the west coast is deep, open bay that is exposed to the southwest and said to be the place where Odysseus' ships departed for Troy. You can sail round the island clockwise from Port Vathi to Polis, stopping at the deserted bay of Ayias Andreas at the south end. There's not much room to swing and the bottom is shingle, but legend has it that this is where Odysseus' son Telemachus landed when he returned from visiting King Nestor at Pylos to the south. His mother's suitors were plotting his murder, so he hid in the faithful swineherd Eumaeus' stables in the hills above the anchorage.

Across the Ithaca Channel to the west lies Cephalonia, the largest of the Ionian Islands, with a peak rising to over 5,000 feet. Do not fail to visit the tiny fishing village of Fiskardo on the northeast shore of the island. A small circular bay is lined with stone houses, many of them in partial ruins. This is a peaceful hamlet, with only two sleepy tavernas, but a secure port in any wind. You can anchor in the bay in about 25 feet (mud), but are probably better off securing stern-to the quay. The best berths are on the south side. Cephalonia is well worth circumnavigating. The capital, Argostoli, is a modern city with wide if dusty boulevards, completely rebuilt after the great earthquake of 1953. The best berths are alongside the new quay. Ample provisions will be found nearby.

Zakinthos is a little far south for most charterers. It was decimated in the same 1953 earthquake, when all the magnificent eighteenth-century buildings were thrown down. The capital, Port Zante, is a modern port of straightforward entrance, but there is little of historical interest to see after the ravages of 1953. Better to head north again to Levkas, not a very attractive town, but a comfortable port, where a cool wind always seems to blow, and, if you have time, as far north as Parga with its superb restaurants and Venetian fortress high on a rock overlooking the central square. This is the most picturesque town on the western mainland. Best to anchor in the sandy western bay near the beaches rather than in the tiny harbor, where depths are uncertain.

An Ionian charter has the advantage of few long passages, but you may encounter sustained calm periods, especially in high summer, for the rising warm air over the land sucks away the breeze during the day. The winds can blow hard without warning, so make sure you find a secure port each night. These quiet islands are less dramatic than the Aegean, but ideal for a first-time charter in the Mediterranean. If you are at all nervous about Greek waters, why not plan on a flotilla cruise in these waters? A very experienced friend of mine recently returned from such a charter in the Ionian. He is so enthusiastic that at least four of his friends are going with him when he returns next year— all the way from California. This is also an ideal area to charter with children, for there are plenty of sandy beaches and interesting ports to explore. Many yachts you charter here come with their own windsurfers at no additional charge, a nice touch in these days of extra after optional extra.

Words cannot possibly convey the magic of these very special cruising grounds. There are evenings of boisterous eating and drinking, hard slogs to windward against the persistent *meltemi*, but above all the moments when the setting sun makes ancient temple columns radiate with a reddish glow, or when a shepherd plays his pipe on the hillside that looks down on your island anchorage. The past reaches out to touch you, and you are never quite the same again.

PART VI: SOUTH PACIFIC

21 Pacific Islands and Australasia

The islands of the South Pacific have enchanted sailors ever since Captain Cook and other European explorers came to Tahiti more than 200 years ago. The South Pacific has lured artists, beachcombers, and cruising people to its tropical lagoons ever since. But the islands were far off the beaten track for most people until the 1950s, when the intercontinental jet brought Hawaii, Fiji, Tahiti, and Australasia within reach. A generation ago, it took weeks to reach Polynesia or New Zealand. Now you can fly from Los Angeles to Papeete in seven and a half hours and on to Auckland, New Zealand, in another five. Luxury hotels line quiet lagoons, air-conditioned buses greet the passengers on every jumbo jet.

Cruising people have discovered the South Pacific, too. In the 1960s, only a handful of ocean voyagers tied up in Papeete or waited out the cyclone season in New Zealand. Now there's congestion in Tahiti and plenty of company in Suva. Some of these people are circumnavigators, living permanently aboard their boats, but many more are sailors who have taken a year or two away from the land on a leisurely, circular cruise from Canada or the United States to the islands, then south and west to New Zealand or even Australia before turning home. Such cruises require either a permanent commitment to the cruising life or extraordinary disruptions in one's working life—sabbaticals, leaves of absence, and so on. Only a tiny minority of sailors can afford to spend months sailing to the islands and exploring the South Pacific. For most of us, a prolonged cruise like this is merely a dream.

The South Pacific is still a rapidly expanding tourist market, one that offers endless possibilities for so-called adventure holidays. The area suffers from several disadvantages from the package-tour perspective. The distances between islands are often enormous; four-to-seven-hour flights between major destinations, commonplace. Load factors and operating costs make for astronomic airline fares compared with those across the Atlantic or in more traveled areas. Except for low-cost, highly packaged airline and bus tours that spin the unfortunate tourist around the Pacific in a breathtakingly few days, most travelers to this area are more affluent explorers, many of them avid skiers, sailors, or

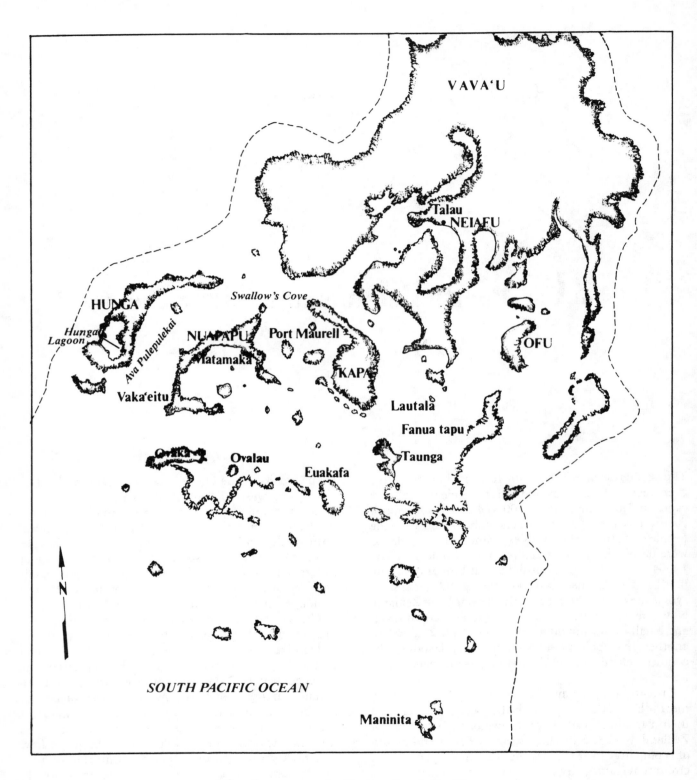

The charter area in Tonga, South Pacific

perhaps divers. Adventure holidays combine some conventional land traveling with a variety of other activities: skiing in New Zealand's Southern Alps, diving on Australia's Great Barrier Reef, exploring World War II battlefields and sunken wrecks.

Fortunately for cruising sailors, bareboating has come to the South Pacific as well. You can charter in Tahiti and Tonga, explore New Zealand's Bay of Islands, or bareboat inside Australia's Great Barrier Reef. Inevitably, these charter operations cater to people who are prepared to spend thousands of dollars to sail in exotic waters, but it is surprising how cheaply you can charter in the South Pacific if you take advantage of special excursion fares and prorate the cost of the yacht among a crew of four or six people.

This chapter explores some of the chartering opportunities available in the South Pacific. The reader is warned that the situation is changing constantly. Of all the bareboating regions of the world, this is the one where it pays to book your trip through a travel agent specializing in the area. We make specific suggestions for each area.

Tonga

South Pacific Yacht Charters was founded by Betty and Lynn Leasure in 1979. Experienced travel agents and expedition guides, they set up shop in, of all places, Logan, Utah. Why Utah? Because they like skiing and horseback riding. In any case, almost all their customer contact is by telephone, so it doesn't matter where they live. The Leasures took a long, hard look at the bareboating business, saw the overcrowding in the Caribbean, and decided to open up a charter operation in the unspoiled South Pacific that would cater to experienced sailors. They modeled their operations on the CSY concept that has worked so well in the Virgins and Grenadines. Their first yachts were CSY-44s, proven charter vessels acquired on a lease-back arrangement from private owners. South Pacific has subsequently diversified its fleet to include Endeavor 37s, Peterson 44s, and other designs. Anyone who has chartered in the Caribbean will be comfortable with this company's approach. It is virtually identical to many West Indies operations.

The Leasures looked long and hard for an unspoiled charter area. They settled on the Vava'u Islands of Tonga. The Tonga government was so delighted at the prospect of much needed foreign exchange and cash employment that they gave the company some valuable tax breaks and other incentives to operate in their waters. As a result, you can charter in one of the most beautiful and remote parts of the South Pacific. South Pacific's venture was an instant success. In 1981, they expanded to a second charter base on the island of Raiatea in French Polynesia. A charter in either of these areas is an opportunity to experience both island and open-water tropical sailing at their best. Above all, the anchorages are uncongested and the people friendly.

Both the Vava'u Islands and Raiatea are somewhat off the beaten track, so it's essential that you make your travel arrangements through the charter company. South Pacific Yacht Charters (Box 6, Smithfield, UT 84335) operates its own travel agency with a toll-free number (800-453-2730). They specialize not only in long-distance excursion rates, but in all the intricacies of local carriers. Your greatest problem may be choosing where to go first. Tonga is the more remote and unspoiled, a small cruising ground with endless possibilities for snorkeling and diving. The distances are short. Few passages are more than two to three hours long. The Leewards are a large charter area consisting of four offshore islands separated by distances of about 20 miles. Raiatea and its neighbors will appeal to those who like open-water passages and sheltered lagoon sailing, with many of the amenities of civilization relatively close to hand. You can charter for a week in both places, if you wish, which will give you a tantalizing sample of two very different cruising grounds.

Getting to Tonga is quite an adventure. You normally fly out of Los Angeles International to Hawaii, Fiji, or American Samoa, then connect to a local flight to Tongatapu, where you take yet another hop to the airstrip near the marina at Neiafu, the main town on Vava'u. Incidentally, Vava'u is so remote that provisions are often difficult to come by. The charter company supplies a provisioning package of imported foods, which they supplement with all sorts of local fruit and vegetables. The cost is surprisingly modest (about $20 a day per person).

When Captain James Cook visited Tonga in 1773, he commented on the friendliness of the people and the beautiful scenery. "Nature, assisted by a little art, no where appears in a more florishing state than at this isle," he wrote of Tongatapu. He would have applied the same description to Vava'u had he visited it. The islands are a scenic mixture of the Bahamas and Virgins. This is a deep-water cruising ground among mountainous islands, but with a profusion of shallow coral reefs and fine, white beaches. Add friendly people who welcome visitors, and you have an irresistible mix for a successful charter.

Tonga is the last independent monarchy in the Pacific, 1,000 miles from New Zealand and yet virtually

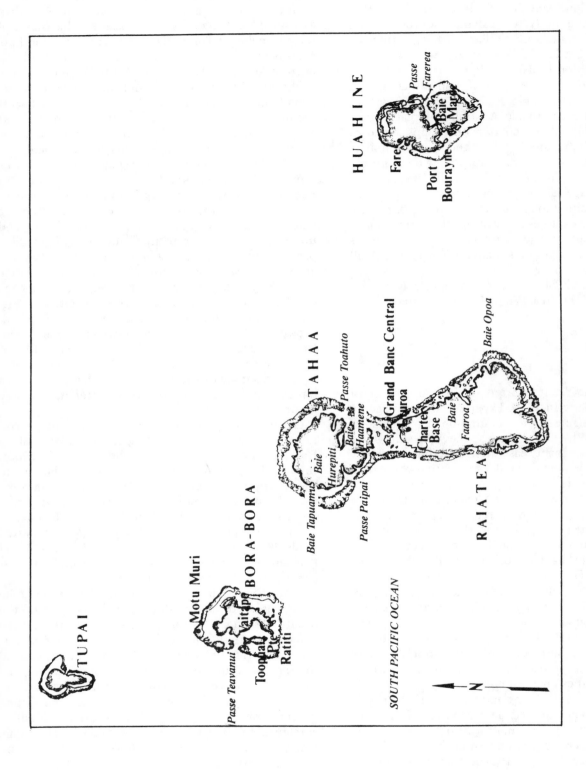

TUPAI

Passe Teavanui

Motu Muri

BORA-BORA

Vaitape

Toopua Pte.
Ratiti

TAHAA

Baie Tapuamu

Baie
Hurepiti

Baie
Haamene

Passe Toahuto

Passe Paipai

Grand Banc Central

Faaroa

Charter
Base

Baie
Faaroa

Baie Opoa

RAIATEA

HUAHINE

Passe
Farerea

Fare

Port
Bourayne

Baie Maroe

SOUTH PACIFIC OCEAN

N

Les Îles sous Le Vent, Polynesia

Vav'au. (Courtesy FPG Fred J. Eckert)

untouched by modern industrial civilization. Only the missionary influence is strong. The islanders observe the Sabbath with Victorian rigor: no swimming, fishing, or games are allowed. Charterers are exempt from the restrictions. Tonga's islands extend like a net some 175 miles north to south, cast on the ocean, as it were, in three clusters. The capital is at Tongatapu in the south, the central group is named Ha'apai, while you charter in the compact Vava'u group in the north. The entire charter area is about the size of the Virgins, consisting of a multitude of low-lying islands with gentle contours. The highest islands lie in the northern and western part of the group, intersected by deep channels. They offer plenty of well-protected anchorages. The scenery is inviting—an ever-changing vista of cliffs, beaches, and sheltered coves. The people live in small clusters of huts among extensive copra plantations. To the east lie the great coral reefs that protect

Vava'u. The deep-blue Pacific swells crash on their eastern bastions. Inside, you sail among tiny cays and islets capped with a few palm trees and surrounded with gleaming white beaches. The diving and snorkeling are without peer. The unspoiled reefs support a magnificent array of tropical fish. Many charters spend the night in sheltered anchorages to the north and west, then sail down to the reef for the day. The small islands offer a great variety of lunch stops and some of the finest shelling in the Pacific. Best of all, you have the reefs almost to yourself.

Tonga has a tropical climate that tends to be slightly cooler and less humid than the rest of Polynesia. The weather in Vava'u is dominated by the southeasterly trades, which blow at a predictable 13 to 18 knots for much of the year. The hurricane season lasts from January to March, but tropical storms are very rare indeed. The sailing is still good, but the winds are more variable and there are occasional rainy days with strong northwesterly winds. But such conditions rarely last long. This is an area where you can count on ideal sailing weather nearly all the time. The charter company asks you to keep in daily touch with base by VHF, so that they know where you are anchored for the night. Because these are remote waters, this is a good idea—invaluable during hurricane season.

Navigationally, Vava'u is straightforward, provided you are intelligent about eyeballing among the reefs and take note of the tides and currents. The eastern cays and reefs need an experienced eye, careful use of the high sun, and a constant lookout on the bow. The tidal range is about 3.3 feet at neaps and up to 5 feet at springs, with two high and two low tides a day. In some narrow defiles, the current can run as strong as 3 to 5 knots. You should pull your dinghy well above high-water mark at all times. In places like the entrance to Hunga Lagoon, you should plan to use the high tide to avoid the danger of running aground on the ebb. Anchoring presents few problems in these waters, provided you take care to set the hook in sandy spots and avoid fouling the line on coral heads.

As elsewhere, your cruise plan will be affected by the prevailing winds. Although the distances are small, the usual advice of making distance early on and then coming back slowly against the wind makes good sense here. I would certainly plan on spending some time around Vava'u, for it must rank among the most interesting islands in the entire Pacific. The 5-mile-long, fjordlike waterway that leads to Neiafu and the charter base offers smooth, deep water in any conditions. You can anchor safely on either side of the "fjord," but Talau is a pleasant spot bounded by two hills. Land on the south side and climb a trail to the summit of Talau, which offers a magnificent view of the islands below you.

Talau is a good first-night stop, as is Port Maurell on Kapa Island at the entrance to the waterway. Be sure to anchor outside the coral heads in deep water. From there, you can dinghy 1.5 miles up the coast to Swallow's Cave, which you are bound to have noticed as you rounded the northwest corner of the island. During the late afternoon, the sunlight illuminates the water inside, as well as the stalactites and coral formations deep below the water. Hundreds of starlings build mud nests in the roof. You can swim to a large dry chamber at the back of the cave and picnic there in complete seclusion. Alternatively, you might care to try out your snorkeling skills on the reef on the north side of the pretty island of Nuku, where you can also anchor for the night.

The Kapa anchorages are a good starting point for your cruise. Many charterers head out from here to the reefs around Ovaka, Ovalau, and Taunga. The latter is under 3 miles from Nuku, one of the smallest inhabited islands in the Vava'u group and the estate of the noble Akau'ola, "Navigator to the King." The only overnight anchorage lies on the northeast side, but the cove off the village on the west side is well worth a visit for lunch. Anchor in about 30 feet well clear of the stakes that mark the channel to the wharf. The best snorkeling and diving lie close to temporary anchorages at the south end of Taunga. The beaches off Ngau and Pau are some of the best in the group.

"Going E at longitude 174 deg. is similar to moving from the West Indies to the Bahamas," says the charter company's admirable cruising guide. You sail from deep-water conditions typical of the Virgins to a world of white sand, light-blue water, and low-lying reefs, where eyeballing is the name of the game. I would not be too ambitious for a couple of days. Take the time to get your sea legs, then head for the Fanua Tapu Passage that takes you into the heart of the reefs. Choose a time of day when the tide is rising and the sun is overhead, so that the dangers are well marked. The two entrance markers are sometimes hard to see, until you pick up the small island of Lautala and the S-shaped channel passing south of Fanua Tapu. Once through the channel, you should decide where your overnight base should be. Many people prefer the village of Makave, 4 miles north of the channel, where the shelter is excellent in easterly conditions. At least four temporary anchorages are within easy reach, one of which, Ofu, is famous for its shelling. Ofu village is a marvelous example of Tongan life, thatched houses spread out around a gently curving beach where fishermen mend their nets.

If the weather is sunny and eyeballing easy, you can spend a fascinating day sailing south inside the chain of islands and reefs to Maninita. This 10-mile passage needs considerable care, for the chart is only approximate. The anchorage at Maninita itself is so difficult that the company restricts visiting to yachts with a guide. But the island is well worth a visit, if only to enjoy its white beaches and the shady puko trees. Your guide will eyeball the yacht into a small sandy cove surrounded by coral heads and a beach, so you can row ashore and stroll under the lattice shade of the trees and admire the reefs on the eastern side. There are some temporary anchorages for snorkelers off the small uninhabited islands to the west, but the coral bottom can be a real anchor grabber. If you have the slightest doubt about anchorage, it's best to head for Euakafa, a high island some 5 miles northwest, where you can spend a happy day snorkeling and swimming, or tramping over the 300-foot-high plateau on the summit. There's a comfortable daytime anchorage on the north side, provided conditions are settled and you aim your anchor for a sandy patch on the bottom. Best head back to Taunga or over to Nuapapu for the night.

Nuapapu is famous for its large bight and Mariner's Cave on the western shore, a domed underwater cavern accessible only to divers. You need a guide, and even then the expedition is not for the novice. Local traditions tell of a young Tongan chief who hid his sweetheart from danger in the cave until they were able to escape to Fiji. Vaka'eitu on the west side of the bight is an excellent overnight anchorage, provided you approach close to the island of Lape and anchor clear of the extensive shallows. There's a German-owned plantation ashore. Many people prefer to anchor at Matamaka on the northeast side, where you can anchor north of the pier in anything but strong southerly and westerly conditions. The village and beach are worth a visit.

The ambitious charterer may venture to the westernmost island of Hunga, whose lagoon has a tricky entrance. You sail 2 miles west across Ava Pulepulekai, around the southern end of Hunga, and spot the 150-foot-wide entrance 1.5 miles north, bounded on its south side by a high cliff. The main danger is a 10-foot-high rock in the entrance, which you leave to port as you traverse the narrow channel. The charter company has tried to improve the channel with dynamite, but it still remains dangerous and should only be attempted at high tide, in good light. The anchorage inside is ample compensation for the hazards of the entrance, for you lie in an absolutely calm lagoon off the village in the northeast corner. The Hunga lagoon was once a refuge for people from outlying islands who were in danger of being captured and sold into slavery by white men in earlier times. You may be tempted to linger here for a couple of days. After all, the charter area is so compact that you are only some 10 miles from home base.

Vava'u is the ultimate in get-away-from-it-all charter areas. Fua'amotu, Fonua 'one 'one, Sisia, and Tefitomaka—the names of dozens of islands and villages roll off the tongue with musical resonance. This is the timeless South Seas, truly a tropical paradise.

The Leeward Islands, French Polynesia

South Pacific Yacht Charters runs its second operation in the Leeward Islands, an archipelago of four islands—Raiatea, Tahaa, Huahine, and, most famous of all, Bora-Bora, lying some 137 miles northwest of Tahiti. Ever since the eighteenth century, Tahiti has been the symbol of everything gracious and inviting about the Pacific. Thousands of World War II servicemen were charmed by Bora-Bora. Even in the days of the jumbo jet, the legend lives on. You arrive in the early morning hours, emerge from an atmosphere of steel and plastic into a fragrant world of hibiscus and swaying palm trees. Papeete, like most larger tropical towns, tends to be noisy and dirty. The real charm of Polynesia lies in the offshore islands. As a result, most charterers spend at most a day on Tahiti itself, then hop across to the charter base on Raiatea.

The Leeward Islands lie halfway between California and Australia in the easterly tradewind belt. They are much easier to reach than Vava'u. You can fly from Los Angeles International to Papeete in seven and a half hours. Air New Zealand, Qantas, and the French airline UTA offer admirable overnight service. From there, it's a short commuter hop to the Leewards. South Pacific maintains quite a varied fleet at Raiatea, among them Peterson 44s, Nautical 39s, Endeavor 37s and 40s, all of which perform well to windward, a necessary quality in waters where you have to make open-water passages against the trades. Unlike Tonga, there are stores and hotels at several small towns and resorts, so it is possible to charter this area without a provisioning package. Personally, I prefer to take the company's stores, simply because I hate shopping after an overnight flight. One does not come to Polynesia to haul bags of groceries. But be sure to pick up some French bread, pate, and cheese for your picnic lunches. And the vin ordinaire in plastic bottles is cheap and easily stowed below. Take along more than you think you will need. It will certainly vanish. The local Hinano beer is strongly recommended, too.

These are French-governed waters, so the Iles Sous le Vent (Leeward Islands) are subject to somewhat different navigational terminology. The charter company has put together an excellent guide, summarizing the main navigational problems and translating such French terms as *feux* (light), *arbre* (tree), and *recif* (reef). In general, French charts are superior to most others, so you should have no trouble finding your way around. American charterers should remember that port is to red when you enter harbor ("Red to red on return"). The Leewards lie in the easterly tradewind belt, so there's relatively little variation between the seasons. December through March tend to be wetter and more humid, with periods when the trades are down and the air is hot and sticky. Although you can charter year round, I would recommend April through November, when conditions are drier and the trades more predictable.

Bora Bora. (Courtesy FPG Werner Stoy, Camera Hawaii)

You'll have temperatures between 70 and 85 degrees year round, with the hottest weather when the trades are down. The last time I was in Tahiti was in March. It was horrendously sticky when we arrived, but the weather cleared next morning, the trades returned, and one could breathe again. So go for the dry months. The trades average between 10 and 15 knots, although they can blow considerably harder on occasion.

Unlike Vava'u, the Leewards are very much a deep-water cruising area, covering some 2,500 square miles. You will make several inter-island passages during your charter, which will take you into open water. You will need some deep-water sailing experience, even if the distances between the islands are little more than 20 miles. The Leewards have some special conditions, which are worth mentioning:

● Open-water sailing experience is essential for island-to-island passages. The essence is in the timing. Make sure you leave well before 0930, so that you are off the entrance pass through the reefs by 1530 at the latest. This gives you ample time to make a safe entrance, or to stand off if an afternoon squall obscures visibility for a while. Night sailing is suicidal and is forbidden. Since weather forecasts can be easily obtained by telephoning the charter base or from the local police station, you can pick your passage days without too much problem.

● Reef passages are the hardest navigational challenge in the Leewards. Each island is surrounded by a barrier reef, through which only a limited number of deep-water channels pass. Strong currents can run through them, especially on the ebb. These passes are identified on charts and in sailing directions by compass courses. The major entrances are marked with beacons, clearly described in the cruising guide. Entering a pass is easy enough, provided you stay well offshore until you have identified the entrance and you make the transit in good light conditions. Take a careful look around before you enter. Is a squall approaching, that will bear down on you at a critical moment in the narrow pass? Best to stand off until it dissipates. If you are caught in a squall in the inner passages, best anchor if there is swinging room. Pushing on in poor visibility is at best a questionable strategy. Bear in mind that strong currents can set through the passes and will tend to push you onto the reefs. An area of disturbed water extends beyond the entrance, so you should maintain your compass course until you are at least a mile outside the reef. In these days of reliable diesels, it is idiotic to enter lagoons under sail, even with a leading breeze. But have sails and anchor ready for use just in case something goes wrong.

● The Leewards are famous for their deep-water anchorages. Anchoring in 80 to 90 feet is pretty spooky at first. You get very tired of hauling in all the scope needed at such depths. The charter company recommends a ratio of three to one in winds under 15 knots, full scope of 350 feet in stronger breezes. And if it really pipes up, they suggest you lay your second, Danforth, anchor over the bow. Incidentally, you should never attempt to fulfill your Polynesian fantasy of tying up to a palm tree ashore. A sudden gust could put you ashore.

Raiatea and Tahaa share a common barrier reef, and you'll probably be navigating inside it for your first few days. The chart and cruising guide delineate the complex routes that take you between the reefs, especially around the Grand Banc Central between the two major islands. What may seem confusing at first is in fact relatively simple, provided that you realize that the marked channels are all oriented toward the port of Uturoa on the northeast corner of Raiatea. The main channels are well marked with beacons (balises) and there are plenty of landmarks such as hills and headlands to help you on your way. The charter marina is at Oporo on the northwest corner of Raiatea, so you will probably spend your first few days exploring some of the anchorages on the west coast. There are several overnight spots along this stretch of coast. I have spent a pleasant night in Baie Faafau in easterly weather in no less than 90 feet. There's only swinging room for a single yacht, so be prepared to move on to Tevaitoa village, where there is a well preserved marae, a pre-European religious shrine.

Uturoa lies only 3 nautical miles east of Oporo, so many people visit the port early on in their charter. The best days to visit are Wednesday, Friday, or early Sunday morning, when the market is open. You tie up to the northern end of the commercial wharf or anchor off and get a grandstand view of all the bustle, as the inter-island steamers arrive and depart. The market offers excellent fish, local produce, and the most delicious fruit pies I have ever tasted. You have to get up early for the best produce, but there's incentive—a delicious breakfast ashore at a local restaurant. Uturoa is a very civilized place, with plenty of Chinese stores with all the food and liquor supplies you could possibly

want, to say nothing of both cheap and expensive restaurants. Some people rave about the local marinated raw fish (poisson cru), but I must confess that I am not a raw-fish fanatic. This pleasant port is a good place to stop before taking either the Passe Teavapiti or Passe Irihu for Huahine. You can also anchor at Baie Vairahi 3 miles south of the town, where there are three marae to explore.

The archaeologically minded should sail south to Baie Opoa, pass carefully between the shoals at the entrance, and anchor off the village in 90 feet. Both the settlement and the bay are hallowed ground, part of the religious complex centered on the marae known as Taputapuatea, "an inmost heart." You can walk to the ruins, which lie close to Pointe Atiapiti. Tahitian maraes were cult places of ancient gods like the warrior deity 'Oro. Here were sung the ancient chants commemorating tribal gods. "The sea rolled, and the tides succeeded each other for a period of nights. It was the birth night of a god....'Oro-taua (Warrior-at-war) was the god born that night...." The songs rolled mellifluously off the priests' tongues. Wander among the courts and terraces of black coral stones, the ancient altar stones standing out like headstones. Tahitian maraes may disappoint when compared to the spectacular columns of the Parthenon or the Pyramids of Giza on the Nile. But shut your eyes and listen for a moment. Perhaps the presence of the gods will come drifting down to you across the centuries. The Tahitians themselves may not have been great architects, but the maraes had intense symbolic significance to people living all over Polynesia. Many of the great canoe voyages started at Opoa, including, legend has it, the voyage that led to the Maori settlement of New Zealand. The Raiateans were famous canoe builders in Captain Cook's time. Cook himself admired some ocean canoes and measured them at Opoa.

The combined effects of jet lag and an overnight flight send many charterers north from home base to spend their first few days in the quiet anchorages of Tahaa. Tahaa is round, about 6 miles across, and deeply indented with sheltered anchorages. You can find shelter in almost any conditions, provided you keep to the leeward side of the island. The chart shows you a number of places where you can put down a lunch hook and go snorkeling or diving on the inside of the barrier reef. This quiet island is well worth leisurely exploration ashore, too. If you have time, walk the beautiful trail from the head of Baie Haamane over the edge of Mount Taira to Baie Hurepiti.

Baie Haamane is a good place to lie up, provided the wind is not blowing too strongly from the east, funneling down the deep fjordlike bay. Haamane has the advantage of being easy of access and within close reach of excellent day anchorages for snorkeling. It's also close to Passe Toahotu, a logical exit when crossing to Huahine. From here, you can circumnavigate the island inside the reef, with plenty of good temporary stops off isolated islets called *motus*, where you can dinghy to snorkeling places. The passage between Tatoora and Pointe Tahuaotaha on the north coast needs good light and prudence, especially when strong currents are running. You can overnight safely at Baie Tupuamu or Hurepiti, except when westerlies are blowing. The latter is very convenient when you are waiting for suitable conditions to cross to Bora-Bora. You can buy some supplies in the village of Tiva close by, where there is also a fine church. By the way, if you are ever near a Tahitian church on a Sunday, attend the service if only to hear the magnificent, sonorous hymn singing. The fishermen among the crew will enjoy the Hurepiti fish cages, where you can identify many species of local fish as well as sharks.

Everyone who spends any time chartering the Leewards makes the almost obligatory passage some 18 miles northwest to Bora-Bora. Bora-Bora is everyone's tropical paradise, a quiet island only 17 miles around, where time stops, the sunsets are spectacular, and the drinks always cool. Thousands of tourists fly in every year to stay at the island resorts. Best enjoy Bora-Bora before the pressures of modernization overwhelm the inhabitants.

Bora-Bora's distinctive twin peaks rear up from the ocean. They once inspired the mythical Bali Hai in *South Pacific*. Whatever their associations, they are one of the finest landfalls in the Pacific. You'll probably carry the easterly trades when westbound and have little to worry about except occasional squalls. If the trades are down, the passage may be downright uncomfortable. The swell will bump you around and you may have to beat against light headwinds, or motor and change sail as squall after fluky squall crosses your path. It will take at least five or six hours to make the crossing, so plan to leave early to reach the entrance to Passe Teavanui by 1530 at the latest. Be sure to stay way south and west of the barrier reefs until you are well around Pointe Teturiroa. The low-lying reef extends farther out to sea than might be apparent.

Passe Teavanui is easy of access—a course of 090 degrees magnetic will take you safely through the entrance. Once inside, secure alongside the Vaitape town pier to check in at the *gendarmerie* (police station). There are a handful of shops and boutiques in this pleasant community. Most cruising boats and charters end up anchoring in the deep water off the Bora-Bora Yacht Club just north of the pass, a mecca for cruising boats from all over the South Pacific. You'll have lots of company here, so take care when you lay out your anchor, use plenty of scope, and make sure you swing clear of your neighbors.

The yacht club is run on a very informal basis. Everyone is on trust, so you simply open an account at the bar and help yourself. The laundry service is cheap, freshwater showers are available, and you can eat ashore any day except Sunday, when they often organize a potluck. Every crew that attends brings a favorite dish, which is added to the buffet. The result— a wonderful evening, where you can meet sailors from all over the world.

You can spend days exploring the reefs and bays on the north and west coasts of Bora-Bora. Some people enjoy visiting the various hotels close to Pointe Ratiti. You can rent bicycles to tour the island, take an ocean fishing trip, or walk ashore. Most yachts spend several days exploring the reefs around Topua, where there are excellent anchorages in good weather. Be careful! You need good light and high sun to make the narrow pass between Topua Iti and the reef. The islet of Teveiroa has good beaches on the western side, which you can visit by dinghy or by walking through thick brush. The Bora-Bora airport is on Motu Mute. You can anchor off the islet if you wish, but there are better berths around the corner in Baie Paorie and Baie Taihoo in southerly conditions. The charts and cruising guide supplied by the charter company give detailed information on daytime anchorages in this general area. You are not allowed to visit the eastern shore, where local knowledge is required.

Most people spend all their time at Bora-Bora. I think this is a mistake, for Huahine offers many unspoiled delights. It's a 19-mile passage from Tahaa to Huahine, normally a sail to windward. But the effort's well worth it. The two reef passes that lead to the principal town of Fare are easily traversed in good light. Both are well marked. You check in at Fare police station. The best anchorages lie off the Bali Hai Hotel or near the Huahine Shack close to town, where most sailors congregate. Fare itself is a pleasant little village with some excellent stores, banks, and a post office. Again, the market is well worth visiting. There is even a Tahitian disco, which offers hectic entertainment several nights a week. Next morning, exercise your aching head by walking or cycling 2 miles north to the village of Maeva, where some ancient *marae*s are to be seen. If you want a quieter berth near Fare, try Baie Haavai, where you can lie in 75 feet close to a small village with an interesting church.

Huahine is quiet and easygoing, but most people visit it for the pleasures of the inner pass that runs down the

Petersen 46. An earlier version, the Petersen 44, has proved a popular charter design in the Caribbean and Pacific. We can be certain that the 46 will be the next generation. This is a true performance cruising boat, with an easily handled cutter rig on roller furlers, so you can shorten sail in a few seconds. A six-cylinder diesel provides ample performance under power.

I like the interior layout of the Petersen 44, with its two staterooms and cleverly designed galley that is right out of the way to port. You can sleep six people very comfortably, yet a couple can handle the yacht. (Courtesy Jack Kelly Yacht Sales)

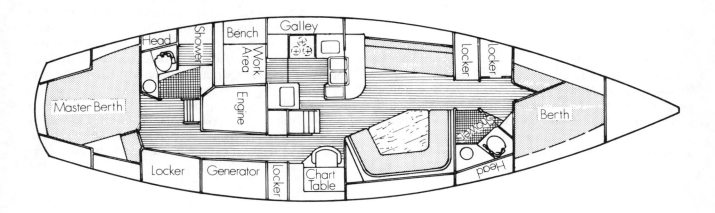

western side. The passage is well marked as far south as Baie Haapu, but the scenic highlight is Port Bourayne, a deep calm bay ringed by steep, densely wooded, and often cloud-shrouded hills. Port Bourayne by moonlight reminds one of a placid Scottish loch. Even the occasional gusts of wind off the hills sound authentic! The senery remains attractive all the way down to the day anchorage in Baie de'Avea, where the inner passage ends.

You may be tempted to sail home after visiting Port Bourayne. But if you have three or four more days, take time to sail around to the eastern shore. There's no inner passage, so you have to make an outside passage around the island. This can be bumpy even in fine conditions, but is well worth the effort. Things will be much more comfortable if you stay a little offshore to escape the ocean swells reflecting from the barrier reefs. The passage will be both uncomfortable and dangerous in strong easterlies, so forget it in such weather. Provided you reach the entrance to Passe Farerea by 1530, you should have no trouble coming in on the black beacon that marks the entrance. Once again, you will find yourself in Scottish loch-like conditions, with a superb rock pillar known as Le Doigt ("the finger") overlooking the deep bay. You can anchor off Maroe village, where there's a store. Wherever you spend the night, keep an eye out for winds funneling down the hills, just as you would in Scotland. Some people anchor in Baie Apoomati, just southeast of the pass, a good place to leave your yacht while you explore the reefs between Motu Mahora and the main island in your dinghy. You could spend days here and never visit the same area twice.

The Leewards are a cruising ground of deep-water anchorages and open-water, tradewind passages, a place where you can enjoy the delights of tropical islands under the most civilized and uncongested conditions possible. Americans and Europeans alike have become used to cruising in company most of the time, whether they like it or not. Les Iles Sous le Vent and Vava'u are two places where you can still sail alone.

Bay of Islands, New Zealand

A generation ago, only a handful of ocean sailors ventured from Europe or North America to New Zealand waters. Now the trickle has become a minor flood. Several hundred yachts from all over the world check into North Island's Bay of Islands every year, a cruising ground that must rank among the most attractive in the world. The advent of the jumbo jet and the worldwide explosion of bareboat chartering have made it possible to realize one's dream of cruising the Bay of Islands or exploring the Marlborough Sound area on the shores of Cook Strait in South Island. Instead of taking months to reach southern latitudes, you can jet to Auckland from Los Angeles in about 13 hours, and from Australia in two.

Even in these days of 747s and intercontinental airlines, New Zealand is far away. The very remoteness of the land adds much to its charm, but also to the cost of getting there. A trip to New Zealand is likely to be the vacation of a lifetime. Most overseas charterers combine their sailing with at least a week of land travel so that they can explore more of the country at the same time. You can choose from a whole range of attractive packages that enable you to see a great deal of this fascinating country within two or three weeks. Here's how it works. You purchase a round-trip excursion ticket on Air New Zealand (they are by far the best carrier across the Pacific), book your charter, then buy special motel and rental car vouchers for each day you spend on land. These give you overnight accommodation and a car at a guaranteed rate. All you have to do is to arrive in Auckland, pick up your car, and call ahead for a motel reservation. You pay for your food and gasoline; everything else is settled up before you depart. The vouchers are usually contracted with motel chains, of which Best Western is by far the largest. We found their motels to be comfortable and the owners extremely friendly. They are glad to call ahead for your next night's reservation. You'll love driving in New Zealand. The roads are mostly uncongested and in superb condition. We were given a Honda, which handled well around mountain bends.

Nearly everyone who goes to New Zealand complains of running out of time. We spent three and a half weeks there, somewhat longer than most tourists, and still felt rushed. New Zealand is unique among tourist destinations for the incredible variety it offers. You can walk in a subtropical rain forest one day and be skiing on an Alpine glacier the next. Quite apart from the magnificent sightseeing, you can fly-fish for rainbow trout that will have your friends back home gasping in amazement, or ride horses on deserted park trails. You can land on a mountain snow pack, take a helicopter ride over rugged glaciers, walk for miles on remote trails without seeing another soul. You have only a few precious days to experience a fraction of all this, so plan carefully.

The main thing is to find a travel agent who really knows not only New Zealand, but local sailing conditions as well. Your vacation plans should be tailor-made to your specification, so use an expert rather than your local travel agency. We found some real professionals—Rainbow Adventure Holidays, 23241 Ventura Blvd., Suite 216, Woodland Hills, CA 91364, (800-227-5317). They have firsthand knowledge of local conditions and close links with the charter company in the Bay of Islands. Furthermore, they are experts on yacht chartering all over the world. Ask their advice about itineraries. Here, for what they are worth, are my recommendations:

First, take your bareboat charter early on in the trip. Most charterers land at Auckland, spend a day there, and then drive three and a half hours north to the Bay of Islands, where they swap their car for a yacht. They then relax afloat and pick up a car again when they return.

Second, head for South Island as soon as you come ashore. The main scenic attractions are down south. If you can, fly from Auckland to Christchurch and pick up a car there. The fare is expensive, but you will make it up in saved time. Christchurch is just a day's drive from the fjords and mountains. If you fly south, you can then dawdle in magnificent scenery before visiting North Island at the end of your trip.

Third, leave North Island to the end. This is the place for trout fishing, Maori culture, and geysers. Of course, there's a great deal more to see, but most visitors drive north to Picton, take the ferry across Cook Strait, then drive to Lake Taupo and Rotorua before flying out of Auckland on the last evening. If you have the time and are interested in fishing, spend the money and give over a day to fly fishing. We splurged on two nights at Tongariro Lodge at the south end of Lake Taupo, where we spent a morning horseback riding and a day learning how to fly-fish with an expert guide. Fly-fishing is a real art, requiring infinite patience and a delicate touch. It was just our luck that the fish were not biting! The lodge itself was a wonderful experience. Only 16 people can stay there at a time. The tradition of the house is that everyone eats dinner at communal tables. The result is a wonderful mix of New Zealanders, Americans, Australians, and others, and a thoroughly entertaining evening.

Lastly, go out of your way to meet people. New Zealanders are the friendliest, most relaxed people on earth. They love meeting visitors from overseas, will invite you to their homes, and smother you with hospitality. We met all sorts of Kiwis during our stay— sheep farmers, innkeepers, big-game fishermen, insurance men, Maori dancers, even bull-semen salesmen. They gave us insights into their country that we would never have obtained otherwise. You can talk about scenery all you like, but what makes New Zealand in the final analysis is the people.

All of this may seem irrelevant to bareboating, but it's not. You are crazy if you do not combine your New Zealand cruise with some time ashore. Every moment spent planning ahead of time will be richly rewarded at the other end.

Bareboating is a very new sport in New Zealand, nearly all of it centered in the Bay of Islands close to the northern tip of North Island. You can charter a trailer boat on Lake Rotorua, or 28- or 30-footers in Queen Charlotte Sound (contact Southern Marine Charters, PO Box 246, Picton, South Island, for information), but these are very much local operations tailored to the domestic market. Queen Charlotte Sound is a scenic cruising ground somewhat like the Pacific Northwest, with a relatively short summer season. It has historical associations with Captain Cook and other early explorers, but probably less to offer the overseas visitor than the Bay of Islands, where the major New Zealand charter company operates.

Rainbow Yachts was founded at Russell in 1976 and now maintains a fleet of more than 20 boats, ranging in size from 20 to 38 feet. They also run 36-foot launches and a 46-foot skippered yacht. This is a company with high standards of client service and maintenance, accustomed to dealing with oveseas visitors. Their boats are government licensed and subject to stringent inspection during construction and operation. You can be sure that they will stand up to severe conditions and hard use. Most overseas charterers are likely to choose the Davidson 28 or Chieftain 38, both New Zealand–designed and built to very tough specifications. We chose a Davidson 28, a Laurie Davidson design that can sleep four comfortably in two double berths. *Cherita* was a fast sailor, with a large cockpit, well-equipped galley, and dinette saloon that was luxurious with only two aboard. Her Bukh one-cylinder diesel drove her along comfortably at 6 knots in calm water. When the wind squalled up to 30 knots plus, we tucked in a single reef, set the working jib, and make excellent time to windward.

We were able to visit one of the Chieftain 38s, a weatherly, center-cockpit design with huge aft cabin and all the luxuries. A charter party of six could cruise up the coast from the Bay of Islands to Whangaroa in great comfort. Whatever your choice of yacht, the specifications include anything you could possibly need, including plenty of safety gear, comprehensively equipped galleys, and refrigerators. The company provides a provisioning starter pack, bedding, masks, fins, and snorkels, and—best of all—a 9-foot sailing dinghy. New Zealand yacht interiors are not as luxurious as the coordinated "home afloat" effect that you find on many American boats these days, but we

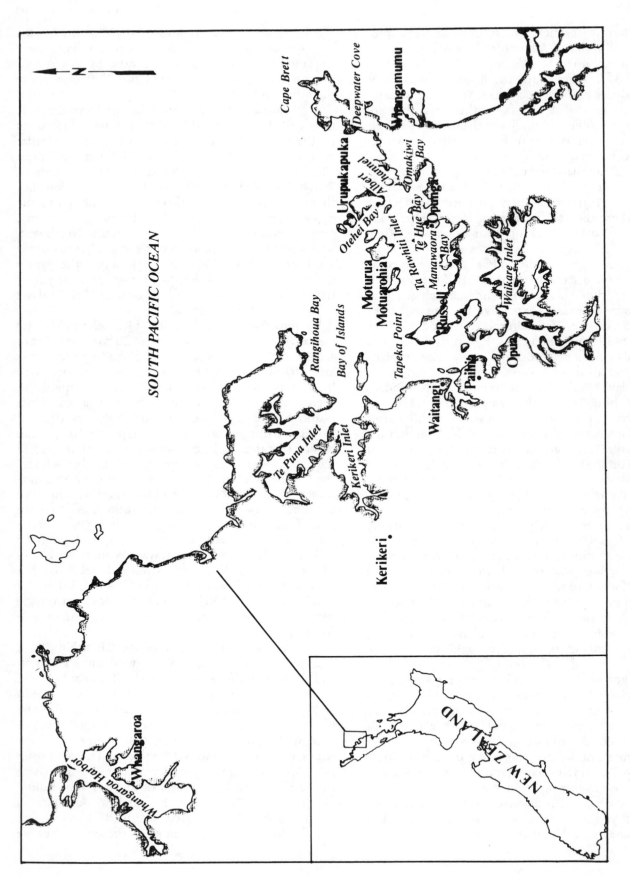

SOUTH PACIFIC OCEAN

Cape Brett
Deepwater Cove
Whangamumu

Urupukapuka
Omakiwi Bay
Albert Channel
Te Hue Bay
Otehei Bay
Opunga
Manawaora Bay
Ta Rawhiti Inlet
Moturua
Motuarohia
Tapeka Point
Russell
Waikare Inlet
Rangihoua Bay
Bay of Islands
Opua
Waitangi
Paihia

Te Puna Inlet
Kerikeri Inlet

Kerikeri

Whangaroa
Whangaroa Harbor

NEW ZEALAND

Bay of Islands, New Zealand

chartered in complete comfort. Both the designs and the equipment specifications are ideal for Bay of Islands waters.

The Bay of Islands lies 35 degrees south of the Equator and enjoys a moderate, subtropical climate. The summer months from late November through early April coincide with the northern winter. The warm months are normally fine. There are long periods of settled weather, with northeasterly sea breezes during the day and gentle land airs from the southwest at night. The winds tend to be stronger in March and April, with the windiest weather between June and September. Most of the rainfall comes during the winter when temperatures are much cooler, with occasional cloudy, rainy weather from the north. You can sail year round here, but the charter season lasts about 20 weeks a year, from spring to fall. The best chartering conditions are in late spring, early summer, and after the main holiday rush between December and February, when the Bay of Islands is literally paved with yachts from Auckland. An overseas visitor can expect fine sailing and relatively predictable weather slightly off season. Many people feel that March is the best month, although we had unusually squally weather in 1984. Even if the weather is windy, you can sail between the islands in smooth water on most days, so your cruise may be curtailed but certainly not stopped dead in the water.

At first sight, the Bay of Islands is such a jumble of islands and anchorages that it's difficult to plan a week's cruise. Roger Miles of Rainbow Yachts suggested that we drive to the summit of Mount Bledisloe beyond Waitangi, on the northwest side of the bay. A broad panorama of green hills, deeply indented bays, and inviting islands lay at our feet. Deep inlets fingered into the land. White puffy clouds chased one another over the evening sky, laying alternating patterns of light and shadow over the white houses of the old whaling settlement of Russell across the bay. Few cruising grounds ever looked so enticing.

Rainbow Yachts is based on the long pier at Opua at the mouth of Waikare Inlet, close to a store and small take-out restaurant, where you can refresh yourself while waiting to board your yacht on the pontoon nearby. Roger Miles suggested that we make a lunch stop at Russell, only 45 minutes away by boat, to view the audio-visual presentation on the Bay of Islands at the Park Visitor Center. We anchored off the town with its historic waterfront and were soon transported into the rich history of the islands. Captain Cook was the first European to sail into the bay. He landed on Motuarohia Island in the center of the bay, climbed to the summit and admired the landlocked anchorages at his feet. There were "large Indian towns" all around him.

Cook's "Indians" were Maori, who had settled in the Bay of Islands centuries before. These ferocious, brave people greeted Cook wearing feathered capes, their faces deeply tattooed with curvilinear designs. Cook managed to avoid trouble, but a French explorer named Marion du Fresne and 27 men were murdered three years later. In a fury of revenge, the surviving Frenchmen burned several Maori villages and killed scores of the local people. Many European ships kept away, believing that the Maori would eat them. So it was not until 1814 that missionaries settled in the bay. Whalers rested their crews at Kororareka (now known as Russell), and a few European traders and farmers came to stay. There were inevitable conflicts over land, so the British government signed the Treaty of Waitangi with the Maori on February 6, 1840. Waitangi lies across the water from Russell. Its Treaty House and Maori meeting house are the nearest thing to a national shrine New Zealanders share. The stirring events of the early days are but dim memories today, but you can easily spend a week chasing the past at Russell, at the early mission station at Kerikeri, and in the islands. There's so much to do ashore in the bay that it's sometimes hard to find time to sail.

Russell itself is a charming little place. The town clusters behind Kororareka Bay. You can land your dinghy on the same beach that the whalers used. The waterside taverns once had an international reputation for drunken roistering and prostitution. As many as 150 ships a year were calling at the port by midcentury. Relations between Maori and settlers became so bad that the town was attacked and burned by the Maori chief Hone Heke in 1845. You can see some of the musket-ball holes in the church walls to this day. High above the town is a hilltop flagpole that was cut down repeatedly by the Maori during those uneasy years. Take the time to climb up to the site and photograph the town at your feet. Russell Church is the oldest in New Zealand, erected in 1835 by public subscription. The naturalist Charles Darwin, who visited Russell in HMS *Beagle*, was one of the subscribers. Both Europeans and Maori lie buried in the churchyard. Their gravestones are a fascinating vignette of New Zealand's past. Do visit the Captain Cook Memorial Museum in town as well. It's a curious jumble of historical objects and features a miniature replica of his ship *Endeavour*.

The anchorage off Russell can be uncomfortable, so you are best off sailing round the corner into the sheltered waters of the islands themselves. In fine weather, the prevailing winds will be blowing into the bay, so you will have a beat out of Russell. Give Tapeka

Opua. (Lesley Newhart)

Point a wide berth, then head eastward on a close fetch into Manawaora Bay, which boasts of at least six excellent anchorages. Ancient Maori forts, known as *pas*, look out over Manawaora from strategic headlands, in the area where Marion du Fresne and his men were killed. You can climb up to one of the Maori forts, settlements destroyed by the avenging French two centuries ago. Most yachts make a beeline for Opunga Cove at the southern end of the bay, a fine sheltered roadstead with ample space to anchor off a sandy beach in 20 feet. But I prefer Te Hue Bay, also called Assassination Cove on account of the monument to du Fresne and his men that lies ashore. The surroundings are more picturesque, the anchorage very sheltered, and you can walk across a narrow spit of land to a superb beach facing Te Rawhiti Inlet.

The longer we stayed at Te Hue, the more convenient we realized it was. We sailed the dinghy down to nearby Orokawa Bay, an exposed beach, but well worth exploring if only for the climb up to the Maori *pa* perched on the peninsula of the same name. The *pa* is sited brilliantly, protected on three sides by precipitous cliffs with the waters of the bay far below. One can imagine the densely packed stake fences, the low grass-and-thatch huts inside, the tattooed warriors gathering at the fortifications in times of war. Another fine *pa* lies across the water on the northeast side of Paroa Bay, where you can anchor under the cliffs in moderate depths. Here as elsewhere, there are sandy beaches in abundance, guarded by massive *pohutukawa*, "New Zealand Christmas trees." They are ablaze with crimson flowers during the festive season. Their roots cling to the cliffs and sprawl on the beach in intricate profusion.

One arm of Manawaora forms the western arm of Te Rawhiti Inlet, which runs between a chain of six islands and the mainland shore. You are bound to enjoy some superb sailing between the islands. The wind can funnel between the cliffs even on fine days and you can enjoy a stiff punch to windward. We sailed up to Omakiwi Cove on a squally day with gusts of 30 knots or more. *Cherita* asked for a reef and the working jib and eagerly heeled to her work. Occasional bursts of spray reached the cockpit as grey clouds, bright sunlight, and heavy rain showers chased us over the water. At times, we could see only a few yards; at others, a deep-green panorama of hills and farmland unfolded in front of us. It was blowing hard outside, but here we were able to enjoy a magnificent sail.

Had the weather been more settled, we could have diverted to literally dozens of anchorages among the islands. First you pass Motuarohia, the place where Cook first landed. The anchorage at the east end is a good lunch stop in calm weather. You can climb to the top of the very hill where Cook and Banks gazed out over the unknown bay in 1769. Moturua is next, with three fine anchorages at its southern end. The Park Service maintains a water buoy in Waipao Bay on the southwest shore, where you can replenish your tanks without going back to Russell. This unique and civilized idea is complemented by another—a garbage barge moored at the southeast end of the island during the season. I only wish other charter areas offered such facilities. The barge is close to Pipi Bay, a well-sheltered anchorage safe in all but southeasterly winds.

The islands farther to the east are worth several days. You can find remote, usually deserted anchorages off Urupukapuka or Waewaetoria in almost any weather. The most famous is Otehei Bay, a cozy spot associated with the American author and sportsman Zane Grey in the 1920s. Otehei is still a private resort, but you can anchor off the pier. The deepest water lies on the southeast side of the bay. You should hug this shore when entering, for a shallow patch blocks much of the entrance. Otehei is easy to find. Just look for the small rocky island with a light tripod on it on the north side of Poroporo Island and you are there. Unfortunately, this charming spot is often crowded. But do not despair, for there are many anchorages elsewhere on Urupukapuka. Indico, Oneura, and Urupukapuka all offer fine sandy beaches and a chance to tramp ashore. I think this is about the finest island in the bay for exploring ashore.

Te Rawhiti Inlet ends in the narrow defile of the Albert Channel that separates Urupukapuka and the Hauai Peninsula. This is a valuable short cut to Cape Brett. At first sight, the passage between Rawhiti Point and Orerewai Rock is intimidating, but in fact there's 19 feet in the middle. You'll see Deep Water Cove straight ahead as you leave the channel, lined by forbidding cliffs. This is a good lunch stop. Maunganui Bay at the northwest corner is the best berth, a deep, narrow inlet that was once the site of a sportfishing camp in the 1920s and 1930s. There's not much to see ashore now, but the cliffs seem to crowd in on you here, in an anchorage that is totally unlike any other in the bay. I was reminded of some of the smaller coves at Santa Cruz Island in Southern California.

If you have the time and the weather's settled, make a point of rounding Cape Brett and sailing south along the peninsula to explore Whangamumu Harbor. The entrance is about 6 miles from the cape and is a little hard to find until 1,100-foot-high Pukehuia peak is abeam. The best anchorage lies off the beach, which is lined with pohutukawa trees. Whangamumu was once the site of a whaling station with its own pier. The Cook family (no relation) operated the station from 1893 until the early 1930s. They pursued humpback whales, but found that open rowing boats were too slow for catching them. So they assembled a massive gill net that was set in the path of the migrating whales. A whale would become entangled in the net, the rowing boats would approach, and the whalers would throw their harpoons at close range. The Cooks landed hundreds of whales over the years, 74 in 1927 alone. They went out of business five years later as the demand for whale oil declined. Today, few humpbacks are to be seen off the Bay of Islands. They have been hunted out.

With luck, the weather will still be fine when you leave Whangamumu. Take the opportunity to sail across the mouth of the bay, pausing to anchor off the commemorative cross in Rangihoua Bay, the place where missionary Samuel Marsden landed in 1814. "Behold, I bring you good tidings of great joy," preached Marsden on Christmas Day of that year. A Celtic cross records this event. But a new and more lasting mission station was founded at nearby Kerikeri in 1819 under the protection of the great Maori chief Hongi Hika, whose strongly fortified pa looked down on the tiny settlement. (Before visiting Kerikeri, you should try to spare a day for Te Puna Inlet, which has the advantage of being less crowded in high season. Wharengaere anchorage, sometimes called Crater Bay, on the east side of the inlet, is an excellent berth in most weather and is almost completely circular.)

Back to Hongi Hika. He had sailed aboard whaling ships and visited Samuel Marsden in Australia. A shrewd, ruthless chief, Hika encouraged the missionaries, seeing in them a chance to acquire firearms and other European goods that would give him strategic advantage in his constant rivalries with his powerful neighbors. He traveled to England in 1820, where he worked with the Church Missionary Society and was showered with gifts, among them a suit of armor. He traded most of these in Sydney and returned with a load of muskets that he used with devastating effect against his Maori neighbors. The missionaries lived in uneasy proximity to Hongi Hika, especially since the chief demanded muskets for food. But for all these difficulties, the tiny mission station flourished until 1848, when it was closed in favor of other locations. The

earliest European houses in New Zealand rose by the shores of the Kerikeri Inlet. Two of them, the Kemp house, which was once the mission residence, and a stone store, still stand. They overlook the calm tidal pool where Maori canoes once berthed in complete shelter.

A visit to Kerikeri is a highlight of any bay charter. The inlet itself is entered between Motupapa Island and Akeake Point. You can anchor in several bays inside the entrance, the best being Opito. The others tend to be congested with moorings. The inlet shallows quickly, but there is a buoyed channel that leads to the basin upstream. You need at least half-tide to take your boat up the channel, so you will have to plan your day to carry the flood between the beacons. Provided you watch the markers and the chart, you should enjoy a gentle passage in delightful scenery. The final bends take you through wooded meadows, past the foot of

Hongi Hika's *pa*, to the mooring posts in the basin. This may be crowded in summer, but the inconvenience is well worth it. You can visit both the store, which is now a shop, and the mission house, as well as exploring the *pa* and a replica of a pre-European Maori village on the opposite shore. The modern town of Kerikeri lies an easy walk inland from the basin. You can buy any provisions you want here, and the French restaurant in town is unpretentious and excellent. Next day, you cast off on the last of the flood and return to deep water with the first of the ebb.

Kerikeri Inlet is only 7 miles from Russell and about the same distance from Waitangi, where the story of European settlement really began. Unfortunately, Waitangi is an uncomfortable, rather exposed berth much of the time, but you can lie to the mooring posts provided for visitors at the river mouth. Everything interesting is within easy walking distance. The

Kerikeri Pool. (Lesley Newhart)

Waitangi Visitor Center tells how Lieutenant Governor William Hobson and 45 Maori chiefs signed a treaty on February 6, 1840, ceding New Zealand to the Queen of England. You can walk from the center to the great 119-foot Maori war canoe, Te Ana o Maikuku, with its intricate bow and stern carvings. Her canoe house lies close to the place where Hobson landed on Treaty Day. A well-manicured path leads to the green meadow, with its enormous flagpole, where the treaty was signed. You can tour the Treaty House (1833), a fine Georgian-style house that was once the British Resident's home, now a museum. Nearby stands the Maori National *Marae* (meeting house), built on the place where the local chiefs gathered to discuss the treaty and its implications.

By this time, you may be itching for some exercise. The beginning of a trail to the Haruru Falls lies opposite the entrance to the Visitor Center. This is a marvelous forest walk that passes over a golf course, traverses a boardwalk through some mangrove swamps, and climbs above the river valley to emerge at the falls just under 4 miles inland. The return hike takes about two moderately strenuous hours and offers fine views over the estuary as well as a close look at the local flora. If you are lucky enough to make the walk on a rainy day, you'll enjoy the sight of delicate veil clouds of rain passing over the river valley and tracing the forest ferns in patterns of raindrops. Haruru is a small waterfall by New Zealand standards, but nevertheless a pretty spot that is well worth the effort.

Waitangi brings you full circle, from deserted anchorages and long-abandoned Maori *pas*, to historic mission stations and to the birthplace of a modern nation. Few charter areas offer such magnificent sailing in sheltered water, with so many unique sights and fine beaches close at hand. Here, as in Greece, the charterer is at an advantage, seeing the life of an area from the ocean, as its earliest settlers did. Only in this way can one appreciate the full historical impact of places like the Bay of Islands.

Australia

After the intimate friendship of New Zealand or the

Pacific islands, the size of Australia comes as a distinct surprise. One tends to forget that it is a continent almost the size of the 48 contiguous American states, with a vast, almost empty desert interior. Australia is a land of coastal city dwellers, a country difficult to understand without taking the time to explore not only the large population centers like Sydney, Adelaide, and Perth, but the vast loneliness of the outback as well. The people are boisterous, friendly, and always generous. Unfortunately, I have not had the chance to sail there yet. It is therefore difficult to write about bareboating in Australia with the authority of firsthand knowledge. But Australia is high on my list of cruising priorities.

Australia is so far from America or Europe that you need at least three weeks, preferably a month, if you plan to combine some bareboating with travel ashore. You'll almost certainly fly into Sydney, an international city with every facility imaginable. You can bareboat in Sydney Harbor or on the protected waters of Broken Bay, some 50 miles up the coast. Most of the companies that work there are small operations, whose facilities are atuned to the local market. The Australian Tourist Commission, PO Box A-1, Addison, IL 60101, should be able to give you a list of them and of companies operating in more remote places like Tasmania or Queensland.

Most tourist itineraries "down under" take in several major cities and a quick trip to Alice Springs and Ayres Rock in the far interior. There's usually a chance to visit the Great Barrier Reef, the 1,200-mile reef that runs up the northeast shores of the continent. This is where the major bareboating area lies, centered on the Whitsunday Islands near Townsville in northern Queensland. You can easily fit in a week or more of sailing into a longer Australian holiday. I would allow at least three or four days, if not a week, before flying up to the Whitsundays. This will give you time to adjust to the time change and to recover from the long flight. Then hop on a plane from Sydney to Brisbane and Shute Harbor, where the Whitsunday fleets are based. There are several companies to choose from. Most of the yachts are in the 30-to-40-foot range.

It seems that wherever you charter in the South Pacific, you are in the company of Captain Cook. He traversed the Whitsunday Passage on June 3, 1770, passing between the Cumberland Islands and the mainland on a fine day. A week later he was to run aground on top of the tide. It took him 23 hours to haul *Endeavour* off, after she had been lightened of more than 50 tons of stores. Even today, the Great Barrier Reef is a potentially hazardous cruising ground, one where many small yachts have come to grief over the years. Cook and his men admired the islands lying parallel to the coast, the deep bays and coves, the green vegetation ashore. You can enjoy the same scenery today, for the Whitsundays have changed little since the eighteenth century. There are occasional resorts on Hamilton Island and elsewhere, but they are lost among the 74 islands that make up this remote charter area. Here, as in Tahiti, you can find solitude with occasional tastes of civilization at isolated resorts, some of which maintain moorings for floating guests.

The Whitsundays are not part of the Great Barrier Reef. They are craggy islands with indented bays, rugged hills, and snow-white bays, whose waters are protected by the reef far offshore. The tradewinds blow steadily across them, lighter in summer and with greater, more predictable force during the Australian winter (May through August). You can sail here year round, but I would aim for the southern winter months, when the sailing is better. The Whitsundays are no place for first-time bareboaters, for the currents run strongly through the islands and sudden downslope gusts can put you on the coral at the entrance to an anchorage in a few moments. (If you are inexperienced, why not take a skipper for a few days?) You tend to use your engine wisely and well, laying out plenty of scope for the night. The choice of anchorages is unending, including places like Butterfly Bay and Macona Inlet, where you can lie in solitude and snorkel among colorful coral heads or climb ashore to admire the scenery over the islands. The Whitsundays are a "lunch-hook" charter area, where you can anchor off dozens of pristine white beaches and walk ashore with your feet scuffing sand that may well have been untouched by human feet before. In some ways, the scenery, with its hooked pine trees and rocky islands, is reminiscent of the Pacific Northwest or Scandinavia. But the steady trades at your back and the imported coconut palms soon remind you that you are within a few hundred miles of New Guinea.

The Great Barrier Reef lies 15 to 40 miles offshore, so you are actually inside it here. Bareboats are forbidden to visit the reef, but Air Whitsunday will actually bring a seaplane out to your yacht and take you for a morning or afternoon's excursion out to the low sandy cays and reefs far offshore.

By combining a week or more of chartering in the Whitsundays with a longer land vacation, you'll have a chance to extend your Australian adventure to some of the most remote parts of the Southern Hemisphere.

Appendix: An Anthology of Charter Planning Resources

General comments

The writing of this book required not only months of chartering and cruising in all parts of the world, but many hours of library research as well. Like all cruising books, *Bareboating* is based on a mix of book learning and practical experience acquired from a wide variety of sources, many of them relatively inaccessible to the average charterer. Over the years, I have found that a charter is much more enjoyable if you do some planning and basic navigational legwork ahead of time. Some charter companies realize this and send you copies of charts and cruising guides ahead of time. Even then, you may want to dig deeper and to plan a more ambitious, or specialized, itinerary to cater to your crew's individual needs. Thus armed, you can then ask really specific questions at briefing time and make the most of local knowledge.

When compiling the descriptions of the charter areas in Parts III through VI of *Bareboating*, I tried to put myself in the position of a prospective charterer making plans for a cruise in unfamiliar waters. Of course my research was bolstered by firsthand experience and by more comprehensive reading than the average bareboater would undertake. But there are certain fundamental sources on each major area that will save you a great deal of planning time. This anthology will summarize some of these sources for you. My editorial remarks are, of course, my own opinions, and you may not necessarily agree with them.

Caribbean

The Virgins: The charter companies will send you a cruising guide and their own cruise charts about a month ahead of time. Being highly cost-conscious, many of them send you Harry Kline's *Yachtsman's Guide to the Virgin Islands and Puerto Rico* (North Miami: Tropic Island Publishers, annual), a long-established guide that suffers from two major disadvantages. It is filled with advertising, which means it stresses shore facilities rather than navigation. It also tends to be out of date, despite being an annual. The BVI

Bareboat Association has published Simon Scott's *The Cruising Guide to the Virgin Islands* (BVIBA, PO Box 6571, Fort Lauderdale, FL 33316), which is well spoken of by some charterers of my acquaintance. I strongly recommend that you supplement Kline or Scott with Donald Street's *Cruising Guide to the Eastern Caribbean* (vol. II, New York: W.W. Norton, 1980), which covers the Virgins in detail. Street's guides are the absolute best, because the author has been to nearly every anchorage and harbor in the Caribbean repeatedly. Time and time again, he has lead me safely into uncrowded bays. This is a real seaman's guide, and I would spend the money on a copy even if I were going to the islands only once. This contains more than enough information for your purposes.

The flourishing tourist industry has spawned a whole series of pretty photograph-filled guides to the bays and anchorages of the Virgins. Unless you collect such baubles, forget them. Better to buy a local guidebook that deals with sights on land when you arrive.

I found the Better Boating Association's Virgin Islands Chart-Kit a useful supplement to charter company charts. This and other Chart-Kits can be obtained from BBA at PO Box 407, Needham, MA 02192, (800-242-7854).

St. Martin and neighboring islands: William J. Eiman, *St. Maarten/St. Martin Area Cruising Guide* (obtainable from Virgin Island Plus Charters, 239 Delancy St., Philadelphia, PA 19106) covers neighboring Anguilla, St. Barts, and Saba as well. Caripress's *Cruising Guide to Martinique* (30 rue Montesquieu, 97200 Fort-de-France, Martinique) has both an English and French text.

Windward Islands: Again, I like to have Street on board. Volume II of his four-set *Guide* covers Puerto Rico to Dominica, while Volume III will take you down the Windwards to Trinidad. What I like about Street is that he encourages you to try challenging places. That to me is what cruising is all about (within the limits placed on you by the charter company).

Chris Doyle's *Sailor's Guide to the Windward Islands* (obtainable c/o Mrs. Hooper, PO Box 17, Saint Vincent) is a fine local publication. It is at this point, however, that I reach for my Julius Wilensky, *Yachtsman's Guide to the Windward Islands*, which CSY uses as a standard handout (Wescott Cove Publishing Company, PO Box 130, Stamford, CT 06904). Wherever I have used them, I have found Wilensky's books both thorough and practical. He strikes a delicate balance between navigation, sights ashore, and intelligent planning. He is one of the best. Stevens Yachts puts out *Stevens' Cruising Guide to the Windward Islands*, obtainable from their offices. This is excellent for the more conservative charterer.

Bay Islands: Wilensky's *Cruising Guide to the Bay Islands of Honduras* is the only available source, indeed was commissioned by CSY (Wescott, 1979). You will find yourself relying on his sketch charts, for U.S. and Admiralty charts of the islands are effectively useless for a small yacht. The *Guide* is more than adequate and a mine of information about a little-known area.

Belize: There's just one guide, Bill Sorem's *Belize Cruising Guide* (Freewing Development, PO Box 1325, Pinellas Park, FL 33565). This is supplemented with the charter company's admirable local charts, based on Admiralty folios. This being a relatively simple area, little else is needed.

North America

North American waters are covered by a large number of cruising guides and by U.S. government charts. Indeed, there are now so many purported guides to the major cruising areas that it's difficult to know what to recommend. Your first investment should be a Chart-Kit portfolio for your chosen area, if one is available. At the time of writing, you can charter the Bahamas, Florida Keys, Chesapeake, Maine, and Southern California with one aboard. U.S. charts are obtainable from most major marine store outlets or direct from the government in Maryland—the latter is rather a laborious way of obtaining them. The remarks about guides that follow assume that you have the correct chart coverage available.

Incidentally, in U.S. waters I recommend that you purchase your own charts and take them along with you. Charter companies tend to skimp, especially on large-scale plans. If you can, buy the fold-out versions, folio charts that are designed specially for cruising boats. Those for the Intercoastal Waterway and the Florida Keys are ideal for the purpose.

Florida Keys: Frank Papy's *Cruising Guide to the Florida Keys* (Publication Arts Inc., 5700 Green Circle Drive, Minnetonka, MN 55343) is written by an expert charter skipper and revised regularly. Unlike most advertising publications, the author really emphasizes pilotage and anchorages. There is no need to look for more detail. The large-scale plans are very effective when used with government charts, particularly when cruise planning or identifying landmarks in the flat Keys landscape.

Bahamas: The Bahamas as a whole are covered by Harry Kline's *Yachtsman's Guide to the Bahamas* (Tropic Isle Publishers). Although it's revised annually, it suffers from the same disadvantages as the Virgins volume. Last time I used it, it was very out of date. However, the same author's Tropic Island charts are superb large-scale renderings of key passages and anchorages, designed specially for sailors. You are well advised to invest in one or two, especially if you are cruising the Abacos. Kline is sufficient for a Bimini charter, but I would go with Julius Wilensky's *Cruising Guide to the Abacos and the Northern Bahamas* (Wescott, 1981) when cruising the major Bahamas charter area. It is reliable, comprehensive, and very informative for planning purposes.

The Bahamas Chart-Kit is a must in these waters. Invest in your own, it's well worth the $80 or more it costs.

California: Southern California is well covered by a Chart-Kit and my own *Cruising Guide to California's Channel Islands* (Ventura, California: Western Marine Enterprises, 1983). Catalina charterers might like to invest in the *Chartguide to Santa Catalina* (Anaheim: Edmund Winlund), which contains much information on fishing and diving as well as navigational data.

The *Pacific Boating Almanac* (Western Marine, annual) has long been a bible in both Northern and Southern California. This publication carries advertising, lengthy extracts from government sailing directions, and occasional valuable information on local cruising conditions. More of a reference work, it's about the only source on the San Francisco Bay area, except for my *California Coastal Passages* (Santa Barbara: Capra Press, 1981), which is actually a passage guide for coastal cruising.

Pacific Northwest: The *Pacific Boating Almanac* covers some of these waters, but you are better off with local publications, especially Bruce Calhoun's *Cruising the San Juan Islands* (Newfoundland, New Jersey: Haessner Publishing, 1973) and the beautifully illustrated *Pacific Yachting's Cruising Guide to British Columbia*, a multivolume work that covers the Gulf Islands and Desolation Sound. When planning a charter in these waters, buy some charts, otherwise you'll have trouble relating one island group to another. The Canadian charts are excellent and a good buy.

Apostle Islands: Navigation is so simple that you really don't need much more than chart 14973 of the islands. David Strzok's *A Visitor's Guide to the Apostle Islands National Lakeshore* (Superior Printing, 607 East Second Street, Ashland, WI 54806) contains sufficient information to get you about, provided you are careful with charts. It also tells many stories about the islands.

Chesapeake and Maine: Two definitive works will carry you through these two areas, William T. Stone and Fessenden S. Blanchard's *Cruising Guide to the Chesapeake* (New York: Dodd, Mead, latest revision 1983) and Roger F. Duncan and John P. Ware's *A Cruising Guide to the New England Coast* (same publisher, latest edition 1983). Both are cultured,

eloquent volumes that will serve you well under any conditions. You need look no further. If you want information on attractions ashore, wait until your charter begins. You can buy the best selection in local bookstores.

Europe

Scandinavia: Unless you read Danish, German, or Swedish, you are really on your own. A Danish charter company will probably supply a copy of *Danskhavenlods*, a government publication, which does however contain superb harbor plans that are intelligible even to illiterates. The *Baltic Southwest Pilot* by Marc Brackenbury (Stanford Maritime Press, London) is also an excellent source of information. I believe there is a similar government publication for Swedish ports. You will probably have to navigate here without a cruising guide, but take heart, for the Danish and Swedish government charts are among the finest and most accurate anywhere. They come in flip-chart form, spiral-bound, each sheet covering only a few miles. Such charts are bound to be on board, but you will probably find it difficult to obtain your own. You might try J.D. Potter, 145 The Minories, London EC3 1NH, England. They may be able to locate copies for you. Another idea: get hold of a topographic map and do your advance planning with that. Fortunately, there are so many anchorages and ports that you can make last-minute planning choices without any trouble.

Great Britain and Ireland: The British Isles are probably the most thoroughly documented cruising area in the world, and with good reason, since they are among the trickiest to navigate, especially for overseas visitors used to less tidal waters. *The Cruising Association Handbook* (Cruising Association, Ivory House, St. Katherine Dock, London EC1 9AT, England) is a comprehensive guide to British waters that is somewhat clipped in style. It's a book of basic sailing directions plus hundreds of harbor plans, nothing else, and as such is superb. The following are some regional guides to supplement Admiralty charts.

English Channel: K. Adlard Coles was for many years *the* authority on the English Channel and France, but has now largely retired from writing cruising guides. Fortunately, his works are being kept in print. For the Channel Islands, you can do no better than his classic *Channel Harbors and Anchorages* (London: Macmillan), which will also take you to Cherbourg and St.-Malo, and into the most incredible minor anchorages. Malcolm Robson's *Channel Islands Pilot* and his *French Pilot* (both Nautical Publishing Company, London) or David Jefferson's *Brittany and Channel Islands Cruising*

Guide (Stanford, London) will take you west to the Chenal du Four and beyond. So will Adlard Coles' *North Brittany Pilot* (Coles, Lymington). The same author's *Shell Pilot to South Coast Harbors* (Faber, London) is the best source on West Country ports. North Spain and the Bay of Biscay are covered in Adlard Coles and A.C. Black, *North Biscay Pilot* (Coles) and in Robin Brandon's *South Biscay Pilot* (Coles).

Ireland: The best guide is the Irish Cruising Club's *Sailing Directions, South and West Coasts of Ireland* (obtainable from Mrs. J. Guinness, Censure House, Bailey, Co. Dublin 323123, Ireland). This is a compendium of information accumulated by dozens of club members over the years. A marvelous book!

Western Scotland: The Clyde Cruising Club has done the same thing for Scotland—*West Coast of Scotland* (obtainable from R.A. Clement and Co., CA, 62 Glasgow G1 1TX, Scotland). Like the Irish guide, it's based on dozens of sailors' experiences over the years. Also available is *Scottish West Coast Pilot* by Marc Brackenbury and published by Stanford Maritime of London.

East Coast rivers: One small paperback volume has been the authority for years, the *Yachting Monthly Pilot for East Coast Rivers* (Yachting Monthly, London). The *Yachting Monthly* has a long tradition of involvement with the rivers of Essex and Suffolk, reflected in this short, thoroughly practical book. Again, you need look no further.

Mediterranean: For many years, the best guides were Captain H.M. Denham's admirable volumes that took you all over the Mediterranean. He mingled practical navigational information with delightful insights into local history, archaeological sites, traditional sailing craft, and many other topics. They are somewhat out of date these days, but are still worth carrying aboard. Denham's *The Tyrrhenian Sea* (John Murray, London) is still the most widely available guide to Corsica and Sardinia, and you will not go far wrong by using it.

Greek waters are another matter. Rod Heikell's *Greek Waters Pilot* (Imray, Laurie, Norie & Wilson, St. Ives,

England) has no peer. This is worth buying even if you contemplate just a short cruise in Greece. If you're going for any length of time, try to obtain an older edition of the relevant volume of the British Admiralty's *Mediterranean Pilot*. These compendia have no peer for the leisured cruising yacht.

South Pacific

The best general cruising guide to the Pacific is Earl R. Hinz's *Landfalls of Paradise* (Western Marine Enterprises, Ventura, California), but this is intended for the ocean sailor rather than the bareboater. Otherwise, you must rely on local guides.

Tonga and Leeward Islands: South Pacific Yacht Charters has put out its own cruising guides, which are supplied to all charterers when they confirm their reservations. Both the *Tonga Cruising Guide* and *South Pacific Yacht Charters Cruising Guide to Îles Sous le Vent* are simple, mimeographed volumes that are easy to use on board.

Bay of Islands, New Zealand: New Zealand's *Bay of Islands: The Land and Sea Guide* (Roger and Evelyn Miles, Opua, New Zealand) is a practical volume that mixes shore attractions with basic navigational information. Aficionados may want to purchase the *Pickmere Atlas of Northland's East Coast*, a folio volume of very detailed pilot charts available locally, but hardly needed. Guides to Marlborough Sound or to New Zealand waters are generally available locally, but you will not need them in advance.

Australia: The *Complete Yachtsman's Handbook to the Whitsunday Passage* (Whitsunday Yachting World, PO Box 903, Crows Nest, New South Wales 2065, Australia) is the definitive source, but you will have to obtain it from Australia weeks ahead of time.

Readers eager for up-to-date information should consult the annual charter issue of *Cruising World*, which lists cruising guides from all over the world.

Index

276